The Judicial Politics of Abortion in Latin America

The Judicial Politics of Abortion in Latin America

Argentina, Colombia, Costa Rica, and Mexico

JORDI DÍEZ

The University of North Carolina Press
Chapel Hill

Set in Minion Pro by Westchester Publishing Services
Manufactured in the United States of America

Complete Cataloging-in-Publication Data for this title is available from the
Library of Congress at https://lccn.loc.gov/2025015446.
9781469689739 (cloth: alk. paper)
9781469689746 (pbk.: alk. paper)
9781469689753 (epub)
9781469689760 (pdf)

Cover art: *Sketch of Iustitia (Lady Justice) on Caduceus*, by Dhiego Gutierrez
(instagram: @dhiegogutierrez). Used with permission.

For product safety concerns under the European Union's General Product Safety
Regulation (EU GPSR), please contact gpsr@mare-nostrum.co.uk or write to the
University of North Carolina Press and Mare Nostrum Group B.V., Mauritskade 21D,
1091 GC Amsterdam, The Netherlands.

To Dhiego

Contents

Illustrations

Acknowledgments

The publication of this book would not have been possible without the contributions of numerous people and institutions.

Academics in Canada are truly privileged to receive generous support from multiple funding agencies. I thank the Social Sciences and Humanities Research Council for the Insight Grant I earned in the 2016 national competition (435–2016–1106), funding that allowed me to undertake this rather ambitious project. Here's hoping that research funding from federal governments for open research will continue in these rather turbulent times.

I also thank my colleagues in the Department of Political Science at the University of Guelph for their kind encouragement and collegiality. I could not imagine working anywhere else. A special note of thanks must go to Troy Riddell, chair of the department, for rearranging my teaching schedule so that I could take time away from the classroom to carry out essential fieldwork.

I express the warmest thanks to Susan Franceschet, Janine Clark, Candace Johnson, Pascal Lupien, Catalina Smulovitz, Julio Antonio Ríos Figueroa, Pablo Mijangos y González, Camilo Saavedra, Ezequiel González Ocantos, Alba Ruibal, Mariela Daby, Chris Fraresso, Rebecca Cook, Leticia Bonifaz, Ana Cristina González Vélez, Edward Koning, Troy Riddell, Dennis Baker, and Kate Puddister for their support at various stages of the project.

Research assistants are an integral part of research projects. From helping to map out the main actors in the field to retrieving data from archives, they play pivotal roles. In this case, truly fantastic assistance was provided by these individuals: Pablo Gómez Pinilla (Mexico); Marcelo Mangini and Santiago Cunial (Argentina); María Fernanda Valverde Díaz (Costa Rica); Viviana Bohórquez, Nora Picasso Uvalle, and Juliana Jaramillo (Colombia); and Brendan Dell, Brooke Granovsky, Sierra dePass, and Alyssa Hill (Canada).

I thank the faculty and staff at various academic institutions in Latin America for their support while in the field: my most sincere thanks to everyone at the Centro de Estudios de Género at El Colegio de México, my second academic home; the Universidad de los Andes (Colombia); the Universidad de Buenos Aires and the Universidad Torcuato di Tella (Argentina); and the Universidad de Costa Rica. A very special shoutout goes to Felipe Alpizar for having supported and processed my affiliation as a Visiting Scholar at the

Centro de Investigación y Estudios Políticos at the Universidad de Costa Rica in early 2018.

The core of this book is, of course, the information the main actors shared with me during the various interviews I conducted in the four countries. To the many sitting and retired justices and their (truly hardworking) law clerks, thank you from the bottom of my heart for opening windows into the decision-making processes that led to such important rulings. I would like to thank all of their administrative staff for the patience they showed when I contacted them incessantly to secure the interviews.

At the University of North Carolina Press (UNCP), a heartfelt thank-you to the most formidable of duos: Elaine Maisner and Debbie Gershenowitz. It has been a true honor and delight working with both of you. Thank you so very much! Fate somehow decided that the three of us would end up working on this manuscript. A warm thanks to Alexis Dumain, also at UNCP, for her great work and patience.

I thank the four anonymous reviewers for their constructive suggestions. It is rare to receive such in-depth and beneficial feedback. You clearly read every word and thought about the best way to refine my ideas to improve the manuscript. I hope I have done justice to your suggestions as I revised the final version.

To my family and friends, thank you for all your support and patience! Many things delayed the project, including health issues, personal loss, and the pandemic, and I could not have completed this work without you.

I dedicate this book to Dhiego Gutiérrez. Our lives are intrinsically woven with this project, and your steadfast, loving support through the many ups and downs has made it possible.

Toronto, June 2025

The Judicial Politics of Abortion in Latin America

Introduction

Strategy is good if it advances ideology.

—Former Justice, Colombian Constitutional Court,
   Bogotá, June 8, 2018

Latin America has had a significant public health crisis. There are between 730 and 2,000 deaths each year from unsafe abortions, and some 760,000 girls and women are hospitalized because of medical complications (UNFPA 2017; WHO 2012; Guttmacher Institute 2018). There are, further, 3.6 million teenage pregnancies, and approximately 1.65 million unsafe abortions are practiced each year. Indeed, at least 10 percent of all maternal deaths in the region are from unsafe abortions. Most of these cases disproportionately involve poor women and girls who cannot afford access to safe clinics or adequate health care in the region of the world with the widest income disparities. A main reason behind this crisis is that Latin America has historically had one of the strictest regulatory abortion regimes, forcing women and girls to seek the practice in clandestine and unsafe ways and places. In effect, by the turn of the twentieth century, unconditional access to abortion ("abortion on demand") was not available in democratic Latin America, and exceptions to its criminalization existed in some countries only under restrictive humanitarian reasons, such as in cases of rape, incest, fetal deformations, or to save the mother's life. Despite the unprecedented move away from authoritarianism that the region underwent as part of the Third Wave of Democratization during the 1980s and early 1990s, a process that included the notably strong mobilization of women's groups and organizations throughout the region, abortion remained criminalized.

The landscape began to change in 2000, however. With minor reforms introduced in Mexico City that year, several Latin American jurisdictions began to modify abortion regimes. Indeed, the turn of the twentieth century marked the beginning of a significant, if gradual, shift in the regulation of abortion access in some Latin American countries. The process culminated with the complete decriminalization of the practice in Uruguay (2012), Argentina (2020), Colombia (2022), and Mexico (2021, 2023) within the emergence of a strong and visible region-wide pro-choice movement known as the "Green Wave." Yet, along with the liberalization of abortion access in these countries, other countries restricted the practice even further (Dominican Republic, El Salvador, and Nicaragua), while most others opted for policy stasis.

What explains such variance?

Foundational comparative work on gender politics originally offered explanations for the strict abortion policy regimes that characterized the region prior to 2000 (Htun 2003; Blofield 2006). Indeed, work on abortion politics in individual countries followed the common thread of exploring the factors behind generalized policy stasis (Mollmann 2005; Getgen 2007; Kane 2008). Political science scholarship has since then endeavored to explore policy change and identified the role played by various factors, such as political parties and party systems (Haas 2010; Reuterswärd 2019; Blofield and Ewig 2017; Viterna 2012; Lind 2012), the strategic deployment of various policy frames by opponents and proponents of deregulation (Sutton and Borland 2013; Kane 2008; Tabbush et al. 2016; Jesudason and Weitz 2015; Morgan and Roberts 2012; Marcus-Delgado 2020), the influence of feminist mobilization and policy networks (Marcus-Delgado 2020; Kane 2008; Blofield and Ewig 2017; Ruibal and Fernández Anderson 2020), the strength of socially conservative mobilization (Haas 2010; Reuterswärd 2019; Daby and Moseley 2021; Blofield and Ewig 2017; Wood et al. 2016), and federalism in Argentina and Mexico (MacDonald and Mills 2010; Becker and Olavarrieta 2013; Lopreite 2014; Ruibal 2018a, 2018b). However, a key part of policy change has been the role played by the judiciary. Within what is known as the "judicialization of politics" (Tate and Vallinder 1995; Hirschl 2008), which has included Latin America (Smulovitz 2012; Ríos-Figueroa and Pozas-Loyo 2010; Rodríguez-Raga 2011; Rueda 2010; Brinks 2011; González-Ocantos 2019; Smulovitz and Peruzzotti 2003), the region has seen the substantive incursion of high courts into numerous contentious policy arenas, such as sexual and reproductive rights. It has notably included abortion. Table I.1 captures this phenomenon.

In the quarter of a century from 1999 to 2024, twenty major reforms were introduced in Latin American countries that altered (or cemented) abortion regulatory regimes. Fourteen of those cases have in fact involved the active participation of the judiciary and, ultimately, apex courts (presented in bold in table I.1). As attempts at reform became judicialized, constitutional tribunals, as the final arbiters of contentious disputes, have brought down important rulings on the regulation of abortion. These rulings have varied, however. In some cases (Argentina), courts have decided to liberalize restrictions on reproductive rights rather amply. In others (Costa Rica), they have favored the status quo, while in yet others (Dominican Republic), they have restricted access even further. What explains such variance in these high court decisions? In this book, I answer this question by analyzing the decision-making

Table *I.1* Abortion policy reform between 1999 and 2024

	1999			2024		
	AP	RH	OD	AP	RH	OD
Argentina		x			**2012**	2020
Bolivia		x			**2014**	
Brazil		x			**2012, 2016**	
Chile	x				**2017**	
Colombia	x				**2006**	2022
Costa Rica		x			2007, 2009	
Dominican Republic		x		**2016**	2014	
Ecuador		x			**2021**	
El Salvador	x			1999		
Guatemala		x			x	
Honduras	x			2021		
Mexico					2007, **2009**	**2021, 2023**
Nicaragua		x		2006		
Panama		x			x	
Paraguay		x			x	
Peru		x			x	
Uruguay		x				2012
Venezuela		x			x	

AP: absolute prohibition, RH: restricted to humanitarian reasons, OD: on demand.

processes that led to four landmark rulings on abortion during what I call in this book the First Wave of Abortion Decriminalization (2000–2012):

1. **The 2012 FAL Case (*A. F. s/medida autosatisfactiva, F. A. L.*).** In this majority ruling, Argentina's Supreme Court agreed with a 2010 decision made by the Superior Court of Chubut Province, challenged by the province's attorney general, that allowed a fifteen-year-old to have an abortion. The girl had been raped by her stepfather. The court took the controversial step to hear a moot case (the abortion had already been performed) and established a series of expansive rules around reproductive health that went considerably beyond the case at hand. It argued that the Argentine Constitution and international treaties do not prohibit abortion (setting a precedent on the constitutionality of abortion beyond cases of rape); that doctors could not judicialize abortion cases; that a rape victim's sworn declaration was enough to access an abortion (in effect, allowing women and girls to access an abortion by declaring they had been raped); and that judges must guarantee rights and accept any future cases. It also ordered the

national government, all provinces, and the city of Buenos Aires to establish "hospital protocols" that guarantee safe and prompt access to abortion services. Importantly, the decision established that the practice of abortion is not unconstitutional in Argentina.

2. **The 2006 C–355 Case by the Colombian Constitutional Court.** In this case, the court responded to a constitutional challenge submitted by a team of activists led by Mónica Roa. The team argued that the articles in the penal code that criminalized abortion violated the Colombian Constitution as well as numerous international treaties to which the country was signatory. In a narrow (5–3) majority ruling, the court agreed with some of the arguments in the challenge but argued that women's rights must be balanced with competing rights enshrined in the constitution. The court thereby assumed a moderate position by allowing abortion only in three particular cases: when the pregnancy was the result of an unconsented sexual act, incest, or unauthorized fertilization; when, certified by a doctor, the continuation of the pregnancy poses a danger to the woman's life; and, also certified by a doctor, when the fetus's life prospects are inviable, given malformations.

3. **The 2008 Case by Mexico's Supreme Court (*Acción de Inconstitucionalidad 146/2007 y su Acumulada 147/2007*).** In a majority ruling, the court responded to a constitutional challenge submitted by the Office of the Attorney General and the Human Rights Commission that challenged the constitutionality of the decriminalization of abortion enacted by Mexico City the previous year. The court's majority took a moderate position; rather than issuing a broader ruling that would have expanded conceptions of women's health and reproductive rights, as some justices on the bench had pushed for, it mostly limited its arguments to procedural elements by ruling that Mexico City was within its constitutional jurisdiction to legislate on the matter.

4. **The 2007 Case by Costa Rica's Constitutional Chamber (*A.N. v. Costa Rica*).** In this case, the court responded to a constitutional challenge submitted by the legal representatives of a teenager who had been denied a therapeutic abortion by a San José hospital. The plaintiffs argued that the high-risk pregnancy should be terminated because it posed significant health risks. In an unusually lengthy decision, the court decided not to hear the case arguing that, while the pregnancy did cause anxiety and its continuation had risks, the right to life was enshrined in the constitution and had to be protected. It also argued that while the right could be limited under certain

circumstances, it was not up to the court to decide but rather to the National Assembly.

The four rulings capture some of the variance in the liberalization of abortion by apex courts during the First Wave of Abortion Decriminalization in Latin America. I present a comparison of these rulings and explore the factors that drove a majority of justices on each bench to decide the extent to which existing legal frameworks on abortion could be changed. My analysis therefore centers squarely on judicial decision-making: it opens the black box of the discussions that took place inside each one of these high courts to uncover how justices in the four constitutional tribunals arrived at decisions regarding the regulation of abortion.

To explain variance in the decisions made by judges in salient abortion cases, I have selected four rulings handed down by constitutional tribunals that, in comparative terms, have been among the most autonomous and active in the region and that have ruled on abortion within a five-year period. These are Argentina's *Corte Suprema de Justicia de la Nación* (Supreme Court); Colombia's *Corte Constitucional* (Constitutional Court); Mexico's *Suprema Corte Justicia de la Nación* (Supreme Court); and Costa Rica's *Sala Constitucional, Suprema Corte de Justicia* (Constitutional Chamber). The analysis relies on the most similar system design: all four tribunals exhibit an important degree of judicial independence and have the power of judicial review. Yet the decisions they have rendered have varied: ample in Argentina, medium in Colombia and Mexico, and null in Costa Rica.

The selection of the policy area is influenced by a desire to solve real-world puzzles that have significant implications for people. The (de)regulation of reproductive rights is a matter of life or death for millions of girls and women in Latin America. Learning about the political and legal processes that have led to the reform of abortion regimes is therefore of paramount importance because they have real, concrete, and consequential implications. It is also influenced by an interest in the politics of high-profile cases. Abortion is, without a doubt, one of the most controversial issues in most democracies, an issue that ignites strong arguments and divides societies, and, as I argue in chapter 2, access to the procedure is central to the attainment of full democratic citizenship for women and girls. There is therefore a keen interest by academics and the general public in learning how these decisions are made. The analysis that I present in this book seeks to meet that interest.

The research I present builds on our knowledge of the politics of abortion in Latin America and its changing regulatory landscape. Important work has looked at legal changes but has not explored the role judiciaries have played in policy change. To be sure, legal scholars have explored the evolution of national (Bergallo 2014; Bohórquez Monsalve et al. 2019) and international abortion law (Lemaitre 2014; Hessini 2005; Rahman et al. 1998) by, for example, looking at how arguments in favor of deregulation have changed over time through different legal frames. Work has also looked at processes that have led to the judicialization of attempts at deregulation (Machado and Cook 2018). Other scholarship has looked specifically at feminist legal mobilization and its interaction with high courts in their pursuit to influence law reform, offering explanations of the conditions under which they may influence legal change (Ruibal 2014b; Jaramillo and Alfonso 2008). However, this work has not explored the internal processes of constitutional tribunals that have resulted in the rendition of landmark rulings. This gap in the political science literature is actually rather puzzling. While a lot has been written about the struggles over sexual and reproductive rights in Latin America, we know next to nothing about the policymaking role of courts in the area. Moreover, when law and politics scholars write about the increasing role of courts in Latin America, they tend to include abortion as examples of momentous decisions. Courts are a central part of the story. This book fills the gap.

My analysis contributes to the study of judicial politics in Latin America, a dynamic and burgeoning field. The judicialization of politics in the region has produced important work that has explored various aspects of the phenomenon as it has unfolded over the last three decades. A group of scholars has sought to explain the origins of formal judicial empowerment by analyzing the constitutional reforms that endowed courts with ample judicial review powers (Finkel 2004a, 2004b; Nunes 2010a, 2010b; Brinks and Blass 2018). This work attempted to solve the seemingly paradoxical decisions made by domestic elites to undertake reforms that strengthened judiciaries and diminished their own policymaking power. Scholars have also paid significant attention to questions regarding judicial independence by investigating the formal empowerment of courts and their actual performance. Latin American courts may have been given formal autonomy through constitutional reforms, but the extent to which they have exercised it has not only varied across countries but also across time. Some courts are more independent than others, and some courts have become more or less independent over time, depending on political contexts. Scholarship has thus explored the factors behind the observable gaps that have emerged between formal institutional design and the actual exercise of judicial independence (Brinks 2005; Iaryczower et al. 2002; Kapiszewski and Taylor 2008; Ríos-Figueroa 2011; Staton 2010; Ingram 2015; Ruibal 2009; Magaloni 2008; Inclán 2009).

Linked to these debates, some scholars of judicial politics in Latin America turned their attention to an aspect that has been central to the study of judicial politics more generally: judicial behavior. As judges became new and important policy actors, interest grew in exploring how judges make decisions by deploying theoretical and conceptual tools elaborated to study established democracies (reviewed in chapter 1). Latin Americanists have looked at the relationship between a country's degree of political fragmentation and the assertiveness of rulings (Pérez-Liñán and Castagnola 2009; Chávez 2004; Domingo 2000; Ríos-Figueroa 2007). The general theme that emerges from this important work is that pluralistic and fragmented contexts tend to yield more assertive court decisions. Without denying the importance that formal institutions and political environments play in how judges decide, another group of scholars offered alternative explanations by looking at the role played by legal ideas and cultural and professional norms. Identifying a broad generational and legal-cultural change in Latin American judiciaries—induced in part by curricular changes at university law faculties, the international diffusion of norms, and the professionalization of litigation—scholarship has established an association between judicial assertiveness and changing legal preferences. As a new generation of "neo constitutionalist" scholars began to occupy courts, replacing legal-positivist judges, deference to other branches of government decreased and courts began to behave more actively through more expansive rulings (Couso 2010; González-Ocantos 2016). Some literature has identified how a cultural transformation (neoconstitutionalism) has been behind the judicialization of politics in Latin America (González-Ocantos 2016; García Villegas and Uprimny 2004; Gargarella et al. 2006). In addition to the study of origins of judicial empowerment and behavior, scholars have become interested in the impact of courts and whether their interventions, especially in areas of cultural, social, and economic rights, have had tangible effects, especially among marginalized sectors of society (Landau 2012). This research has, so far, pointed to unevenness on this score across the region.

I build on this important literature by presenting a detailed analysis of decisions rendered on abortion in four constitutional tribunals. Explanations of judicial behavior in Latin America and elsewhere tend to make observations through ecological inferences—that is, they look at general patterns in court rulings to establish whether any associations exist between judges' decisions and their ideological leanings or relational positioning vis-à-vis political actors. While useful in detecting broad patterns, they are unable to account for the various factors that judges consider *at the individual level* before they pen a decision and cast a vote. These processes unfold through complex discussions and deliberations. In this book, I present fine-grained accounts of those processes to answer a question that has fascinated scholars of judicial politics for decades: How do justices arrive at the choices they make? Taking a particular policy area, my analysis builds on work that has looked

Actors ──────────▶ Amplitude of Decisions

▲
│
│
│

Political Climate

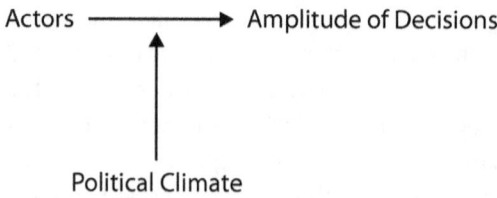

Figure I.1
Explaining Variance
in Court Decisions

at legal mobilization around reproductive rights (Ruibal 2014b; Jaramillo and Alfonso 2008; Machado and Cook 2018) by uncovering the decision-making processes begun once cases reached a constitutional court's docket.

Explaining Variance in Court Decisions: The Argument

What accounts for variance in the amplitude of decisions the four courts made regarding the regulation of abortion? In this book, I answer this question with data collected over a period of three years in the four countries.[1] The data suggest that variance in the type of decisions is explained by the presence of strategic actors—justices and law clerks—who are able to assemble majorities in favor of reducing restrictions on abortion with the strategic deployment of arguments. The crafting and deployment of arguments was in turn influenced by the political climate. Variance is fundamentally the result of strategic agency exercised within junctural contexts, as figure I.1 conveys.

I argue that in cases where high courts ruled in favor of decriminalizing abortion (Argentina, Colombia, and Mexico), a group of justices *and* law clerks took the initiative to convince the largest possible number of justices on each bench to vote in favor of decriminalizing access to abortion by presenting arguments they thought would secure a majority of votes. My research suggests that a small group of entrepreneurial justices and law clerks committed to the expansion of rights and democratic equality—what is generally known in Latin America as being *garantista*—led well-coordinated efforts to build majorities by focusing on moderate justices. The contentiousness of the cases solidified the positions of justices at each end of the political and doctrinal spectra, and efforts to build majorities focused on justices who were less ideologically and doctrinally rigid. The role that law clerks played in these processes was key. Law clerks in Latin American high courts (unlike the US and Canadian Supreme Courts) tend to be career civil servants who spend years, and in some countries decades, in their posts; they are therefore highly experienced and knowledgeable individuals. They are, in fact, the ones who usually pen most rulings. In the cases I study, law clerks were tasked with conducting research and crafting arguments that they knew had the potential to bring nonrigid justices to their side.

Table I.2 Amplitude of decisions

Case	Costa Rica	Colombia	Mexico	Argentina
Strategic actors	No	**Yes**	**Yes**	**Yes**
Political climate	Closed	**Constrained**	**Constrained**	**Open**
Amplitude	Null	**Moderate**	**Moderate**	**High**

Table I.2 illustrates my argument. In the three cases where the rulings re-laxed restrictions to access to abortion (Argentina, Colombia, and Mexico, in bold), the strategic crafting and deployment of arguments by these actors within each court was key to the crafting of majority rulings. This was not the case in Costa Rica, where the bench opted for stasis. However, the political climate in each of the three positive cases influenced both the type of strategic arguments deployed and the final content of each ruling. An analysis of the discussions and negotiations that took place after the cases reached the dockets reveals that, as the main actors carefully calibrated the drafting and deploy-ment of arguments, they considered the political climate, understood as both the position of other state and nonstate actors outside the court (such as presidents and members of Congress) and debates in society at large, in de-ciding the direction and content of each decision. Interviews with these ac-tors suggest that, in garnering a majority of votes, they considered the extent to which political conditions allowed for the deregulation of abortion. Key to these processes were strong attempts at building the largest possible majorities in order to afford both the rulings and the courts themselves the greatest legitimacy possible. By amplitude of decision, I mean the extent to which access to abortion was relaxed.

To my knowledge, this is the first study of its kind as no other work has looked at how strategic planning takes place *within* collegial Latin American courts in the crafting of rulings. Indeed, as Ezequiel González-Ocantos has pointed out, the strategic model's main shortcoming when applied to Latin America is that "it sees the process of judicial decision making as fundamen-tally shaped by external factors" (2016, 31). My analysis fills this gap. I argue in this book that strategy was at the core of assembling the largest possible majorities among liberal and moderate justices in the three high courts of Ar-gentina, Colombia, and Mexico. Internal strategic bargaining was key to the building of majority coalitions in these three cases. Entrepreneurial justices and their law clerks engaged in strategic bargaining in the assembling of ma-jorities that supported their desired direction of the ruling. They considered other justices' policy and legal preferences, past voting behavior, and, yes, even at times their personal traits. This is then an account of collective and not individual endeavor, which speaks to multiple conjunctural causation (Ragin

1987). The answer to the research question is about an interplay between agency and structure; it is about actors pursuing their interests within the constraints of broader political environments. My study falls, then, within the tradition that looks at the behavior of rational actors within institutional and social constraints (Hall and Taylor 1996), an approach that has more recently been used to explain larger processes in comparative politics (Acemoglu and Robinson 2020).

By paying attention to internal strategic bargaining, I therefore challenge accounts of judicial behavior that take the direction of an entire court as a measurement of that behavior, look strictly at external factors in explaining it, or code individual justices' policy and legal positions to predict outcomes in rulings (reviewed in chapter 1). Strategic bargaining is therefore key.

Key to these processes is what could be rather easily called the "art of persuasion." As I show in subsequent chapters, the justices and law clerks who took the lead in assembling majorities carefully and strategically presented arguments they thought would convince wavering justices to their side. Argument framing appears to be a central part of the story. A line of inquiry within the literatures of public policy and social movements has looked at the role the framing of arguments plays in public policy debates. As I have shown elsewhere, policy success is oftentimes linked to the ability of state and non-state actors to frame their policy objectives in a manner that resonates with policymakers and the public at large (Díez 2013, 2015). Framing is equally important during internal bargaining in institutional collegiate settings, such as high courts. My analysis suggests that the framing of arguments plays an important part in persuading other justices to join the direction a ruling begins to take.

While framing is clearly at play, less clear for key actors was which argumentative lines would be effective in the process of persuasion. As we shall see, sometimes leading justices (and their law clerks) decide to present a variety of arguments that they know are *likely* to convince their colleagues to join a majority, but without knowing what their colleagues' reception will exactly be. That applies to the Argentine and Colombian cases. In Argentina, the justification to liberalize the regulation of abortion access was made in an original draft opinion on various lines of argumentation: practical (the Supreme Court had to decide on the case because pregnancies last nine months); jurisdictional (the court had to hear the case because it was under federal jurisdiction); and substantive (abortion in the country had to be understood through a social justice lens). In Colombia, on the other hand, the original arguments were practical (not to antagonize conservative justices to avoid polarization and win moderate justices); technical (deploying a test of proportionality); and jurisdictional (liberalizing abortion under some conditions in an effort to convince moderate justices that preferred judicial restraint). In the case of Mexico, original discussions involved two main lines of argumentation: substantive (justifying the liberalization of abortion along a rights-based reasoning) or jurisdictional (Mexico City had the authority to rule on abortion). As discussions progressed, the leading justice and his law clerks decided to abandon the substantive approach and adhere to the jurisdictional one to secure a majority of votes. None of this occurred in Costa Rica.

While argument framing is important in strategic bargaining, part of strategizing can include other elements, such as considering the personal traits of certain individuals, as we shall see. In the case of Colombia, for example, inviting the only woman justice on the bench to co-draft the majority opinion and delegating the process to a less polarizing junior justice were part of the persuasive strategy. In Argentina, inviting a woman justice to co-draft the opinion was also part of the strategy. The strategy worked in the first instance but did not in the second one.

Nevertheless, judicial decisions are not simply the aggregates of individual strategic decisions resulting from internal institutional constraints, since they take place within broader structural contexts. Scholars who rely on the "strategic model" to explain judicial behavior also incorporate external factors beyond state actors, such as a court's legitimacy in the eyes of the public (chapter 1). My analysis suggests that strategic decision-making plays out both within the courts *as well as* vis-à-vis outside state and nonstate actors. Justices and law clerks are very much attuned to the potential reaction their decisions may provoke. They therefore think carefully about the legal arguments they develop, not only with the intention of earning majority support for their preferences but also in order to afford their decisions the greatest legitimacy before the other branches of government and society at large. Indeed, the elaboration and deployment of arguments leading justices undertake are shaped by their *perceived* openness of the political environment. Justices and their teams seem to be keenly aware of social debates and the positions held by various state and nonstate actors, including not only the "governing majority" in the executive and legislature but members of the legal community, the media, and the positions held by proponents and opponents of the decriminalization of abortion. The political environment not only molded discussions held within the courts on the type of argumentation used by some justices to convince colleagues to join their opinions, but it also shaped the reach of their decisions. The extent to which leading strategic justices within a court saw a favorable political environment shaped the amplitude of each decision.

In the case of Costa Rica, a favorable political environment was perceived to be nonexistent. While some justices within the Constitutional Chamber were sympathetic with the case and are widely seen as liberal in their ideo-logical positioning, they refused even to begin a discussion and, in a lengthy justification, discarded the constitutional challenge. Interviews suggest that the perception among senior justices was that a backlash from government officials and sectors of society would ensue and that the court would be seen as *abortista* (pro-abortion). Costa Rica's Constitutional Chamber is among the most progressive in Latin America as it has taken an overall clear posi-tion in the extension of a variety of socioeconomic rights, yet when it came to reproductive rights, most justices believed that a backlash would be too strong even to begin a discussion.

By contrast, justices perceived political opportunities to be favorable in the constitutional tribunals of Argentina, Colombia, and Mexico. In the three courts, discussions were led primarily by teams of law clerks working for one or two justices once the cases were assigned to a chamber after entering the docket, in what one Argentine law clerk informally, and aptly, referred to as the "bun-ker." A striking similarity among the three cases is that they were led by justices with similar profiles: highly respected judges with a clear academic bent. Dis-cussions within these teams focused on the arguments that could be developed to convince as many of the justices on each bench to allow for the decriminal-ization of abortion, thinking carefully about the extent to which they could go, given the political context.

The most favorable political context of the three was Argentina's. While the then-president of Argentina, Cristina Fernández de Kirchner (2007–15), was known not to be personally supportive of the decriminalization of abor-tion, her administration and that of her husband, Néstor Kirchner (2003–7), had been largely framed around the need to expand human rights. For some of the justices in the court, most of whom were appointed by Kirchner, these clearly included reproductive rights. As a justice put it, "The [political] con-ditions were propitious to go far . . . to establish a framework beyond the partic-ular case." These perceptions allowed for the development of arguments that encouraged the leading drafters of the opinion not only to make the (potentially controversial) decision to rule in the abstract on a case that was moot (the teen-ager's abortion had already been performed) but to establish a series of broad legal criteria around the state of, and access to, abortion in Argentina, as well as mandating the establishment of abortion "protocols" to regulate the practice across the country.

While justices saw favorable conditions in Colombia and Mexico, they were narrower than in Argentina. In the case of Colombia, for the leading Consti-tutional Court justice behind the case, the political opportunities existed to allow for the partial decriminalization of abortion. Discussions among the justices centered mostly around whether abortion should be accessible without restrictions, as the most liberal justice of the bench argued, or whether access should be limited to certain cases, such as when pregnancy was the result nonconsensual sexual intercourse. The lead justice and his team sensed that some of his colleagues would not support a total decriminalization of abortion and argued for restrictions through the application of the proportionality test (the balancing of competing rights). Moderate justices agreed and joined the majority opinion. But he also knew that political conditions would only allow for partial decriminalization. That was, in fact, the position taken by the country's attorney general on the case. Central to their discussions was fear of a backlash should abortion be decriminalized further, given the recent reform of the penal code: following a counter-majoritarian logic, for some justices allowing for unlimited access would overstep the court's remit, thereby challenging its legitimacy. The political opportunities allowed for partial decriminalization. And that is what the ruling did.

Mexico's case is strikingly similar to Colombia's. Once this case reached the Mexican Supreme Court's docket and discussions began among justices and their clerks, the main debate revolved around whether Mexico City had the constitutional jurisdiction to legislate on the decriminalization of abortion or whether decriminalization violated constitutional provisions to the "right to life." For some, engaging the debate on this issue necessarily meant delving into having to balance the "right of the unborn" versus women's rights. For the lead justice of the case and his team, the only way to ensure the largest majority and prevent a backlash from state and nonstate actors outside the court was to opt for the "procedural route"—that is, to restrict arguments in favor for the city's right to regulate the criminality of abortion. As a law clerk in his office stated, "We decided that the only way to get this forward was to limit our arguments to the procedural (*lo procesal*)." Interviews with the key players suggest that opting for such procedural option and not using the case (as in Argentina) to advance a broader agenda would be the best way to ensure a large majority, lessen potential backlash, and, importantly, guard the court's legitimacy given the contentiousness of the file. The final ruling thus reflected such strategic thinking.

This book is divided in two parts. In a first, I set up the theoretical, historical, and contextual elements needed for the comparative analysis I present in the second part. Chapter 1 reviews the academic debate on comparative judicial politics and judicial behavior. I explore the extent to which the modeling developed for studying judicial behavior outside Latin America is transferable to the region's realities. I argue that the strategic model is the most useful in explaining variance across the four cases. The chapter subsequently reviews the historical judicial politics of each of the four countries I compare in this study to provide readers with a fuller understanding of how the four constitutional tribunals assumed such policymaking power. As we shall see, judicial review is nothing new in Latin America. Indeed, elements of that institutional mechanism can be traced back to the birth of some of the republics in the early 1800s. However, political processes that have unfolded in the four countries have resulted in the strengthening of constitutional tribunals, something that is necessary to review before exploring the rulings that I analyze.

Chapter 2 explores the evolution of the legal regulation of abortion in Latin America. This chapter has two main objectives. First, it highlights the various historical specificities of abortion policy in the region. This exercise, I suggest, is important background for readers unfamiliar with either this policy area or the region. I then review the main theoretical debates around abortion politics to remind the reader of the significant implications that access to abortion has for full democratic citizenship. Indeed, while many Latin American countries have made significant strides toward democratization over the last three decades, restrictions to access to abortion can be seen as a "democratic debt" that the region's polities owe women and girls. It is, I argue, one of the last obstacles to achieve full, formal democratic citizenship. To be clear, I do not contend, as a cisgendered man, that I am making any original contributions to the theoretical debates on abortion that feminists have held for decades. In chapter 2, I simply review those debates to remind the reader of the significant implications access to abortion has for democratic citizenship.

In the second part of the book, I present the four cases used in the comparison. The presentation order is based on the amplitude of the decisions: from larger to lower.

Let us begin.

PART I

Setting the Stage

Chapter 1

Courts and Constitutional Review in Latin America

Introduction

The global judicialization of politics has included Latin America. Over the last thirty years, several high courts in the region have emerged as powerful policy actors that have made important and consequential decisions in a variety of areas, from deciding whether presidents can run for reelection to whether the adoption of international free trade agreements is constitutional. Political scientists have given a great deal of scholarly attention to explaining the emergence of more assertive courts and how judges arrive at their decisions. As part of this phenomenon, in what is generally known as "judicial behavior," scholars studying Latin American apex courts have relied on various approaches to explain court behavior (Pérez-Liñán and Castagnola 2009, 2016; Chávez 2004; Domingo 2000; Ríos-Figueroa 2007; Couso 2010; González-Ocantos 2016; García Villegas and Uprimny 2004; Gargarella et al. 2006; Landau 2005). Some of this work has relied on various "models" to explain judicial decision-making. In this chapter, I review the theoretical debates around these models and argue that the strategic model is the most useful in explaining the variance in judicial behavior that I explore in this book. In the second part of the chapter, I overview the emergence of the four constitutional tribunals and engage in an exercise that, I suggest, is essential to understanding the four landmark rulings under study.

Theoretical Debates

While the emergence of comparative judicial politics as a subfield of comparative politics is quite recent—largely the result of scholarly interest in studying the global expansion of judicial review over the last thirty years (Cerar 2009; Ferejohn 2002; Hirschl 2008)—interest by political scientists in courts, law, and judges goes further back in time. Generally known as political jurisprudence or simply judicial politics, scholars primarily housed in US political science departments with an interest in the intersection between law and politics began to turn their attention to the study of courts and particularly judges in the 1940s and 1950s. As the (belated) realization set in that judges are not neutral appliers of the law and that courts are political institutions with significant policymaking powers, political scientists began to turn their attention to the study of the judiciary, with particular attention to the US Supreme Court (SCOTUS). The main discussion has hinged on the "majoritarian debate" sparked by Robert Dahl's foundational analysis (1957). Dahl explored the extent to which the US Supreme Court should and would vote against the "lawmaking majority" (the executive branch and Congress), an important question regarding democratic legitimacy given that its members are appointed and not elected. This debate gained force in the 1960s as politics in the United States became increasingly judicialized, in large part because of growing social mobilization and litigation of the time (Bickel 1962; Horowitz 1977; Casper 1976; Graber 1993; Devins 2004). Another debate central to the study of judicial politics concerns how judges make decisions. This area of study, known as judicial behavior, has been characterized by the development and deployment of various models to explain judicial decision-making.

Attitudes

The first and dominant model is the "attitudinal" model. Traced back to the publication of *The Roosevelt Court* in 1948,[1] and usually identified with the work of Jeffrey Segal and Harold Spaeth, proponents of the attitudinal model argue that the main factor behind the decisions that justices make is their ideological preferences: "This model holds that the [US] Supreme Court decides disputes in light of the facts of the case vis-à-vis the ideological values of the justices" (2002, 86). According to this model, justices resolve disputes based on their "sincere policy preferences" mostly unconstrained by other actors or institutions. Their personal attributes, life experiences, and traits influence how they see the world and filter how they interpret facts and, consequently, how they adjudicate disputes. Proponents of the model suggest that rulings can be predicted based on the ideological positioning of justices. Put simply, the model suggests that liberal justices will vote liberally and conservative justices conservatively.

Despite its appeal (partly due to its simplicity) and dominance (given its rather strong predictive capacity), the attitudinal model exhibits numerous important weaknesses. In addition to some methodological issues,[2] the model suffers from its limited generalizability outside the United States. The model was developed to study a high court that is likely the freest in the world (Schor 2008). Because SCOTUS justices are appointed for life, they are more likely to act according to their policy preferences than justices in courts with term-limits: justices need not fear any repercussions from their voting trajectory when they leave the bench, such as may happen when seeking employment. Moreover, the ideological divide SCOTUS has assumed as a result of the deep political polarization the country has undergone over the last ten years makes it highly incomparable to other high courts. Further, the attitudinal model fails to account for a certain degree of fluidity that exists in individuals' ideological positioning. At the most basic of levels, some people change their views over time as they also oftentimes do when faced with new information or when persuaded by opponents (democracies ultimately depend in part on such fluidity because otherwise one political party would always get elected). Research does show that, even in SCOTUS, there exists some ideological change over time (Martin and Quinn 2002).

In terms of judicial decisions, despite its strong predictive power, the attitudinal model fails to explain swing votes in some courts, changes over time in the number of justices that join majority decisions within a given bench, unanimous rulings, or concurrent opinions. In the last case, for example, if the sole purpose was to meet a policy preference, a justice need not write a concurrent opinion but could simply join the majority one. Something other than ideology may be at play behind that decision. Importantly, the attitudinal model fails to account for the fact that some justices change their votes from the beginning of discussions of a case by a bench until votes for the final rulings are cast (Brenner 1980). Group interactions, negotiations, and argumentation matter. We know that policy preferences tend to be sensitive to how the issue is framed (Zaller 1992). Nevertheless, evidence suggests that the role of ideology varies depending on the salience of the case and that it plays an augmented role in more salient cases (Unah and Hancock 2006; McAtee and McGuire 2007; Hettinger et al. 2004; Sunstein et al. 2004).[3] One would therefore expect ideology to play a central role in decisions regarding reproductive rights.

The role ideological attitudes play in how judges make decisions has been explored in several studies of Latin America, with mixed results (Scribner 2011; Basabe-Serrano 2012; Martin and Quinn 2002; Sánchez et al. 2011; González-Bertomeu 2019; Desposato et al. 2015; Iaryczower et al. 2002). While ideology has been closely associated with voting behavior in high courts (Brazil and Argentina before 1999), in other countries that association was weaker (Mexico, Brazil, Ecuador, and Argentina after 1999), while in others, no association was found (Chile). In this book, I contribute to this important scholarship by showing that ideology mattered in the four rulings under study in varied but also in surprising ways, thereby limiting its predictive capacity.

Confirming previous work on the role ideology plays in salient cases, ideology did in effect play a role in the decisions I study in this book, as may be expected given the nature of the cases: debates over abortion tend to heighten individuals' ideological positioning. Indeed, it is safe to say that debates over abortion are usually the most ideologically driven and incite passionate responses because many individuals tend to hold strong views on the issue. However, while important for some justices in the courts I analyze, ideology is not a consistent part of the story here. In all four cases, the positioning of the most ideologically rigid justices solidified on both sides of the spectrum. The most conservative justices expectedly made clear their opposition to the deregulation of abortion, and the most liberal justices, known in Latin America as *garantistas*,[4] signaled their support. Nevertheless, as we shall see in subsequent chapters, in some cases, women justices considered liberal and with a tradition of supporting women's rights voted against the deregulation of abortion for a variety of (political and doctrinal) reasons. In other cases, conservative justices, who would have been expected to side with their conservative colleagues, joined the majorities. In yet other cases, some justices appear to have traveled over time along the ideological spectrum prior to casting their vote. At the same time, several liberal justices tempered their ideal policy preferences in order to ensure the largest possible majorities. Importantly, a handful of liberal-leaning justices *and* law clerks, who generally describe themselves as committed democrats, were able to convince moderate justices to join majority opinions to decriminalize abortion. Interviews reveal that the outcomes were not assured simply based on justices' ideological leanings but that a great deal of convincing and negotiation took place. In effect, ideology can influence justices' decisions, but a main part of the story from the four cases I analyze in this book is that group interaction matters, and it matters quite significantly: justices change their minds when confronted with new arguments; they can be swayed when presented with technical arguments that do not challenge their ideological positions too much; and they can even be partially convinced to join in the expansion of rights when asked to coauthor a decision. Indeed, while ideology can play a role, sometimes even personality traits matter. As we shall see in the subsequent chapters, the building of majorities around rulings is akin to a process of coalition formation during which a variety of factors play a role, with ideology being but one factor.

The Law

Discussions of the role a judge's ideological bent may play in decision-making do not sit well with some scholars, particularly among those in the legal academy, who have argued that judges are not, and should not, be guided by personal preferences but by the meaning of the text. Judges, in short, should be committed to established legal principles such as stare decisis. In its purest form, early iterations of what is known as the "legal model," associated with Harvard Law School, posited a formal understanding of judicial decision-making whereby judges were seen as mechanical applicants of the law with no discretion (Wasby 1988).[5] That view was subsequently challenged by American jurisprudence and theorization in what is known as legal realism. Associated with the Yale Law School, legal realism called into question the rigidity of legal formalism by arguing that judges make law and are influenced by their personal backgrounds; furthermore, as humans, they simply cannot be separated from their lived experiences in the adjudication of cases (see, for example, Llewellyn 1931). More recently, the dominant view in some advanced democracies, certainly in the United States and Canada, is that of "legal positivism," generally associated with the work of H. L. A. Hart (1961). In general terms, legal positivism sees law as distinct from politics. While acknowledging that judges have a certain degree of discretion when deciding cases, legal positivists emphasize that judicial behavior is constrained by legal precedent, constitutional texts, statutes, and conventions. For some legal scholars, law is the most important factor in judicial decision-making, something that is reflected, for example, by the fact that, in the US Supreme Court, most decisions are in fact unanimous or rendered through large majorities, contrary to what is generally assumed (Corley et al. 2013).

Expectedly, the legal approach has been criticized by (mostly) political scientists. Legal factors such as precedent (stare decisis) is not usually, it is argued, mechanically applied, particularly in cases that are complex and where the law is unclear (Beatty 1990; Howard and Segal 2002; Songer et al. 2012; Sunstein et al. 2004, 302–3). Not only can justices cite precedent to support opposing decisions, which sometimes explains split decisions, but they often differ in their opinions over what constitutes precedent or may give it different weight (Bailey and Maltzman 2011). Perhaps nothing captures this better than the US Senate's confirmation of Justice Amy Coney Barrett to SCOTUS in late 2020 when she referred to cases that formed precedent and those that formed "super-precedent." For some justices, there appears to be a hierarchy. Further, as explored in the conclusion, in the 2022 SCOTUS decision on abortion, the majority of justices appear to have completely forgotten the basic notion of stare decisis.

These criticisms have been countered. On precedent, for example, it is recognized that Supreme Court justices can justifiably oppose precedent when they have already articulated opposition in previous cases (Whittington 2000). Fundamentally, a main source of disagreement within this debate seems to be a methodological one. As has been argued, the reliance on quantitative analyses to test causality is of limited use because operationalizing the meaning of the law distorts what legal scholars believe to be the law's influence (Gillman 2001). Quantitative analyses leave out important information that case study work provides in exploring the relationship (Epstein and Kobylka 1992). More generally, however, contemporary discussions do not suggest that the law is applied mechanically, but rather that texts and precedent serve as guides to judges when making decisions by balancing various factors (Kritzer and Richards 2003).

Regarding Latin America, a handful of studies have explored the role that law, or as Ezequiel González-Ocantos has appropriately termed "legal preferences" (2016), plays in judicial behavior (Huneeus et al. 2010; Ingram 2015, Hilbink 2007; Sánchez et al. 2011). Tied to explanations behind the judicialization of politics in Latin America, these studies have been carried out within a broader shift in constitutional interpretation that has taken place in some judiciaries in the region. That shift has seen a move away from the positivist, formalistic, and nationalistic Latin American legal tradition, which conceived of judging as mere procedural arbitering, toward more expansive and creative reading of the law, or "legal interpretivism" along the Dworkian tradition (González-Ocantos 2014; Couso 2010; López Medina 2004; Nunes 2010a, 2010b; Landau 2005).[6] The move away from legal formalism, known as "neoconstitutionalism" in Latin America, is readily identified with a shift of high courts to more liberal positions. In effect, some explanations of the judicialization of politics in the region see it as being the result of a structural reorientation of judges in the region. Some studies identify the spread of neoconstitutionalist ideas as the main factor behind the shift. In particular, some of this work has attempted to explore how these changes in legal visions have influenced how judges decide cases. For example, studying judicial behavior at Mexico's Supreme Court, Sánchez et al. (2011) captured this shift by coding judges' doctrinal positioning as "interpretivist," defined as a position in favor of expanding the court's jurisdiction by engaging in nonliteral interpretation, challenging precedent, and adopting a generous conception of standing. The study found that the court's justices do in fact divide with respect to judicial philosophy or forms of judicial interpretation.

To the likely dismay of political scientists who tend to like the tidiness of typologies and modeling, my analysis in this book contributes to this debate by complicating the picture. I demonstrate that, in the cases under study, legal preferences, like ideological preferences, can play a role, though in varied and, at times, surprising ways. As I detail in subsequent chapters, variance among justices' decisions is often in fact the result of a judge's doctrinal positioning and approach to legal and constitutional interpretation. However, such variance does not always coincide with ideological leanings. To be clear, the law does matter. Indeed, some justices clearly justified their votes based on their positions on constitutional interpretation. Importantly, in some cases, doctrinal rigidity trumped ideological preferences as justices with an established approach to the interpretation of the law could not justify challenging the positions they had previously taken, or their own precedent.

Nevertheless, there is a commonality among the three cases in which a majority of justices supported the decriminalization of abortion: legal doctrine was used *strategically* in order to assemble personally favorable opinions. Of note is the fact that while in one case (Mexico) justices and law clerks deployed strategic arguments in the process of crafting majorities by relying on positive-legal lines of argument, in two other cases (Argentina and Colombia) they did so by relying on clear interpretivist positions. My analysis builds on scholarship that has found that law is used instrumentally by judges (Lax 2011) and strategically when crafting majority opinions (Maltzman et al. 2000). The evidence that I present suggests that legal doctrine, similar to ideology, is important, yet it was not the most important explanatory factor. The data collected for this book suggest that, in the cases analyzed, the main explanation lies with the process of internal bargaining around efforts by some leading justices to build coalitions on the bench. That process of internal bargaining, I show, is mainly driven by strategic calculations. It is indeed about strategy.

Strategy

Strategic behavior by some justices in the courts I study is the most important factor in explaining the rulings I analyze in this book. The "strategic model" of judicial behavior, I argue, provides the best guidance in explaining the majority opinions of the four high courts. Traced back to Walter Murphy's *Elements of Judicial Strategy* (1964) and usually identified with the work of Lee Epstein and Jack Knight (1998, 2013), the strategic model adopts a rational choice perspective and posits that, while judges do in fact pursue their policy references, they make strategic decisions to accomplish them. Because judges are embedded within institutional settings with other people, the model suggests that they are influenced by others' preferences and are consequently required to compromise on their positions. Judges, therefore, cannot always get what they want; to advance their policy and legal preferences, they need to modulate their positions to achieve them at least partially. Central to this approach is the view that strategic decision-making is greatly influenced by what a judge thinks the majority opinion will be. Supporters of the model thus argue that judging in collegial courts is therefore an interactive process with people who have their own preferences, ideological bents, and doctrinal approaches. Rulings, the model suggests, reflect these interactions. While policy and legal preferences play a role in judicial behavior, judges are seen primarily as strategic maximizers: they prefer opinions and legal rules that reflect their policy positions, and they will try to secure those outcomes, as much as possible, by basing their decisions in part on the decisions and actions of their colleagues (Maltzman et al. 2000).

Strategic bargaining is therefore central to explanations of judicial behavior. As Epstein and Knight argue, court jurisprudence is "the long-term product of short-term and long-term strategic decisions" (1998, 183). A revised version of the model, based on scholarship mostly outside political science, suggests that the judges are not only motivated by policy goals but by factors such as job satisfaction and promotion, which also enter their strategic calculations (Epstein and Knight 2013).[7] However, even with the amplification of the model, strategy remains the primary explanatory factor.

Strategic judicial decision-making has been explored on two levels: within a court and vis-à-vis external political actors. In what sometimes is called the "internal strategic approach," judges are known to make decisions based on the likely votes their colleagues may cast (Wahlbeck 2006; Farhang et al. 2015; Hall 1990; Epstein and Shvestova 2002; Hammond et al. 2005; Maltzman and Wahlbeck 1996). However, judges operate within larger political systems and, scholars suggest, react to the positions held by actors outside courts. In what is sometimes referred to as the "outside strategic approach" or the "separation of power game," justices make decisions considering the potential reaction of other state actors in the other two branches of government (Marks 2012; Gely and Spiller 1990; Eskridge and Ferejohn 1992; Bergara et al. 2003; Eskridge 1991; Garrett et al. 1998; Volcansek 2001; Spiller and Spitzer 1992; Ginsburg 2003; Cooter and Ginsburg 1996; Epstein et al. 2001). The model was mostly developed based on the US Supreme Court, which is one of the most insulated in the world given that its justices have life tenure. However, the model holds that judges will nonetheless consider the positions actors in the other two branches of government hold as they can retaliate to adverse rulings by overturning or failing to implement them. The US Congress, for example, can revise the court's interpretation of a statute. Judges are consequently presumed to be attuned to the positions held by actors in the other two branches of government and take these positions into account when making decisions.

The strategic model has been criticized because of its weak predictive capacity. Political scientists have found evidence in support of strategic judicial behavior, and few would doubt that strategy plays a role in decision-making. However, a review of scholarship on the US Supreme Court reveals that "strategic behavior occurs on the Court, but it takes place much less often than the strategic scholars claim" (Brenner and Whitmeyer 2009, 165). A challenge to the model when, again, looking at the US Supreme Court is that most cases tend to be decided by the preferences of the justice in the ideological middle. Relying on what is called the "median voter theorem," research on judicial behavior has shown that case outcomes are best explained in reference to the median justice (Martin et al. 2005). The research therefore challenges the claim that judges are influenced by internal and external factors. Nevertheless, research has also found that the so-called median justice varies depending on the issue. In fact, there exists a great deal of variance in the identity of the median voter across areas of law and across time (Lauderdale and Clark 2013). Evidence also suggests that the pivotal "swing" justice is not always the median justice (Enns and Wohlfarth 2013). Moreover, scholarship also suggests that majority opinions tend to capture the preferences of the median justice *within* the majority coalition, which means that the content of the opinions will depend on its composition (Bonneau et al. 2007; Clark and Lauderdale 2010; Carubba et al. 2012). Majority coalitions vary, and their members often find legal argumentations that their colleagues can support.

That the strategic model's overall predictability on outcomes may be weak does not mean that strategy may at times play an important role. Indeed, in some landmark cases, it has been central. In *Craig v. Boren*, for example, Justice William Brennan, writing the majority opinion, could not assemble enough votes to support his preferred policy preference (strict scrutiny) on a discrimination case. The justice decided to compromise in the face of opposition and resorted to the use of an alternative legal test (heightened scrutiny), a decision that secured him the additional vote he needed to secure a majority. Such a test has become the legal standard in the United States for equal protection in gender-discrimination cases (Bressman 2007). While the model may have limitations in predicting consistently case outcomes in the US Supreme Court, it does not mean that justices do not engage in strategic negotiations and hedging and, sometimes, in precedent-setting cases. The model can be useful in landmark cases that tend to elicit the most interest given their social import.

As mentioned in the introduction, scholars of Latin America have relied on the strategic model by looking at the behavior of courts vis-à-vis the other two branches of government, exploring the relationship between a country's degree of political fragmentation and the assertiveness of rulings (Pérez-Liñán and Castagnola 2009; 2016, Chávez 2004; Domingo 2000; Ríos-Figueroa 2007). While useful in detecting broad patterns, this work has not looked at the various factors that judges consider *at the individual level* before they pen a decision and cast a vote.

Political Environment

The strategic model posits that one of the most important constraints on judicial behavior concerns perceptions about what constitutes a legitimate court action. Proponents of the model suggest that justices have to, more or less, appear to follow legal principles such as stare decisis. Following on this idea, scholars have explored how social forces in society at large may shape judicial decision-making (Gillman and Clayton 1999; Whittington 2000). For example, work has looked at the relationship between public opinion and judicial behavior, and evidence does in fact suggest that justices are highly responsive to the public mood (McGuire and Stimson 2004).

To capture how broader structural and institutional factors affect judicial behavior, some scholars have relied on institutional approaches to explain judicial decisions (Smith 1988). For example, historical institutionalism considers values, ideas, and norms as part of analyses of political phenomena (Thelen and Steinmo 1992; Hall and Taylor 1996). Students of judicial politics have argued for the inclusion of, for example, how "role perception" may influence a judge's behavior: specifically, how a judge's sense of duty, obligation, and recognition interacts with ideological, doctrinal, and strategic considerations to yield a particular outcome (Gillman and Clayton 1999).

The most prevalent model applied by scholars in the study judicial behavior in Latin American has been the strategic one, and it has strictly relied on external factors. Beyond looking at the dynamics of internal bargaining, my analysis builds on this work and pays attention to the political context to explain variance in the four court decisions. It matters in important ways.

Constitutional Review in Latin America and the Emergence of Four Powerful High Courts

Argentina's Supreme Court

HISTORICAL ORIGINS

In what has been described as "constitutional plagiarism" (Sagüés 1998), the Argentine judicial system is almost identical to its US counterpart. The 1853 Argentine Constitution, which has formed the basis for the country's political development, was modeled after the 1787 US Constitution in both letter and spirit.[8] The text established the Argentine Supreme Court (*Corte Suprema de Justicia de la Nación*, CSJN), whose nine members were to be nominated by the president in turn and confirmed by the Senate. The first justices were appointed a year later but never sat on the bench to hear cases. In 1860, presaging the court's future instability, a constitutional reform required statutory laws, in contrast to constitutional provisions, to delineate the court's functioning, making it prone to changes by simple congressional majorities. Prompted by President Bartolomé Mitre (1862–68), Congress passed legislation in the early 1860s intended to "organize" the country's "national judiciary" as mandated by the constitution. Law 27, enacted in 1862, lowered the number of justices to five. A year later, and modeled after the 1789 US Judiciary Act, the

Argentine Congress adopted Law 48, drafted by the newly confirmed five justices, which organized the jurisdictional responsibilities of federal tribunals, including the court.

While the constitution was silent on judicial review, Law 48 made the court its final interpreter. It established the "extraordinary appeal" procedure (*recurso extraordinario*), which to this day has been the main venue through which decisions rendered by provincial superior courts (Argentina has a federal system) and federal tribunals can be challenged before the CSJN on constitutional grounds.[9] In instances where an appeal to a lower court is denied, the case can be presented by the appellant directly before the court through a "complaint proceeding" (*recurso de queja*). Argentina's CSJN judicial review powers were firmly cemented through the 1887 leading "*Sojo* case," which followed, almost word by word, the famous 1803 US *Marbury v. Madison* decision, in which the court, ruling on a presidential decree, established that Congress cannot alter the court's constitutional jurisdiction.[10] These developments established a decentralized (or diffuse) system of judicial review (*control de constitucionalidad difuso*). Argentine judges from all levels of courts can engage—and are in fact expected to engage—constitutional questions in all cases before them. The judges have the authority to declare executive or legislative acts unconstitutional. While their decisions affect only the parties involved (*inter partes*), the judicial reasoning can influence future cases. Through subsequent appeals, cases can arrive at the court, which can, in turn, establish general jurisprudence at the national level.

In line with Latin American civil law systems, formal precedent (undergirded by the legal principle of stare decisis that is central to Western systems of law) does not exist in Argentina. That is, the principle of *erga omnes* (applicable to all) does not apply, and decisions handed down by the CSJN are not binding on other courts hearing similar cases. However, upon repeated insistence by the CSJN,[11] lower-court judges have an obligation to follow its jurisprudence. Thus, lower courts are generally expected to apply the CSJN's arguments on constitutional matters. Further, lower-level decisions that contradict or deviate from the Supreme Court's jurisprudence are considered meritless unless they disagree based on unengaged or unexamined reasons.

Perhaps not surprisingly given the country's history of political instability, Argentina's Supreme Court had up until recently been characterized by institutional instability that has affected its judicial independence (Kapiszewski and Taylor 2008). After a period of relative stability in the CSJN's composition since its establishment, 1946 saw the beginning of a regular pattern with the court: the executive's manipulation of its membership ("court packing") mostly through forced retirements. Following the court's validation of military governments after the 1930 and 1946 coups through *sua sponte* rulings, in what became known as the "great agreements" (*acordadas*), newly elected President Juan D. Perón, in what it is widely thought to have been unfair accusations and in violation of due process, managed to impeach or force the retirement of all the justices sitting on the court. As seats vacated, in August 1947, Perón began a process of appointing friendly justices that were both loyal to him and had close links to his political party. The impeachment of sitting justices and the subsequent appointment of justices loyal to the president is regarded as an important historical inflection point for the CSJN (Castagnola 2018, 35–36). It began a particular pattern of interaction between its members and executives whereby incoming presidents would pursue the induced retirement of unfriendly justices and appoint loyal ones to create what in Argentina is generally known as "*corte adicta*" (co-opted court).[12] In effect, from 1955 until the end of the last military dictatorship (1976–83), the entire bench was replaced five times and the number of justices filling the court was changed three times.

DEMOCRATIC RULE

While the political manipulation of the CSJN has generally decelerated since the return of democratic rule in 1983, the court's makeup has continued to be marked by rather distinct periods generally associated with each president in turn. However, in the early 2000s, political developments yielded a bench that was likely one of the most independent in Argentine history. It is this bench that rendered a series of important decisions in the 2000s and 2010s, including the 2012 FAL case.

Soon after President Raúl Alfonsín (1983–89) assumed office as the first democratically elected president after the military dictatorship, the composition of the court changed. With their lack of legitimacy, given that the military junta had appointed them, all sitting CSJN justices voluntarily resigned. In a break from the past, and aiming to secure the necessary senatorial votes for confirmation, Alfonsín appointed a more politically diverse bench consisting of prestigious justices, some of whom had clear ties to the opposition (Verbitsky 1993). Of the five vacancies, he appointed three justices (Genaro R. Carrió, José S. Caballero, and Augusto C. Belluscio) with clear ties to his Radical Party (*Unión Cívica Radical*, RP), one (Carlos S. Fayt) with ties to the Socialist Party (*Partido Socialista*), and one (Enrique Petracchi) with ties to the Peronist Justicialist Party (*Partido Justicialista*, PJ) (Verbitsky 1993).

While Alfonsín assembled a bench with a majority of justices sympathetic to his political positioning, the court turned out to be not all that friendly to the president. The two issues that dominated the political agenda during the 1980s were human rights and economic crises. The court's rulings were characterized by rather erratic behavior when it came to economic cases (González-Ocantos 2016, 80), and in fact it struck down some economic emergency measures enacted by the president (Kapiszewski 2011). Indeed, on average, the court ruled against the government 37 precent of the time between 1983 and 1987, and 47 percent during the last two years of Alfonsín's administration (Helmke 2004, 296). Importantly, in what was perhaps the most charged political filing at the time, how to deal with human rights atrocities committed by the military dictatorship, the court refused to bend to the president's wishes. While he may have crafted a "friendly court," the court assumed unprecedented independence. An attempt to continue the Argentine judicial tradition to increase the court's size in 1987 and to pack it failed when the president was unable to secure congressional support. While the idea continued to be harbored by the executive, it was finally abandoned when the justices threatened to resign en masse if pursued further (Verbitsky 1993).

The CSJN's independence was significantly weakened during the administration of Carlos Menem (1989–99) prior to an important resumption in the early 2000s. Menem, from the Justicialist Party, assumed the presidency in the middle of an economic meltdown characterized by running hyperinflation.[13] While he was elected on the PJ ticket, a party that had long maintained an interventionist position on economic policy, soon after his election he began to push for an ambitious economic reform program along market-friendly principles that saw a significant reduction in statal regulation of the economy. Within months of his inauguration, he sent to Congress a battery of bills to privatize the country's main parastatal firms and to reduce government spending (Teichman 2001). Menem's economic reform plans were pursued in tandem with an important concentration of power in the executive, which included the weakening of both the legislature and the judiciary. Regarding the high court, he resumed the country's tradition of manipulating its composition by both forcing the retirement of some justices and enlarging its size. A priority for his administration, as stated by the president's General Secretary, was to "homogenize" the Supreme Court vis-à-vis the executive (González-Ocantos 2016, 84). A captured court would remove any judicial roadblocks that could find his policies unconstitutional.

Menem was successful in co-opting the CSJN and in securing, for his two terms in office, what became known as an "automatic majority." This term refers to a majority of seats on the court that invariably supported the president's policy decisions. Soon after assuming office, his administration began to pressure justices to retire. The effort had limited results as only one justice (Caballero) did so. As a result, Menem resorted to enlarging the court. In April 1990, amid procedural irregularities,[14] Congress approved a bill to increase the court's size from five justices to nine justices.[15] Justice Jorge A. Bacqué resigned in protest,[16] leaving another vacancy. This meant that, with an increased bench, six vacancies became available. Menem moved swiftly to fill these seats, and come the following month, he sent his roster to the Senate. It was approved within twenty-four hours.

The six new justices shared a very similar profile. While they were respected in academic circles, they also had had close personal relationships to the president, which guaranteed their personal loyalty. Moreover, they openly professed a restrained, conservative approach to judicial interpretation. They relied on this approach to justify their deference to the executive branch (González-Ocantos 2016, 77, 85–86). Menem's appointees gave him an automatic majority in the CSJN, as they invariably wrote in concert. The justices' favorable rulings were crucial in pushing through his social and economic programs during his first term in office.

The court's acquiescence is perhaps best illustrated by the then-controversial privatization of the country's national airlines, Aerolineas Argentinas. The constitutionality of the decision was challenged by opposition parties through a writ of amparo because of allegations of fraud and corruption. To prevent the case from landing on a lower court, the CSJN invoked, for the first time, the *per saltum* doctrine, forcing the case to go directly to the high court to be heard (Castagnola 2018, 49). The court expectedly upheld the constitutionality of the airline's privatization.

The second half of Menem's term saw the crystallization of a constitutional reform that affected Argentina's highest court. Menem's economic reform, while controversial, was popular among important sectors of Argentine society given the assumption of macroeconomic stability (reflected by an increase in the PJ's representation in Congress after the 1991 midterm elections). As such, Menem sought to undertake a constitutional reform that would allow him to run for a second term (presidential reelection was constitutionally barred). To accomplish this, he needed the support of the main opposition, the Radical Party,[17] which saw an opportunity to negotiate with Menem to reduce the concentration of power he had amassed in the executive branch. The result was the Olivos Pact (*Pacto de los Olivos*), an agreement between Menem and Alfonsín held at the presidential residence. In the agreement, Alfonsín supported the presidential election in exchange for the decentralization of power, mainly by granting jurisdictional autonomy to Buenos Aires and formal and informal ways through which the Supreme Court could be made more independent. The informal component of the agreement involved relying on the Argentine tradition of forcing some justices to resign to achieve a different political composition on the bench. Both parties agreed to force the retirement of three justices, jointly choose their replacements, and appoint three independent justices. The addition of these new justices would remove the president's automatic majority.

In part because Menem did not respect his end of the Olivos bargain, the court's co-optation continued during the president's second term once re-elected. Indeed, the automatic majority gave way to a more loyal court. One justice, Eduardo Moliné O'Connor, acted as the main operator in the bench. He drafted most decisions, gave instructions to his counterparts on how to vote, and, it has been argued, would often have his chamber draft most individual justices' written opinions (Hauser 2016, 17).

Nevertheless, the Olivos Pact resulted in formal changes to Argentina's judiciary and the CSJN. A new constitution was enacted in 1994, following deliberations by a constitutional convention in which Radicals pushed for a weaker court (Finkel 2004a, 2004b). The new constitution changed the appointment process by increasing the senatorial threshold for the confirmation of justice from a simple majority (with quorum) to two-thirds, making hearings open to the public, and allowing civil society groups to ask questions of nominated justices. It also reduced the justices' tenure from life to seventy-five years of age. Further, it established the National Judicial Council (*Consejo Asesor de la Magistratura*), which was tasked with the selection of federal judges (from which the executive creates a short list to be confirmed by the Senate), their disciplinary control, and the overall administration of the judiciary below the high court. Finally, it also set up an Impeachment Jury (*Jurado de Enjuiciamiento*) to reduce presidential discretion over the appointments and dismissals. However, despite all the informal negotiations and the formal constitutional reform, Argentina's Supreme Court continued to be co-opted right until the end of Menem's second term.

Nevertheless, the 1994 constitutional reform introduced important changes that have had an important effect on the judicialization of politics in Argentina. The first change refers to the inclusion of a variety of new rights in the constitution, ranging from Indigenous rights to environmental rights to consumer and data privacy rights. The second change was the incorporation of international human rights treaties—evidently, only those to which Argentina is a signatory—as part of the country's legal framework by making their provisions legally enforceable on par with the constitution. In what in Latin America is widely referred to as "conventional control" (*control de convencionalidad*), judges in Argentina, according to new provisions included in section 2 of Article 75, must also consider possible violations of human rights listed in international conventions or treaties when adjudicating constitutional cases.[18] Statutory law must therefore be compliant with international law. A year after the reforms, the Supreme Court also established that, when interpreting provisions established in the American Convention on Human Rights, rulings by the Inter-American Court of Human Rights, the main adjudicatory body, should be taken as guides in deciding cases.[19]

The third important element of the reform was the expansion of standing through the formalization of the writs of *amparo*, *habeas corpus*, and *habeas data*, through their incorporation into the constitution. While the writ of amparo had been part of Argentina's jurisprudence for some time,[20] the formal adoption of the three types of writs provided clearer legal tools to individuals and groups seeking remedies to alleged violations of human rights before the courts.[21] The three elements of the 1994 constitutional reform have dramatically increased the litigation of all matters constitutional and have placed human rights at the core of judicial politics in Argentina (Smulovitz 2012). Indeed, discussions about human rights among judges and members of the legal community in Argentina have been infused with constant references to the importance of economic, social, and cultural rights (ESCR) in the litigation and adjudication of cases.

Colombia's Constitutional Court

HISTORICAL ORIGINS

Colombia's Constitutional Court (CCC) has played a central role in the country's politics, and any analysis of it must be placed within a larger historical context. Colloquially known in the region as "the human rights court," the CCC was established in 1991 with the drafting of a new constitution largely intended to solve the country's intractable violence resulting from conflict around socioeconomic distribution, profound disagreements on the separation between church and state, and the confrontation between its liberal and conservative elites. Indeed, perhaps no other country captures these classical features of Latin America's postindependence political development better than Colombia. Similar to other Latin American countries, its political institutions have historically proved unable to mitigate these problems and avoid violence. Yet, Colombia has developed a highly legalistic culture that favors the mediation of conflict through constitutional discussions and reform (Cepeda-Espinosa 2004). In effect, Colombia's history is one punctuated by distinct periods of instability followed by societal regroupings that have yielded new constitutional frameworks.

The first of these periods spanned from 1819,[22] when Colombia gained independence from Spain (when Simón Bolívar's famously expelled the last large contingent of Spaniard soldiers in the Battle of Boyacá), until 1863, when it adopted a new constitution that established the Republic of the United States of Colombia.[23] This period saw four civil wars between the Liberals and the

Conservatives (who established Latin America's oldest political parties) mainly over the role the Catholic Church should play in politics, the state in economic activity, and the levels of centralization (unitary or federal). The triumphant Liberal Party (*Partido Liberal*) enacted a new liberal constitution (*Constitución de Rionegro*) in 1863 intended to bring about peace through the expansion of a variety of progressive civil and political rights (such as the protection of freedom of speech, the press, the right of association, and universal male suffrage and economic liberalization). It also dispersed political power by clearly establishing three branches of government and decentralizing it through a federal system of government that demarcated nine subnational states. Starting a historic cycle, the new constitution failed to bring about stability and the country saw two more civil wars. The Conservative Party (*Partido Conservador*), triumphant after the second conflict, enacted a new conservative constitution in 1886 with a clear traditionalist bent that reestablished church privileges and concentrated political authority, mostly in the hands of the executive. The new constitution was to guide a new period of Colombian history, a period generally known as "Regeneration." Continuing a pattern, it was unable to mitigate conflict, however. Difficulties in asserting control and socioeconomic tensions proved too strong for the political system to mitigate under conservative (1886–1930) and liberal (1930–46) administrations, despite two constitutional reforms introduced by each of them after asserting control (1910 and 1936) (Palacios 2006). Despite the Liberal Party's attempts at calming social unrest resulting from the Great Depression by, for example, responding to the demands of labor and peasant movements, social tensions continued to intensify, setting the stage for sectarian conflict between the two camps that resulted in country's most violent period, *La Violencia* (The Violence), from 1946 until 1953.

La Violencia, which intensified with the assassination in central Bogotá of the highly popular Liberal presidential candidate Jorge Eliécer Gaitán on April 9, 1948, resulted in approximately 170,000 Colombian deaths. Whereas previous conflicts had been limited to shorter periods of time and restricted to some geographical areas, La Violencia spread to most areas controlled by the state, witnessed an intense urban insurrection, and brought into the mix actors (such as large landowners) who had previously stayed mostly out of conflict. The progressive degradation of the conflict prompted the Liberals and a faction of the Conservative Party to support a military coup in 1953, led by General Gustavo Rojas Pinilla, to try to restore social and political order. Despite initial success, and when it became clear that Rojas Pinilla had the ambition to remain in power, both camps established a bipartisan power-sharing agreement to form a civilian government. As part of what had become a well-established tradition, a constitutional reform in 1957 set the stage for the new agreement (endorsed by over 95 percent of eligible voters through a referendum), called The National Front (*Frente Nacional*) that lasted until 1974. The consociational agreement's main elements were an alternation of the presidency between the two parties every four years for a period of sixteen years and an equal distribution of seats in the cabinet, the judiciary, the two chambers of Congress, departmental assemblies, and municipal councils.

Despite both the augured stability the agreement would bring and the steady economic growth Colombia enjoyed in the 1960s and 1970s (gross domestic product grew by 5.5 percent a year from 1957 until 1981), the country's sociopolitical situation progressively deteriorated during this period, setting the stage for the establishment of the most recent constitutional social contract in the early 1990s (Gutiérrez Sanín 2002). Perhaps inevitably, the guaranteed rotation of power fostered a decrease in programmatic differences between the two parties as political ideology became less important to gain office. While the Liberal Party had traditionally defended the interests of socially excluded sectors of society, both parties became more attentive to the interests of the upper classes. The political regime thus became highly exclusionary and, by the early 1980s, began to bleed legitimacy. Colombia entered a new cycle of political instability as sectors of society began to pull away from the system (captured by higher electoral abstention rates and declining levels of party identification) and to mobilize to place their demands directly on the state. Protests, strikes, and unrest intensified, and organized violence against the regime erupted once again. As has been argued, a main issue was that the National Front's main agreement did not allow for the emergence of new political parties, though because of discontent, factions within the two parties and new social movement did emerge (Duque Daza 2019).

Two additional elements plunged Colombia into another deep crisis by the late 1980s. On the one hand, the country's three main guerrilla groups (FARC, M-19, and ELN), whose leaders were formed during La Violencia, strengthened during this time because of growing social discontent. Indeed, whereas they had previously operated at the margins of mainstream society, the unresponsiveness of the political regime encouraged the sympathy of broader sectors of society, including parts of the middle class. Violence thus became generalized and spread in the country, and that included urban areas (Bushnell 1993). Organized violence became thus increasingly supported by more Colombians (Gutiérrez Sanín 2002). The second element, which contributed to a rather toxic combination, was the incursion of the drug trade. It, in effect, fundamentally altered politics in Colombia. While drug-trafficking activities had previously existed, they were dispersed to rural areas and mostly devoted to the production and transportation of marijuana (Carroll 2011). The increased demand for cocaine, mostly in the United States, during the late

1970s and 1980s changed things dramatically as a new political economy emerged that anchored violence in the country. By the mid-1980s, a duopoly made up of the Cali and Medellín cartels controlled an estimated 80 percent of the world's cocaine traffic, employed more than 100,000 Colombians, and generated upwards of $4 billion in revenue (Hartlyn and Dugas 1999). Beyond the violence associated with the trafficking and exporting of an illicit product, one of the most important effects of the drug trade was political as cartel leadership essentially mounted an attack on the state to guarantee their continued operations (Bejarano 2011). This attack culminated in the assassination of various high-profile political leaders and justices, including the favored presidential candidate Luis Carlos Galán.

Perhaps nothing captures better the climax of the most recent violent period in Colombian history than the dramatic 1985 attack on the country's Supreme Court by a guerrilla group. Members of the M-19 guerrilla group stormed the Supreme Court in an attempt to kidnap sitting justices. The armed forces entered the building as a response and almost half of the court's twenty-five sitting justices and many others were killed or "disappeared."[24] Almost a hundred years after the enactment of Colombia's last constitution of 1886, the country's political institutions had proved, yet again, unable to mitigate conflict. The intensity of violence and social fatigue after these one hundred years of solitude and violence pushed various sectors of Colombian society to regroup and negotiate a new social contract that would refound the political system in fundamental ways. The result was the drafting of Colombia's most recent constitution in 1991, which made the CCC a central protagonist in the country's political life.

CONSTITUTIONAL REFORM AND THE NEW COURT

The previous (and unjustly brief) overview of Colombia's political history set the stage for the enactment of Colombia's new constitution, a process driven by a genuine desire to establish a more inclusionary political system. Originally spurred by a student movement, subsequently labeled The Seventh Ballot (*La Séptima Papeleta*), an initiative to establish a constitutional assembly was tagged onto the ballot for the legislative elections of 1990 (Lemaitre 2009). While the Electoral Council (*Consejo Electoral*) rejected the inclusion of the additional ballot for the elections, the results—in which 86 percent of voters supported the initiative—were nonetheless counted and the Supreme Court (*Corte Suprema de Justicia*) subsequently validated the vote. It paved the way for the election, in December 1990, of the delegates that made up the National Constituent Assembly (*Asamblea Nacional Constituyente*). The assembly, tasked with deepening Colombian democracy, worked for five months and presented the new draft constitution. It was adopted on July 4, 1991.[25]

Colombia's constitution established a rather progressive "social and legal" political system (*Estado Social de Derecho*) whose main objective is to guarantee its people's welfare.[26] The constitutional text explicitly refers to ideas of social justice and enumerates a battery of socioeconomic rights that the state is tasked with guaranteeing. Framed around the idea of human dignity, these rights are listed along seventy-seven articles and range from the right to health care and education to the right to a safe environment and pensions. Moreover, Article 93 makes it mandatory to reference international treaties when interpreting these rights. Importantly, for our purposes, the constitution contains several gender justice provisions, since it included most of the demands presented by women's movements (Lemaitre 2009). For example, it prohibits discrimination against women and includes a reproductive freedom clause that guarantees "the couple" the right "to decide freely and responsibly the number of their children" (Articles 13 and 42). Colombia's political (conservative and liberal) elites, after having dominated the country's politics for decades, appear to have realized that a new, progressive social contract was necessary, a change of heart that was partly brought about by the presence of leftist and alternative voices during the constitution-making process (Bushnell 1993).

Structurally, the constitution established a republican, centralized unitary state that provides some autonomy to its "territorial entities" made up of 32 departments and 1,123 municipalities. Nationally, power is divided among three branches of government made up of the executive, the legislative, and the judiciary. The executive branch is led by the head of government and state, the president. The constitution established that the president would be elected by national vote for one nonrenewable four-year term.[27] As is the case with many Latin American countries, if no presidential candidate wins an overall majority, a runoff election is held between the two leading candidates. While the new constitution weakened somewhat the power of the presidency (by, for example, decreasing the president's ability to declare states of siege), the president still wields significant power and conforms to the Latin American norm of *presidencialismo* (Díez 2012). For example, presidents possess significant fiscal power: all budgetary bills must emanate from their office. The legislative branch of government is made up of a bicameral congress composed of a Senate and a Chamber of Representatives. Members of both chambers are elected for unlimited four-year terms through proportional representation. However, to curb the historically strong presidential powers, the 1991 constitution allows Congress to override some presidential vetoes and to modify their decrees. It also took away the special status the Catholic Church had and established freedom of worship, granting all religions the same legal status (Lombo 2021).

In terms of the judiciary, the drafters of the new constitution placed high courts at the center of Colombia's new political regime, expectedly given the country's rather long tradition of judicial independence. As has been pointed out (Landau 2005), since its establishment in 1886, Colombia's Supreme Court (*Corte Suprema de Justicia de Colombia*) has been part of state building and entrusted with an important role in national politics. The court built experience dealing with political matters, and most major political controversies were judicialized (Landau 2015). In a country with a highly legalistic political culture and a strong Supreme Court, the judiciary became, understandably, a key political actor. However, in part due to a generalized feeling of distrust of old institutions, especially Congress, and to make institutions more pluralistic and accessible to citizens given the ossification of the old political system, the constituents decided to create a new specialized court: the Constitutional Court. It was seen as a mechanism of access to the political system and prime site of conflict mitigation.[28] It was given sweeping powers because constituents saw the judiciary and the law as the best ways to solve Colombia's problems (Landau 2015, 28).

The CCC is one of three apex courts in Colombia, along with the Supreme Court and the Council of State (*Consejo de Estado*). They are structurally organized according to their functional jurisdictions. The twenty-three-member Supreme Court deals with disputes in ordinary areas of the law, such as criminal, family, and labor law. It is the highest appellate court in these matters and reviews decisions from municipal, circuit, and superior courts. Importantly, and similarly to some post-transition courts in Latin America, the Supreme Court was given important investigative and prosecutorial powers, including the power to investigate the president and members of Congress. The (prestigious) Council of State, the oldest judicial institution in Latin America founded by Simón Bolívar in 1817, has twenty-seven members and is the highest administrative court in Colombia. It has jurisdiction over all public and private administrative issues. It reviews decisions from departmental courts.[29]

In the country with the longest history of de jure (i.e., legally mandated) judicial review in Latin America (and, likely, the world),[30] the CCC was expectedly given strong judicial review powers (both abstract and concrete) to decide on the constitutionality of bills, laws, and referenda (Rozo Barragán 1997; Mendieta González 2010; Uprimny and Villegas 2004).[31] The court was designed to strike a delicate balance between preventing it from being overly politicized and making it accessible to the public. On the first aspect, the constituents adopted a hybrid appointment process that allows for broad representation of various political forces in the country, making it impossible for political elites to "capture" a majority of seats on the court (Tiede 2022;

Lamprea 2010; Schor 2008). The nine justices (*magistrados*) are elected by the Senate from slates of three candidates nominated by the president, the Supreme Court, and the Council of State.[32] Since its establishment, the court has guarded against court packing by bolstering its own legitimacy among the middle class and the legal academy (Landau 2015).

In terms of accessibility, the new Colombian Constitution retained its powerful public action (*acto popularis*) review mechanism (*Acción Pública de Inconstitucionalidad*), which is, to my knowledge, the first individual constitutional review mechanism in Latin America and one of the most powerful in the world.[33] An abstract review instrument, the public action motion can be used by any citizen and submitted directly to the court to compel it to review the constitutionality of any part of legislation, regulations, and decrees. Rulings resulting from public actions have *erga omnes* effects, affecting all Colombian citizens.[34] The public action mechanism eliminates any requirements for standing. Under this mechanism, any Colombian citizen can submit a public action without an attorney and without having to demonstrate a specific legal interest in the subject matter of the claim. The court must hear all cases and issue a ruling either upholding or striking down the impugned law.[35]

A second mechanism is an individual complaint called the writ of *tutela* (*acción de tutela*). A tutela provides quick relief to individuals whose constitutional rights have been violated by state or nonstate actors. Tutelas can also be filed by any citizen and brought before any court, also without the need of an attorney. All lower-level tutela decisions reach the CCC, which has discretion over which tutela cases it takes up. This discretion prevents the CCC from becoming overwhelmed and allows it to ensure consistency across its decisions. Tutelas confer the power to individuals to request relief directly from the CCC. This mechanism has been the primary conduit through which individual Colombians have sought redress for the violation of numerous socioeconomic constitutional rights.[36] Judges are legally bound to prioritize these files above any other business and provide an answer within ten days.[37]

Colombia's CCC has become one of the most powerful and assertive high courts in the world since its establishment. Despite challenges to its independence, the CCC has both retained its activism and maintained a great deal of legitimacy among Colombians (Botero 2020). It has also become a central player in Colombian politics. Indeed, it has been critical in checking excesses committed by the executive (famously denying a president's wishes for reelection in 2010) and taken vital steps in transforming the country socially through the confirmation of many socioeconomic rights and the expansion of others. For example, the CCC ruled in favor of the legalization of the personal possession of illicit drugs in 1994 (Decision C-221) and euthanasia in 1997 (C-239), years before the issues were placed atop national agendas in many countries.[38] It has also taken substantial steps at including marginalized groups into the policymaking process. In a 2010 ruling, for example, it strengthened Indigenous autonomy rights by requiring that major extractive operations include significant prior consultation with Indigenous peoples in the region. Moreover, in 1999, the court ruled, in a landmark decision that gained global attention (SU-337–99) on intersexual rights (establishing that surgery cannot be performed without the express consent of minors).[39] Also, in 1998, the CCC ruled (SU-642–098) that educational institutions cannot impose any restrictions on students' personal appearance because it violates their constitutional right to the free development of personality.

The progressive nature of Latin America's "human rights court" is explained by its design and composition, which were set upon the court's establishment. This is key in understanding any of the CCC's subsequent landmark rulings. It is, in a way, an essential part of the court's DNA. Along with the inclusion of an extensive list of rights into the new constitution, discussions among constituents during the assembly's deliberations included a new conception of rights that regarded them as real power assigned to individuals (Cepeda-Espinosa 1993). The idea was that they would not be remote legal concepts but rather directly and immediately enforceable, and they would protect the most essential needs of people. Rights, according to this new conception, were about empowering people to transform Colombian society into a more just society. Importantly, this view had support from leaders of both the Liberal and Conservative Parties. While this view was pursued by the Liberal President César Gaviria and advisers close to him (Nunes 2010a), it was eventually also supported by prominent Conservative Party figures, such as former president and conservative delegate Misael Pastrana (1970–74).

The court's progressive tilt is also inextricably linked to the composition of its first bench in 1991, which consisted of three progressive legal scholars with expertise in constitutional law. As agreed upon, the court began to operate with a "temporary" bench of seven justices for a full year in February 1992.[40] The new bench included a group of three justices who, along with their law clerks, had international experience, came from an elite law school in Colombia, and possessed a sense of purpose to make of the court an active supporter of human rights (Nunes 2010a; Landau 2015).[41] While not a majority, the three justices were supported by the president and acted effectively as a bloc. An integral component of their legal preferences and philosophy involved a more substantive and interpretive legal doctrine aligned with Latin America's neoconstitutionalism. Convinced that the dysfunction of the old political regime was linked to the formal way the Supreme Court had interpreted rights, this group of legal entrepreneurs pushed away from legal formalism and toward a new way of conceptualizing rights that would be closer to people's realities. For the three justices, it was about bringing constitutional rights closer to the people. The CCC abandoned formalism and adopted a realist approach that emphasized balancing tests in accord with a progressive, neoconstitutional political agenda (Landau 2005; Lemaitre 2009, 146–49). The drastic break from formalism was sustained among an important cohort of justices in subsequent years. The court's new-constitutionalist position has been challenged, inside and outside the court, by jurists and political actors with a more formalist approach to the law, such as those who have been career judges or conservative actors. However, they have for the most part operated with an understanding that the court's main role is to materialize the rights enumerated in the constitution.

THE COURT'S STRUCTURE AND FUNCTIONING

Since the "first court" was confirmed (on March 31, 1993), Colombia's Constitutional Court has had nine justices who serve for one eight-year nonrenewable term. Each justice leads an "office" (chamber) (*despacho*) usually made up of two senior law clerks (*magistrados auxiliares*), three junior law clerks (*auxiliaries judiciales*), and a legal counsel (*abogado sustanciador*). The number of staff has increased over time, as has the workload. These teams oversee the development of a justice's decisions (*ponencias*). Like the Argentine case, law clerks perform powerful roles since most of them spend more time at the court than the justices themselves, and they are also in charge of drafting most decisions (Agudelo 2010). Law clerks also develop close, personal relationships with the justices, and a couple of them have in fact become justices themselves. They are, in a way, career civil-judicial servants. There were, by 2000, approximately 140 staff personnel at the court. Through a vote, the nine justices select a president and a vice president of the court. Both justices are in charge of the internal administration of the court, which outside the nine chambers is made up of six administrative offices, such as the press office and the powerful General Secretariat (*Secretaría General*) and, likely surprising for those who are not observers, Monitoring Chambers (*Salas de Seguimiento*). Made up of three justices, these chambers are set up by the court itself and tasked with monitoring the implementation of landmark decisions. The first one was set up in 2004.

Most of the court's decisions relate to the resolutions of tutelas and constitutional public actions. To maximize efficiency, tutelas are processed by small chambers. A Selection Chamber of two justices decides whether a tutela should be chosen for discussion. Recall that all of the country's tutelas end up at the CCC. If selected, the file is distributed to (one of nine) Revision Chambers, which are made up of three justices and presided by one of them. Any justice, the Ombudsperson Office (*Defensor del Pueblo*), the Attorney General Office, and the National Agency for the Legal Defense of the State (*Agencia Nacional de Defensa Jurídica del Estado*)—that is, those tasked with defending subnational levels of government in judicial processes—can insist on the exclusion of a tutela from process. The distribution of files is carried out in alphabetical order. A simple majority of two of the Revision Chamber is required to decide on a case. When there may exist more than one tutela whose contents may be contradictory or unclear, or when there is no consensus among the three on any other case, the entire bench meets to set jurisprudence through a Unification Ruling (*Sentencia de Unificación de Tutela*). Decisions on tutelas make up, by far, the bulk of the court's workload: by 2002, close to 70 percent (784) of the 1,123 cases decided on by the CCC were tutelas, with the rest being abstract review decisions. Since the CCC's establishment, 58 percent of all tutelas were granted by the court.[42] These relate mostly to issues around health care and pensions (López Bajo 2017).

Constitutional public actions are heard by the court's highest chamber, the Plenum (*Sala Plena*). Public actions are distributed to all justices, but each file is assigned to one justice at a time, in alphabetical order. This Justice Rapporteur (*Magistrado Ponente*) oversees the writing of a draft decision after evaluating the case. Decisions are adopted by an affirmative vote with a single majority of five. Justices can draft concurring opinions (*aclaraciones de voto*) and dissenting opinions (*salvamentos de voto*).

As part of the objective to make the court more accessible to citizens, the 1991 Constitution established mechanisms for public participation and consultation periods leading up to decisions: a mandatory ten-day period for public actions and one determined at the discretion of the Revision Chamber for tutelas. The Justice Rapporteur is responsible for holding these consultations, which are usually attended by experts, state actors, and nongovernmental organizations. Any citizen can submit an opinion on the case, and *amicus curiae* (advisory briefs) are also accepted. The opinion of the attorney general (*Procurador General de la Nación*) is mandatory in public actions. The court may also solicit the opinion of cabinet justices and other state actors.

Mexico's Supreme Court

HISTORICAL ORIGINS

A schematic reading of scholarly work on the judicialization of politics in Mexico would lead one to believe that the story begins with the 1994 constitutional reform that cemented the autonomy of Mexico's Supreme Court (*Suprema Corte de Justicia de la Nación*, SCJN) and strengthened its power of judicial review. While there is a consensus that during the almost sixty years of dominant one-party rule (1939–97) the SCJN played a subservient role vis-à-vis the executive (Caballero 2009; Ríos-Figueroa 2007; Finkel 2003, 2004a; Domingo 2000; Magaloni 2008; Fix-Zamudio 1990), judicial review has been a central part of judicial politics in Mexico for a long time. Dismissing this history would convey an incomplete picture of judicial politics in Mexico. In the country where the *juicio de amparo* (writ of amparo) was created, the idea that individuals and jurisdictions can seek redress through courts when their constitutional rights have been violated has been long in the making. This is perhaps best captured by the expression *me voy a amparar* (I will seek an amparo), used colloquially by Mexicans when a perceived injustice has been committed against them. Mexico's conception of judicial review unfolded through conversations among constitutional drafters at important historical junctures about the proper role of the Supreme Court in Mexican politics. A brief historical overview is thus in order.

Mexico's one hundred years of solitude (of violent state formation) spanned roughly from 1824, with the adoption of its first national constitution, until 1917, when the postrevolutionary political elite (the "revolutionary family") enacted a new constitution intended to bring about stability and foster socioeconomic development. During this period and through various regimes, political elites entertained different ideas about the role of the judiciary in upholding constitutional principles. The 1824 Constitution established the first Supreme Court (*Corte Suprema de la República*) as an appellate court on jurisdictional matters.[43] As various political forces settled in the early postindependence period, the court was established primarily to mitigate conflict among the various levels of government in the new federal state. Eleven justices were selected from lists of elected candidates supplied by state legislatures and computed by the lower chamber of Congress (except for Mexico City). The court was thus placed as an important arbiter among jurisdictional actors under the new political pact.

Ideas of judicial review first emerged in colonial Mexico.[44] Then the 1824 Constitution gave the court the power to establish constitutional delimitations among levels of government. However, judicial review proper was not adopted until 1836. After another period of instability, a new constitution established a high tribunal (*Supremo Poder Conservador*) tasked with the augmented responsibilities of mediating conflict among the branches of government *and* nullifying laws, executive actions, and even rulings from the Supreme Court that are incompatible with Mexico's constitution.[45] Moreover, the new constitution augmented the power of the Supreme Court, which, through an injunction mechanism called "nullity recourse" (*recurso the nulidad*), reviewed rulings handed down by departmental high courts.[46] The court was also given the power to review whether decisions regarding the expropriation of property violated the constitutional right to private property. It in fact ruled four times on the issue over the next several years (Mijangos y González 2022, 30).

These early efforts to establish judicial review were the precursors of the writ of amparo, introduced by Mariano Otero in the constitutional reforms of 1847.[47] According to Article 25 of the text, the judiciary may *amparar* (protect) any inhabitant in the exercise and enjoyment of their constitutional rights against any "attack from the Legislative and Executive Powers, from the Federation or the States." From the beginning, the amparo was established with a limited inter partes scope: (federal) courts' rulings applied only to "the particular case related to the process, without making any general declaration in respect to the law or act that provoked it." Since its initial adoption in 1847, the amparo has been the main mechanism through which Mexican citizens (and subsequently jurisdictions) have been able to seek redress, directly through the courts, when their constitutional rights have been violated. The amparo mechanism was kept in the 1917 rewrite of the constitution, and the mechanism's importance has expanded over the years, even today. While it was primarily intended to have inter partes effects, the amparo gained wider applicability through the enactment of legislation in 1936. The legislation, intended to regulate the amparo, allowed the mechanism to have far-reaching *erga omnes* effects by expressly binding lower courts to the decisions made by the Supreme Court.[48] The system established an exclusive diffuse system of judicial review; the 1936 changes to the amparo were thus binding on future constitutional disputes.

In terms of the Supreme Court, the 1857 Constitution, on which the 1917 Constitution was based, brought about important changes to the court. It gave the judiciary a more prominent role against the backdrop of Mexico's burgeoning legal culture and expansion of civil and political rights. The 1917 Constitution enumerated a battery of rights in twenty-nine articles—thereby expanding the grounds on which parties could seek judicial review and expanding the sites of constitutional contention. The 1917 changes also broadened the areas on which the amparo could be sought: parties could use the amparo to challenge the constitutionality of *any* state action that violated individual freedoms, as well as any federal law or action that violated the sovereignty of states, and any state law or action that violated the sovereignty of the federal government. These changes thus made judicial review available for the decisions of various levels of government. The Supreme Court, as the ultimate appellate court, was therefore granted the final word on amparo cases and a range of issues related to federal law. Regarding its structure, the court's eleven justices were to be appointed through an indirect system managed by Congress for limited periods of six years.

It is within this new legal framework, and during the period of Mexican history called the Restored Republic (1867–76), that judicial review was cemented in Mexico. This occurred with the Vega Case (*Caso Vega*), Mexico's own version of the famous *Marbury v. Madison* case that established a system of judicial review in the United States. The Vega case arose following changes to the amparo system. To facilitate access to the amparo, a law was introduced in 1869 to clarify the amparo's applicability and limits.[49] An important part of this statue was the requirement that the court hear all cases ruled on by district courts. The rationale for this change was to enhance jurisprudential stability, maintain a uniform application of the constitution, and, importantly, ensure that the Supreme Court would become the "depository of constitutional interpretation" (Mijangos y González 2022, 64). The new legal framework empowered the court in an unprecedented way, and it asserted this power that same year in the Vega case. The Vega case concerned a dispute over sanctions to a lower-level judge from Sinaloa State. The dispute turned on a disagreement over the interpretation of judicial jurisdiction between the federal and state courts. The Supreme Court responded to a challenge from the lower chamber of Congress (calling for the impeachment of seven justices with whose votes they disagreed) by affirming the court's ultimate authority on all matters of judicial review. The court held that Congress did not have the ability to review the court's decisions and declared that the court had "the constitutional prerogative" to declare that a "law may not be applied when it is contrary to the Constitution." Judicial review was thus anchored, and the court's judicial independence was born. It is unsurprising that legal historians tend to look at this period of judicial politics in Mexico with a heavy dose of nostalgia.

This nostalgia may be justified because judicial independence was not only short-lived but would not resurface in Mexican politics until after the 1994 reforms. The court was weakened with a reform introduced in 1878 and became essentially subservient vis-à-vis the executive during the dictatorial period called the *Porfiriato* (1876–80, 1884–1911). While the court rarely countered Porfirio Díaz's major decisions, it nonetheless continued to exercise its powers of judicial review. The court enjoyed a period of stability and dealt with a significant increase in the processing of amparos. Indeed, the number of amparo cases that the court resolved increased from 123 in 1869 to 2,108 in 1880 and to over 4,000 cases a year in 1906 (Mijangos y González 2022, 96–97). Mexican citizens made ample use of their country's primary mechanism of judicial review, even during one of the least democratic periods in their country's history.

As is well known, widespread discontent with the inequalities and injustices created by the Porfiriato created the conditions for the uprising that led to the Mexican Revolution. The revolution lasted from 1910 until 1917, during which more than a tenth of the population died. The year 1917 marked the beginning of a new period in contemporary Mexican history. A political pact was reached with the enactment of the 1917 constitution, one of the first "social democratic" constitutions in the world. The 1917 Constitution was one of the first to explicitly task the state with positive obligations to guarantee socioeconomic rights. The 1917 Constitution, which has formed the basis for Mexico's political order, was meant to facilitate the ideological goals of the revolution—namely, economic development and social justice.

The 1917 Constitution adopted several features of the 1857 constitution. It established a federal and presidential system of government with a clear division of powers along three levels of government (federal, state, and municipal). It also dispersed power among three branches of government: the executive branch; the legislature (a bicameral legislative branch of government made of the upper Senate, which represented the thirty-two states, and a Chamber of Deputies); and the judiciary. Regarding the high court, and in an attempt to recover some of the independence it had previously enjoyed, the 1917 Constitution established the SCJN) consisting of eleven justices (later increased to twenty-one) with life appointments. Justices were elected by an absolute majority of Congress in a secret ballot, from lists drafted by state legislatures. As for the judiciary, the new text included three main mechanisms of judicial review. Not surprisingly, the 1917 Constitution kept the *juicio de amparo* with some minor changes. The constitution allowed the court to review rulings by federal tribunals related to the implementation of federal law and international treaties through a mechanism called *recurso de súplica* (appeal recourse). Finally, the 1917 Constitution maintained the Supreme Court's position as jurisdictional arbiter by giving it the power to resolve "constitutional controversies" between the federal government and one or more states, between states, and between branches of state at the state level (Ovalle Favela 2011). This power included "constitutional controversies" in the abstract, where the court could issue an advisory opinion on the constitutionality of a prospective law or policy. The system could be described as a mixed one of abstract and concrete judicial review (López-Ayllón and Fix-Fierro 2003).

While this institutional design was meant to foster judicial independence and constitutionalism, it was not all that successful given the rise of one-party authoritarian rule under Mexico's Institutional Revolutionary Party (*Partido Revolucionario Institucional*, PRI). Mostly through changes made by President Lázaro Cárdenas (1934–40), the political system that emerged after the Great Depression was a highly centralized one built around corporatist structures in which the main social groups were vertically incorporated into the PRI's leadership (Díez 2006, 13–15). In this system, which essentially became a gigantic pork-barreling machine, the leaders of the various corporate groups exchanged party loyalty for material benefits. The system guaranteed stability, as a new political pact guaranteed that the official party could rely on the corporate groups to win elections in exchange for economic and political benefits. In what has been termed as a "partisan system of elite circulation" (Magaloni 2003), vertical and horizontal conflict was resolved in the president's office under PRI rule. This rendered both the legislative and the judiciary mostly rubber-stamp institutions (Casar 1999; Domingo 2000). The Supreme Court was a layover in trajectories of political careers: justices would go on to assume state governorships or seats in Congress (Magaloni 2003).

In terms of the court, and in addition to corporatist forms of state-society relations, a series of reforms introduced in the late 1920s and 1930s weakened severely its judicial independence.[50] By the end of the decade, the Supreme Court had become a "simple appendage of the Executive, in charge of legitimating its decisions" (Mijangos y González 2022, 147). Nevertheless, continuing with a historic trend of changes to degrees of the court's judicial independence over time, the amparo continued to be an important mechanism for constitutional remedy, even during PRI rule, though mostly for controversies dealing with commercial and administrative law. Some work points to high levels of success in amparo proceedings in some cases.[51] Judicial review, then, continued to be part of the Mexican legal-political system.[52]

THE 1994 REFORM AND THE NINTH ERA COURT

One-party rule in Mexico weakened by the late 1980s and accelerated during the 1990s, a process that saw the introduction of a major constitutional reform in 1994 that placed the Supreme Court at the center of Mexican politics. The reform was largely an attempt to restore legitimacy to a system that had suffered major challenges in previous years.

On the political front, the PRI suffered a real challenge to its rule when a splinter group—which opposed the neoliberal economic direction the regime adopted in the 1980s—formed a political party and its leader, Cuauhtémoc Cárdenas, ran against the establishment in the 1988 general elections. While the PRI *officially* won those elections, they were marred by widespread allegations of fraud. It is widely believed that the opposition leader obtained a higher percentage of votes than the official candidate, which severely eroded the PRI's legitimacy. Faced with declining popular support, and within a context of increased mass mobilization, the administration of Carlos Salinas de Gortari (1988–94) attempted to regain legitimacy by introducing a series of political reforms that, among other things, established an independent electoral institute (*Instituto Federal Electoral*), which allowed for the participation of international observers, and a national human rights institute

(*Comisión Nacional de Derechos Humanos*). He also made concessions to the opposition by allowing greater minority representation and by recognizing opposition gubernatorial electoral victories, especially by the main conservative opposition party, National Action (*Partido Acción Nacional*, PAN).

While these efforts appeared to have been partially successful in restoring support for the regime in the 1991 midterm elections, when the PRI gained 61 percent of the vote, they were short-lived as turmoil heightened. Weak economic growth exacerbated economic inequalities, partly fueling further mass mobilization. The media became increasingly critical of the government, and opposition parties began to look like viable governments-in-waiting. In 1994, a guerrilla movement emerged in the southern state of Chiapas, and the political infighting that began in the 1980s culminated in the assassination of two senior party officials, including the PRI presidential candidate for the 1994 elections. Political chaos deepened when, in late 1994, Mexico's economy was thrust into crisis. Mexico's banking sector collapsed, prompting a precipitous devaluation of the peso. By the end of the Salinas administration, the country was experiencing armed conflict, an unprecedented increase in violence, the worst economic crisis in decades, and rumors of a possible coup.[53]

It is against this backdrop of political and economic turmoil that President Ernesto Zedillo (1994–2000) began his administration on December 1, 1994. For Zedillo, it was imperative to restore confidence in the political system. This included a new national social contract in the form of major constitutional reform, in which the judiciary would play a central role. From Zedillo's perspective, achieving democratic legitimacy in a more competitive Mexico required a trustworthy and impartial arbiter, and that could no longer be the president: it had to be Mexico's Supreme Court (Mijangos y González 2022, 202). Such was the urgency of acting on it that, four days after his inauguration, Zedillo sent to Congress a package of constitutional reforms to the judiciary. These reforms significantly changed the role of Mexico's Supreme Court. The reforms aimed at turning the constitution into "real law" intended to provide the basis for "a safe, orderly, and tranquil" coexistence. The Supreme Court was, according to the proposed reform, central to this plan. It meant turning the Supreme Court into a constitutional tribunal, which included expanding the strength of its decisions and letting it rule on the constitutionality of statues with broad effects to reduce conflict and to act as guarantor of federalism. The proposed reforms were speedily approved and came into effect four weeks after their submission to Congress.

The reforms brought about several important changes that established what is generally known in Mexico as the Ninth Era Supreme Court (*La Corte de la Novena Época*).[54] The size of the bench was reduced from twenty-six to eleven justices (*Ministros*), the original number established in the 1917 constitution.[55]

Judicial candidates were required to possess "recognized professional prestige" and "high moral virtues," as well as having earned a law degree at least ten years before. Candidates were barred from having held a political position in the year before their nomination. In terms of the appointment process, the Senate selects a candidate from a list (*terna*) of three names submitted by the president.[56] Those selected seek confirmation by a simple two-thirds majority of the upper chamber of the legislature.[57] Candidates must answer questions from senators in public hearings. Justices serve for staggered and nonrenewable fifteen-year terms. The reform also created the seven-member Federal Judicial Council (*Consejo Federal de la Judicatura*) to oversee the administration of the federal judiciary and relieve the court of a heavy administrative load (Jiménez Remus 1996).[58] Finally, the reform reduced the number of specialized benches (*salas*) from four to two, made up of five ministers each. The First Chamber (*Primera Sala*) hears criminal and civil cases and the other (*Segunda Sala*) hears labor and administrative cases. The court's *presidente* (chief justice) is elected through a secret ballot process by their peers for a nonrenewable four-year term. Most sessions are public and, since 2006, accessible through the court's TV channel (*Canal Judicial*) and website.[59]

In terms of judicial review, the reform kept the amparo, with some modifications. Beyond changes clarifying standing and transferring the responsibility to resolve *contradicciones de tesis* (jurisprudential conflict) to the full plenary bench, the reform made it easier for the court to implement amparo decisions by establishing clear mechanisms.[60] The reform also amplified the nature of "constitutional controversies" by expanding the state actors (various branches and levels of government) that have standing and by clarifying the process through which they can challenge the validity of statues and acts that infringe on their jurisdictional competencies (Article 105). Intended to solve disputes between branches and levels of government, the Supreme Court has sole jurisdiction over a posteriori judicial review and hears concrete cases. Depending on the type of the challenged action or statue, it can have limited inter partes effects or systemic *erga omnes* effects.[61]

The most important change to the court's constitutional jurisdiction brought about by the 1994 reform was the introduction of the constitutional action (*acto de constitucionalidad*). Like Argentina's amparo and Colombia's "public action," the constitutional action granted Mexico's Supreme Court the exclusive power of abstract review over the constitutionality of state and federal laws. Intended to provide minority parties access to judicial review, constitutional actions allowed state actors to bring challenges to the court. Actions could be brought by 33 percent of legislators of the chamber that approved the statue; 33 percent of either congressional chamber against statues passed by the federal government and Mexico City; the attorney general;

registered political parties; the National Human Rights Commission; and the state human rights commissions. Individuals do not therefore have standing in acts of constitutionality. Applicants must submit their constitutional action to the court within thirty days of the challenged law's enactment. A supermajority of eight justices is required to declare the invalidity of a statue and for the decision to have *erga omnes* effects. This datum is important to our story, as we shall see.

Finally, the reform strengthened the ability of the court to select and hear amparo cases from circuit courts through the *Facultad de Atracción* (*hearing prerogative*). Historically, and in an attempt to lessen the court's workload, most amparo cases have been heard by circuit courts. The 1987 constitutional reform reaffirmed the practice. The 1994 reform, however, allowed the court to hear amparo cases from the circuit courts' dockets. A type of writ of *certiorari*, this institutional feature can be activated at the request of any Supreme Court justice, at the request of a circuit court magistrate or the attorney general, or when the case was deemed to be of national "importance or transcendence." Once the case is selected or literally "attracted" by the court, justices decide whether the case should be heard by the bench. This mechanism gives justices a great deal of power because they can choose which cases they hear from among the many amparos being processed by circuit courts. The 1994 reform thus left Mexico's Supreme Court with a complex constellation of judicial review mechanisms that contains abstract, concrete, and diffuse features.[62]

While there exists disagreement around the factors behind Zedillo's decision to give the court expanded de jure judicial review powers,[63] there is a consensus that the SCJN has become a more assertive constitutional tribunal because of the 1994 reforms and that it has become an important policymaker in post-transitional Mexico (Fix-Fierro 2003; Ríos-Figueroa 2007; Finkel 2003, 2004a; Cossío Díaz 2001; Staton 2010). In its early years, the Ninth Era Court tended to prefer resolving jurisdictional and electoral disputes. However, it became progressively more interested in using its judicial review power to expand human rights protections (Madrazo and Vela 2011; Bustillos 2009; Bárcena Arévalo 2018; López Aylón and Valladares 2009; Castillejos-Aragón 2014; Vela 2011). Indeed, during the mid-2000s and before another important reform undertaken in 2011,[64] the court decided on several controversial human rights cases, including cases involving sexual and reproductive rights. This incipient change includes abortion, as we shall see in chapter 5. Its more prominent role as a human rights protector has come with increasing public approval rates (Mijangos y González 2022). Some polling has the court enjoying higher approval ratings than other political institutions: 63 percent (*El Financiero*, March 21, 2023).

Costa Rica's Constitutional Chamber

Costa Rica's Constitutional Chamber is widely regarded as one of the most independent and active in Latin America (in fact, it might be one of the most independent and active in the world).[65] Since its creation in 1989, the chamber has become an active policy actor, a major player in the country's national politics, and one of the most trusted institutions in this Central American country (Gutiérrez de Colmenares 2006; Ríos-Figueroa and Pozas-Loyo 2010; Wilson 2007, 2011; Lösing 2002). However, despite its importance in the country's contemporary politics, the chamber's role in expanding sexual and reproductive rights has been, until recently, insignificant—standing out in stark contrast with the three other courts I analyze in this book. Indeed, the chamber's 2007 decision under study (chapter 6) is the "non-case" in my comparative analysis, given that it supported the status quo on access to abortion. The chamber's support for policy stasis within what I call the First Wave of Abortion Decriminalization is rather puzzling given that, as scholarship has shown (Wilson 2007; Wilson and Rodríguez Cordero 2006), its active role has included the expansion of a variety of socioeconomic rights, some of which have been extended to previously marginalized groups. This inaction is partly explained, as data reveal, by a particular historical legacy of judicial politics in the country: a generalized tendency by Costa Rican judges to defer to the Legislative Assembly (*Asamblea Legislativa*) on moral issues. Therefore, a brief journey through Costa Rica's history of judicial politics is necessary before analyzing the 2007 decision, as this context is vital for providing a more thorough explanation.

HISTORICAL ORIGINS

A cursory glance at Costa Rica's history may prompt some readers to draw parallels with most other countries in the region, including the three that I have just reviewed. The country underwent a long period of instability after independence from Spain, followed by various attempts at forging new social contracts through constitution-making in the latter part of the nineteenth century, subsequently followed by democratic rule by the turn of the twenty-first century. A similarly quick glance at the country's history of judicial politics would likely prompt the same readers to identify further similarities: the early establishment of a Supreme Court with some judicial review powers, fluctuation over time in the high court's independence and policymaking role, ultimately followed by constitutional reforms in the latter part of the twentieth century that empowered its highest constitutional court. Nevertheless, as any introductory textbook to Latin American politics would also suggest, Costa Rica is, along with Uruguay and Chile, an exception to broader general political trends in the region given its many particularities. It is, after all, the longest-standing democracy in the region and the only country without a standing military. Some of these particularities, derived from historical developments, are essential in understanding the country's contemporary judicial politics and politics more broadly. Indeed, one of the country's many exceptional characteristics appears to involve a particular judicial tradition.

As one of six colonies (along with Chiapas, which later joined Mexico, Guatemala, Honduras, El Salvador, and Nicaragua) that belonged to Captaincy General of Guatemala (which was under the administrative authority of New Spain, current-day Mexico) during Spanish colonial rule, Costa Rica officially gained independence from Spain in 1821, when Mexico did. The five other provinces broke away from Mexico and formed a new polity in 1823 called the Central American Federal Republic, with its capital in Guatemala. Like in many other parts of postindependence Latin America, tensions between various political forces—in this case between liberals and conservatives, Guatemala and the provinces, centrists and local nationalists, and key political figures (Booth 1998, 19)—forced the collapse of the new country in 1839. Five new independent nations emerged, among which was Costa Rica.

Unlike the other Central American countries, deep divisions between the elite liberals and conservatives did not exist, since conservative forces dominated national politics. Yet the country did not completely escape Latin America's one hundred years of solitude. From 1824 to 1949, only 16 percent of all presidents got to power through fair elections, and there were twenty-one insurrections every two years between 1882 and 1938 (Lehoucq 1998, 28). Nevertheless, with the region ushering in its era of "Order and Progress" in the latter part of the nineteenth century, Costa Ricans elected a constituent assembly to draft a new constitution in 1870 following a coup d'état. It was adopted in December of the following year. A liberal document, the constitution was in place, with brief interruptions, until 1949. The 1871 document was progressive for its time. It abolished the death penalty, established freedom of religion, extended some socioeconomic rights, such as education, and established a separation of powers between three branches of government. The constitution set the basis for relative political stability in the country as it established a more inclusive political system that saw an expansion in social spending, especially in health and education (Díaz 2003).

Concerning the judiciary, Costa Rica established three branches of government as early as 1824 while it was a province of the Central American Federal Republic. It had a high court sitting above all lower courts, and justices were elected through popular vote.[66] In 1825, a superior court was set up with "five to seven" justices (*magistrados*) (Article 132). It began to function formally in 1826 with five justices. However, as the remotest province of the republic, colonial laws continued to be generally applied over the next two decades.

It was not until 1841, after Costa Rica separated from the federation in 1838, that under the (authoritarian) government of jurist Braulio Carillo Colina (known as "the architect of the Costa Rican State"), the country adopted its own legal system. It did so through the General Code that regulated criminal, civil, and procedural matters. Regarding judicial review, just four months before Costa Rica's separation, a law was passed by the federation that adopted an ambiguous notion of judicial review: it stipulated that it would be the federal Supreme Court's role to annul acts passed by federal or state governments that contravene fundamental rights (Sáenz Carbonell and Masís Pinto 2006, 19). This idea was vaguely taken up by Costa Rica's first autonomous constitution (*Decreto de Bases y Garantías*) adopted in 1841 with a newly created Judicial Chamber (*Cámara Judicial*) and a subsequent, newly drafted constitution (1844) that established a Supreme Court. A Judiciary Act (*Ley Reglamentaria de Justicia*) was passed in 1845 and reintroduced over the next three decades after constitutional reforms.

Costa Rica's 1871 Constitution set the foundation for judicial independence in the country as it opened what has been termed the "first era of constitutional maturity" (Sáenz Carbonell and Masís Pinto 2006). The document set up a republican system of government that clearly divided power horizontally among three branches of government (executive, legislative, and the judiciary) and reintroduced an independent Supreme Court. As part of an intergenerational conversation among the elites, the constitution contained several features from previous texts. The court comprised a chief justice (*regente*), five justices, one prosecutor (*fiscal*), and five substitute justices selected by a unicameral legislature—the Legislative Assembly. Justices would serve for as long as they exhibited "good performance." The text was also influenced by an earlier idea of dividing the court's work into specialized chambers (*salas*) to engage different areas of the law, similar to the Mexican case.[67] This time around, however, the court was given explicit judicial review powers: the constitution assigned it the authority to strike down legislation, through unanimity, in order to stop "the implementation of laws contrary to the Constitution" when requested by the attorney general or "any citizen" as well as to strike down any bylaws (*ordenanzas*) or "municipals acts" contrary to the Constitutions and Laws of the Republic (Article 62). The newly empowered court began to sit in May 1872. Its internal responsibilities and reach were regulated by a series of statutory acts, among which is the 1888 Judiciary Act (*Ley Orgánica de Tribunales*). This act was followed by other statutes that reinforced judicial independence (1937 and 1940). Of note was the 1937 reform that established concentrated judicial review—a feature that characterizes the type of judicial review Costa Rica has to this very day: it transferred this authority from the country's tribunals to the Supreme Court.[68] Nevertheless, and this is a key point, despite the changes to the legal framework that increased its de jure judicial independence, the Supreme Court acted in a restrained manner and with deference to the legislature from the beginning (Hernández Valle 1978; Gutiérrez de Colmenares 2006). Such attitude would continue to guide the chamber's behavior in subsequent years.

The 1871 Constitution was suspended after Costa Rica's short (forty-four-day) Civil War of 1948 and replaced by a new constitution that remains in force to this day. The war was provoked by the Teodoro Picado Michalski administration (1944–48) attempting to have the Legislative Assembly, dominated by his political party, nullify the election won by the opposition party's candidate, Otilio Ulate Blanco. Backed by communists and elements from Guatemala and other Central American countries, the National Liberation Army (*Ejercito de Liberación Nacional*), led by José Figueres Ferrer, fought against the (weak) army and deposed the sitting government. The victorious National Liberation Movement called for a new constituent assembly to draft a new constitution after the end of the conflict. Made up mostly of a new generation of political actors, the assembly drafted a new constitution that set the basis for the longest uninterrupted democracy in Latin America (and one of the most successful). It came into effect on November 7, 1949. The new constitution expanded political participation (it, for example, introduced women's suffrage) and enshrined numerous socioeconomic rights. It has contributed to the country's stability ever since.[69]

The document established a "Liberal and Social Democratic State" in charge of guaranteeing numerous civil, political, and economic rights. According to Articles 20–74, the constitution provides an array of civil rights that range from the prohibition of capital punishment to freedom of movement and the right of habeas corpus. Adopting the idea of "un-renounceable rights," the constitution commits the state to pursuing the "greatest well-being of all inhabitants of the nation" as well as to "organizing and stimulating production and the most appropriate distribution of wealth." As such, it makes the state responsible for guaranteeing the stipulated socioeconomic rights, several labor rights (including a decent minimum wage, equal pay for equal work, two weeks of paid vacation a year, and collective bargaining rights, among many others), and the right to education and social security, which includes health care through the national social security system, the *Caja Costarricense de Seguro Social* (CCSS), which is colloquially known as *la caja* by Costa Ricans. While there has tended to be a gap between legal formalism and compliance with the law in Latin America, most observers would agree that Costa Rica has been generally successful in guaranteeing its people's rights.

The 1949 Constitution reestablished a republican system of government based on the notion of "popular sovereignty" (the right to rule resides in equal citizens). It adopted a unitary system with seven provinces with relatively limited power and eighty-one cantons (*cantones*), or municipal governments, headed by mayors. Partly because of the events leading up to the Civil War, the document did not establish an army and, innovatively, set up what essentially amounts to a horizontal division of power among four branches of government: the executive (led by a president to serve for only one four-year term),[70] the legislature (reintroducing a unicameral Congress in the form of the Legislative Assembly made up of fifty-seven deputies (*diputados*), the judiciary, and an independent Electoral Tribunal (*Tribunal Supremo Electoral*, TSE) in charge of organizing and overseeing elections and settling electoral disputes.

Straying from a historical and persistent regional trend, Costa Rica's constitution established a presidential system that is an oddity in Latin America: a (comparatively) weak presidency and a powerful legislature. A main objective among many of the constitutional drafters was to diminish the power of the presidency to prevent the return of caudillo rule and ultimately civil conflict (Gutiérrez Gutiérrez 1999). The result was a constitution that established one of the weakest executives in Latin America (Mainwaring and Shugart 1997). Beyond the non-reelection clause and the establishment of autonomous institutions in charge of some important areas of social policy, such as the CCSS, there are few formal powers exercised by the president alone: they include naming and removing cabinet ministers as well as serving as the head of state and commander-in-chief of the National Police and Civil Guard (Booth 1998, 62–63). Other powers must be shared with other actors. For example, veto power on legislation is shared with the cabinet minister in charge of the subject matter. Further, a Council of Government (*Consejo de Gobierno*) is tasked with many important responsibilities, such as naming ambassadors (a traditional Latin American means of rewarding political loyalty). Finally, there are several important checks on the presidential office: the Legislative Assembly must approve the president's suggested budget, has the power to impeach presidents and cabinet ministers, and appoints a national comptroller (*Contralor General*) who oversees budget spending.

In what may remind some readers of discussions surrounding "parliamentary supremacy" in comparative politics, Costa Rica's constitution essentially adopted such an idea in a presidential system: the Legislative Assembly was designed to be the most powerful institution in the country. The *presi-*

dencialismo (strong executive) pattern that has characterized postindependence Latin American political history (Díez 2012, 37–40) was therefore not part of the deal here. In effect, whereas in presidential systems, the three branches of government are seen as being the depositories of popular sovereignty, Article 105 of the Costa Rican Constitution explicitly states that the "power to legislate resides in its people, who delegate it, by means of the vote, to the Legislative Assembly." The Costa Rican legislature was thus granted a great deal of power. Beyond legislating and the powers vis-à-vis the president mentioned above, it has the power to amend the constitution (with a two-thirds majority);[71] it can declare war, ratify treaties, expropriate property, suspend constitutional rights in times of crisis, grant amnesty for some crimes, and authorize public debt; and it has significant powers over the appropriation of local infrastructure projects (in a unitary system) (Booth 1998, 59–61).

A strong legislature necessarily means a weaker executive but also a weaker judiciary, and this has involved the Supreme Court. The 1949 Constitution maintained de jure judicial independence and continued to give the Supreme Court the power to check the other two branches with strong judicial review powers in the form of constitutional actions. It also adopted the writs of habeas corpus and amparo. Specifically, it maintained the Kelsenian model of a concentrated form of judicial review lodging this power in the Supreme Court (Article 124). Importantly, the constitution also made explicit that the court's declarations of unconstitutionality have *erga omnes* effects. Perhaps expectedly, given the country's historical proximity to Mexico, it gave the court the power to decide on amparos to protect individual constitutional rights not protected by habeas corpus.[72] Moreover, Article 128 also adopted a priori judicial review whereby, with a two-thirds majority of Legislative Assembly deputies, the court can reject a bill on constitutional grounds. Finally and very importantly, the 1949 document explicitly states that the judiciary must obtain a set percentage of the national budget, which, since 1957, has been set at 6 percent.

The Supreme Court's strength was reinforced by several formal and informal factors that were at play before the constitutional reform of 1989. However, despite the judicial independence guaranteed by the 1949 Constitution and the de jure judicial review powers it extended to the Supreme Court, the legislature was designed to be the strongest branch of government. While the constitutional drafters intended to maintain judicial independence, they also kept important mechanisms to make the court accountable to the legislature by allowing it to remove justices easily (Cascante Segura 2014). They did so by continuing to have the Legislative Assembly be responsible for setting the number of justices on the bench and their appointment for renewable eight-year terms pending "good performance."[73] Justices were therefore accountable to the legislature through their reelection every eight years. Moreover, introducing a priori judicial review allowed legislators to act preemptively on the court's potential decisions by adjusting bills before their final adoption (Wilson 2005). Further, a two-thirds majority of the bench (twelve votes out of seventeen) was required to rule on the constitutionality of legislation, making such an action rather onerous.

The constitutionally designed strength of Costa Rica's Legislative Assembly was reinforced by a variety of informal mechanisms, in what could be called a type of Costa Rican judicial tradition. This contributed to a restrained Supreme Court before 1989. Indeed, the court's behavior during this time has been described as if it had been in a "slumber" (Wilson 2005). Because of their training in civil law, Costa Rica justices tended to be more inward-looking and aligned with the continental European civil law tradition, an approach that made them less "activist" (Mora Mora 2001). While this may have been the case, Costa Rican judicial culture also built on a longer tradition predating the 1949 Constitution of deference to the legislature. In effect, observers have noted that there was a general sense among deputies that "their power to legislate was absolute" (Urcuyo Fournier 1995, 44, cited by Wilson 2005, 52) and that there was a presumption of constitutionality in the laws they enacted, which meant that justices exercised judicial review with "excessive timidity" (Gutiérrez Gutiérrez 1999, 49). Costa Rican judicial culture meant that judges tended to defer to the legislature and adhere to the concept we essentially know as parliamentary supremacy. The chamber thus rarely ruled against the other two branches of government and tended to make decisions on technical rather than legal grounds. It effectively removed itself from engaging with legal and political issues (Wilson et al. 2004). The result was a rather restrained court that it heard 150 actions of constitutionality by 1989 (out of which only seven were found unconstitutional). This compares to the 228 cases it reviewed during the first two years after the Costa Rica's Constitutional Chamber was established (Feoli Villalobos 2012).

THE 1989 REFORM AND THE CREATION OF THE CONSTITUTIONAL CHAMBER

Constitutional Reform The court's judicial review "slumber" ended with reforms to the constitution and the Judiciary Act (*Ley de la Jurisdicción Constitucional*) carried out in 1989. After a decade of discussions, in August 1989, the Legislative Assembly approved the reforms that created the Constitutional Chamber as a fourth chamber. The assembly confirmed its members on September 15, 1989. It began operating for the first time two days later. The reforms created one of the most powerful and active high courts in Latin America.

After years of discussions among national and international jurists and the Costa Rican political elite, the idea to establish a constitutional court crystallized under the first administration of Oscar Arias Sánchez (1986–90). Arias signed an executive decree in late 1988 that established a special committee tasked with assessing the state of the judiciary in Costa Rica to provide suggestions to improve its efficiency. One of the main proposals advanced by the committee's final report was the establishment of a separate chamber with ample judicial review powers.[74] The proposal was taken up quickly by several deputies from both main parties—the National Liberation Party (*Liberación Nacional*, LN) and the Christian Social Unity Party (*Partido Unidad Social Cristiana*, PSUC)—and it was fast-tracked (*dispensa de trámites*) by the Legislative Assembly and adopted with an overwhelming majority.[75] Unlike other Latin American countries, and certainly the three we have explored in this book, the establishment of Costa Rica's Constitutional Chamber was not part of a broader renegotiation of a national social contract. While part of the motivation behind its establishment appears to have been the desire to restore some legitimacy to the judiciary after some corruption scandals (which affected the Supreme Court), and a potential erosion of democratic legitimacy more broadly as a result of the economic crisis Costa Rica underwent in the 1980s (Wilson 2005, 48), it also appears that the Costa Rican political elite did not fully anticipate the consequences of establishing a specialized court with strong judicial review powers (Wilson 2011, 58). Deviating from another regional trend, explanations for the judicialization of politics applied to other Latin American countries did not seem to have been present in Costa Rica. The Costa Rican experience seems to be a clear case of institutional design with unintended consequences.

The reform picked up on several elements Costa Rica's elites have had in their historical constitutional conversations. The establishment of a fourth chamber saw an increase of the justices on the Supreme Court's bench from seventeen to twenty-two, of which seven (*ministros proprietarios*) were assigned to the constitutional chamber. Continuing with a long tradition, the reforms established that justices in the chamber must be selected by the Legislative Assembly through a single majority,[76] for renewable eight-year terms based on performance, barring a two-thirds majority negative vote by deputies. Twelve substitute judges were assigned, also elected by the assembly for four-year terms. Substitute justices cast a vote when a justice is unable to or absent.

The judicial review powers lodged with the chamber are significant, culminating a process that started in 1871. As set out in Articles 10 and 48 of the constitution, the Judicial Act (Article 73), and an accompanying statute (*Ley Orgánica del Poder Judicial*, Article 57), Costa Rica's Constitutional Chamber has the power to strike down any bill, statute, regulation, international treaty responsibilities, or administrative action it considers unconstitutional. This includes constitutional changes based on faulty legislative procedure. The last point is an important one, given the power the 1949 Constitution gave the legislature.

The reforms lowered the required majority threshold from two-thirds (of the full bench of seventeen justices) to a simple majority of the chamber's four justices, making it easier to reach the threshold. It does not have to consult the Supreme Court's full bench. It also can settle disputes between the various branches of government, including the Electoral Tribunal. Its decisions have *erga omnes* effects (Article 10). As a result of the reforms, Costa Rica has one of the strongest judicial review powers in Latin America (Wilson et al. 2004; Navia and Rios-Figueroa 2005). Calling it the "repairing control" (*control reparador*), Articles 10 and 48 of the constitution established a concentrated system of abstract and concrete judicial review.[77] Specifically, the reforms kept the action of constitutionality, which can be brought against any statute or executive regulation (or international treaty) considered contrary to the constitution, and they can be brought by state actors, which include the comptroller general, the attorney general, the public prosecutor, and the people's defendant (Article 75).[78] Regulated by various provisions of the Judiciary Act, the reforms kept both the writs of habeas corpus and amparo. The first can be filed at the Constitutional Chamber when basic civil and political rights have been violated (i.e., physical liberty) and the second when a right not covered by habeas corpus is violated (i.e., health care). Amparos can be filed against a provision, decision, resolution, or public administrative action or omission that is thought to have violated a constitutional right.[79] Famously, these recourses can be brought to the chamber by any individual in Costa Rica (even nonnationals) without the need for a lawyer; the chamber, also famously, has a reception wicket. Claims can be handwritten. In both cases, the chamber must establish a remedy for the violation of a right. Importantly, the effects of both recourses have inter partes effects and are unappealable. It may well be the most accessible constitutional tribunal in the world.

A new fourth mechanism introduced by the reforms was a priori abstract judicial review through advisory opinions (*consultas*). There are two types. The first (*consulta perceptiva*) requires the assembly to consult the Constitutional Chamber when discussing constitutional reforms, approval of international treaties, and reforms to the Judiciary Act. The second (*consulta facultativa*) allows deputies to seek the chamber's opinion on the potential constitutionality of a bill discussed in the assembly when supported by at least ten deputies.

Finally, in terms of international law, the 1989 constitutional reform (Article 48) maintained the principle (established by Article 8 of the 1949 Constitution and Article 1 of the Judiciary Act) that the "interpretation" of statutes when adjudicating disputes must consider norms present in international treaties to which Costa Rica is signatory. This principle, called conventional control, was solidified when the Constitutional Chamber ruled in 1990 (in its V-282–90 decision) and subsequently in 2003 (2794–03 decision) that when a conflict exists between national statutes and international norms, the latter must prevail.

The Chamber's Functioning After Its Creation The 1989 reforms created one of the most powerful constitutional tribunals in Latin America and likely the world. As we have seen, the judicial review powers lodged with Costa Rica's Constitutional Chamber were significant. The high tribunal began to exercise those powers rather amply after its establishment, a trend that continued over time, making it one of the most powerful judicial policy actors in the region if only by the sheer number of cases it resolves and some decisions it has made since its creation. Nevertheless, the chamber's activism was limited to areas that justices on the bench saw as having broad social support, a sort of national consensus, in the period leading up to the decision chapter 6 analyzes. Continuing with the long tradition of judicial deference to the legislature that characterized Costa Rica's judicial culture, justices have tended to be rather reticent about expanding rights not already conferred by the constitution. Unlike the other three countries in this book, justices at Costa Rica's highest constitutional tribunal did not appear to have taken an "interpretivist" turn by the time the 2007 decision was handed down. The Constitutional Chamber had certainly challenged the other two branches of government through many important decisions it made, but it was, until recently, more timid in the expansion of new rights, including sexual and reproductive rights.

The judicial review powers granted to the Constitutional Chamber were promptly exercised by its justices. Setting the tone for what was to come, the chamber ruled soon after its establishment that an executive decree (*Acuerdo Ejecutivo 268*) that altered the country's telecommunications system was unconstitutional. Supported by the Legislative Assembly, the decree, issued in 1987 (*before* the chamber was established), broke the monopoly over the provision of telephone mobility services by granting a private firm (Celulares Comcel) the license to use four of the system's frequencies to sell services. In its ruling (5386–93), the chamber argued in a majority opinion that wireless services provided by the public telecommunications network are a national public good and, as such, are protected by the constitution. Public goods, it argued, are "imprescriptible and inalienable." In a neoliberal time when the privatization of public assets was at its height in Latin America, such a decision was quite significant. It was followed by several other important rulings. In a historic decision (9992–04), the chamber ruled in 2004 against a presidential declaration supporting the US invasion of Iraq. Responding to several actions of constitutionality that were filed, it ruled that the presidential decision violated the constitution, international treaties that Costa Rica had signed, and the principles established by the UN-based international system that uphold "peace" as a common value. It declared peace to be a "founding value" of the Costa Rican nation as well as a constitutional one. In the lead-up to the 2007 opinion I look at in chapter 6, the Constitutional Chamber ruled against policy decisions made by the executive on constitutional grounds in several other landmark rulings. There was a 2004 decision (2004–07378) against a presidential decree that had allowed beachfront areas to be developed by private business and a 2006 ruling (R-15245–2006) against an executive decree that allowed Costa Ricans to participate in foreign military parades. In the same year, it decided (DE 33240-S) against a presidential decree that allowed for the extraction of minerals for making armament (Wilson 2010, 64–65).

The Constitutional Chamber also exercised its judicial review prerogatives against the powerful Legislative Assembly during this time, but to a much lesser extent. Perhaps no other case captures such an exercise of judicial review against parliamentary supremacy than its 2771 ruling of 2003. In it, the chamber declared that the non-reelection clause, reformed by the assembly in 1969,[80] was unconstitutional on the grounds that it violated the fundamental right of Costa Ricans to be elected based on provisions found in the American Convention on Human Rights (colloquially known as the *Pacto de San José*). In the majority opinion, the chamber argued that according to the "preeminence" principle established by the *Pacto de San José*, partial constitutional reforms cannot limit or reduce fundamental rights recognized by the original constitutional drafters (Cruz Castro 2007, 573–75).[81]

Regardless, the area in which the Constitutional Chamber has most notably asserted its judicial review powers, by far, has been in decisions regarding individual rights, mostly in the form of hearing citizens' submissions of amparo cases. The sheer numbers speak for themselves. Whereas in the first full year of operation (1990) the chamber heard 1,600 cases, the number jumped to 7,000 by 1997; to 10,000 in 2000; and 17,000 by 2008 (Wilson 2011, 70), where they have essentially remained since then.[82] The vast majority of these cases (85–90 percent, depending on the year) are amparo cases, with approximately half of them addressing issues related to health care rights (with access to medicines being an important component).[83] Approximately 50 percent of amparo cases are rejected *ad portas* (upon receipt and based on procedural grounds), and only 25 percent of them are successful (Hernández Valle 2009). However, they nonetheless make up a significant number and speak of a highly active court exercising its judicial review powers amply to guarantee individual rights.

The Constitutional Chamber's ample use of judicial review powers since its establishment is generally cited by scholars as an example of a highly independent and active Latin American high court and the prototype behind the judicialization of politics in the region (Uprimny 2014; Ansolabehere 2008; Domingo 1999). Indeed, the chamber has been identified as the protagonist behind Costa Rica's "rights revolution" (Wilson 2009). However, while the chamber's expanding activism in guaranteeing rights is undeniable, it appears that it has taken place within the bounds of a (growing) national consensus around the importance of guaranteeing individual human rights. In particular, while the emergence of powerful high courts in other Latin American countries, including the other three analyzed in this book, has resulted from changes to institutional design (i.e., the constitutional empowerment of high courts with judicial review), the adoption of conventional control mechanisms, and the growing influence of neoconstitutionalism, it appears that the last element has not been as discernably present in the case of Costa Rica. In effect, to my knowledge, there exists no academic work that identifies a clear change in the "policy preferences" of justices and judges at the individual level away from legal positivism and to a more interpretivist approach to reading the law, which, as we have seen, has been an important driver behind the expansion of rights elsewhere.[84] In Costa Rica, there exists a certain (paradoxical) continuity in the profiles of justices appointed to the Supreme Court after the chamber's creation. Unlike in other courts, the ideologies and policy preferences of individual justices do not seem to play a central role in explaining court decisions: "a magistrate-level explanation for the existence of the Sala IV's hyperactivity in the protection of individual rights and assertive exercise of its accountability function is highly incomplete" (Wilson 2010, 61).

The judicialization of politics in Costa Rica appears to be partly the result of the establishment of a new and powerful high court whose members are nonetheless keenly aware of the limits to their actions and areas where there appear to be a national consensus, such as guaranteeing individual socioeconomic rights through the granting of amparo cases. In effect, criticism of the chamber's judicial activism has mostly emanated from the other two branches of government when their policy decisions have been affected and from non-state sectors and society at large when it makes unpopular decisions on political issues. The court's decision to declare the 1969 non-reelection reform unconstitutional is a clear case in point of backlash from state actors: it was followed by stern criticism, especially from deputies (Díaz 2003). Similar reactions followed two 2010 decisions: a ruling (2010–14821) that limited the use of police checkpoints on roads (an executive decision) and one (2010–1282) that suspended an investigation by the TSE into a deputy's undue use of public resources for electoral purposes.[85] In both cases, reactions were swift and harsh from members of the executive and legislative branches as they argued that the court was overstepping its role (*La Nación*, July 3, 2010; *La República*, September 24, 2010). The backlash to unpopular decisions also came from the public, such as an important and highly controversial 2008 ruling (2009–6922) that allowed open-pit mining in a forest (known as *the Crucitas* project). Polling from the time showed generalized dissatisfaction with this type of unpopular decision made by the Constitutional Chamber, with 58 percent of Costa Ricans saying that the court was meddling in issues outside its remit (*La República*, September 24, 2010). However, this does not appear to be the case regarding its active role in the processing of amparo and habeas corpus cases.[86]

Essentially, there appears to be a view, certainly among some justices and clerks, that hearing and deciding these types of cases is one of the most important functions the chamber performs; something that, they sense, is widely accepted by society. Indeed, interviews reveal a clear perception of the limits justices have in their judicial review powers: they portray a certain aversion to going beyond what is established in the constitution and to pushing the limits of a perceived national consensus—which includes reading new rights into the constitution. Costa Rica's judges did not appear to have moved away from legal positivism as clearly as some justices in Argentina, Colombia, and Mexico had by the time the 2007 decision was made. Despite the Constitutional Chamber's important role in national politics and the clear references justices make to a "living constitution" (Cruz Castro 2007, 570), they appear to follow a long tradition of judicial restraint and are inclined to be deferential to the legislature when big decisions are made. This certainly includes the area of sexual and reproductive rights, as we shall see in chapter 6. Interviews reveal a clear sense of what their "field of action" is, and it appears to be restrained by what a justice referred to as a "national consensus." To wit:

> We have a constitution, and our job is to make sure its rights are accessed by people. That is our job. But we cannot go beyond that. We cannot create new rights. That is why there is a constitution. Yes, of course, we grant health amparos, and they are a priority, and most of them are granted. But that has to do with a social agreement, a national consensus that in Costa Rica health is a basic human right, and so it

cannot be denied. We all know that health amparos will be granted, especially the ones dealing with medicines . . . that is our main field of action (*campo de acción*). . . . We are criticized sometimes because of some of the big decisions we have made, such as on free trade, but those cases come to us, we do not seek them out.[87]

Of course, we pay attention to what happens in the assembly. It is the repository of popular sovereignty. That is what is established in the constitution. We decide on cases, but the legislator oversees the making of policy. We are bound by the constitution. It is a straitjacket for the political class, and that includes the chamber [*La Sala*], us. We have limits.[88]

The chamber deals with a lot of cases because people realized that we are the first barrier to access rights. It is a victim of its own success. It has become [an escape] valve for society. But that is in the area of basic rights, such as health. We are an active tribunal, but [we] are also limited in our actions. It is up to [the] Legislative Assembly to make decisions on hard topics, on new areas of rights.[89]

Justices vote according to what is best for the parliamentary majority. They will not vote against it, because there would be pushback. They know how far to go.[90]

Costa Rica's constitutional tribunal therefore shows a certain paradox. While it is one of the most active and independent in the world, its members seem to have a very clear idea of what their limits are. It is thus both independent and timid. Both personae seem to be linked to a tradition of judicial restraint among justices, as well as the appointment process, which we take up in chapter 6.

Chapter 2

The Long Road to Abortion Reform and Democratic Citizenship

Introduction

Few policy issues have been as divisive in contemporary democratic societies as abortion. While people may hold opinions on a variety of other policy areas, such as the acceptable levels of migration and poverty, attitudes toward abortion tend to come down to strongly held binary opinions on whether it should be accessible to women and girls. Even within what Merike Blofield has classically referred to as "moral policies" (2006), which include the broader areas of sexual and reproductive rights and family planning, people tend to have stronger and at times more stubborn preferences on abortion policy. Indeed, while we have seen polling move on issues such as same-sex marriage, the same is not the case for abortion. One of the reasons behind the strength of opposing positions is, of course, the role that religion and morality have historically played in opinion formation. While for some people abortion is simply a matter of public and reproductive health, for others the practice is linked to morality and religious principles. For the "anti-choice" folk, abortion is not just another policy area; it is about deeply held religious beliefs regarding life and who has the right to decide when life starts and when it ends. It can be more about a worldview than public policy. (For the anti-choice camp, though, the discussions of life tend to be skewed toward the unborn and away from the thousands of women and girls who die each year seeking abortions in highly risky and unsanitary settings.) Strong positions on abortion tend to yield seemingly intractable debates that often produce policy stalemate. Abortion policy is therefore a rather specific policy area that clearly stands out from most others.

It is also complex because it overlaps with a host of other social and policy issues. It straddles the public and private spheres, involving both profoundly consequential and deeply personal decisions made by individuals as well as public health policy that encompasses family planning, access to medical care, and public health expenditures. It is also about the criminal justice system, which involves security forces, prisons, and the judiciary. Further, it is a policy area that has historically been dictated by men, who have dominated politics and the policymaking process, yet it affects women and girls. Finally, and most importantly for many, it is also about inequalities; it is a policy area whose negative results are inordinately suffered by the most marginalized sectors of society because it is the poorest women and girls who die disproportionately at higher rates, given their more limited access to safer procedures.

In the case of Latin America, the specificities of abortion policy are amplified by three important factors. The first concerns the strong influence the Catholic Church has had in public policy discussions. While there is an academic debate around whether levels of religiosity are related to the strict abortion policy regimes (Htun 2003; Blofield 2006), the Catholic Church has deployed significant resources, both material and discursive, to counter every and all efforts to liberalize abortion policy regimes in a part of the world where it has its largest presence. Second, the disparities in access to abortion tend to be wider given that it is the most socioeconomic unequal part of the world and where access to health care is far from universal. Lastly, Latin America was a main protagonist of the Third Wave of Democratization, a phenomenon that at least allowed for an opportunity to renegotiate social contracts and the terms of citizenship and to extend, finally, full democratic citizenship to all. Abortion is, after all, about bodily autonomy, a long-standing cornerstone of democratic citizenship and its most basic of negative rights.

This short chapter has two main objectives. It first aims to highlight, in a succinct way, the various historical specificities of abortion policy in Latin America. This is important background for readers unfamiliar with either this policy area or the region. The second is to overview the main theoretical debates around abortion politics. As mentioned in the introduction, I do not contend, as a cis-gendered man, to claim that I am making any original contributions to the theoretical debates on abortion that feminists have held for decades. While a devout feminist, I simply propose to review those debates to remind the reader of the significant implications access to abortion has for democratic citizenship. Indeed, while many Latin American countries have made significant strides toward democratization over the last three decades, restrictions to access to abortion can be seen as a "democratic debt" that the region's polities owe women and girls. It indeed is one of the last obstacles to achieve full, formal democratic citizenship. These implications are important to keep in mind as the reader delves into the four cases I present in subsequent chapters at a time when the world is experiencing serious challenges to democratic governance and citizenship.

Women, Patriarchy, and Reproductive Rights in Latin America

Historical Background

There is little research on the history of what we today call "abortion" in pre-independent Latin America. In very general (and clearly cursory) terms, we know that the voluntary termination of pregnancy through the consumption of different natural products (abortifacients) was a practice among many pre-Columbian societies in the Americas (Acevedo 1979; Koblitz 2014), but research is scant. While the practice continued during the colonial period among religious and laypeople alike (Schiebinger 2004), some research suggests that there was far from a consensus on the prohibition of the practice. In effect, abortion was not a debated national policy issue well until the new republics emerged (Müller 2012; Noonan 1967).

Latin America's "one hundred years of solitude," the violent and unstable years of the nineteenth century, saw significant sociopolitical change as the colonies gained independence and attempted to build liberal republics. Yet, independence did not fundamentally change important elements of the social organization of the new republics. Stark class stratification and the continued dominant position of powerful social actors, such as the landed elite and the military, remained virtually intact. In terms of gender roles, the years that followed independence witnessed the replication of the patriarchal family as the main unit of social organization, which gave men socioeconomic and political privileges that were legally protected and socially sanctioned. Despite the liberal bent of the independent *criollo* leadership, the legal systems, particularly civil codes, adopted by the incipient republics were influenced by Catholic ideas that outlined the clear gender roles that women and men were to play in society and politics. Women (officially thought by Catholic dicta to be innately inferior and subordinate to men) were prohibited from participating in the public realm, and their access to legal and social rights, such as property and inheritance, was severely curtailed. These restricted liberal states essentially excluded half of the population by enshrining patriarchy in constitutions and legal systems. Women continued to be noncitizens within formal independent and semi-democratic polities.

As liberal forces gained strength in the mid-nineteenth century, some leaders attempted to secularize the regimes and pursued the separation of church and state. They forced the Catholic Church, which had had a monopoly of the market (of souls) during colonial times, to transfer important prerogatives it had retained since independence, such as the administration of school systems, cemeteries, hospitals, and jails. A central element of this process was the secularization of legal systems through the creation of the legal entity of civil marriage, which took away from the Church one of its most important roles: the administration of marriages. Nevertheless, the new legal systems reproduced Catholic (Thomist) ideas of family by upholding the monogamous and indissoluble nature of marriage, reaffirming the patriarchal and reproductive nature of the family, and gave men authority over women and children. A main social function of marriage thus became reproduction. The legal subordination of women and reproduction thus continued, and the patriarchal family caried on being the locus of activity and the entity through which society would (formally) interact with the state. In most liberal constitutions of nineteenth-century Latin America, the concept of the family was enshrined and declared to be one of the foundational blocks of the new regimes and political units to be protected. However, within the context of state formation, the new political regimes excluded most Latin American women who lived in rural areas and were dominated by clientelist relations in the haciendas and fincas.

Toward the end of the nineteenth century, Latin America's era of Order and Progress, which saw the rise of positivism as the region became more integrated with the world's capitalist system, women began to organize and mobilize and to place demands directly on states. Within what is known as "American feminism" (*Feminismo americano*), elite urban women, empowered by the opportunities provided by increased education and employment, began to articulate some of the first criticisms of patriarchal domination (Miller 1990). Framed around concepts of maternity, women engaged in a variety of social activities to push for health and childcare services. While their demands were restricted to social policy change, this incipient activism formed the basis for larger-scale mobilization in the early part of the twentieth century to petition for a change in the limits of democratic citizenship.

The Latin American socioeconomic and political landscape underwent profound changes in the early twentieth century, and that included the flourishing of American feminism (what elsewhere has generally been termed first-wave feminism). On the economic front, the era of Order and Progress brought about economic stability and prosperity (albeit rather skewed) to many Latin American countries. With it, the establishment of political party systems and workers' rights provided activists with opportunities for mobilization.

Similar to what was occurring in North America and Europe at the time, in Latin America, feminists were pushing for an expansion of citizenship rights in the electoral arena. While women's mobilization varied in objectives, a main target among mainstream first-wave feminists was a call for a renegotiation of citizenship through the demand for electoral enfranchisement. As occurred in other parts of the world, some Latin American activist leaders began the region's suffragist movement asking for the right to be included in politics through voting. Starting with Uruguayan Paulina Luisi, who established the first suffragist organization in South America in 1916, activists across the region organized and mobilized demanding the right to vote. These activists included Clara González (Panama), Bertha Lutz (Brazil), Ofelia Domínguez Navarro (Cuba), Marta Vergara (Chile), Minerva Bernardino (Dominican Republic), and Margarita Robles de Mendoza and Hermilia Galindo (Mexico). Panamanian feminists even created a pro-suffragist political party in 1923, the National Feminist Party (*Partido Feminista Nacional*). Efforts led by activists crossed borders and strengthened mobilization, articulating regionwide demands. Starting with the first Feminist Congress of Buenos Aires in 1910, activists began holding regular regional meetings and established regional organizations, such as the Pan-American Association for the Advancement of Women in 1922 and the first intergovernmental organization for women's rights in the world, the Inter-American Commission of Women in 1928 (Marino 2019).

These efforts paid off. Starting with Ecuador in 1929, women earned suffrage in the region, a process that can be regarded as a major alteration of national social contracts and the expansion of citizenship status to women. Patriarchy ceased to be the only mechanism through which women could interact directly with the state.

As countries adopted new, socially progressive constitutions, emulating Mexico's rather advanced 1917 text, some Latin American feminists began to petition for social and economic justice. And, as Katherine M. Marino (2019) has shown, they did so innovatively (when compared with mobilization elsewhere), framing women's rights as social rather than individual. Their demands for citizenship went beyond enfranchisement and included substantive rights in the form of socioeconomic and welfare protections, including access to social services. Ideas around gender equality in early American feminism encompassed larger notions of citizenship, beyond elections.

Yet, paradoxically, during this time, some Latin American states increased their intervention into women's lives because of the elites' desire to control public health, establishing clear boundaries around morality as part of larger projects of nation-building within a context of incipient industrialization. While prostitution had been tolerated, for example, within the larger Latin American tradition of *Obedezco pero no Cumplo* (I obey but do not comply with), and inspired by French policy, governments began to police and regulate sex workers. In Peru, for instance, as part of population control and health policy, sex workers were required to undergo medical checkups and keep registries (Drinot 2020).

Latin American states thus took an active role in controlling women's lives through their medicalization and the criminalization of certain activities. Fertility control thus became a central element of state policy in many countries in the region. Two important developments affected women's reproductive lives. As part of nation-building, women's sexual and reproductive lives became matters of state guided by what Linda Kerber (1980) has called "Republican motherhood"—that is, women were seen as being responsible of nurturing good citizens to uphold the well-being of the new republics. As such, fertility control became government policy as elites began to require health institutions to regulate abortion to prevent the practice (Roth 2020). Women's role was seen as contributing offspring to the nation, and any interruption to the cause was to be avoided. The curbing of women's citizenship rights was therefore done through the regulation of reproductive lives as motherhood was promoted by the state (Roth 2020). The state then took firm control over women's lives, despite their electoral enfranchisement.

The second development relates to Catholic Church doctrine. While the Church's position varied since Thomist ideas were adopted, in 1869 Pope Pius IX, regarding it as homicide and a sin, prohibited *any* form of abortion for Catholics the world over, stating that life began at conception. Several of the new Latin American republics had managed to reduce the political influence of the Catholic Church as liberals won the battle for the separation of church and state, but the Vatican's position on abortion hardened.

It is within this context that Latin American states began to craft laws to regulate abortion designed to oversee women's health and have them contribute to nation-building (Roth 2020), all while being guided by Church dictates. In some cases, their reach was constrained. As Mala Htun (2003) has shown, some legislation introduced at the time was rather progressive, comparatively speaking. For example, Argentina, one of the first countries to include abortion regulation in its criminal code (in 1921), permitted abortions of medical necessity in the case of rape, including the presumed raped of disabled women (Htun 2003, 145). However, in general, and directly influenced by religious postulates, which considered abortion a sin, abortion came to be seen as a crime against human life. As such, the defense of life of the unborn became a component of legal systems (Lemaitre 2014), without considering a woman's life or her health. It is important to underline, however, that even in cases in which "therapeutic abortions" were allowed by legislation, access to the procedure was only possible upon the advice of certified (men) medical doctors.

Once legislation was introduced in the first part of the twentieth century, minor changes were undertaken over the next several decades, as we shall see in the next chapters. Nevertheless, feminists in many Latin American countries mobilized and took up the cause of repealing of some of this legislation. In Mexico, for example, at a 1936 government-organized convention intended to harmonize legislation across its federal system, feminists demanded the repeal of provisions on subnational legislation that criminalized abortion. In that case, Ofelia Domínguez Navarro gave a presentation, titled "Abortion due to Social and Economic Reasons" (*Aborto por Causas Sociales y Económicas*), asking for the repeal of those criminal code provisions (Cano 1990). Importantly, and within the framing of the movement's demands for social rights, Domínguez Navarro argued that abortion was the result of unequal social and economic conditions and, as such, that it was an issue of public health and not one to be dealt with by the criminal code (Lamas 2017, 12). Underlying the social and economic dimensions of abortion, first-wave feminists also demanded the decriminalization of abortion. As we shall see in chapters to come, these very arguments will be picked up again decades later, to successful ends. Nevertheless, abortion subsided as a main political demand by first-wave feminism, in Latin America (and elsewhere), as the debate focused on suffrage rights.

Second-Wave Feminism and Contemporary Regulation

Also like with developments elsewhere, and within a context of a global wave of mass mobilization, Latin American women organized collectively in the early 1970s in what is commonly known as second-wave feminism. In many countries of the region, feminists advanced a series of demands that included changes to discriminatory legislation and the provision of social services such as day care. However, access to abortion became a central policy objective at this time. Organizations such as the *Frente Unico por los Derechos de la Mujer* (Common Front for the Rights of Women) in Mexico and the *Movimiento de Liberación Femenina* (Movement for Women's Liberation) and the *Unión Feminista Argentina* (Argentine Feminist Union) returned to the decriminalization of abortion as a policy objective. Their demands were framed around ideas of bodily autonomy and personal choice. Bringing into the debate lived experiences and stigmatized practices, feminists placed the personal on the political agenda with the famous slogan "the personal is political." They thus attempted to shift the debate away from when life starts and into the politics of women's personal lives (Bohórquez Monsalve et al. 2019). Demanding greater personal autonomy, second-wave feminists fought for reproductive and sexual freedom within broader demands to establish greater autonomy from political parties and other organizations, such as unions, which did not support birth-control policies because they were seen as imperialist policies (Ruibal 2014b, 15). For feminists, abortion became a central demand and has remained so ever since. Access to abortion, in Latin America as elsewhere, was articulated as "abortion on demand" (without restrictions), which meant a focus on decriminalizing the procedure.

Based on ideas of personal dignity and moving away from debates about when life starts, second-wave feminism demanded that the state stop making decisions about women's bodies and family planning and reproduction. These demands were articulated at a time when in most Latin American countries the restricted access to abortion (under some circumstances, such as in cases of unviable pregnancies or when the woman's life was in danger) was only possible when health experts authorized the procedure. What this essentially meant is that women were not considered to be autonomous agents and sufficiently responsible to make free decisions: it was up to the state, when advised by third parties, to make the decision. This, of course, meant that women were not able to exercise full citizenship rights for agency over one's body, which is at the core of democratic citizenship. Feminists were therefore demanding democratic citizenship. Arguments in favor of access to abortion therefore asked for an expansion of citizenship rights.

In the case of Latin America, however, second-wave feminism encountered two important obstacles. The first was, of course, the onset of military regimes. With the objective of depoliticizing societies and cleansing through the elimination of "subversive leftist" organizations at a time of political instability and guerrilla mobilization, democracies across the region succumbed to military coups. What ensued were concerted efforts by military juntas and generals to demobilize societies through grotesque repression and systematic violation of human rights. In several countries of the region, especially in the Southern Cone, feminists were therefore forced to organize in private through discussion groups and curb the public articulation of their demands. Women's mobilization thus weakened at the time.

The second obstacle was the arrival of a Vatican hard-liner in the late 1970s, Pope John Paul II. A self-confessed conservative with a clear animosity toward structural explanations for social injustice, his papacy managed to gain a great deal of influence over Latin America's Catholic leadership through the appointment of ultraconservative cardinals and bishops. The pope's personal ideology had a big impact on public debates on abortion policy in the region. His papacy prioritized a strict adherence to the Church's sexual and moral dogmas, making divorce and abortion the most visible issues engaged by Catholic leaders. Indeed, the pope popularized the term "culture of death" to refer to countries that allowed contraception and legal abortion (Blofield 2006, 26). This conservative turn made it a lot more difficult for feminists to push for the decriminalization of abortion in Latin America (Blofield 2001).

Democratization and Reproductive Justice

The debate over abortion policy reform in Latin America underwent important changes in the late 1980s and early 1990s. On the one hand, the region saw the collapse of military regimes in several countries in the region and the liberalization of politics in others, such as Mexico. Latin America's process of democratization provided opportunities for feminists to organize collectively and advance publicly a variety of demands as state repression lessened; in addition, it allowed them to reframe the demands for women's rights expansion within larger debates on human rights. In effect, in several countries of the region, activists belonging to a variety of social movements successfully framed democratization as being about expanding and guaranteeing human rights (Díez 2006, 2015). Latin American feminists reframed their demands, too; they rearticulated their notions of autonomy and agency (earlier understood as being independent from political and state actors) and began to interact more closely with the state. Calls for the decriminalization of abortion were articulated within a larger and more collaborative policy frame.

The link between women's rights and human rights also strengthened at the international level. Human rights assumed an importance during the 1990s in international relations, extending to gender issues. The notion of viewing women's rights as human rights crystalized with the 1994 International Conference on Population and Development held in Cairo and the 1995 Fourth World Conference on Women held in Beijing. The two meetings produced declaratory documents that urged signatory countries to address women's public health concerns. In terms of abortion, signatory countries were asked to tackle the health consequences of unsafe abortions and to help in the prevention of unwanted pregnancies. Of particular significance was the document developed after the Beijing conference that specifically called on signatory countries to "consider reviewing laws containing punitive measures against women who have undergone illegal abortions" (United Nations 1995, para. 106k).While the documents produced at the conferences were not binding, they nonetheless legitimized feminist demands for the decriminalization of abortion at the domestic level and helped with consciousness-raising and political mobilization (Htun 2003, 150). Indeed, the documents became a road map for Latin American feminists for years to come. Importantly, they cemented the idea that women's rights were intrinsically human rights and helped frame the concept of reproductive rights (Bohórquez Monsalve et al. 2019). The Beijing declaration, for example, states that "women's human rights include the right to have control and decide freely and responsibly on matters related to their sexuality, including sexual and reproductive health, free of coercion, discrimination and violence" (United Nations 1995, 96).

These discussions at the international level provided the context for the crystallization of the concept of "reproductive justice." Defined and promoted by a US organization, SisterSong Women of Color Reproductive Justice Collective, created by Black American women in 1997, the concept referred to "the human right to maintain personal bodily autonomy, have children, not have children, and parent the children we have in safe and sustainable communities" (Ross and Solinger 2017, 12). Based on the concept of human rights, reproductive justice is more expansive and includes socioeconomic and personal aspects of women's lives. As Loretta Ross and Rickie Solinger point out, at the heart of reproductive justice is the claim that all persons who reproduce and become parents require a safe and dignified context for these most fundamental of experiences, and this goal requires access to specific community-based resources, including "high-quality care, housing and education, a living wage, a healthy environment and a safety net for times when these resources fail" (2017, 9). In the case of Latin America, the concept has been a natural fit. As the alert reader may recall, the framing of demands by first- and second-wave feminists have carried an important social component, one that in fact aligns well with Latin America's tradition of incorporating socioeconomic rights in constitution-making (Gargarella 2019). And this is an important point to remember as we navigate the analyses in the pages to come: the demands for the decriminalization of abortion have been framed as a human but also a social right by many Latin American feminists over the last quarter of a century.

Not surprisingly and given the Latin American context of deep socioeconomic inequality and high levels of poverty, the new, more robust understanding of women's reproductive autonomy has included an important access-to-health dimension. In the region, women's organizations have emphasized the importance of including discussions of health care in debates over abortion policy reform as it relates to the need to reduce maternal morbidity and mortality rates as a result of unsafe and clandestine abortions (Bohórquez Monsalve et al. 2019). Arguments for the liberalization of access to abortion have been based on the need to promote and protect women's health. By the end of the twentieth century, feminists called for the need for allowing abortions at least when a woman's life was in danger. While there has evidently been variation in the way Latin American women's groups have deployed the health policy frame, an important element has been the desire to medicalize the debates in an attempt to depoliticize them (Sheldon 1997).

The development of these concepts occurred at a time of significant mobilization by Latin American women within the context of democratization (Alvarez 1990). Beginning in the 1980s, Latin American feminists have been national and regional networks of activism, some of which have focused specifically on reproductive rights (Ruibal 2014b). In 1987, feminist lawyers established the Latin American Committee for the Defense of Women's Rights with the intention of expanding women's rights. Its foundation was followed by the establishment of many other prominent ones, such as Catholics for the Choice in Montevideo (1987), which subsequently established a regional network, and the Latin American and Caribbean Health and Reproductive Rights Network. These organizations have been active in coordinating transnational activities and mobilizing grassroots organizations at the national level. In effect, these organizations reached throughout the region and have organized collectively to push for the decriminalization of abortion, all while developing and deploying a common conceptualization of the health exception within a human rights frame (Ruibal 2014b, 16).

Pro-choice movements in Latin America quickly encountered a significant growth of anti-choice countermobilization, which was connected to a larger, international antiabortion movement. Partly mobilized by the historic 1973 *Roe v. Wade* decision in the United States, which turned access to abortion into a constitutional right, antiabortion activists organized to fight against the liberalization of abortion in the United States and internationally. This mobilization helped organize antiabortion groups in Latin America through, for example, the establishment of a regional office by the Human Life International (*Vida Humana Internacional*) network. With the rhetorical and ideological support of the increasingly conservative Catholic Church and greater resources from national and international sources, anti-choice mobilization gained an important presence in national debates around family planning and reproductive justice. Much of that presence was taken up by organizations established by the Church to promote antiabortion activism: namely, the Pontifical Council for the Family and the Pontifical Academy for Life. In effect, the conservative papacy of John Paul II led campaigns throughout the region to introduce constitutional amendments to protect the right to life from "the moment of conception until natural death."

Abortion Policy at the Turn of the Century

The emergence and strengthening of the abortion and antiabortion movements in the 1980s and 1990s yielded a stalemate and policy stasis on abortion regulation by the turn of the twentieth century. Attempts at liberalizing one of the strictest regulatory regimes in the world were successfully countered by antiabortion mobilization and lobbying that in fact managed to create a climate of fear in which even discussing abortion actually became stigmatized (Htun 2003, 152). The result was that, unlike what occurred in other democratic countries, the new Latin American democracies failed to bring about abortion reform by the end the century, despite the embrace of a human rights discourse by many elites. By 1999, policy stasis continued. By then, seven countries (Chile, the Dominican Republic, El Salvador, Haiti, Honduras, Nicaragua, and Surinam) had complete bans of abortions without any exceptions. Except for Guyana, where abortion on demand was legalized in 1995, all the other then-democratic countries considered abortion a crime against human life with only three exceptions: when a woman's life is in danger, when the pregnancy in not viable, or in cases of rape. As Alba Ruibal (2014b) has importantly reminded us, even in many of these countries, restricted access to abortion was in reality generally unavailable because governments failed to implement these exceptions. Indeed, given that most legislation regarding abortion in Latin America did not undergo reform by the turn of the century, work on abortion politics in individual countries followed the common thread of exploring the factors behind generalized policy stasis (Htun 2003; Blofield 2006; Mollmann 2005; Getgen 2007; Kane 2008).

The result has been tragic: Hundreds of women died every year in Latin America. In effect, the region had at the time the highest rate of unsafe abortions in world.

The landscape began to change in what I call in this book the First Wave of Abortion Decriminalization in Latin America. Beginning with a reform passed by Mexico City in 2000 (analyzed in chapter 5), which waived some penalties on the procedure, in several countries of the region, women's mobilization appears to have tilted the balance of the previously entrenched status quo and began to achieve important policy objectives. These changes have attracted important scholarly attention. Political science scholarship has explored policy change during the First Wave of Abortion Decriminalization and identified the role played by various forces, as reviewed in the introduction. However, that foundational work has not explored the role judiciaries have played in policy change. This is the aim of this book. The next four chapters analyze the factors that explain variance in the decriminalization of abortion reform in four countries by opening the black box that yielded some of the most important landmark rulings on abortion.

Abortion and Democratic Citizenship: The Democratic Debt

Democracy and Citizenship

As I have written elsewhere (Díez 2015), the study of democratization in Latin America has mainly focused on the conditions that allowed for democratic transition and consolidation, the institutional performance of new democracies, and the quality of democracy in the region. With some exceptions (Jelin and Hershberg1996; Dagnino 2003; Fox 1994; Yashar 2005), political scientists have generally ignored the relationship between democratization and citizenship. Yet, as Frances Hagopian (2007) forcefully reminded us, citizenship is central to democracy. While definitions of democracy vary, all include a combination of basic civil and political rights, and these rights make up a fundamental dimension of citizenship. Citizenship, at its most basic level, refers to an individual's membership in a polity and, in essence, to the enjoyment of rights and the assumption of responsibilities such membership confers. It is about belonging. In democratic systems, citizenship membership necessarily entails the possession of civil and political rights. Because an equal distribution of power among citizens is central to all conceptualizations of democracy, the extent to which individuals possess the legal entitlements to interact with the state and one another on an equal basis is therefore central to the democratic process. The study of democratization is consequently incomplete without the incorporation of citizenship, given that it involves the acquisition and exercise of rights needed to enjoy equality.

Nevertheless, while there may be a consensus that democracy entails rights, there is a great deal of debate regarding which rights it ought to include. According to liberal democratic theory, democracy requires the enshrinement of civic and political rights as a means of protecting individual freedoms from interference by other individuals or the authorities themselves (Walzer 1989). For liberal democrats, citizenship is essentially about political freedom, and democracy is equated with suffrage and civil rights and freedoms. For others, who belong to what can be termed a social democratic tradition, citizenship rights encompass more than civil and political rights and freedoms and should include social rights. The most influential conceptualization of such view has been T. H. Marshall's *Citizenship and Social Class* (1950). According to Marshall, citizenship is about ensuring that everyone is treated as a full and equal member of society, and the only way to achieve this is through a constant expansion in the number of rights to citizens. Based on his appreciation of the evolution of rights in England, which he saw as having evolved in successive stages, Marshall divided citizenship into three categories: civil rights, political rights, and social rights. For him, a full expression of citizenship requires a liberal democratic welfare state that must guarantee not only civil and political rights but also social rights—such as, for example, public education, health care, and unemployment insurance.

The view that social rights are integral components of democracy became accepted as early as 1917 in Latin America, with the adoption of Mexico's social constitution. It also became mainstream when accepted by many theorists and policymakers during the postwar period, especially in Western Europe. However, the equation of citizenship to these three "levels" of rights is contested. Some who see democracy in minimalist terms argue that the welfare state creates a culture of passivity among citizens and a dependence on the state. For them, the full integration of the citizenry, particularly the poor, depends on going beyond the "entitlement" of rights and, instead, on their responsibility to make a living. According to this view, social rights are in fact an impediment to the attainment of citizenship. Others have argued that the enshrinement of social rights by a polity is not sufficient for the expansion of citizenship membership to all groups. Marshall believed that the expansion of social rights in England would foster a shared identity, a "common culture," which would integrate previously excluded groups, especially the working classes. Citizenship for him was also about an expression of one's membership in a community.

However, Marshall's prediction was dampened by the fact that a variety of groups, such as Indigenous peoples and peoples of African descent, felt excluded from common group membership, despite their legal entitlement to the possession of the three levels of rights he had identified. These groups' difference from the majority was a source of exclusion. As a result, some theorists have argued—all while accepting that social rights are indeed part of citizenship—that citizenship membership must account for these differences in order for individuals to be able to exercise the various levels of rights (Minow 1987). According to what Iris Marion Young (1990) has called "differentiated citizenship," members of certain groups can only be fully incorporated into a society if these differences are considered. For Young, the establishment of genuine citizenship equality can only be guaranteed through the affirmation of group differences because culturally excluded groups are at a disadvantage in the political process and have distinctive needs. Accordingly, the state ought to encourage mechanisms of group representation and adopt group-differentiated policies. The concept of differentiated citizenship has expectedly been criticized. Critics have argued that differentiated-group rights violate the principle of equality, making some citizens "more equal" than others; that they are arbitrary because there is no "objective" way to determine which groups are deserving of differentiated rights; and that they fracture a sense of community and common purpose, which can lead to mistrust and even conflict (Cairns 1993; Offe 1998; Waldron 2002).

Such criticisms notwithstanding, Young's work has contributed to a broadening of the conception of citizenship in recent decades, and it is within these debates of what citizenship is about that some feminist theorists and activists have called attention to the gendered assumptions that have characterized debates around the components of citizenship (Friedman 2005; Okin 1979; Pateman 1988). Undergirding historically gendered understandings of citizenship, going back to ancient Athens, is the public-private divide according to which women have (and continue to be in some areas) relegated to the private realm and whereby citizenship has been connected to the public space and limited to a few. (As we saw earlier, such divide was foundational to the Latin American republics.) Since then, women have been (and continue to be in some countries) dependent on male relatives for representation in the public sphere, "and their exclusion of the polis was based on socially constructed roles of mother, wife and daughter, which limited them to performing duties in the private sphere of the family" (Abraham et al. 2011, 3). Women's mobilization has challenged this divide, and it has gradually earned inclusion into the polis. But it has not been full. In many areas, even in democratic societies, many women, such as migrants and refugees, have been excluded from the full range of benefits citizenship confers (Dobrowolsky and Tastsoglou 2006).

Access to abortion has been (and continues to be in Latin America and the United States) an obstacle to the attainment of full citizenship. As Rachael Johnstone has argued, abortion "is not a stand-alone topic but a procedure inextricably tied to the status of women citizens. Whether the state provides access to abortion services and how those services are framed, is a direct reflection of the status of women in that state" (2017, 15). While debates over the conferral of citizenship to women in many areas, such as voting or running for office, have been settled for the most part, abortion continues to be a part of the debates over the "woman question," as Reva Siegel has argued (2012). It is *the* area where some members of democratic societies continue to believe— paternalistically—that women are not capable of making decisions about their own bodies, so the state should make those decisions for them by limiting access to the procedure through its criminalization. This view suggests that women are not responsible enough to make these decisions (Bohórquez Monsalve et al. 2019). The rights and responsibilities associated with liberal democratic notions of citizenship have historically been based on a genderless idea of membership modeled after a universal male citizen and fail to take into account the special needs that women have, such as reproduction (Johnstone 2017, 18). While women have slowly gained greater access to citizenship through mobilization, de jure citizenship assumes masculine norms that create barriers, making it difficult for women to exercise the rights associated with citizenship (Friedman 2005). Adherence to universalistic norms has ignored specific needs women have. Restrictive abortion laws are a result of this male universalistic approach to citizenship. They are based on religious beliefs that have formed traditional attitudes about women in their roles as wives and mothers (Johnstone 2017, 17). Basic citizenship rights, such as the right to privacy and equality, are abridged when a woman becomes pregnant because states assume the responsibility of overseeing a woman's reproduction with the support of physicians (Nossiff 2007).

Seeing access to abortion as part of full citizenship not only requires, of course, a more robust definition of democracy, one which some sexual and reproductive rights theorists have pushed for; it also requires attention to the rather specific needs women have and, as a result, the particular relationship they have with the state. Following Young's idea of differentiated citizenship, scholars have called for moving away from universalistic and merely legal conceptions of citizenship and looking at the structural and societal contexts in which women live to enable them to exercise their citizenship. In terms of abortion, a robust and *practicable* conception of citizen requires seeing abortion as related to women's equality and paying attention to the barriers that exist to attain such equality. Johnstone has lucidly argued that "recognizing abortion as inextricably tied to women's equality, and their equal citizenship, not only situates the denial of abortion access in broader denial of women's equality but ties these issues to women's experiences as members of a political community, opening the door for broader considerations of how reproduction implicates women's equal citizenship" (2017, 19).

The reader must clearly see the link between these broader considerations needed for women to exercise their citizenship and the concept of reproductive justice covered earlier. The concept is not restricted to the immediate aspects of reproduction but considers broader aspects of women's lives, such as access to health care and support, in order to determine whether there is any (reproductive) justice. It follows, then, that any robust definition of citizenship that takes women's equality seriously can rely on the idea of reproductive justice to make it practicable. As we shall see in the following chapters, women's movements and some justices atop judiciaries in Latin America have recognized the clear connection between the two, which has resulted in the lifting of restrictions on access to abortion and, as a consequence, the expansion of further citizenship rights for women.

For Latin America, the fact that the region had the most restrictive abortion regulatory system in the world by the end of the last century meant that women had not attained full citizenship—despite strong mobilization, a dramatic increase in positions of political power, the acquisition of a variety of rights, and all within the context of an unprecedented transition to democracy. That is why women activists and scholars (and allies) in the region tend to refer to it as the "democratic debt." In the pages that follow, we shall see how far such debt has (finally) been settled and the factors behind such settlement.

The Critique "de Moda"

This book would be remiss if it did not address one of the main criticisms of analyzing women's equality through a rights lens: that the rights discourse is a "Western" notion (Crowley 2014; Mohanty 1995; Bashin and Khan 1986). On a very simple and practical level, these arguments of course give ample ammunition to dictators the world over to suppress their people and for authoritarians to take rights away. But, for our purposes, and as has been argued by some (including some "colonized" feminists, such as Sonia Corrêa), the criticism does not offer alternative discourses for social movements to make practical political claims (Corrêa and Petchesky 2006). More importantly, in relation to Latin America, such criticism ignores the fact that feminists in the region have, for at least a century, advanced the demands for fuller incorporation into the polis through a rights-claim approach. As seen earlier, the construction of their demands as part of the subject of rights has been central to American feminism since the latter part of the nineteenth century. As we also saw, Latin American feminists adopted, early on, a broader conception of rights that included a social dimension.

Rather than rejecting a rights-based discourse, Corrêa and Rosalind Petchesky have proposed reconstructing the area of sexual and reproductive rights by taking into account power and resource dynamics and how they intersect with gender, class, culture, and other differences. They argue, "Our principal point is that sexual and reproductive (and any other) rights, understood as private 'liberties or choices,' are meaningless especially for the poorest and most disenfranchised without the *enabling conditions* through which they can be realized. These conditions constitute *social rights* and involve social welfare, personal security, and political freedom. Their provision is essential to the democratic transformation of societies to abolish gender, class, racial and ethnic injustice" (2006, 298, emphasis in original).

For them, such reconstruction rests on four component principles: bodily integrity, personhood, equality, and respect for diversity. These are, in short, main elements of any robust conception of citizenship. And, as we now know, a conception of citizenship with a social dimension is as old as Latin American feminism itself. In a part of the world that has the starkest social inequalities, how can a social dimension not be part of discussions over democratic citizenship?

Conclusion

As one of the main protagonists of the Third Wave of Democratization, Latin America experienced an unprecedented expansion of democratic rights in the 1980s and 1990s. Political scientists had moved away from discussions centered on the conditions that would sustain democracy and toward a discussion of the "quality" of the region's democracies, signaling the important progress many of these countries had made. However, the many victories women have won in the acquisition of rights as part of that process of democratization, building on a decades-old tradition of mobilization, meant that by the turn of the century, Latin America owed them a significant debt: unrestricted access to abortion. As feminists have argued, unless that democratic debt is settled, women cannot be considered full democratic citizens. Nevertheless, things began to turn early in the twenty-first century. Starting with some minor reforms in Mexico City in 2000, several jurisdictions in Latin America began to relax penalties and restrictions on abortion in what I call the First Wave of Abortion Decriminalization. High courts in the region have played a central role in this process, as we will see in the following pages.

PART II

The Cases

Explaining Variance

Chapter 3

Argentina

Strategizing Ample Reform

Introduction

The chapter shows that the 2012 ruling in *A. F. s/medida autosatisfactiva, F. A. L.* (FAL case) by Argentina's Supreme Court (*Corte Suprema de Justicia de la Nación*, CSJN) was the result of the strategic calibration primarily undertaken by the chambers (*vocalías*) of Justices Eugenio Raúl Zaffaroni and Ricardo Luis Lorenzetti. A law clerk representing both chambers was tasked with exploring possible lines of argumentation once the case began to circulate among the justices' teams. Through the strategic deployment of arguments, the two chambers were able to build majority support from the bench to pursue an ample reform that liberalized access to abortion in Argentina. The decision was made not only to hear the case (which was moot since the abortion had already been carried out) but also to argue that the court had to pronounce itself on the constitutionality of the issue because it was an urgent matter of public health and socioeconomic inequalities (given that it disproportionally affected poor women and girls) that went beyond the specific case. These arguments were critical in securing a 5–2 majority from the bench.

Further, given that the two Kirchner administrations (2003–15) framed their presidents as defenders of human rights and that they were widely perceived as socially liberal, the political opportunity existed to push for the establishment of a legal framework to address the systemic inequities in abortion access across the country. For some justices and clerks, the political opportunity also encompassed their perception of the public mood. They sensed that Argentine society would approve of allowing mostly poor women terminate their pregnancies, even in cases beyond rape. As such, the decision laid down a series of legal directives and protocols to guarantee access to abortion in cases of rape without judicializing them. Importantly, the ruling established that a rape victim's sworn declaration was enough to access an abortion, thereby allowing women and girls wide to access an abortion by declaring they had been raped.

The Crafting of the "Golden Court"

As is well known, Argentina faced a severe crisis during the first several years of the twenty-first century. This crisis forced significant changes to its political landscape. As we saw in chapter 1, Argentina's historical political instability tended to reduce the independence of its Supreme Court. However, the political context early this century led to the emergence of what has likely been the most respected and independent bench at the high court: informally (in Argentina's hallways of power) known as the "golden court."

Exhausted from a decade of *Menemísmo* (chapter 1), in 1999, Argentines elected Fernando de la Rúa (1999–2001) from the Radical Party (*Partido Radical*). De la Rúa ran in an alliance with several opposition and dissenting Peronist parties. His election marked the beginning of a series of events that threw the country into turmoil. Ongoing economic stagnation, squabbling within the ruling coalition (the vice president resigned ten months into the job), and government's inaction in dealing with glaring corruption cases (involving former Argentine president Carlos Menem himself) made the de la Rúa's administration highly unpopular rather quickly. The pegging of the peso to the US dollar, a staple of the Menem years introduced in 1991, worsened the country's economic situation as exports became uncompetitive. In an attempt to prevent further deterioration, the de la Rúa government introduced measures to stop a bank run by freezing bank account withdrawals for ninety days. The so-called *corralito* (small corral) sparked anger and fear, especially among the middle class whose life savings were at risk, and provoked massive riots and protests. Demanding that the entire political class leave—*¡Qué se vayan todos! (To hell with them all!)*—some of this anger was directed at the Supreme Court since it ruled the controversial economic measures to be constitutional. Protesters gathered daily in front of the court building (colloquially known as *Tribunales*) demanding the justices' resignations (Castagnola 2018, 51). Unable to deal with the deteriorating situation, the president declared a state of emergency, which led to instances of police brutality and resulted in thirty-nine deaths. On December 20, 2000, de la Rúa left the *Casa Rosada* (presidential palace) in a helicopter and formally resigned the following day.

De la Rúa's resignation plunged the country into a severe political crisis. The absence of a vice president complicated the succession plan and led to congressional efforts to find a suitable candidate. In just a few days, three presidents were elected, inaugurated, and resigned because of their inability to deal with the multiple crises. On the economic front, the country announced a default on its foreign debt obligations. Within a worsening context, congressional leaders supported the appointment of Peronist Eduardo Duhalde (2002–3) as president. Duhalde, a former governor of Buenos Aires Province and failed presidential candidate in 1999, was inaugurated on January 1, 2002.

Duhalde proved adept at calming the economic situation. He instituted a series of economic measurements (informally referred as the *corralón*, big corral),[1] which stabilized the peso. He then initiated negotiations with international financial institutions to restructure the national debt, thereby restoring economic confidence. Duhalde also expanded social spending, including the provision of direct payments to the unemployed.

On the political front, Duhalde skillfully brought in stability. He presented himself as managing a caretaking government and promised not to run in the 2003 elections. Instead, Duhalde allowed various political forces to start positioning themselves for the presidential elections, all while supporting his administration.

Despite the turmoil, the Supreme Court's composition remained relatively stable. It had changed very little by the time Duhalde left office. Attempts by de la Rúa to force vacancies at the court and to continue Argentina's long tradition of court-packing (chapter 1) failed. Further attempts at forcing the resignation of justices during Duhalde's eighteen months in office also failed.[2] By the end of his term, Duhalde was only able to appoint the replacement of Justice Gustavo Bossert, who resigned, alleging political persecution. Duhalde replaced Bossert with Juan Carlos Maqueda, a loyal and committed Peronist who, at the time of confirmation, was in fact the Peronist Justicialist Party (*Partido Justicialista*, PJ) president in the Senate.

Duhalde's transitional administration gave way to a new era in Argentine politics. In a widely dispersed vote, the relatively obscure governor of the southern Santa Cruz Province, Néstor Kirchner (2003-7), from the PJ, won the 2003 presidential election and was inaugurated president on May 25.[3] Kirchner brought about significant changes to the country. On the economic front, he reversed the market-friendly policies introduced in the 1990s by implementing a series of redistributive policies that expanded state expenditures; in addition, he launched programs that promoted job creation, even while facing pressure from international lenders not to do so. Because of high demand for commodities during this time (referred to as Latin America's "commodity boom"), the economy recovered rapidly as unemployment fell and consumer spending increased. On the political front, Kirchner led an administration that would be characterized by substantive policies around human rights. Central to his government was a significant push for transitional justice. While Menem and de la Rúa refused to look at the past, Kirchner came in with a decisive push for criminal accountability for human rights violations committed during the military dictatorship (González-Ocantos 2016; Kapiszewski 2011; Helmke 2004). In addition to the building of museums and memorial sites to remember victims of state atrocities and the official recognition of the role human rights organizations played in the defense of human rights in one of the darkest periods in Argentina's history, he retired generals that expressed support for the dictatorship, pushed for the repeal of the amnesty laws passed in the 1980s, formed a special team within the Solicitor General's Office charged with monitoring investigations, and had the human rights minister act as claimant in federal court cases (González-Ocantos 2016, 116–17). Argentina soon became the country with the largest number of criminal court cases against human rights violations in the world.

The Supreme Court became a central player in Kirchner's plans to advance a more robust respect for human rights and transitional justice. The court's rehabilitation thus became a priority. However, this required a delicate balancing act. While public support for the Supreme Court was low, and there was generalized support to replace co-opted justices (Hauser 2016) as captured by the public sentiment of *¡qué se vayan todos!*, a blatant exercise in court-packing would not help to restore the court's legitimacy. As a result, Kirchner established a more transparent nomination process. Within hours of assuming office, he formed a team called a "court for democracy" that was tasked with changing the nomination process for the court's justices. Led by his minister of justice and human rights, Gustavo Béliz, the team was made up of highly respected lawyers, academics, and activists who sought to make changes that would limit the power of the executive and make the process more transparent.[4] A core objective for the team was to establish a process that could restore some of the significant legitimacy the court had lost during the 1990s as a *corte adicta*. The team's work led to the drafting of Decree 222, which was signed by President Kirchner, the justice minister, and the chief of cabinet ministers,[5] Alberto Fernández, on June 16, 2003, less than a month after Kirchner's inauguration.

The decree brought about important changes. Within thirty days of an open vacancy, the president must nominate a candidate by publishing their names and curricula vitae in the official gazette and in at least two national newspapers. Candidates should reflect gender and regional diversity. Once nominated, they must release to the public an account of their assets, as well as those of their spouses and minor children. Further, the justice minister would solicit commentary on the nominees from average citizens, human rights organizations, academia, and nongovernmental organizations. Individuals from the public and these organizations can ask direct questions to nominees in publicly held confirmation hearings in the Senate.[6] The required two-thirds majority in the upper chamber was kept.

As the new nomination process was developed, the Kirchner administration began to plan the replacement of justices that had formed the "automatic majority" during the Menem years (chapter 1). Ten days after his inauguration, and in one of only a handful of broadcasts he gave on national television during his administration, he called publicly for the impeachment of some justices and made explicit references to a co-opted court (*Clarín*, June 5, 2003).

During the same time, the justice minister made several public statements suggesting that the justices could avoid impeachment by resigning. Resorting to the Argentine tradition of forcing unfriendly Supreme Court justices from the bench, within the first two years of his government, Kirchner induced the resignation or impeached five justices that had been loyal to Menem (Justices Nazareno, Moliné O'Connor, López, Vázquez, and Boggiano) and a sixth (Justice Belluscio) retired.

Kirchner was forced to continue to play a careful balancing act in filling the vacated seats on the bench. Owing to the 2003 elections yielding a fragmented Congress, fissures that existed within Peronism, and his weak mandate, Kirchner did not have an assured two-thirds majority in the Senate and could not pursue the strategy of nominating loyal and/or politically inexperienced justices (Kapiszewski 2011, 86). Within two years, as each of the *Menemista* justices left the court, Kirchner filled four vacancies with highly respected lawyers known for their independent minds. None of the new justices, who included the first two women to be appointed to the high court, had any political links to the PJ or personal connections to Kirchner. However, Kirchner sought individuals who were generally sympathetic to his positioning, especially regarding the importance of human rights. Kirchner sought support on two particular issues: the constitutionality of emergency measures introduced during the economic crises, particularly the pegging of the Argentine peso to the dollar, and the unconstitutionality of the amnesty laws passed in the 1980s, which would clear the way to bring perpetrators to justice. Kirchner's administration vetted potential candidates with those two issues in mind. In fact, a series of informal meetings with three of the candidates were held in the private home of Kirchner's chief of cabinet ministers to determine their positions on the two issues (Hauser 2016, 42).[7]

The first new justice, confirmed by the Senate on October 16, 2003, was Eugenio Raúl Zaffaroni. A prestigious, well-known, and highly respected jurist (especially in the legal academy) with a career in the federal judiciary and a brief stint in electoral politics, Zaffaroni had only met Kirchner once and had no ties to the PJ. An expert in criminal law, Zaffaroni had a special interest in the improvement of carceral social conditions. Known for his creative legal thinking and outspoken independent mind,[8] he was what in Latin America is generally called a *garantista* (someone committed to upholding civil and human rights). Zaffaroni's judicial career had focused on issues of social injustice (Hauser 2016). His trajectory worried conservative actors. These concerns were reflected in the long questioning during the senatorial confirmation hearings, which focused on Zaffaroni's (favorable) position on sexual minority rights and abortion, and in the 16 nay votes he received (versus 43 in favor).

The second vacancy was filled by Elena Highton de Nolasco, who was confirmed by the Senate on June 9, 2004, and became the first woman to be appointed to the court under a democratic government in Argentina. An expert on civil law, Highton had a traditional career within the judiciary. After pursuing postgraduate degrees in law at Harvard Law and the University of Nevada's Faculty of Law, Highton practiced as a defense lawyer. She subsequently joined the judiciary after being confirmed as a judge in the National Appeals Court in the early 1990s. Like Zaffaroni, Highton was respected among legal scholars and taught at the Faculty of Law of the University of Buenos Aires. Because of her career within the judiciary, she was reserved about her sociopolitical views but generally considered to have espoused liberal views (Hauser 2016).

The third vacancy was filled by Ricardo Lorenzetti, who was confirmed by the Senate on December 12, 2004. A prolific author and lecturer at the Litoral University in Santa Fé Province, Lorenzetti was widely respected in political and academic circles. With a doctoral degree in law, he was well known for giving regular public lectures and talks to members of Congress, which eventually led to a biyearly conference of Argentine lawyers. While he had sympathized with Peronism in his youth, he had no formal ties to the PJ and was generally regarded as a political pragmatist. However, Lorenzetti's legal career and his numerous publications demonstrated a focus on the most vulnerable sectors of society and on human rights.

The fourth and last Kirchner nominee appointed to fill a vacant seat at the court (on February 3, 2005) was Carmen María Argibay, the second woman to do so. A well-respected lawyer, Argibay had a well-defined professional, national, and international trajectory around social justice issues, especially on gender. She was a cofounder of the International Association of Women Justices as well as the first president of the Argentina's Association of Women Justices. She had also sat on the International Criminal Court for the former Yugoslavia, where she had been key in challenging gender stereotypes in judging women's experiences of war (Ruibal 2014b, 185). As a feminist, Argibay's nomination sparked opposition from socially conservative groups, and questioning during her confirmation hearings was characterized by pointed queries on her position on abortion (*Página 12*, June 24, 2004). She received the required two-thirds majority support by a mere two-vote margin.

While the newly appointed justices did not have any personal or political relationships with Kirchner, they shared a similar socially liberal political ideology and the same interest in the protection and expansion of human rights and civil liberties (Castagnola 2018, 56). However, the golden court exercised unprecedented judicial independence. While it sided with the Kirchners on their two most important policy goals,[9] it ruled in favor of the executive only

62.50 percent of the time (in salient cases) during Néstor Kirchner's administration and 43.75 percent during Cristina Fernández de Kirchner's term (2007–15) (Arballo 2015, 9).[10] These numbers contrast with the favorable rulings the court handed down 85.71 percent of the time during President Raúl Alfonsín's term and the 100 percent automatic majority during *Menemísmo*. This golden court, one clearly more independent and made up of highly respected jurists, is the one that ruled on abortion in Argentina for the first time.

Decriminalizing Abortion: Strategic Negotiation

On March 13, 2012, Argentina's Supreme Court issued the landmark FAL decision regarding a fifteen-year-old girl who had sought an abortion after having been raped by her stepfather. The legal case began two years earlier in lower courts, in the province of Chubut, in Argentina's Patagonian region. This case marked the first time the country's highest court had the opportunity to take a position on one of the most controversial issues in any jurisdiction. By the time the case reached the Supreme Court, the case's central issue—of whether the young girl could seek an abortion—was, in effect, moot. The young girl had already undergone an abortion. Nevertheless, the court decided to hear the case in the abstract and rule on it. This section details the internal process that led to this ruling and suggests that it was primarily characterized by the strategic negotiation among a handful of law clerks and justices.

The Regulation of Abortion in Argentina before 2012

With what were, at the time, innovative reforms undertaken in 1921,[11] paragraph 2 of Article 86 of Argentina's criminal code established abortion as a crime, punishable by up to four years in prison. This prohibition applied to all stages of pregnancy, with only two exceptions. When practiced by a certified medical doctor and with the patient's consent, an abortion could be performed if either the life or the health of the pregnant person was at risk or the pregnancy was the result of "rape or indecent assault against a mentally handicapped or mentally ill person."[12] While the criminal code underwent several reforms prior to 2012, the article's wording remained the same as the original (Bergallo and Ramón Michel 2016; Htun 2003). Despite the exceptions the code provided, research shows that they were rarely invoked or applied until the 2000s (Ruibal 2014b).

The judicialization of abortion in Argentina began with the emblematic 2006 LMR case. VDA, on behalf of her disabled daughter, LMR, requested an abortion after testing confirmed that she had become pregnant as a result of having been raped by her uncle (*Página 12*, November 26, 2007). LMR filed a police complaint on June 24, 2006, and scheduled an abortion at a hospital. VDA qualified for the two exceptions under section 86.2 of the criminal code: rape and mental disabilities. Despite the code's exceptions, antiabortionists were able to secure an injunction against the hospital and prevented the procedure from going ahead. LMR appealed unsuccessfully to the civil court. Because the injunction argued that section 66.2 was unconstitutional, the case was subsequently heard by the Buenos Aires Superior Court (*Suprema Corte de Justicia de Buenos Aires*), which rather expeditiously ruled that the abortion should proceed and reiterated that judicial authorization was unnecessary (Causa Ac. 98.830). However, again under pressure by antiabortionist groups, the hospital refused to perform the abortion because, it argued, the pregnancy was too far advanced. LMR was forced to obtain an illegal abortion at a private clinic, with the support of feminist groups.

Also with the support of paralegal organizations, VDA took her case to the United Nations Human Rights Committee arguing that LMR's rights under the International Covenant on Civil and Political Rights had been violated—specifically, the right to freedom from torture or other cruel, inhuman, or degrading treatment; the right to privacy; and the right to access medical care. The committee ruled on April 26, 2011, that the Argentina state had indeed violated LMR's rights under the covenant and asked it to provide compensation as a remedy and to take steps to ensure that similar violations not reoccur (No. 1608/2007).[13] The case contributed to a growing consensus in international law that restricting a women's access to abortion may be considered cruel or torture. While LMR's case worked itself through the UN committee, another case began to transpire.

The Judicial Road to the FAL Decision

In November 2009, a fifteen-year-old girl, identified by Argentina's judicial system as A.G., was raped, again, by her stepfather, Orlando Nahuelmir.[14] On December 3, A.G.'s mother, identified as ALF, lodged a formal legal complaint before the Prosecutor's Office of Chubut Province (*Ministerio Fiscal de la Provincia de Chubut*). Twenty days later, ALF obtained a medical certificate proving that the girl was eight weeks pregnant.

In early 2010, with the legal support of women's nongovernmental organizations and represented by lawyer Sandra Grilli from the small town of Cholila, ALF submitted a request to the first instance criminal court of the city of Comodoro Rivadavia to allow for an abortion in the city's public hospital (Hospital Zonal de la Ciudad de Comodoro Rivadavia). The girl's legal team argued that her situation qualified for an exception to the prohibitions against abortion, detailed above. The main argument in the request submission was that the procedure should be allowed because the girl was showing depressive and suicidal symptoms, and that "the continuation of the pregnancy against the girl's will entail a grave risk to her psychophysical health, including her own life." On January 22, the criminal court declined the request on the grounds that such a decision was outside its jurisdiction. It instead turned the case over to the Public Prosecutor's Office (*Fiscalía*). That office also declared that it did not have jurisdictional competency and declined to hear the case.

Following that decision and after consulting with A.G. and her mother, Grilli decided to seek a "self-executing" emergency injunction (*medida autosatisfactiva*) before the province's family court.[15] On February 16, 2010, the court's judge, Verónica Robert, rejected the request on the grounds that allowing the abortion to proceed would "irredeemably violate the unborn's fundamental right to life, judicially recognized as a person in the current legal framework." Grilli appealed the decision before the province's appeals court (*Cámara de Apelaciones de la Circunscripción Judicial de Cmodoro Rivadavia*) and reiterated the arguments from the initial submission. However, nine days later, chamber B of the appeals court declined to grant the emergency injunction. Echoing the lower court, the appeals court redeployed and reinforced the arguments around the fetus's right to life.

Undeterred, Gillis took the case to the province's highest court, the Chubut Superior Court (*Tribunal Superior de Justicia de Chubut*). In a surprising and significant decision, on March 8, the Superior Court overturned the appeals court's ruling and authorized A.G. to obtain an abortion. The Superior Court determined that the case fit (*encuadra*) within Article 86 of the criminal code, allowing for an abortion when the individual's health is in danger or when the pregnancy resulted from the rape of a disabled person. The court found that A.G.'s arguments were compatible with the country's constitutional and conventional framework. It thus deemed that A.G. could seek an abortion without judicial authorization; as a result, the procedure could occur as scheduled. And it did: three days later, A.G. obtained an abortion and terminated her pregnancy at a hospital in the city of Trelew (*Centro Materno Infantil del Hospital Zonal de Trelew*).

The province's Office of the Ombudsperson (*Ministerio de la Defensa Pública*) appealed the case before the Supreme Court, the country's final arbiter. The office's Subrogation General Counselor (*Asesor General Subrogrante*), Dr. Alfredo M. Pérez Galimberti, on behalf of "the rights of the unborn," submitted an extraordinary appeal to the Supreme Court challenging the Chubut Superior Court's decision. As the unborn's guardian ad litem (advocate in place of), the claimant requested that the decision be declared unconstitutional given the Superior Court's broad interpretation of the exception of rape in the criminal code. While the case had become moot—A.G. had already obtained an abortion—the appellant argued that the exception had significantly challenged Argentina's constitutional legal framework and conventional obligations, which, it was argued, protect life from the time of conception. The appellant argued that the court should take a position to resolve these important contradictions and clarify the jurisprudence on exceptions to the crime of abortion.

The Case Arrives at the Court

The file officially entered Argentina's Supreme Court in August 2010. Customarily, files are admitted by the court's reception desk. Once processed (i.e., given a file number), files are sent to one of the various judicial secretariats for consideration.[16] These units are organized according to various areas of the law (e.g., administrative or criminal) and are led by law clerks (*secretarios letrados*).

The power that law clerks have in Argentina's highest court, and many other Latin American apex courts, must be underlined for they play a critical role in the crafting of decisions. Given the extraordinary number of cases the CSJN reviews every year (approximately 15,000) due to broad standing—let us recall that every Argentine citizen can submit an extraordinary appeal or an amparo (chapter 1), the number of law clerks has increased significantly since the 1994 constitutional reforms: from approximately 30 in 1990 to 200 by 2014 (Barrera 2014, 76–80). Importantly, and unlike at US or Canadian apex courts, in Latin America, law clerks tend to be career civil servants. They can spend decades working for different justices over their professional lifetimes. Given both their accumulation of knowledge and the significant number of cases the court reviews, law clerks are indeed quite powerful: in fact, they draft most of their justices' decisions. As one justice intimated: "I do not look at 90 percent of the files due to the large workload. The law clerks do most of the work. They know where I stand on the various issues. I look at a decision before signing it."[17] While justices tend to provide a general indication of their likely vote, law clerks can wield significant discretion when drafting decisions, essentially holding the same power as first instance judges.

Given its potential jurisprudential consequences, the FAL file assumed a rather particular processing route once it entered the court. Because the case's appellant framed his arguments as a rights claim ("the right to life"), once admitted, the reception desk turned the file over to the Human Rights and Labor Judicial Secretariat (#6). At the time, this secretariat was led by a highly socially conservative law clerk, Dr. Rolando Gialdino. Gialdino's views against the decriminalization of abortion were widely known inside the court and in legal circles outside it. Interviews with several law clerks and a review of the case's trajectory within the court suggest that the file languished in the secretariat for several months in what some think was an effort to "bury" the case among the thousands that are processed every year.[18] However, through routine reviews of the cases, law clerks from Justice Carlos Fayt's chamber "rescued" the file from the (literal) piles of paper files at the secretariat and alerted Justice Fayt. As recounted by one of his law clerks:

> I showed the justice the file. When I saw it for the first time, I got goose bumps (*se me puso la piel de gallina*). I showed it to the Justice, and he was also surprised (*se le pusieron los pelos de punta*). We read the details of the case and thought that what the girl had suffered was a barbarity. We had actually never discussed abortion. And there was a sense of where he may stand given his position on equal marriage. I would not dare say that it was on his agenda, but once he read the particularities of the case, he said that it had to be heard (*hay que tomarlo*). We then drafted the memo to be circulated justifying that it should be heard [given what A.G. had undergone] and to ask formally for the attorney general's position.[19]

While files are generally administered by a judicial secretariat, in this instance photocopies were circulated simultaneously by Fayt's chamber to the other justices' chambers. Initial discussions among some justices and their law clerks arrived at the conclusion that the file should be pulled from the Human Rights and Labor Judicial Secretariat and transferred to Judicial Secretariat #5 (Landmark Cases), which was led by the highly respected law professor Dr. Cristian Abritta. As a law clerk stated, "Some justices believed that there was not only a conflict of perspectives but a conflict of interest, given that Gialdino had intervened in some cases on reproductive rights."[20]

At this stage of the process, the discussion began to be permeated by Justice Zaffaroni's view on criminal law. His view was based on the *ultima ratio* principle: the idea that there should be limitations on the extent to which states can criminalize individual's actions, and that sanctions should be the last resort in shaping social behavior. According to interviews, discussions were influenced by the deployment of Zaffaroni's academic arguments around this principle and his views on the use of criminal law to address social issues. For Justice Zaffaroni, the debate had to take place outside the criminal code and within the administrative realm. Regarding abortion, the justice's position was that debates about criminalization had been dealt with in other cases (such as the Tejerina case),[21] even if in a tangential manner, and that the important point was to distinguish between abortion as a practice and abortion as an individual's voluntary decision to end a pregnancy. Abortion, the actual procedure, was technically a criminal activity. However, the decision to have one was not.[22] According to a law clerk: "As the expert on criminal law, we all listened. That is why the file was not submitted to the Criminal Law Secretariat (*Secretaría Judicial Penal*)."[23]

On the Admissibility of the Case

Following the decision to transfer the file to Judicial Secretariat #5, the discussion centered on whether the case was justiciable. Led by law clerks from three chambers (Zaffaroni, Lorenzetti, and Maqueda), the informal discussions pondered arguments on the case's admissibility, given its complexities and novelty. As a law clerk put it, "Its admissibility was problematic. There wasn't strictly a legal requirement to hear the case in the abstract. From an orthodox stance, the file was not admissible. From an equality perspective and access to justice, there were important arguments to be made, to say something on the particularities of the case . . . on the judicial maze, on what [the court called] the [judicial] architectural barriers (*barreras arquitectónicas*) and on the revictimization of the person."[24] According to another clerk, "There was no basis to hear the case. There had not been repeated cases previously . . . where a realized action (*hecho concluido*) violated constitutional rights (*con afectación de derechos constitucionales*)."[25]

Interviews reveal that the discussion about admissibility revolved around three main concerns. The first was the actual mootness of the case, given the particularities of abortion. On that issue, the arguments in favor of hearing the case focused on the conflict between the urgency required to terminate a pregnancy versus the considerable time it takes for cases to work through the judicial system. In essence, the view for some was that the court could only take a position on abortion by ruling on the abstract because by the time a ruling could be made, cases would always be moot. As a law clerk put it: "In this secretariat, the average number of days to process a file is 323, given the court's workload . . . a pregnancy takes an average of 270 days. If the court wanted to pronounce itself on abortion, and clean up inconsistencies in the system [regarding its criminalization], it had to be in the abstract."[26]

The second area of argumentation related to *certiorari* (a writ or order by which a higher court reviews a decision of a lower court). The Supreme Court could review cases from lower courts if there was a federal question at stake or if the issue was relevant to the higher court's jurisdiction (Sagüés 1998, 96). While the issue's relevance could be debated (given its mootness), its federal aspect was clearer. The appellant framed their arguments around how the authorization of abortion by the Chubut Superior Court had challenged

Argentina's constitutional and conventional legal framework. On this issue, law clerks from two chambers noted and argued with their colleagues that there was a clear federal question at stake. The federal question arose because of the appellant's references to a "right to life" in international conventions to which Argentina had subscribed. As mentioned in chapter 1, the 1994 constitutional reform introduced the mechanism of "conventional control" into Argentine law. This mechanism stated that international conventions had to be considered when deciding domestic cases. As such, Argentina, as a state, had an obligation to take a position on whether the lower courts' decision was compatible with Argentina's legal obligation to apply certain international conventions on the right to life.

The third, and what appears to have been the main, area of discussion referred to ideas around social justice. While the technical debates were important, for Justice Zaffaroni and several law clerks, a key factor was the case's potential impact on social justice and equality, and importantly, on addressing an issue that affected disproportionately poor women and girls.[27] Ruling for the first time on abortion gave the court "a rare opportunity to pronounce itself," given how exceptional it was that a case of this type would arise and given the importance of the political context. According to a clerk, "The court had a social agenda. After the 2001 crisis, there was a lot of dialogue between the court and society, in addition (*sumado*) to the agenda being pushed by the *Kirchenrista* governments."[28] Another law clerk explained: "The court did not differ much from the government's agenda to draw attention (*visibilizar*) and push (*avanzar*) issues related to access to economic, social, and cultural rights in general. From this human rights perspective, abortion was one of the most unjust. And we had already had the discussion on equal marriage."[29] It therefore appears that the political context was an important consideration in these preliminary discussions, as was, for some of those involved, their view of the proper role of the court in the policymaking process. As a law clerk from Fayt's chamber stated, "When thinking about the case, the idea was not about judicial activism but immersing oneself into the democratic argument, seeing the court as a co-maker (*co-productor*) of public policy within a presidential system."[30]

These discussions, which seem to have lasted for several months, led to the drafting of a memorandum to capture each justice's position. The memorandum was circulated among all the justices' chambers. According to interviews, two justices, Zaffaroni and Lorenzetti, were in favor of hearing the case. Three others (Argibay and Petrachi and an undetermined one) were not in favor. It was at this point that Justice Maqueda (who had not taken a position) argued with other ministers at a regular Tuesday meeting in the conference room (*Sala de Acuerdos*) that the bench should not only hear the case but also engage fully (*de fondo*) with the substantive legal issues.[31] For Maqueda, hearing the case was a question of social justice, given that the current legal framework disproportionately affected poor women and girls.

At this point, news of a leak got out, alerting the press and some nongovernmental organizations that the file was being circulated in the court, so pressure mounted to decide on whether to hear the case.[32] Discussions continued, and several options were considered, including the possibility of not hearing the case because it was too abstract according to "technical justifications" (*salidas técnicas*).[33] However, once Maqueda decided to engage the file fully, several of his colleagues decided to press ahead (*ir para adelante*).[34] Interviews revealed that four justices (Zaffaroni, Highton de Nolasco, Lorenzetti, and Enrique Santiago Petracchi) agreed with Maqueda that the case should be heard. Discussions *de fondo* thus began in early March 2011.[35]

Nevertheless, once the decision to move ahead was made, the justices took the unusual step of establishing a working group (*mesa de trabajo*) made up of law clerks with an expertise in criminal law, one from each chamber, to explore possible lines of argumentation.[36]

The Strategic Crafting of Arguments

Upon agreement between Justices Lorenzetti and Zaffaroni, a law clerk (hereafter, the lead law clerk) from the former's chamber was designated to lead the working group and to represent Zaffaroni's chamber as well. This decision was not surprising: beyond the fact that he had an expertise in criminal law, interviews suggest that the clerk was highly respected and trusted among his peers. Moreover, he had a close personal and professional relationship with Justice Zaffaroni, with whom he had collaborated at the University of Buenos Aires Faculty of Law.[37] Further, he was tasked to represent two chambers that had traditionally voted together and were known to work together in assembling majority decisions by persuading others to sign on to the majority opinion. Indeed, the two justices had the highest rate of voting in the same direction on the bench, 71.53 percent of the time, and were among the justices with the highest rates of joining majority opinions: 89.5 percent for Lorenzetti and 92.55 percent for Zaffaroni (Arballo 2015). Interviews reveal that law clerks and justices were quite comfortable deferring to the aforementioned law clerk for the initial engagement of the case. Such deference also appears to be due to the significant presence Justice Zaffaroni carried at the court given his renown as a jurist and expertise in criminal law, not only in Argentina but in Latin America more widely.[38] According to a law clerk, "It was normal to send files to those with expertise in the area. In criminal law cases, they went to

Zaffaroni. We all listened to [what] he had to say."[39] Another clerk mentioned that Zaffaroni was the "center of gravity" when it came to criminal law cases.[40]

The designated law clerk's office became the main operational center for the case once the working group was established. According to individuals involved, original discussions among members of both justices' chambers agreed on three main points. The first was that a ruling had to justify the admissibility of the case. On that point, discussions narrowed from the more general discussions previously held (on whether the case should be heard) to Article 75 of the constitution, which mandated that all statutory laws comply with international treaties. Given the appellants' argumentation that the Chubut Superior Court violated the country's constitutional and conventional legal framework, admissibility could be justified because the matter had federal import. The Supreme Court could therefore pronounce itself on the matter. The second point, heavily influenced by Zaffaroni's judicial philosophy, revolved around the need to engage *ultima ratio* principle in the ruling. This line of argument aimed to prevent the overall judicialization of abortion.

The last point of agreement concerned the adoption of a robust definition of health, such as the one advanced by the World Health Organization and Pan-American Health Organization (which incorporate physical, mental, and social elements, not only medical), to justify a broad ruling that would turn the case into a public health issue. Specifically, the clerks wanted to emphasize the psychological damage inflicted on those denied abortions. Framing abortion as a public health issue would move the debate away from criminalization and into health care policy, in line with discussions on abortion at the regional and international levels. This approach would also allow for abortions in situations where nonmedical aspects of a pregnant person's health— that is physical, mental, and social aspects—would be affected by the continuation of a pregnancy. As mentioned above, Argentina's criminal code allowed for exceptions in cases in which an individual's "life or health" was in danger, in addition to when the pregnancy was the result of a rape of a disabled woman. Adopting a public health frame would therefore decriminalize abortion in a variety of situations beyond the risk of death or severe illness, such as when the pregnancy would have negative psychological effects. Further, given that the Argentine Constitution guarantees the universal right to health care,[41] participants thought, abortion would also have to be guaranteed by public hospitals in the country. According to a law clerk privy to those discussions, "The justices instructed us (*dieron la consigna*) to elaborate arguments that would go far. To craft (*armar*) something flexible that would allow us to find a guiding principle (*principio rector*) to avoid the judicialization of matter in the future. To do it in the amplest way possible. We essentially elaborated two arguments . . . around taking it out of the criminal code and health."[42]

The three agreed-on points were subsequently presented by the law clerks to Justice Zaffaroni, who endorsed them and fleshed out the arguments to support them (*les puso gancho*).[43] The points were subsequently endorsed by Supreme Court Chief Justice Lorenzetti. At this point, the group sought support from other justices. As the lead law clerk stated: "We already had half of a majority, two of the four we needed."[44] Armed with the arguments to start discussions, the law clerk made sure that the presentation of his ideas on a ruling was couched in socioeconomic terms. Specifically, the idea was that, when engaging in discussions, one had to be thinking about the reality of abortion in Argentina: unequal access to abortion predominantly affects poor and marginalized women. Because the justices had expressed empathy when the case was originally presented, the clerk inferred that this was the best way to set up the discussion and generate support. According to the clerk, "It was about understanding women's reality. It is a matter of class. If in any of the provinces, for whatever reason, the service is not available, the closest hospital is 1,200 kilometers away."[45] Importantly, when considering the framing of the arguments, the law clerk referred to the "favorable conditions" (*condiciones propicias*) to incorporate an expansive ruling, highlighting the favorable political environment and the Kirchnerista emphasis on human rights. Embedding the discussions within a social justice approach, the clerk recounted, "would allow us to go far."[46]

The search for additional votes turned to Justice Maqueda's chamber for discussions, and, in particular, to the law clerk with an expertise in criminal law (also seemingly widely respected at the court). Maqueda's chamber appears to have been the most logical to address first, before speaking with the other justices. Maqueda frequently voted in the same direction as Lorenzetti (70.51 percent of the time) and Zaffaroni (69.27 percent) in court rulings. He in fact had the highest incidence of joining majority opinions with Zaffaroni out of the seven justices—92.50 percent of the time. These numbers are not surprising considering Maqueda's progressive political leanings. An expert in constitutional law, Maqueda was the first justice appointed to the bench after a decade of *Menemísmo* and had close ties with *Kirchnerísmo*. Maqueda and some of his family members (two brothers) were in fact openly Peronists, and he had been officially a member of the PJ since 1983 (Hauser 2016). With a political career, Maqueda also had a personal relationship with President Fernández de Kirchner—they had previously served as Peronist senators together—and was known to be a *garantista*.[47] When appointed to the bench (at age 53), Justice Maqueda favored a restrained role for the court, but his position changed over time, and after the landmark 2006 ruling related to conditions in prisons,[48] began to vote with Zaffaroni.[49]

The lead law clerk briefed Maqueda's point law clerk on the lines of argumentation created by his office. In ensuing discussions, Maqueda's chamber agreed with the first two items (regarding admissibility and *ultima ratio*) but rejected the adoption of a broader legal definition of health. On reflection, the lead law clerk said, "I launched the idea that we define health in an ampler manner, so as to give the ruling a broad reach, but they rejected it and decided to limit the discussion to the question of rape."[50] However, while favoring a narrower reach, Maqueda's chamber accepted the idea of working on a ruling that would extend beyond the case at hand. Maqueda's chamber expanded the argument and proposed that the only requirement to obtain an abortion should be the victim's sworn declaration of rape. According to one of Maqueda's law clerks:

> Justice Maqueda proposed the idea of a sworn declaration. He had a commitment to the issue. He had read a lot about the case and developed his own analysis. He tasked us to study comparative law on abortion. We knew that a sworn declaration would open the door [to possible cases of false declarations], but victims had to be trusted. . . . He instructed us to work on overcoming institutional barriers. The idea was that the ruling could irradiate, set broad guidelines [on access to abortion]. But we had to play a double argumentative game. How do we push for social justice while avoiding criticism of meddling with statutory law? There was a precedent with the ALITT case. Everything is calibrated.[51]

Maqueda's mindfulness of perceived judicial overreach thus appears to have shut down the idea of adopting a robust definition of health. Nonetheless, his chamber agreed to work on crafting a ruling that would establish a basis against the judicialization of abortion in future cases and expand abortion access by removing institutional barriers. The sworn declaration seems to have been central to this additional goal. As a clerk stated: "He [Maqueda] wanted to avoid barriers. When he proposed the idea of a sworn declaration, another clerk [name withheld] and I asked, 'Is this not too much?' But he had the absolute conviction."[52] From these discussions, the lead law clerk dropped the idea of deploying a robust definition of health and accepted the incorporation of a sworn declaration as a tool to liberalize access to abortion as much as possible.[53]

While the objective was to craft a far-reaching progressive ruling, the lead law clerk presenting the objective to the chambers as crafting a ruling with the endorsement of as many justices as possible, even if this would limit the scope of the ruling. As he explained, "We could agree on some items and vote on a concurrent vote on others, but we worked for a majority [opinion]. Because of the matter at hand (*tema*), the court had to be united."[54] This line of thinking appears to have been influenced by a desire to present a common front against possible criticisms from social conservative actors, as well as by the ongoing desire of several justices, especially the chief justice, to restore as much legitimacy to the court as possible after the crises of 2001 and 2002.[55]

The discussion over arguments that could garner as many adherents as possible while weaving a majority opinion turned to the two logical allies: the two women justices, Justices Argibay and Highton de Velasco. The idea was to have the two justices take a prominent role in the development of the majority opinion. "I approached Argibay's and Highton's chambers to share with them the direction in which we were going. As women, I thought the subject was ideal for them, so that they could feast on it (*para que hagan una panzada*)."[56] To the clerk's declared surprise, Justice Argibay's chamber refused to join (*sumarse*).[57] Such surprise, however, would not appear to have been shared by many at the court. While Justice Argibay was ideologically a *garantista* (Castagnola 2018, 56; González-Ocantos 2016; 130, Hauser 2016, 38–39) and a known feminist,[58] she believed in a limited role of courts in the political process and in a restrained interpretation of the law. Additionally, her position was well known at the court. Indeed, she was informally referred to as "Dr. 280" in the hallways of Argentina's highest court, in reference to Article 280 of the Procedural and Commercial Code (*Código Procesal Civil y Comercial Nacional*), which she regularly invoked to refuse to hear cases.[59] Her position was well summarized by one of her own law clerks: "She had an orthodox position on the judicial system. She believed that courts should have a limited role . . . conscious of the counter-majoritarian effect. She believed that they [the justices] should not be hearing that many cases. She thought that it had to be limited to 100 cases [a year]. We cannot invent new rules. It is about seeing whether the decisions of the other institutions conform with the constitution. She was against the arbitrariness principle."[60] Justice Argibay's doctrinal approach to hearing cases resulted in her being a true lonely actor on the bench. Indeed, she had the lowest vote coincidence levels relative to her colleagues (from a low of 25.33 percent with Zaffaroni to a high of 40.58 percent with Petracchi), and the highest number of individual votes (40.91 percent) (Arballo 2015). According to a law clerk in her chamber, "Her position was very clear, and our job was a lot about questioning Zaffaroni's laxer doctrine. She could agree with the case, but not on doctrine. [Regarding abortion] she was deeply conflicted between her jurisprudence and her feminism, where her heart was."[61]

Consequently, many anticipated her chamber's reaction to the draft opinion. Once reviewed, her chamber relayed the justice's position not to join the draft opinion. According to one of her law clerks:

> We were clear in the chamber what her position was because the road had been paved (*camino hecho*) from our internal discussions. We knew her, and we were clear on what her position was. . . . For her, this was just another case. . . . She was opposed to the arguments presented by Zaffaroni's chamber on three fronts: on the manner in which the file was accepted [through the Human Rights and Labor Judicial Secretariats], on the prism [it was a matter of statutory law that had been decided by the legislator], and on the operative part (*la dispositiva*), the reach they wanted to give it.[62]

Justice Highton's reaction to the lead law clerk's presentation of arguments in the draft opinion differed from Argibay's. An expert in public law (*civilista*) with a career in the judiciary, Highton was widely perceived as being a "traditionalist" in her approach to the law. While, similar to Argibay, she had demonstrated a commitment to human rights and civil liberties (Castagnola 2018, 56; González-Ocantos 2016, 130) and was also generally perceived to tilt to the *garantista* side (Hauser 2016). Her position on abortion was more difficult to determine because she had not made it known publicly. When, during her senatorial confirmation hearing, she was accused by socially conservative associations of being in favor of decriminalizing abortion, she categorially declared that she had never taken a position on the issue.[63] Highton decided not to take a leading role in the case, but unlike Argibay, she agreed to join the majority opinion and to have her chamber work on the arguments. However, like Maqueda, Highton did not support the adoption of a robust definition of health to develop a broad ruling. Instead, she was sympathetic to the socioeconomic arguments and receptive to the need to prevent the judicialization of future cases given the psychological impact revictimization has on predominantly lower-income persons seeking abortion.[64] In particular, Highton's chamber agreed that a sworn declaration should be enough to allow access to abortion citing the court's jurisprudence on the issue and referring to the Albarracini case, which revolved around the need to believe and respect individuals' sworn declarations.[65]

Having two justices, Maqueda and Highton, join the draft opinion meant that a majority of votes (four out of seven) had been secured. While both justices rejected the adoption of a broad definition of health and rejected a draft that would force public hospitals to provide abortions, their chambers agreed that the court should go beyond the case. Their chambers agreed that the ruling should liberalize access to abortion by preventing its future judicialization, allowing future abortion-seekers to obtain the procedure without going through the court system. Interviews reveal that, in discussions, the lead law clerk's framing of arguments around the need to take into account socioeconomic conditions of marginalized girls and women, and their unequal access to abortion, played a key role in persuading the two justices to support the underlying direction of the draft's lines of argument.

The support of these two chambers was key, as the positions of the two remaining justices, Fayt and Petracchi, were more predictable. In terms of the former, Justice Fayt had indicated, on first looking at the file, that it should be heard and engaged. Fayt, a longtime member of the Socialist Party and a senior member on the bench, was known to be of an independent mind. While mostly in favor of judicial restraint (González-Ocantos 2016, 130), as a socialist, he tended to be sympathetic to issues of social justice.[66] For him, the "barbarity" the girl in the case had undergone had to be prevented in the future. Further, within the court, Justice Fayt was known for deferring the crafting of arguments once a majority had crystallized. According to a law clerk from Justice Highton's chamber: "[Fayt] was the eldest in the court, and in cases where he saw that there was going to be a majority, he did not get involved. And he did not participate in many discussions."[67] His chamber indicated that they would join in the majority draft. As a law clerk stated, "He was convinced. He had no doubts."[68]

Justice Petracchi's reaction to the draft ruling was also expected, but in stark opposition to Fayt's. Also appointed by President Alfonsín upon the return to democracy in 1983, Petracchi, the most senior member on the bench, belonged to the more liberal wing of the Peronist movement and openly professed an interest in social justice issues. According to the justice: "I am Liberal in the English style. . . . I was always considered a Peronist, not because I belonged to the Peronist Party, but because there is one thing in the Peronist Party that I accept, and that is social justice" (*Página 12*, October 13, 2014). Petracchi's interest in social justice issues concretely translated into advocating for the expansion of rights early on, especially around issues of nondiscrimination and the right to privacy, even years before these issues made it atop national agendas.[69] Importantly, the justice tended to vote in the minority during the socially conservative Menem years.[70] Petracchi's "English liberalism" included a gender dimension: during a two-year stint as the court's chief justice (2004–6), he oversaw the establishment of the Office of Domestic Violence. Nevertheless, even while having famously admitted that "judges are politicians, whether people like it or not" (UBA Derecho 1998), Petracchi supported a limited scope of judicial authority and deference to legislators on matter of policy. As he penned: "This Court cannot ignore that irrespective of the letter of the law, there is a clear political decision on the side of the legislator, which the judicial branch should not evaluate" (as cited by González-Ocantos 2016, 80). The justice's approach to the law saw him having among the highest levels of individual votes cast at the court (Arballo 2015). In the words of one of his law clerks:

> He designated me to work in the working group. He was against those arguments because of his vision on judicial activism. The legislator [had] already settled it. He had a reticent position regarding what justices can do. His opposition was a technical matter. . . . Petracchi asked why seven judges who nobody voted for would decide on the matter. It was for Congress to decide. For him, this was a question of access to the court. It is not about a liberal issue or not. He in fact ruled in favor of very controversial issues. He was respectful of rights (*garantista*), but there had to be respect for the legislator. He was restrictive around admissibility. Similar to Argibay.[71]

Justice Petracchi's reaction to the working draft opinion was therefore not surprising. According to the same law clerk:

> When the file arrived, he asked us what we thought. We did not take a position. For me, who was in favor [of abortion], the case was going to leave us behind because it would force women to say that they had been raped. I shared his opposition but from a different angle. That bothered me (*me chocaba*) . . . he said that statutory law had settled the matter. In this case he asked, What do you think? Is it not too much? He decided not to join [the ongoing discussions] . . . and we turned to how to reject the case.[72]

After these informal discussions, the position from each chamber became clear. By late March, 2011, the working group began fleshing out the ruling's main arguments. However, because of the reluctance of Justices Argibay and Petracchi to support the main direction of the draft ruling, their chambers left the process at this point. They began to work on their own, in what they said would ultimately be individual decisions. According to a law clerk form Justice Highton's chamber, "We worked among ourselves once it was clear they [Argibay and Petracchi] said they would not join (*sumarse*)."[73]

As the formal writing process began, the court asked for intervenors' legal opinions. The intervenors consisted of formal state agencies and *amicus curiae* (briefs submitted by groups with strong interests in the case). Formally, the court was legally obligated to ask the Office of the Attorney General (*Ministerio Público Fiscal*) for the government's position on the case. The office, through its attorney before the court (*Procurador Fiscal*), Dr. Eduardo Casal, released its opinion the following month (April 14, 2011), arguing that the case should not be heard on the abstract (author's copy). The office also asked for the opinions of those who represented each side. The Public Advocate's Office for Minors (*Defensoría Pública de Menores*) submitted in defense of the appellant, the guardian ad litem for the unborn. The General Ombudsperson's Office (*Defensoría General de la Nación*) submitted in defense of the respondent, the Attorney General's Office.[74] In the case of the former, the opinion essentially restated arguments previously made. In the case of the latter, however, the office director, Stella Maris Martínez, submitted a broad and progressive opinion. She not only recommended that the court affirm constitutional access to abortion for all cases of rape, but she also advanced several arguments that reflected a gender-sensitive position and that had been part of feminist mobilization for some time, such as the understanding that sexual violence includes an inherent risk to women's physical health (Ruibal 2014b, 202).

As for amicus curiae, the court received an unprecedented number of responses. The amicus briefs came from prestigious national, regional, and international organizations, mostly in support of the respondent (the Attorney General). Nationally, organizations supporting women's rights included research institutes such as the prestigious Centre for Legal and Social Studies (*Centro de Estudios Legales y Sociales*) and renowned nongovernmental organizations such as the Association for Civil Rights (*Asociación por los Derechos Civiles*). Regional representation was heard through the Brazil-based Reproductive Health Research Center (*Centro de Pesquisas em Saúde Reproductiva*); the Peru-based Center for the Promotion of and Defense of Sexual and Reproductive Rights (*Centro de Promoción y Defensa de los Derechos Sexuales y Reproductivos*); the Latin American Consortium against Unsafe Abortions (*Consorcio Latinoamericano contra el Aborto Inseguro*); and the Colombian chapter of Women's Link Worldwide. Internationally, the group included briefs from Human Rights Watch and the Centre for International Reproductive and the Sexual Rights Program from the University of Toronto's Faculty of Law. On the antiabortionist side, there were national organizations such the Corporation for Catholic Lawyers (*Corporación de Abogados Católicos*), Austral University's Faculty of Law, the nongovernmental association Nativity (*Portal de Belén*), and internationally, Americans United for Life and the Alliance Defense Fund.

While the legal opinions trickled in, the working group, made up of four law clerks representing five chambers (Zaffaroni, Lorenzetti, Maqueda, Highton, and Fayt),[75] worked for several months to develop the majority opinion. They held approximately six formal meetings, at which the lines of argumentation, supported by the five chambers, were developed.[76] These discussions focused again on the three main areas—two of which had previously been informally discussed among law clerks.

The first area was the question of admissibility, given the abstractness of the case. On this issue, the consensus among the five chambers on hearing the case in the abstract required the group to look at arguments justifying the case's admissibility. While influenced by arguments on the same issue in the landmark US *Roe v. Wade* case, and by the reality of the protracted nature of judicial case processing times, interviews point to a decision to base the justification strictly on technical-legal grounds. Specifically, the group decided to accept the suggestion, previously made by the lead law clerk, to rely on Article 75 of the Argentine Constitution to argue that the Chubut Superior Court's decision had federal import and, consequently, that the case could be admitted.

The decision to base the justification on technical-legal grounds seems to have partially been made out of a desire to shield the court from criticism. As a clerk stated: "The ruling had to be tidy (*prolijo*) and well-justified. We could not afford questioning." Further, reliance on Article 75 could serve as the basis for engaging the specific constitutional challenges presented in the extraordinary appeal. Underlying these discussions was the intention to move the jurisprudence away from the concept of the "right to life," which was the central element in the extraordinary appeal's arguments against abortion, and toward other concepts in national and international human rights law, such as "personal dignity."

The second area was the objective to prevent the judicialization of future cases. The original idea, emanating from the Zaffaroni and Lorenzetti chambers, was to adopt a broad definition of health. As mentioned, Justices Maqueda and Highton rejected this plan, but their chambers agreed on preventing the judicialization of the procedure. Discussions yielded an agreement to stick to the issue of rape—consequently, to drop the argument about a broader definition of health—as well as to include Justice Maqueda's original idea of only requiring the individual's sworn declaration. According to a law clerk, "We wanted the victim not to feel judged and for her to be free to decide, that she have as much information as possible."[77] Adopting the sworn declaration addressed Justice Highton's interest in preventing revictimization. Interviews suggest that the sworn declaration was central to these discussions. According to a law clerk, "We all looked for a solution. Basing it (*basándonos*) on rape, the debate centered on arguments around the medical certification, when we decided that it would not be necessary. This gave it complete amplitude. Someone said, 'but they can lie' . . . and, yes, we knew that it would open that door."[78]

Guided by the ultima ratio principle, law clerks decided to rely on the notion of "privacy" to bring it all together. Specifically, they agreed to ground their arguments in the "legality or reserve principle" (*principio de legalidad o reserva*) included in Article 19 of the constitution. This principle states that no action is punishable if it does not affect the "moral or public order" or a third party.[79]

The third area pertained to the "operational" issue. On this point, discussions centered around the need to have the court establish mechanisms to ensure the implementation of what had been decided regarding the prevention of judicialization on the sworn declaration. The discussions on this area appear to have been largely shaped by two main factors. The first was the perceived need to ensure that the decisions taken be implemented not only because of the controversial nature of the case but also because of the country's history of weak policy implementation. Several interviewees, including with law clerks belonging to the working group, made references to the precedent set by the *Riachuelo* case, where the court took on the unusual step of getting involved in policy implementation.[80] The second factor refers to the political opportunity that existed to go farther than what had been decided. Let us recall that the various justices had given instructions to work on a ruling with ample reach. Given the importance the two Kirchner governments gave to human rights, the working group saw an opportunity to deliver a broad ruling. As described by a law clerk: "We were given free rein to do it in the amplest possible way . . . because this was a government that wanted to push for human rights, and given that the fundamentalist mobilization of the country is less than 5 percent . . . we were not afraid of social repercussions."[81]

Discussions among the law clerks resulted in an agreement to frame the implementation part of the draft decision within a broader need to protect the rights of domestic violence victims and, specifically, to anchor its justification in Argentina's 2009 domestic violence law, the Women's Integral Protection Law (24.485). According to a law clerk, "We had to give certainty to the medical community because they tend to judicialize."[82] The law, beyond addressing the issue of physical domestic violence, listed several rights that victims must be guaranteed. It also advanced a broad definition of what "the protection" of victims required. This definition included protecting victims' mental and physical health and made the state responsible for implementing a number of specific policies to prevent, punish, and eradicate domestic violence. Engaging this law would compel the state to take an active role in eliminating all institutional barriers to ensure the protection of victims of sexual violence. As recounted by a law clerk, "We went far. We knew we would not solve the world's problems, but we wanted it to have a durable effect. We were also required to be prudent. We wanted to avoid useless judicializations in the future, to avoid a weak attempt (*acto barato*). They [justices] asked us to offer a solution to the problem, that is what we discussed. We had to set broad guidelines."[83]

Discussions then turned to the development of guidelines to "exhort" the provinces and the city of Buenos Aires to take concrete action at hospitals to prevent administrative obstacles to allow girls and women to access abortion services. Once the main argumentative lines were agreed upon, the working group asked the law clerks with expertise in administrative law for input on the administrative aspects of the implementation section in the draft opinion. According to one of the clerks:

> Work focused on (*se abocó a*) making precisions on the implementation and to convince [others] of the results. To demand an actual way not to revictimize women. There was a lot of detailed work. We had to make sure that there would not be any way to allow for any tricks (*trampas*) and to avoid conscientious objection. To find an equilibrium. We looked at comparative and international law to give us legal principles (*criterio legales*) to avoid trickery. We knew that there was going to be pushback (*reticencias*), not only from institutions but [from] ultramontanist groups, but not from the executive, because we had not had the [public] debate . . . the justices were willing to pay the cost.[84]

Once the draft opinion was finalized, it was sent to each justice for a final look and then sent back to its original judicial secretariat for a final revision. The law clerk in charge subsequently received the two individual opinions from Justices Argibay and Petracchi, who included them into the final document.

The Ruling(s)

The ruling was handed down on March 13, 2012. The rather short (by Argentine standards) fifty-two-page document contained, expectedly, a majority opinion signed by Justices Lorenzetti, Zaffaroni, Maqueda, Highton, and Fayt and two partially concurring opinions by Justices Argibay and Petracchi. Rather surprisingly, given the analysis of the process presented thus far, *all* seven justices upheld the Chubut Superior Court's decision as constitutional, though each justice gave different reasons for the decision.

The majority opinion, as expected, had three main components. In the first and much longer section, the justices rather succinctly (in one short paragraph) declared the admissibility of the case. They wrote that given the appellant's reference to international legal agreements, "the appellant's grounds for appeal raise a federal issue appropriate for review in this appellate instance, given that, in interpreting article 86, paragraph 2 of the Penal Code . . . , the superior court in this case comprised provisions recognized by the National Constitution and by international treaties of equal hierarchy" (FAL, p. 6). The justices then proceeded to declare the importance of pronouncing on these issues in order to "harmonize" interpretations of national and international law (the plexus) "invoked as breached." The court then ruled, in a thorough analysis of Article 86 of the criminal code, citing both the constitutional and international treaties (the American Convention of Human Rights, the Universal Declaration of Human Rights, the Convention on the Rights of the Child, the International Covenant on Civil and Political Rights, as well as expressions made by the United Nations Human Rights Committee), that the code did not allow for a restrictive interpretation of the rape exceptions established therein.

Interestingly, the court interpreted the code by considering the drafters' intention at the time: "It cannot be validly asserted that it was the will of the authors of the Constitution to limit in any way the reach of the definition of non-punishable abortion to the case of a rape victim who is mentally incompetent" (FAL, p. 9). The decision made explicit references to the principle of equality and nondiscrimination, arguing that these principles were central to the country's constitutional framework. The decision also used the right to personal dignity, as established by international treaties, to argue that forcing a woman to bring a pregnancy to term against her wishes violated her fundamental rights. Based on its reading of national and international law and relying on the *pro homine* legal principle, the decision declared that not only was Article 86 not to be interpreted in a restrictive manner, but it also ought to be interpreted broadly. The section ended by clearly stating "therefore, this systematic analysis of article 86, paragraph 2 of the Penal Code, in conjunction with the provisions defining scenarios of sexual violence that would trigger their application should they cause a pregnancy, confirms that any victim of these scenarios who may be found in that circumstance may have a non-punishable abortion" (p. 20).

The second part of the ruling tackled the issues of judicialization. Starting with a reference to the "the young A.G., who had to travel a long judicial road to secure her right to obtain the interruption of pregnancy that was the result of rape" (p. 20), the opinion asserted that such judicialization was questionable as the victim was forced to expose her private life, and that the delay in such practice placed her health at risk (pp. 20–21). Thus, the court argued that it was "compelled to remind both health professionals and adjudicators" of Article 19 of the constitution, "which enshrines the constitutional principle of legal reserve as complementary to penal legality" (p. 21). And, in (unusual) italics, the court cited, verbatim, the core of the principle: *"No inhabitant of the*

Nation shall be obliged to perform the law that does not demand nor deprived of what it does not prohibit" (p. 21). As a result, it followed that "a person who finds herself in the circumstances therein, cannot and must not be required to request a judicial authorization to interrupt her pregnancy, given that the law does not require it" (p. 22). Consequently, the court noted that "the absence of specific rules on access to permissible abortion in the case of a rape only supposed a need for the victim of this wrongful act, or her representative, to state to the attending professional (through a sworn declaration) that such wrongful act is the cause of pregnancy, given that the imposition of any other proceeding will not be appropriate because it would entail incorporating requirements additional to those strictly provided by the legislator" (p. 25). Addressing the risk of "fabricated cases," the opinion stated that this risk could "never be a sufficient reason for imposing obstacles to victims of sexual crimes that violate the effective enjoyment of their legitimate rights or that they may constitute a risk to their health" (p. 26). Importantly, the decision directed health service providers to guarantee the right of conscientious objection insofar as it did not impede the proper provision of legal abortions in all institutions.

The final and shortest part of the majority decision was devoted to "exhortations." In it, the opinion urged national, provincial, and Buenos Aires city authorities to implement and carry out hospital protocols of "the highest level" and to provide "comprehensive" support to victims of sexual violence, removing all administrative or real (*fácticas*) obstacles to access to medical services to guarantee their physical, psychological, sexual, and reproductive health. Lastly, the opinion urged the same authorities to launch information campaigns, with a special focus on vulnerable groups, on the rights of the victims and to provide training programs so that police and health and educational authorities could provide assistance to sexual violence victims.

In a concurring opinion, Justice Argibay dismissed the extraordinary appeal and confirmed the Chubut Province decision, thereby also declaring the constitutionality of abortion in Argentina. In her tightly written opinion, Argibay argued that the appellant had not demonstrated why access to abortion should be limited to victims of rape who also had mental disabilities given that the girl in this case had also been victim of an attack to her "sexual integrity." Further, and deferring to Congress, the justice noted that the appeal had not demonstrated that the legislator's decision to balance two competing rights was unconstitutional: the right of the unborn and the right of the individual whose pregnancy is the result of rape. Finally, she argued that while a sworn declaration was not needed to access abortion, a medical certificate confirming the rape must be required.

Justice Petracchi also confirmed the constitutionality of abortion and offered arguments similar to Argibay's in dismissing the extraordinary appeal from the Chubut Province's counsel. In a rather short opinion of five pages, the justice argued that the appellant had not duly justified why abortion should only be made accessible to individuals who have been victims of rape and who had mental disabilities given that, fundamentally, in the A.G. case, her integral health had been violated. Also deferring to Congress, Petracchi argued that the appeal presented a biased argument by only focusing on the rights of the unborn. The appellant had therefore failed to demonstrate why the legislators' decision to balance the two competing rights (the unborn's right to life and the right of a victim of sexual violence who as a result becomes pregnant) through Article 86 of the criminal code was unconstitutional.

The three opinions in this landmark ruling raised several interesting issues. First, despite their views on judicial restraint, both Justices Argibay and Petracchi decided to address the constitutionality of abortion in Argentina and ultimately sided with the majority. As a result, Argentina's highest court unanimously ruled that there was nothing in the country's legal "plexus" that deemed access to abortion as unconstitutional. As we shall see, this ruling formed the basis for later arguments in favor of the complete decriminalization of abortion, which the Argentine Congress did in December 2020.

Second, and in line with the discussions that unfolded within the court, the majority opinion moved the debate outside the usual conflict between two competing rights. It did not mention once the "right of the unborn" and instead framed abortion as an issue of public health. This framing was also used to justify "exhorting" national and subnational governments to guarantee access to abortions. On this point, it is interesting to note that, despite Justice Highton's reluctance to adopt a broad definition of health in the attempt to dejudicialize the process, she paradoxically supported references to the World Health Organization's definition, which advanced that exact argument.

Third, the majority opinion achieved its main goal of dejudicializing the process by moving it away from domain of the criminal law and into administrative law. Justice Zaffaroni's stance on criminalization as a last resort to deal with social issues was clearly reflected in the ruling.

Fourth, in light of the discussions held within the court, the opinion's rather short length, clear language, and concise justification for why the case should be heard in the abstract reflected several of the working group's objectives. These points reflected the desire of the justices and clerks to clarify the scope of the rape exception, as well as their desire to shield the court from potential criticism.

Finally, Justice Argibay's individual opinion stands out. While she decided not to hear the case because of her doctrinal approach, she nonetheless decided to take a position on the constitutionality of the case, even if her position was to defer to decisions made by the legislature. Further, and as has been pointed out (Ruibal 2014b), her opinion engaged "the rights of the unborn" and frequently referred to the right of the "unborn person," something that pro-choice circles in Latin America had strategically avoided. Moreover, despite her early discussions with clerks from the working group, Argibay included a need for a physician's certification that a rape had taken place, thereby ignoring calls for the need to avoid revictimizing victims. Notably, the other woman justice, Justice Highton, viewed this issue as a priority and as central to debates around sexual violence.

Abortion Politics Post-FAL

It is generally recognized that the historic FAL decision marked an important shift as it reframed the country's debate on abortion, setting the stage for further liberalization. In particular, the ruling argued that abortion, as a practice, was not unconstitutional. Despite the mootness of the case, the court decided to pronounce itself clearly on the constitutionality and interpretation of the criminal code and to put an end to the historic judicialization and lack of implementation of lawful abortions in line with international law. The decision is important for several reasons. It referred to the legal interruption of pregnancy, shifting the debate away from "non-punishable abortion"; it declared, based on equality, nondiscrimination, and *pro homine* principles in national and international law, that abortion access in cases of rape should not be limited to mentally disabled people; it framed the debate around women's health adopting a broad definition of health and includes a social inequality dimension; and it took up the idea of "protocols" exhorting all provinces in the country to adopt them based on women's right to health.

In practical terms, the ruling had mixed results. Research suggests that access to abortion increased in the following years, but that, in line with the Latin American tradition of poor policy implementation, the court's decision was not fully implemented across the country. By 2015, eight provinces had protocols that met the court's directives, seven provinces and Buenos Aires had protocols that partially complied with the court's criteria, and eight provinces had not adopted any protocols (Ruibal 2018a). However, in 2015, the national Ministry of Health updated its protocol to ensure compliance with the ruling and other statues and recent medical recommendations developed by the World Health Organization. Importantly, it changed the framework from "non-punishable abortion" to the "legal interruption of pregnancy."

FAL was thus significant at the practical and discursive levels; it moved the debate's framing away from a moral discussion and into a broader definition of health and socioeconomic disparities. Indeed, the FAL ruling provided pro-abortion actors with legal and discursive tools to advance the cause through

Congress, partly encouraged by significant progress made in other moral policy areas, such as the adoption of same-sex marriage in 2010 and the most advanced (at the time) gender-identity law in 2012 (Saldivia Menajovsky 2021). Importantly, neighboring Uruguay's Congress passed the first bill in the region decriminalizing abortion on demand in 2012 (Fernández Anderson 2016). Encouraged by these legislative changes, Argentine activists introduced several bills attempting to liberalize abortion during the years following the FAL ruling. However, largely because of lack of support from President Cristina Fernández de Kirchner (2007–15), who had an ambivalent position on the issue, the bills stalled in Congress (often for lack of quorum at the committee level).

However, upon the completion of Fernández de Kirchner's term, the sociopolitical environment began to change. Seven months before leaving office, the body of Chiara Páez was found buried in the house of her boyfriend, who was sixteen years old. Páez, fourteen years of age, was a few weeks pregnant. She had been beaten to death after having been forced to take medication to terminate her pregnancy (*The Guardian*, June 8, 2015). The grotesqueness of the case prompted mass mobilization in Argentina, which birthed the movement known as *Ni Una Más* (NUM), or Not One (Woman) Less. The movement strengthened as several cases of gender violence came to public attention after Páez's assassination. Indeed, it gathered force spreading throughout Argentina and the rest of Latin America (Daby and Moseley 2024). Within a year of its emergence, the movement included abortion on demand as a main objective, adopting the now-famous call, "Without legal abortion, there is no *ni una menos*." An abortion campaign was thus born. As Mariela Daby and Mason Moseley show, by 2017, a strong abortion rights campaign crystallized: "the long-taboo subject of women's reproductive rights had made its way into the mainstream, a topic of debate at high schools and universities, cafés and nighty talk shows that reached millions of Argentines at their dinner tables" (2024, 3). Over the next couple of years, the number of public protests demanding abortion rights increased significantly.

The NUM mobilization in turn gave birth to a broader and transnational abortion rights campaign known as the Green Wave. The name derives from a green handkerchief pro-abortion activists and allies began to wear in public signaling their support for abortion access. They borrowed from the staple handkerchief used by the "mothers" and "grandmothers" of the Plaza de Mayo. The Green Wave swept Argentina and the region; indeed, the green handkerchief was worn by feminists from Chile to Mexico and even the United States (after the overturn of *Roe*) and in France when the debate over the constitutionalization of abortion access took place (Felitti and Ramírez Morales 2020). It soon included famous writers, actresses, and organized groups of women from various sectors of society and different social classes. Such was the intensity and spread of the movement, that Daby and Moseley (2024) have termed the Green Wave more of a "community movement" rather than a social movement. Importantly, the Green Wave continued to move the framing of debate away from moral issues to women's right to health care and to class differences around economic inequality and social justice. Focusing on the consequences of seeking unsafe, clandestine abortions for poor women and girls, the movement captured that new reality with the chant: "The rich abort, the poor die!" (¡Las ricas abortan, las pobres mueren!).

It is within the new context that, in 2018, the movement introduced a new bill to the Chamber of Deputies to decriminalize abortion during the first fourteen weeks of pregnancy (Ley de Interrupción Legal del Embarazo, ILE). While the bill passed the lower chamber, it was defeated in the Senate largely because of the lack of support from conservative president Mauricio Macri (2015–19). He may have allowed the debate to take place but did not ask his coalition's deputies to support the bill. Despite the defeat, women had changed the terms of the debate, moving away from whether abortion should be legal to a focus on trying to prevent the oftentimes lethal consequences of obtaining abortions in clandestine conditions. Moreover, they double downed and argued that they had been successful in changing the terms of the debate, adopting the hashtag #SeráLey (It will be law).

The opportunity to push for abortion opened up with the election of (Peronist) Alberto Fernández in 2019. Known for his progressive views, and unlike Fernández de Kirchner, he had publicly declared that he was in favor of abortion during his election campaign. Once elected, he continued to make clear his support, but suggested that because of the economic crisis, it was not a priority. He nonetheless promised that he would introduce a bill that would legalize abortion, along with another bill called the "1,000-day plan" that would provide support for women during pregnancy, childbirth, and the first few years of childrearing. Importantly, Fernández justified the need to legislate on abortion on both health care and socioeconomic grounds: It was a public health issue that disproportionately affected poorer women and girls (Daby and Moseley 2024).

In close collaboration with his legal counsel, Vilma Ibarra—a key actor in the passages of both same-sex marriage and gender-identity legislation while a legislator herself (Díez 2015)—Fernández's office sent a revised version of ILE (Ley 27.610) to the Chamber of Deputies in November 2020 requesting both congressional chambers to vote on the bill before year's end. With a 131–117 margin, the lower chamber approved the bill—which was a margin close to the 2018 vote. Because of overrepresentation of conservative forces in the Senate, mostly from the provinces, the upper chamber tends to be more conservative on moral issues and is in fact pressured by the executive to pass moral policies, such as the 2010 same-sex marriage bill (Díez 2015). Nevertheless, on December 30, and in line with the Argentine tradition of having thousands of activists in front of the majestic Congress building awaiting the result, the Senate supported, with a 38–29 vote, the new ILE. The new law decriminalized abortion during the first fourteen weeks of pregnancy and set no time limits when a continued pregnancy threatens the pregnant person's life, their mental or physical health, and in cases of rape.

In 2022, 96,664 abortions were performed in the public sector, reducing fertility rates and preventable deaths among girls ages 10 to 14 (Pianesi 2024).

The passage of the new ILE in late 2020 is directly related to the pressure exerted by the Green Wave in Argentina, as has been amply shown (Daby and Moseley 2024). However, part of the success can be attributed to both the declaration in the FAL ruling that access to abortion is not unconstitutional and the adoption of new frames that changed the debate (Díez and Ruibal 2025). The court settled the debate on the constitutionality question and shifted it to issues of public health, human rights, and socioeconomic disparities. These are the frames that the 2012 FAL ruling began to articulate. As has been argued, it was a paradigm shift (Yamin and Ramón Michel 2023). Indeed, analyses of the debate in Congress show that the arguments deployed by pro-abortion legislators revolved mostly around three areas: health and prevention (23.39 percent of interventions), women's rights and autonomy (18.07 percent), and unsafe conditions to seek abortions (13.49 percent) (CEDES 2001, 14).

The 2020 policy change was built largely on the road the FAL ruling first began to pave.

Conclusion

The FAL decision was, at the time, a landmark ruling in Argentina. It was the first major step in the liberalization of abortion in the twenty-first century, and it formed the basis for the discussion in the Argentine Congress that decriminalized abortion completely in December 2020. The analysis presented in this chapter suggests that the ruling is the culmination of the acumen of a handful of justices and law clerks. These justices and clerks worked strategically in calibrating arguments through discussions with their peers in order to gain the necessary support to obtain a majority of votes. It appears that framing the discussion around the issue of class was key in that process. While the general tilt of the bench was toward the *garantista* side, the strategic actors behind the crafting of the majority ruling appear to have compromised part of their original policy preferences—that of framing the entire ruling as a matter of public health by relying on a robust definition of health—in order to earn two critical adherents: Justices Highton and Maqueda. Narrowing the scope to the issue of rape was, according to the key players, key.

The analysis also suggests that actors at the court, beyond those playing key roles, were attuned to the political context and knew they could aim for an expansive ruling. Their reading of the political context seems to have been based on the pro–human rights approach the Kirchner governments had adopted, which was not simply discursive as demonstrated by the concrete steps they took to bring perpetrators of human rights abuses during the dictatorship to trial and the perceived public empathy for the conditions of poor and marginalized girls and women. Finally, as part of the decision justices made, including the two who filed partially concurring opinions, it seems that the perception of the court by other branches of government and the public in general, and its proper role, was considered as being important. Concern for the court's legitimacy thus appears to have been part of the strategic calculi. Getting as strong a majority as possible and presenting a tightly written and clear decision seems to have been a component.

Chapter 4

Colombia

Strategy behind Moderate Decriminalization

Introduction

This chapter shows that the 2006 decision (C-355) by the Colombian Constitutional Court (CCC) was the result of the strategic deployment of arguments by Justice Manuel José Cepeda Espinosa and his law clerks. Once the constitutional challenge (Unconstitutional Action, *Acción pública de Inconstitucionalidad*) was resubmitted by legal activist Mónica Roa a second time (it had been rejected earlier that year on procedural grounds), a discussion began within the court on the extent to which the restrictions to abortion in the criminal code violated the constitution. While Justice Jaime Araújo Rentería argued that all restrictions were unconstitutional infringements on women's reproductive rights and urged complete decriminalization, Justice Cepeda and his team strategically took a moderate approach to secure a majority. They argued for balancing the right of a woman to obtain an abortion with the unborn's right to life. Cepeda's chamber convinced some of his peers to deploy the "proportionality test" to argue for partial decriminalization when the pregnancy was the result of an unconsented sexual act, incest, or unauthorized fertilization; when the continuation of the pregnancy posed a danger to the woman's life; or when the life prospects of the fetus are inviable due to malformation. Partial decriminalization secured a 5–3 majority ruling. The analysis in this chapter shows that some justices were keenly attuned to the political context and anticipated that broader decriminalization would ignite a backlash from state actors, especially the executive and the Catholic Church, given a recent reform of the penal code. Two justices believed that such decision would have been considered counter majoritarian. It also shows that drafting of the legal argumentation in the majority opinion was done with utmost care to ensure the ruling's legitimacy and preempt any possible critiques from opponents.

Composition of the "Second Court"

The CCC's 2006 landmark decision on abortion was made by what is colloquially known in Colombian legal circles as "the second court"—that is, the nine justices who replaced the vacancies left in the bench by those who made up the first permanent bench in 1993 after their eight-year terms were up. As we saw in chapter 1, the new constitution established a hybrid appointment system in which the president, the Supreme Court and the Council of State present three candidate lists (called *ternas*), which are then voted on by the Senate, to fill three vacancies each. Most of the new bench was installed between mid-1999 and early 2001. The new justices assumed a profile that could be described as fragmented given the presence of clearly liberal and conservative justices and a couple of moderate ones.

The court's makeup stemmed from two important elements. The first was its institutional design. The selection process makes it difficult for any political actor to pack the court because the responsibility is shared among three political institutions. Indeed, ideological and doctrinal diversity is one of the objectives behind the adoption of a hybrid model, and that was certainly the case in Colombia (Lamprea 2010; Tiede 2022). One of the direct consequences of the adoption of this model has been that the ideological positions of the candidates proposed by the Supreme Court and the Council of State are usually not known.[1] However, since the court's establishment, candidates appointed by these two institutions have tended to prefer a restrained role of the court (Landau 2005, 319). Their positions on the role of the court in Colombian politics have contrasted markedly with neoconstitutionalist justices, who have pursued a more expansive role since the court's creation.

The second element was the election of conservative President Andrés Pastrana Arango (1998–2002) in 1998. After a twelve-year period of three consecutive Liberal Party administrations,[2] Colombians elected Pastrana in what would be the last president elected on Colombia's Conservative Party (*Partido Conservador*) ticket. His election took place within a larger context of a deinstitutionalization and fragmentation of Colombia's historic two-party system. Largely because of the widely perceived mismanagement of the security situation in the country by both traditional parties and a handful of corruption scandals, competition for the presidency and Congress increased as new political forces, promising a change to the status quo, gathered support and became more successful electorally (Albarracín et al. 2018; Pizarro Leongomez 2002). For conservative forces in Colombia, some of whom were critical of the newly empowered court, Pastrana was seen as the last conduit through which they could rebalance its makeup. However, because of the fragmented makeup of Congress, Pastrana had to strike a delicate balance in the development of his court candidate lists to be able to push his agenda through the legislature. During his administration, his Conservative Party held 28 out of the 102 Senate seats, compared to the 58 held by the Liberal Party and 16 held by other parties. He thus produced lists that contained a mix of conservative and liberal candidates during his administration.[3] Nevertheless, while he did present some known liberal candidates, his lists would ultimately bring to the bench some of the most conservative justices the court has seen, such as Marco Gerardo Monroy (as we shall see below).

The first two justices to be confirmed to the "second court" within this context were Alfredo Beltrán Sierra (1998–2006) and Álvaro Tafur Galvis (1999–2007). Proposed by the Supreme Court on its candidate list, Beltrán was the first justice confirmed to the second court. Beltrán was a highly educated and respected jurist with expertise in administrative law from the prestigious and traditional Universidad Libre in Bogotá, where he also taught law.[4] Given his reputation, Beltrán's confirmation in the Senate was noncontroversial, as reflected by the wide majority of votes his candidacy received: 50 votes in favor and 4 against, while 2 votes were cast for his competitors. His profile captures quite well the perspectives of some justices who reach the CCC from within the judiciary—he served as judge at a Superior Tribunal in Bogotá and subsequently as a law clerk at the Supreme Court prior to his nomination—in that they can, at times, take a rather restrictive approach to the law. At times detached from their ideological leanings, some of these career judges tend to reject an interpretivist approach to the constitution and, like Beltrán, profess a preference for deferring to the legislator.[5] In terms of his ideological position, Beltrán would be best described as a "moderate liberal." An admirer of some of Colombia's most prominent historical liberal figures, such as independence hero Antonio Nariño, assassinated presidential candidate Jorge Eliécer Gaitán, and President Alfonso López Pumarejo (1934–38, 1942–45), Beltrán had close ties to Colombia's Liberal Party (*Partido Liberal*). Indeed, his candidacy was supported by Liberal Senator José Name Terán (*El Tiempo*, May 6, 1998).[6] Expectedly, Beltrán took clear liberal positions during his term at the court when voting on some salient cases,[7] and he has therefore been located on the liberal side of the bench: *La Silla Vacía* (LSV) assigned him a score of 2, where 1 is the most liberal and 10 the most conservative (2012),[8] and Juan Carlos Rodríguez-Raga's survey rated him at 3.6 (2011).[9] However, he also joined the more conservative wing of the court in controversial social issues, such as decisions on LGBTQ+ rights.[10] As a result, some observers have labeled him a "conservative" on social issues (Lemaitre 2005) or a "moderate" liberal (Rubiano 2009).

Replacing Justice Hernando Herrera Vergara, Justice Tafur was the second justice confirmed to this bench. Tarfur was proposed to the Senate in 1999 by Pastrana, whose preferred candidate and legal adviser was Jaime Arrubla. The president asked conservative senators to support Arrubla's nomination (*El Tiempo*, April 7, 1999). However, liberal and independent senators rejected Arrubla and, in a 45–29 vote, confirmed Tafur. While conservative, Tafur had no personal ties with the president. A former Supreme Court justice, Tafur was widely known to be conservative and openly Catholic (Azuero Quijano 2006). An expert on administrative law, Tafur had been president (*rector*) of Rosario University, a traditionalist institution with historical close ties to the Catholic Church, and he was seen as an old-guard *Rosarista*. Tarfur was a renowned academic and jurist with a doctorate in law (Rosario University) and personal connections with members of France's *Conseil Constitutionnel*. While described as independent in his thinking by the press (*Semana*, June 20, 1999), experts generally agree that his ideological position was primarily conservative on most issues (Lemaitre 2005; Azuero Quijano 2006; Rubiano 2009). He would indeed eventually form part of a conservative bloc in the second court, along with Justices Marco Gerardo Monroy and Justice Rodrigo Escobar Gil (2001–9).[11] According to scores developed by observers, his ideological scores are 7.0 (LSV) and 7.01 (Rodríguez-Raga 2011). Regarding his legal doctrine, Tafur was considered a positivist, traditionally characteristic in Latin America, and rejected an interpretivist reading of the law (Azuero Quijano 2006). Unlike Latin American neoconstitutionalists, Tarfur considered Colombia's commitments to international regimes as the only legitimate foreign influence on judicial decision-making.[12]

The next two justices to be confirmed to the bench were Cepeda Espinosa (2001–9) and Escobar. Cepeda was likely the best-known justice to be confirmed to this bench because of his political trajectory and prominence as a jurist in Colombia and in Latin America more broadly. An expert on constitutional law, Cepeda formed part of what was known at the court as the *andinistas* ("Andeanists") or *red uniandina* ("UniAndean Network"), referring to individuals who attended and taught at Bogotá's prestigious Faculty of Law at Los Andes University. This network of jurists, lawyers, and academics is considered responsible for imbuing the CCC with a neoconstitutional approach to the law (Lamprea 2010; Landau 2005; Azuero Quijano 2006; Jaramillo and Alfonso 2008). At times, this network was said to belong to a "liberal Anglo-Saxon" tradition (Azuero Quijano 2006) because of its close association with Harvard Law and other law faculties in the United States, drawing inspiration from common law. The network is characterized by individuals who view the constitution and the law as tools through which to advance human rights, especially in the socioeconomic arena. Cepeda is widely regarded as one of the most influential leaders in the network. Rather prolific academically, he earned a law degree from Los Andes University and an LLM from Harvard and served both as a faculty member and as dean of the Los Andes Faculty of Law. Politically, Cepeda had close connection to Colombia's Liberal Party. Indeed, he was one of President César Gaviria's legal advisers during his administration and lead adviser to Gaviria during the 1991

Constituent Assembly. Cepeda has been identified as a key actor in the establishment of a constitutional court and an expansive enumeration of rights in the constitution as well as the main architect of Colombia's *tutela* (Azuero Quijano 2006, 2009; Landau 2015).

After serving at the court as an Adjunct Replacement Justice (*Conjuez*),[13] Cepeda was presented by Pastrana as a candidate on one of his lists alongside another liberal jurist (Álvaro Tirado Mejía) and a conservative law clerk (Cristina Pardo Schlesinger) to replace the *andinista* Eduardo Cifuentes.[14] While conservative, Pastrana is believed to have chosen Cepeda because of his influence in the drafting of the new constitution and the establishment of the court and advice he had given the president on important political matters (Rubiano 2009).[15] Cepeda was confirmed with 51 votes compared to Tirado's 48, mainly because of the influence that former president Gaviria exerted on the liberal bench in the Senate, which supported his candidacy (liberals controlled a plurality of seats) (Azuero Quijano 2006, 120; *El Tiempo*, December 14, 2000). Ideologically, Cepeda has been placed at the center of the political spectrum: LSV assigned him a score of 4, while Rodríguez-Raga's survey gave him a score of 5.5. However, he has also been labeled as "progressive" (Lemaitre 2005; Jaramillo and Alfonso 2008), "moderate" and "pragmatic" (Rubiano 2009), and a "progressive liberal" (Lamprea 2010). These adjectives reflect the clearly liberal positions Cepeda took on divisive social issues, such as LGBTQ+ rights, which brought him to the liberal side of the bench along with Justices Jaime Araújo Rentería (2001–9) and Jaime Córdoba Triviño (2001–9).

Cepeda's approach to the law is of particular interest for our purposes. In his academic work, he has articulated an approach to the interpretation of constitutional texts through what he calls "responsive constitutionalism" (Cepeda-Espinosa 2019). Influenced by the work of legal theorists Philip Selznick and Phillipe Nonet, Cepeda has argued that the law must be used as a mechanism to respond to citizens' demands to improve their livelihoods in concrete ways (2019, 34–36). The adjudicator, he goes on, ought to consider the social context when engaging the constitution in order to guarantee the "effective enjoyment of rights" and undertake a "differential approach" focused on fundamental rights with "responsive constitutional adjudication" that would protect vulnerable groups in "need of special protection" (2019, 37). In sum, he wrote, "All of these notions evolved into doctrines that require positive actions from a state responsive to real situations faced by diverse human beings, with the aim of transforming the actual conditions in which they live in such a way that they actually enjoy their fundamental rights" (2019, 37).

Cepeda's variant of neoconstitutionalism relied heavily on comparative law for constitutional interpretation and on tests (such as proportionality) for argumentative development. As he declared: "In my case, I tend to explain comparative law and to use it in my decisions. Sometimes it is accepted, but sometimes it is not" (Azuero Quijano 2006, 129). Accepted or not, his reliance on comparative law was key to his work as a constitutional judge.[16] To the attentive reader, Cepeda's profile is strikingly similar to that of Justice Eugenio Raúl Zaffaroni of Argentina, analyzed in chapter 3: an acclaimed jurist with a strong academic bent who sees the law as a mechanism to expand social justice. Like Zaffaroni, Cepeda was a key player in assembling a majority in favor of decriminalizing abortion in 2006, as we will see below.

The next candidate to be confirmed was Justice Escobar Gil, a conservative judge who would sit on the right side of the bench, ideologically, along with Tafur and Justice Gerardo Monroy Cabra (2001–9). Escobar was proposed by the Council of State in what was widely regarded as one of the most conservative lists made up of Jorge Enrique Ibáñez Najar and the candidate backed by the Catholic Church, Ilva Myriam Hoyos (*El Tiempo*, December 15, 2000). A graduate of law from the Catholic Javeriana University of Bogotá (*Pontífica Universidad Javeriana*), Escobar earned a doctorate from Madrid's Complutense University in administrative law and would subsequently teach at conservative universities, including Javeriana, La Sabana University (linked to Opus Dei), and Sergio Arboleda University. Politically, Escobar had close connections to the Conservative Party (as a card-carrying member) and specifically with the prominent former presidential candidate Álvaro Gómez Hurtado (who was assassinated by a guerrilla group in 1995 as he walked out of the Sergio Arboleda University campus in Bogotá). His nomination was backed by most conservative and liberal senators with 71 votes, compared to Ibáñez's 16 and Hoyos's 13. His candidacy was supported by liberal senators,[17] as he was seen as the least conservative of the *terna* (*El Tiempo*, December 15, 2000). Escobar has been identified as having a "conservative orientation" (Rubiano 2009) and a clear "conservative training" (Jaramillo and Alfonso 2008) and being an engaged member of the Conservative Party (Lamprea 2010). On social issues, before the 2006 decision of abortion, Escobar dissented, along with Tafur and Monroy, from majority opinions that advanced LGBTQ+ rights as well as from the 2004 divorce majority decision (C-074-04). LSV consequently assigned him an ideological score of 8, and the Rodríguez-Raga survey rated him a 7.5. As for his legal approach, while influenced by European Continental law, Escobar espoused a literalist interpretation of the law and believed in a restrained role of constitutional courts.[18]

The next set of confirmed justices consisted of Monroy Cabra, Clara Inés Vargas Hernández, Jaime Araújo Rentería, and Jaime Córdoba Triviño (all serving from 2001 to 2009). As mentioned, Monroy was part of a conservative triad that consistently voted against the expansion of LGBTQ+ and divorce rights, and he was perhaps the most conservative justice the CCC had seen at the time of his confirmation. In effect, both LSV and the Rodríguez-Raga survey assigned him the highest scores on their indices: 9 and 8.1, respectively. Replacing a liberal justice, Monroy was named by President Pastrana on another clearly conservative list (*El Tiempo*, November 23 and December 15, 2000). Monroy received the most votes in the Senate (63) compared to the two other conservative candidates (who received 22 and 13 votes each), seemingly because of his established expertise in international law (Rubiano 2009). Monroy undertook his legal training at conservative universities (Rosario and Javeriana), specializing in international law. His links with Rosario University were particularly strong: upon graduation, he became a professor and dean of law, serving from the 1960s until the mid-1990s. Prior to his nomination, Monroy served as a judge in a Superior Court (*Tribunal Superior del Distrito Judicial de Bogotá*) and was a member and subsequently president of the Inter-American Commission on Human Rights. While his training and experience in international law and forums gave his ideological positioning a certain liberal and social vein—which may explain why he took a more liberal approach toward the end of his term at the court—there is a consensus among observers that he was a conservative judge (La Silla Vacía 2012; Lemaitre 2005; Rubiano 2009; *El Espectador*, December 20, 2019), and he was the most consistent conservative judge during his tenure (Lamprea 2010).[19] His conservatism was colloquially referred to as *Católico-Rosarista* (Catholic-Rosarist). In terms of his approach to the law, Justice Monroy rejected the use of comparative and international law in the interpretation of legal texts, leaning toward legal positivism and a restrictive view of legislative-judicial "dialogue" (Azuero Quijano 2006).[20] Monroy would thus make up the conservative pole of the bench with Tafur and Escobar.

Making history, Vargas was the first woman justice to be confirmed to the court in 2000 and became the first woman chief justice in 2004. Proposed by the Supreme Court on one of its rosters, Vargas was supported by liberal and independent senators against Pastrana's preferred candidate, Alberto Rojas Ríos. She won confirmation with a comparatively narrow margin, with 49 votes (compared to Rojas's 31 and 20 for the third candidate).[21] Vargas made her career as a civil judge before becoming a magistrate in Bogotá's Superior Court and subsequently as a representative attorney (*Procuradora Delegada*) before the Supreme Court. As an expert in civil and commercial law, Vargas earned a law degree and a doctorate in law at Colombia's prestigious and left-leaning centrist National University (*Universidad Nacional de Colombia*).[22] Vargas is best described as a centrist judge, both politically and doctrinally. Several justices and clerks interviewed referred to her as having been "undecipherable" at the beginning of her term. Before the 2006 decision, her record on abortion was mixed on social issues. While she wrote the majority opinion in the 2004 divorce ruling, she voted against the expansion of LGBTQ+ rights in the two 2001 rulings. She was supported by various liberal factions, but, given her voting record, there is no consensus on her ideological placement: observers have labeled her as a "conservative judge" (Lemaitre 2005), a "moderate liberal" (Rubiano 2009), and simply a "conservative" (Lamprea 2010). Her scores are 3 (LSV) and 5.8 (Rodríguez-Raga's survey). In terms of her approach to the law and judging, Vargas adopted a moderate view on legal interpretation and believed in a restrained form of judicial review. In defense of "moderate judicial activism," Vargas has argued in various decisions that Colombia's tutela filled an important void because of government inaction (in protecting rights), something that had led to a "Pacific revolution." However, she goes on, judicial review must be moderate and constitutional judges, while addressing unconstitutional issues, must do so in a moderate manner, must self-limit themselves, and "in the Anglo-Saxon tradition," apply the principle of "self-restraint." She argued, upon leaving the bench, that the legislator's activity assumes a more active and positive role than the court, which in turn must assume a position of "self-control" and "self-contention" (Azuero Quijano 2006). She has been identified as having belonged to judges that have an innovative and nonorthodox approach to the law, yet her training in private law may have resulted in the adoption of conservative positions at times (López Bajo 2017).

Vargas's position on gender issues is of particular interest in any analysis of abortion decisions. Vargas was also a moderate advocate of women's issues. Her candidacy was not particularly supported by the feminist movement or women senators, and her jurisprudential production during her tenure was characterized by a lack of attempts to address gender disparities or contribute to the debates that feminist movements were having abroad in terms of gender justice (Azuero Quijano 2006). Yet her involvement with some women's groups may have progressively convinced her to incorporate a gender perspective into her judicial work. She has declared that, in meetings organized by these organizations, "a gender perspective with which one wants to imbue jurisprudence is strengthened . . . [and] if you go to give a paper at an international conference, you have to be prepared, and that will necessarily benefit you when drafting a ruling" (Azuero Quijano 2009).

Justice Araújo, likely the most liberal judge on that bench, was confirmed by the Senate at the same time. Replacing the progressive Carlos Gaviria, Araújo was proposed by the Council of State and received multipartisan support in the upper chamber, with a backing of 84 votes compared to 12 and 4 votes, respectively, for his competitors (Jaime Buenahora Febres and Dolly Pedraza Arenas). Araújo developed expertise in criminal and administrative law at the Externado and Los Andes universities in Bogotá. He subsequently taught at Externado University Faculty of Law, widely known as one of the most liberal law schools in Colombia. Known for his plainspokenness, Araújo, a *costeño* (from the coast), was a longtime socialist and served as a magistrate at the National Electoral Council (*Consejo Nacional Electoral*). Politically, Araújo had personal and professional links with politicians who belonged to leftist movements and parties, such as Senator Iván Moreno Rojas from the Democratic Pole (*Polo Democrático*), whom he represented legally in a case, and Senator Piedad Córdoba from the Citizens Power Movement (*Movimiento Poder Ciudadano*), the leftist faction of the Liberal Party.[23] His clear leftist ideological orientation explained the wide support he received from the Liberal Party and independents (*El Tiempo*, December 15, 2000; *Acta del Congreso, Plenaria 27*, December 13, 2000). Known for his passionate tone in plenary sessions (sometimes called "tantrums" by people at the court), Araújo voted consistently in favor of the expansion of rights. He was a clear *garantista*. In effect, he joined the majority opinion on the 2004 divorce ruling and, characteristically, drafted a concurrent opinion on the 2001 rulings on LGBTQ+ rights with an ampler reach.[24] Such positional consistency logically explains a consensus among observers on his ideological qualification: he has been described as a "progressive justice" (Lemaitre 2005, 210; Jaramillo and Alfonso 2008, 142), a "leftist liberal" (Rubiano 2009), and a "liberal" (Lamprea 2010). Unsurprisingly, Araújo has been given the most liberal scores—a score of 1 (according to LSV) and 3.8 (according to Rodríguez-Raga). Although he is also considered to have an innovative and interpretivist approach to the law, his chamber's incorporation of comparative law into decisions was limited. He is said to have had a conservative and parochial approach to the value of international ideas (Azuero Quijano 2006). In effect, his arguments assumed a nationalist tone. In the words of one of his law clerks, "We were instructed to limit ourselves [in the development of opinions] to Colombian jurisprudence and arguments and not to look at foreign ideas. Internationally, we were limited to international commitments."[25]

The fourth justice of the tranche to be confirmed to the court in late 2000 was Córdoba, another progressive judge. Córdoba was proposed by the Supreme Court and backed by senators in the second chamber with the largest margin, receiving 89 votes, compared to 5 votes for each of the other candidates. Córdoba belonged to the liberal wing of the second court and was chief justice when the 2006 abortion ruling was handed down. However, given his direct involvement with the reform of the criminal code in 2001, he recused himself from the discussion on the case and from casting a vote.[26] His role in the process was therefore nonexistent, and his profile is of limited use for our purposes. He consistently voted with Cepeda on social issues and was a firm advocate of human rights expansions.[27]

The last justice to be confirmed to the bench that decided C-355 was Humberto Sierra Porto (2004–12). Sierra Porto was confirmed in 2004 to fill a vacancy left by Justice Eduardo Montealegre Lynett (2001–4), who retired for personal reasons. A native of Cartagena, he won a tightly contested vote in the Senate against the conservative candidate (Consuelo Caldas) who was favored by President Álvaro Uribe Vélez (2002–10).[28] He was backed by liberal senators, independents, and dissident members of Uribe's coalition in the upper chamber (Rubiano 2009). Like Araújo, Sierra Porto earned a law degree from Externado University Faculty of Law. He subsequently studied in Spain, specializing in political science and constitutional law at Madrid's well-known Center for Political and Constitutional Studies (*Centro de Estudios Políticos y Constitucionales de España*), and he earned a doctorate in law at Madrid's Autonomous University (*Universidad Autónoma de Madrid*). His training in Spain is relevant because it seems to have influenced his approach to the law. Known for their traditional and conservative treatment of constitutional law and based on civil law's deductive logic, Sierra Porto's decisions as a judge affirmed a rather limited role for judicial review and deference to decisions made by Congress. While he has supported an active role of the court in guaranteeing fundamental rights—"it is about an innovative and *garantista* Court" (Sierra Porto et al. 2022, 13),[29] he has also argued that the court must limit itself in the protection of socioeconomic rights when budgetary issues are involved (Galdámez Zelada 2014). Observers have therefore noted that Sierra Porto's chamber adopted a position closer to the civil law tradition and to "Continental Europe's jurisprudence" in contrast to Cepeda's affiliation with the common law tradition (Azuero Quijano 2006). Nevertheless, Sierra Porto's jurisprudence shows a clear respect for international law and treaties, and he supported the idea of a hierarchy of laws by defending the *bloque de constitucionalidad*.[30] Ideologically, Sierra Porto is considered a moderate based on his voting record. He has been labeled "liberal" (LSV) but has been said to have taken "moderate and independent" positions (Rubiano 2009). Sierra Porto's score by LSV is a 5 and 5.8 in the Rodríguez-Raga survey, placing him squarely in the middle.

These justices decided the C-355 landmark ruling. Their profiles highlight certain important general characteristics in toto. Ideologically, it can be said that the court was made up of three distinct wings: liberal (Córdoba, Cepeda, and Araújo); conservative (Tafur, Monroy, and Escobar); and moderate (Vargas, Beltrán, and Sierra Porto). These divisions will be of importance when analyzing the 2006 decision on abortion. Doctrinally, most of the justices can be placed in the two categories developed by David Landau (2005) to describe the court's legal traditions since its creation: traditional-positivist and neo-constitutionalist. For Landau, justices that came to the bench through the judiciary tend to prefer a more traditional-positivist approach. Escobar and Vargas would fall in this category. Justices with a more academic profile, on the other hand, tend to adopt a neoconstitutionalist approach, according to Landau. Justice Cepeda would fall in this category.

The justices of the second bench could also be placed along Alejandra Azuero Quijano's typology (2006). For her, the justices can be placed into three distinct doctrinal categories: liberal Anglo-Saxon, liberal European, and conservative Catholic. Cepeda would belong to the first, Sierra Porto to the second, and Monroy to the third. Both ideological and doctrinal positions will help explain the strategizing behind C-355, as the next section details.

Decriminalizing Abortion: Strategic Negotiation and Moderate Decriminalization

The Regulation of Abortion in Colombia before 2006

The Colombian Constitutional Court's C-355 decision was the first major ruling to decriminalize abortion in Latin America in the twenty-first century, in what I have called in this book the First Wave of Abortion Decriminalization. The ruling partially decriminalized access to abortion by girls and women in a country that, at the time, had one of the region's strictest regimes (González Vélez 2005). As was the case in Latin America and elsewhere, prior to the C-355 decision, abortion in Colombia was regulated by the criminal code, which was last reformed on July 24, 2000. The code defined abortion as a crime against life and personal integrity. The criminal prohibitions were under Articles 122 to 125. Article 122 made it a crime both to obtain or perform an abortion, setting a penalty of one to three years in prison. Article 123 made it a crime to perform an abortion on anyone under the age of 14 or without consent, setting the penalty from four to ten years in prison. Article 124 established the circumstances under which penalties can be "attenuated." It essentially referenced the idea of graduated sentencing: penalties can be reduced by "three-quarters" or "not applied" in cases where the woman is found in "extraordinary and abnormal conditions of motivation."

While for most of its history, abortion has been criminalized in Colombia, a therapeutic exception was allowed in the mid-nineteenth century. However, this exception was eliminated in 1980. This had the effect of making abortion a crime in all circumstances (Jaramillo and Alfonso 2008, 230–31). An important reform to the code in 2000 allowed justices to waive criminal charges in extraordinary circumstances (Article 124) but introduced, for the first time, criminal charges for harms committed against the fetus (Article 125).

The rigidity of abortion regulation notwithstanding, important changes in the court's jurisprudence took place in the lead-up to the 2006 decision—changes that are important to keep in mind. While earlier abortion cases upheld rigid standards supporting the right to life and of the fetus (C-133–94),[31] the CCC gradually embraced more flexibility. In a 1997 ruling (C-013–97) on the constitutionality of criminalizing abortion, the court upheld the sentencing regime as constitutional.[32] The CCC maintained its previous position that abortion was a criminally punishable act that should be "repudiated." But the CCC also found that graduated sentencing was appropriate and constitutionally compliant where the pregnancy was the result of violence and deceit, as is the case in sexual assault or nonconsensual artificial insemination.[33] The majority held that the graduating sentencing regime was within the legislator's policymaking authority, as the sentencing framework was proportionate and reasonable.[34] In a 2001 ruling (C-647–01) challenging the constitutionality of waiving of penalties by judges, the court reaffirmed that this practice was constitutional in the exceptional circumstances set out by the code (and also affirmed the power of the state to determine what are punishable acts and to establish applicable sentencing regimes).[35] However, in a concurrent opinion to the C-647–01 ruling, signed by Justices Vargas, Araújo, Beltrán, and Cepeda, the court introduced the idea of having to weigh conflicting rights in discussions around reproductive justice. The concurrent opinion noted that the constitution protects the right to life, but that the legislator cannot go "to the other extreme" of ignoring a woman's right to human dignity, personal autonomy, privacy, and free conscience, or the rights of a pregnant woman, such as the right to life, integrity, health, and equality. As a result, the legislator's criminal policymaking ability was constrained by the need to balance these competing interests and guarantee the fundamental rights of all parties.[36] Further, the concurrent opinion argued that the access to abortion was constitutionally protected in particular cases when the pregnant person's rights outweighed the fetal life's rights—for example, when a woman's autonomy was violated or there was a diminished interest in protecting fetal life (e.g., due to the inability of the fetus to survive outside the womb, as in cases of severe malformation). It is interesting to note that the concurrent opinion was signed by four justices, denoting increasing support for the idea. It also, importantly, includes doctors performing the procedure, stating that they, too, just like pregnant women, should not be penalized when "attenuating" conditions are present).

The weighing of rights that undergirded the concurrent opinion's argumentation in this last decision is part of an increased reliance on proportionality analysis by some justices as a tool for adjudicating cases.[37] While the Co-lombian judiciary has long engaged in proportionality arguments (Barreto Rozo and González-Jácome 2022),[38] the formal proportionality test emerged in the 1990s and early 2000s in decisions around socioeconomic rights, which, as we saw in chapter 1, formed the bulk of the court's tutela decisions. Partly because of the influence that European constitutional theory has had on some justices and law clerks in Colombia,[39] and partly as a result of the view (es-poused by some justices and law clerks) that the adjudication of constitutional matters must adopt a technical approach, proportionality became central to the argumentative logic behind many of the court's decisions.[40] The propor-tionality analysis was central to the strategy pursued by some justices to assemble the majority behind the C-355 decision, a process to which we now turn.

The Judicial Road to the C-355 Decision

The CCC's C-355 decision was the result of discussions, strategic planning, and a concrete second attempt mounted by civil-society actors to challenge the constitutionality of criminalizing abortion access in Colombia. In April 2003, a group of three women, all Los Andes University alumnae—Mónica Roa (then an LLM candidate at New York University), Isabel Cris-tina Jaramillo (then a doctoral candidate at Harvard University), and Andrea Parra (then employed at a firm in defense of migrant rights in Seattle)—began discussions about the possibility of using a constitutional public action to challenge the articles of the criminal code that criminalized abortion. In light of the 2001 CCC decision upholding the constitutionality of discretionary waivers of penalties in certain abortion cases, Roa saw an opportunity to use the concurrent opinion's reasons to challenge the remaining criminal prohi-bitions of abortion. Roa believed that it would be reasonable, based on this concurrent opinion, to expect that some justices would declare unconstitu-tional barring women from accessing abortion services in cases of rape, un-consented insemination, or when the woman's life is in danger (Jaramillo and Alfonso 2008, 36). However, Jaramillo and Parra were not convinced, given potential pitfalls, among which were the possibility of losing the case and the issue becoming res judicata (a settled dispute that cannot be relitigated). The round of discussions ended with no concrete steps.

Roa pressed on, however. In 2004, she released a document she had writ-ten based on her own research. Titled Gender Justice Project, the document presented patterns of judicial decisions related to women's rights in several countries with input from judges and activists. It identified opportunities and challenges in relying on the judiciary to push for the decriminalization of abortion. Roa subsequently joined the New York City–based Women's Link Worldwide, a nongovernmental organization that supported a litigation strategy to push for the decriminalization of abortion through Colombia's Constitutional Court based on the *Gender Justice Project* document. The project was titled LAICIA—*Litigio de Alto Impacto en Colombia por la Incostitucionalidad del Aborto* (High Impact Litigation in Colombia for the Unconstitutionality of Abortion). LAICIA was officially unveiled in September 2004. Women's Link, with financial support from the Global Fund for Women and the Urgent Action Fund for Women, opened an office in Bogotá in 2005, which was administered by Claudia Gómez. Roa, Gómez, and Viviana Waisman would lead the project (Jaramillo and Alfonso 2008, 42–43).

LAICIA's strategic litigation officially launched in April 2005. It aimed to bring about legal change and a shift in societal attitudes about abortion. The last point is an important one. For the main actors, the aim was to reframe the social discussion on access to abortion in Colombia through the deployment of a clear communication strategy (Ruibal 2014a). Whereas abortion had been a taboo subject in the country, the campaign sought to frame the discussion as an issue of public health, human rights, gender equality, and social justice more broadly. To accomplish this, the campaign advanced two main arguments: first, a public health argument highlighting the high levels of maternal mortality from unsafe clandestine abortions and the associated costs to the health system, and second, the fact that Colombia had not met its international commitments to women's health issues (Ruibal 2014a). The campaign would subsequently include an argument regarding social justice. These are the arguments that drove the discourse surrounding the LAICIA challenge to the constitutionality of the criminal code's prohibitions on abortion.

The challenge came on April 14, 2005, when Roa submitted a constitutional public action to the CCC. The action asserted that the complete criminalization of abortion was unconstitutional because it violated individuals' constitutional rights to dignity (as established by the constitution's preamble and Article 1), life (Article 11), personal integrity (Article 12), equality and freedom (Article 13), the free development of personality (Article 16), reproductive freedom (Article 42), and health (Article 49) (C-1299–05). The public action further argued that the Colombian state had the duty to comply its international obligations to human rights treaties. The demand asked the court to strike down the criminal prohibitions on abortion under the criminal code and, in the alternative, to strike down the criminalization of abortion in three circumstances: in the case of rape, fetal malformation, and when a girl's or a woman's life is in danger.

The challenge did not proceed, however. On December 7 of the same year, the court released a communiqué declaring that the action could not proceed on procedural grounds. Particularly, it said that the demand could not ask for a "conditioned" invalidation of a statute, referring to the action's request to strike down criminal prohibitions on abortion in certain circumstances. The court held that the claim did not demonstrate the existence of new international norms within the "constitutional block" that forced the Colombian state to decriminalize abortion (C-1299–05). Nevertheless, in an unusual move, the court indicated that a new public action could be submitted, and it provided rather specific instructions on how to do so. Procedural issues notwithstanding, the interviews with justices and law clerks suggest that the decision to reject the demand had more to do with internal court dynamics than with legal technicalities. Indeed, interviewees revealed that the bench was not prepared to engage a debate on another contentious issue following the discussion that led to the C-1047 handed down two months earlier. The decision—announced by then-Chief Justice Cepeda on October 19, 2005, at a news conference—upheld the constitutionality of a reform that allowed for a presidential reelection.

The C-1047 ruling was controversial, given the country's long history of not allowing for consecutive reelections and the social polarization that Uribe's conservative administration provoked. The discussions over the decision inside the court sparked a great deal of debate. Importantly, they appear to have split the liberal wing of the bench as Justice Araújo, who cast the only dissenting vote in the ruling, split from the other two known liberals: Justices Cepeda and Córdoba. In effect, such was the heat of the debate that an interviewee present at the main plenary session declared: "I had never seen this before . . . it was intense . . . I had never seen a justice shout to another across the table and storm out of the room, with personal insults."[41] Data collected from interviewees suggest that the decision not to hear the case marked the beginning of a strategy to persuade justices to support the decriminalization of abortion, and that the votes were not yet there because of internal divisions. This was only the prelude to a broader strategy that began to crystallize with the submission of a revised challenge.

The Case Is Admitted by the Court

Roa submitted the revised challenge on December 12, 2005 (D-6122). It asked the court to declare the unconstitutionality of criminalizing abortion in the three cases previously mentioned (rape, fetal malformation, and health risks of bringing a pregnancy to term) and mentioned all the statues that could be challenged, based on the court's previous declaration. The public action challenged Article 122 and sections of Articles 123 and 124 of the criminal code, arguing that it violated specific rights and principles: the rights to liberty, autonomy, and the free development of personality; the principle of proportionality (citing the 2001 ruling); the equality principle; and the violation of the prohibition of cruel, inhuman, and degrading treatment of people (C-355-06).[42] After Roa made her request, three Los Andes University students submitted, on the same day, two very similar public actions to the court, underlining the main arguments presented. The three public demands were received by General Secretariat and assigned a file number (*radicación*). At a plenary session on the next day, the justices made the decision that the three demands be merged (*unificadas*) into one. The file was distributed to the nine justice chambers by the General Secretariat. In a subsequent plenary session, held on December 16, the case was assigned to Justice Araújo by draw, as publicly communicated by the court through a communiqué (*Auto*) and the file's Justice Rapporteur (*Magistrado Ponente*). On the very same day, Justice Araújo decided to hear the case.[43] The process to decide whether to decriminalize abortion in Colombia had begun.

The admission of the public action ignited a strong public debate. Socially conservative groups mobilized to exert pressure on the court to rule against the challenge. The main opposition came from a network of Catholic groups partially financed by international donors such as Human Life International (Ruibal 2014a) and allied individuals. This network mounted a strong campaign on several fronts. First, the network deployed a visible campaign through mainstream media outlets intended to sway public opinion, and indirectly influence the court's decision, by framing their argument around the right to life and the country's traditional values (Jaramillo and Alfonso 2008). Pressure on other branches of government was also part of the campaign. For example, José Galat Noumer, a well-known and conservative academic who was president (*rector*) of the La Gran Colombia University, organized the collection of two million signatures opposing the constitutional challenge and marched with a group of people to present the list to Congress. On the legal front, the network, which included representatives of the Catholic Church's Family Planning Centre, submitted various demands to the court asking for the nullification of the public action based on procedural reasons (Jaramillo and Alfonso 2008, 72–74). Each of these were discarded by the court. Finally, the campaign attempted to influence the process directly by having the Church's hierarchy threaten to excommunicate the justices (Ruibal 2014a). It also launched personal attacks against Roa to discredit the challenge (Kane 2008). According to a justice, "Conservative groups applied a lot of pressure. They tried to nullify the public action with different arguments, procedural arguments. Their plan was to hinder (*entorpecer*) and delay (*prolongar*). They wanted to delay and wait until [Justice Nilson] Pinilla arrived. They were banking on that (*se la estaban jugando a eso*)."[44]

The Strategic Crafting of Arguments

The assignment of the case to Araújo's chamber sparked additional opposition because of the justice's known liberal positions. As the court's most liberal justice, keen observers (correctly) assumed that his chamber's draft opinion would call for the unconstitutionality of the challenged provisions. Indeed, because of Araújo's previous pro-abortion statements, during the weeks following the case's admission, private citizens submitted several requests (*demandas*) to the court asking that the justice recuse himself from discussions and voting.[45] The demands were dismissed by a majority of the bench. Nevertheless, the designation of Araújo as Justice Rapporteur set the tone of the case's discussions during a first phase, one that led to a stalemate.

From the procedural side, Araújo's chamber managed the required first steps of the process. Upon the case's admission, his chamber issued a formal statement indicating that its treatment had begun (*Auto admisorio*). As required, within ten days, his office forwarded the file to Attorney General Edgardo José Maya Villazón for an opinion. The Office of the Attorney General released its opinion (No. 4024) five days later, advocating for the partial decriminalization of abortion.[46] As established by the court's procedures, Araújo's chamber solicited the submission of any pertinent additional information (*pruebas*) to the case, as well as interventions and *amicus curiae* advisory briefs from national and international organizations (Maldonado Castañeda 2014). This step was characterized by significant activity: over the next several weeks, the court received the largest number of amicus curiae briefs in its history (Ruibal 2014b, 155). Some key intervenors, including the National Medical Academy (*Academia Nacional de Medicina*), argued in favor of decriminalizing abortion. The Institute for Family Welfare (*Instituto Colombiano de Bienestar Familiar*), one of Colombia's main welfare institutions, sided with the attorney general's opinion. While the organization did not support abortion as a family planning tool, they supported its decriminalization under some circumstances. The organization also argued that the voluntary termination of pregnancy was not enough to guarantee women's well-being and that a comprehensive health approach had to be provided by the National Health Service (*Sistema General de Seguridad Social en Salud*). Colombia's Ombudsman's Office (*Defensoría del Pueblo*) and the Ministry of Social Protection (*Ministerio de Protección Social*), for their part, went further. They urged the court to strike down impugned articles of the criminal code, arguing that the articles violated women's constitutional rights, including the fundamental rights to life, health, integrity, self-determination, and the free development of personality and dignity. Finally, during the court's first plenary session of the year, on January 26, the bench unanimously supported Justice Córdoba's request to recuse himself from intervening in the discussion and from final voting on the case (due to his previous involvement in the reform of the criminal code six years earlier as vice-National Public Prosecutor).

Once Araújo's chamber shepherded the case through the initial technical requirements, the justice himself took a keen personal interest in the development of the draft opinion. As in Argentina, law clerks at Colombia's Constitutional Court tend to play significant roles in the internal judicial process. Law clerks who are career judicial servants contribute to the selection of cases, the development of lines of argumentation, and the provision of bibliographic material to support arguments (Agudelo 2010). Given the social salience of this case, Justice Araújo decided to get personally involved and work with two of his law clerks to develop the draft opinion.[47] In the words of one law clerk, "As a general rule, law clerks contribute to the support of an opinion's defense (*sustentación*). In this case, Araújo took it on personally (*se apersonó*). This tends to happen in cases that deal with moral issues of high impact or [that are] very political."[48] Led by the justice himself, the team of three worked over several weeks on possible lines of argumentation—work guided by clear strategic thinking.

On a practical level, Justice Araújo instructed his clerks not to discuss the case with anyone, including family members. As one law clerk recalled, "I was told not to discuss it even with my wife, who is also a lawyer. The justice had a sign on his door that read 'This must not be discussed with anyone' (*de esto no se habla con nadie*). He would point to it every time we met to discuss the case."[49] The point of working behind closed doors was for the law clerks to avoid interacting with others, including law clerks from other chambers, who might prompt them to rethink the justice's main position on abortion—namely, that Colombia's criminal prohibitions on abortion were unconstitutional. According to one law clerk, "There was pressure, especially from [Justice] Tafur's chamber. They even asked him [Justice Araújo] to recuse himself from the case given that his position on the issue was clear. And it was clear. Araújo's position was very clear, and he was in favor . . . it was clear what his line of thinking was. He was for the complete decriminalization of abortion, and the model we adopted was that of *Roe v. Wade*. We worked together in the argumentation. We read up on [legal theorist Ronald] Dworkin. This was the argumentation that best responded to the Colombian constitutional context."[50]

According to the second law clerk:

He was a liberal. He believed in all rights and full liberties (*libertades plenas*). In all fundamental rights. He was very excited (*acelerado*) [about rights]. . . . Given his training, he was in favor of the full protection of rights. He studied all the time. I rarely saw justices studying as much. He took his library to his office. He was a good argumentator. He called me and [the other law clerk], and we developed the draft (*proyecto*). Araújo said that he wanted to go for the full decriminalization—that that was the general idea—and [he] asked us to look for its [argumentative] support (*sustento*). He instructed us not to speak with anyone and to develop a draft that would be impeccable, that would not have any errors, not a misplaced comma. . . . It was about looking for arguments for a preconceived idea.[51]

Justice Araújo's position on abortion consequently guided the general direction that the draft opinion would take, and he instructed his law clerks accordingly. But Araújo's larger idea was to bring the discussion on the bench closer to his position. Because the attorney general's position on the file was to decriminalize abortion under certain circumstances—a position that other justices were likely to support, given their signing of the 2001 dissent—the justice aimed to bring the discussion as close as possible to the complete decriminalization of abortion.[52] Entertaining the possibility of declaring the partial unconstitutionality of the challenged elements of the criminal code would shift the discussion to a debate over whether to decriminalize under certain circumstances or not at all. According to a law clerk, "The butting (*el cabezazo*) [total decriminalization] was to bring the debate (*correr el debate*) [to his side]. If he had started with conditions (*causales*), he would have come up short."[53]

Once the general direction of the draft opinion was set, the two law clerks began to work on lines of argumentation. According to one of the law clerks:

We worked a lot on the draft. We worked really hard. We ended up with forty booklets (*cuadernos*) of information. Enormous. I was in charge of organizing our tasks. I divided the research and delegated it to other people in the chamber. We worked hard until we finished the draft. The Justice believed in full liberties, and the work of Isaiah Berlin was very useful. His idea on liberty was very influential . . . for liberty to exist there must be two options. The idea of Berlin was that liberty means to have the option to decide. In terms of abortion, this would support (*dar sustento*) the argument that the woman has to have an option.[54]

In terms of the lines of argumentation, the group worked on three areas. The first was on the challenging the idea that the issue had been settled by the Court in previous rulings (C-133–94, C-647–01 and C-198–02, referred to previously). On this, the team developed an argument around the idea that the principle of res judicata applied only to rulings that resulted from similar challenges to the constitutionality of statues. In this case, the public action submitted by the plaintiffs presented different arguments. The second was the justification of arguing for the unconstitutionality of the challenged articles of the criminal code based on two main points: freedom and a comprehensive understanding of health. On the first point, the group developed an argument underlining the importance of a pregnant woman's autonomy. Team members drew on the Kantian idea that humans have the obligation to be guided by their own reasoning.[55] Accordingly, the state must therefore guarantee the fundamental right of autonomy as it is the basis for real liberty. This means, the argument-in-progress suggested, that there is a need to restrain the legislator's authority to act when it affects fundamental rights. The team connected these points with fuller conceptions of democracy as stated in the constitution's guiding principle of a Social Legal State. The guiding principle here presumed that the state had to protect the free development of a woman's personhood, which is part of a democratic system. In terms of health care, and upon the direction of the justice himself, the team relied on a fuller definition of health to argue for the unconstitutionality of all the challenged elements of the criminal code: "The justice insisted that we should use the conception of health [adopted] by the WHO [World Health Organization] because with it, it is very easy to diagnose the psychological damage [of forcing a woman to give birth without her will]."[56]

The third line of argumentation revolved around the right of the *nasciturus* (unborn). In discussions, the team knew that they had to advance a defense to counter their opponents' main argument on the unborn's right to life.[57] As a result, the team developed the notion that the unborn is not a person and, as a result, cannot be entitled to rights under a liberal conception of human beings as capable of self-determination and self-government.

After several weeks of teamwork, the two main law clerks presented a draft opinion to the justice. They met in his office and discussed the opinion. The justice made some changes and "approved it (*lo chuleó*)." One law clerk recalled, "He [Justice Araújo] then made eight copies, placed them in manila envelopes, sealed them, [and] gave them to me, and I took them personally to the justices."[58] As required, the final version of the draft opinion was registered with the General Secretariat (on March 24, 2006). Perhaps the most liberal justice to have sat on Colombia's Constitutional Court had thus begun the debate.

Nevertheless, Araújo failed to convince his peers to support his proposed opinion, and the discussion soon stalled. In the weeks following its release, informal discussions (mostly) among law clerks allowed for the crystallization of positions by the justices on the bench.[59] As expected, the three conservative justices (Monroy, Tafur, and Escobar) did not support the draft opinion given their strong opposition to abortion. Interviews reveal that two of the court's centrists (Beltrán and Vargas) did not support a complete decriminalization of abortion either. Because Córdoba had recused himself from the process, the liberal wing of the bench was reduced to two justices: Cepeda and Araújo. However, the dynamics between these two justices meant that there was no room for discussion, negotiation, or strategizing. As you may recall, Cepeda's decision to vote for the constitutional change in the 2005 ruling that allowed for Uribe's reelection created a rift between the two justices—a rift so profound that they stopped speaking to each other.[60] This situation was compounded by three additional factors that prevented the two justices from seeing eye to eye. First, as two of the most respected jurists on the bench, a certain intellectual rivalry existed between them. The two tried to present sophisticated arguments to stand out, and negotiation could at times be interpreted as conceding to the strength of the other's argument. Indeed, interviews with justices and law clerks, similar to the Argentine case, show the importance of the justices' intellectual personae and standing in interactions. These differences were clear between these two justices. As interviewees put it:

> There were important differences between Cepeda and Araújo. He [Araújo] believed in full fundamental rights, and for him these were nonnegotiable. He was not mellifluous in his positions and was proud of his arguments. . . . Cepeda was brilliant and a conciliator.[61]
>
> They were the more studious on the court, and there was an intellectual rivalry between the two which had to do with their egos because they were frequently in disagreement, which in a way did not make sense, given their [liberal] positions.[62]
>
> There was a disagreement (*riña*) between Araújo and Cepeda for intellectual and egotistical reasons.[63]

The second factor refers to doctrinal differences. As mentioned earlier in this chapter, the two justices diverged in their interpretation of the law: Cepeda is widely regarded as a neoconstitutionalist; Araújo, while an interpretivist, had a more traditional approach. Araújo's approach meant that, for him, one could not interpret constitutional rights partially:

> His attitude was [that] if they disagree with my arguments, if they defeat me, they defeat me, but there is no negotiation of rights.[64]
>
> He was congruent and did not negotiate. He did not negotiate principles. Cepeda was a negotiator. If he [Araújo] had to lose, he would lose. He had an axiological position on rights. They were a sacred thing. He

was a little radical . . . and he had no plans for after [when he left the court], and he would not move on his position. He used to say that once he left the court, he would go back to academia, his profession. He was clear where he stood (*tenía claro el norte*) and did not care (*no le importaba ni cinco*).[65]

One of the differences between the two is that Araújo takes very seriously class issues, and he criticized very heavily the neo-liberalization of Colombian constitutionalism—its Americanization [Cepeda's approach].[66]

The third factor was Araújo's strong personality. In the words of justices, law clerks, and court staff:

He was a very difficult person. He spoke roughly and debated strongly . . . he would lose his temper easily (*se dejaba sacar de sus casillas*).[67]

The justice was not easy to deal with. He comes from a part of Colombia [Valledupar] that is characterized by very direct ways of speaking. His manners clashed with those from Bogotá, who are more diplomatic . . . he was not prone to engage in debate. . . . He had a bad temper. He would confront justices in a direct manner.[68]

He did not know how to negotiate. He was a very difficult person to deal with.[69]

Araújo did not take to negotiating. He preferred to immolate himself by himself. He was a difficult person. In various occasions, we would storm out of the plenary.[70]

Araújo's position on the full liberalization of abortion access was not supported by other justices. In the words of one justice, "Araújo's position was too much for the bench. He said that he was a liberal, but it was not the case because he was unwilling to compromise on this file and he would lose."[71] Between Araújo's fraught relationship with Cepeda and his doctrinal unwillingness to compromise, any possible negotiations or informal discussions "stalled (*se empantanaron*)," according to another justice.[72]

It is in this context of stalled discussions that, in the lead-up to plenary sessions to be held on the case in early May 2006, the known conciliator and respected Justice Cepeda and his law clerks devised a plan to assemble the necessary votes. For this group, interviews suggest, the main goal was to get Beltrán's and Vargas's votes to assemble a majority. They suspected that Araújo's position could change if his vote was the last one needed to assemble such a majority. As one team member suggested, "The internal strategy was to get the majority of the five votes. We needed all of them because Córdoba was not there. It was about opening up a big [discussion] space to build a majority."[73] The main idea was to seek a middle ground and argue for the partial decriminalization of abortion under some circumstances (*causales*). Their plan had several main components.

The first was to take conservatives' arguments seriously and not to dismiss their assertions that the state had the responsibility to protect fetal life. According to someone privy to the discussions, "The strategy consisted in not disqualifying the arguments from the [conservative] majority, thereby avoiding the hard arguments during the [forthcoming] discussions in the plenary session."[74] Taking that argument seriously, they thought, would make apparent a tension between the rights of the fetus and the rights of a woman's life when in danger. For Justice Cepeda, the idea was to ground the discussion around how best to reconcile this tension, and for him, the best way to approach it was to see how other countries had done so. Justice Cepeda thus instructed one of his law clerks to research jurisdictions that had decriminalized abortion and prepare a comparative analysis assessing how those jurisdictions balanced the competing rights at issue. (The law clerk tasked with this endeavor was eventually asked, jokingly in the halls of the court by law clerks from other chambers, how Fiji dealt with the tension—an obvious tongue-in-cheek comment that tried to capture how far afield Cepeda's chamber had gone looking for answers.) This exercise would, according to the justice's thinking, allow for the deployment of a test of proportionality. As explained:

> Neither Vargas nor Beltrán were in favor of total decriminalization. Of total liberty. The idea was how to have a moderate debate. Respectful. . . . It had to be a technical discussion. And that it is how the debate about the weighing (*ponderación*) of rights begins. Most justices agreed that a woman should decide. But it could not be absolute. It was about confronting one hypothesis against another hypothesis. What was the margin? . . . That is when we carried out a study of comparative law to see how other countries had interpreted those tensions . . . and [through the study] three tensions are detected: the three exceptions (*causales*). . . . The idea [is] that the legislator cannot punish in these three instances. The legislator cannot punish. We then change the debate about the fetus having a fundamental right. We had a duty to protect life. Vargas and Beltrán thought so, too. But this right is not absolute. This debate is difficult in Colombia, given the violence. This would convince the two justices. It was about argumentative strategy. We had Walter Murphy's work in mind.[75]

The idea of weighing rights and the application of a "proportionality test" was then seen as a way to gain the two votes needed and to persuade Justice Araújo to join the majority's opinion. And, for Justice Cepeda, this was a golden opportunity to rely on a proportionality analysis. As someone in his chamber put it:

The idea of weighing rights was supported by a liberal minority. There is also a generational aspect (*tema generacional*). A minority group takes the idea up. I am speaking about how a more traditional understanding of the law becomes difficult in societies where there is a gap between the law and reality. This is what [Samuel] Huntington showed in *The Promise of Disharmony*. The issue is how we interpret the constitution to change reality. It is a matter of [seeing] rationality in the constitution. There are rights in conflict, and these must be weighed against each other (*ponderarse*). We distributed papers [to other chambers] that we called New Law (*Nuevo Derecho*) to begin the debate. This approach enters into conflict with a more traditional view of the law, represented by [Justice] Araújo. He is against reasonableness (*racionabilidad*) . . . It was a debate about [different] ways to interpret the constitution. The weighing of rights is a German tradition where the concept of proportionality was adopted. It aids in Colombia to adopt a structure for the weighing of rights. There was a confluence of factors that helped in Colombia [to adopt the idea]. This is overcome (*superado*) by 2009. . . . The 2001 ruling was fundamental because it opened the discussions on the weighing of rights. There we saw the various positions from the justices. There was a new bench. At first, you do not know what they think. At the beginning, it is about knowing the possibilities. That ruling opened the door to the debate around the weighing of rights.[76]

Another component of the strategy, according to those close to its development, was to have Justice Sierra Porto lead the discussion and support the use of a proportionality test. As you may recall, Sierra Porto joined the bench in 2004, less than two years before the challenge under study arrived at the court. As such, and according to multiple interviewees, he had not been part of some of the interpersonal dynamics that had developed among justices. As a junior, highly educated, and technically oriented judge, Sierra Porto's legal expertise was well respected, and he was seen as the best person to lead a discussion on a technical level (and help assemble the required majority). According to someone in Justice Sierra Porto's chamber, "Vargas and Sierra Porto had been voting together on several cases. . . . He was against the weighing of rights when he arrived at the court. At the beginning, he cast dissenting votes on occasion because he was against that test. He had to be convinced to go to the other side. He had built bridges with Araújo, and he could move him; the idea was to start cooking (*que se fuera cociendo*) a certain position. He could convince Vargas."[77]

The last component of the strategy involved engaging the two centrist justices, Vargas and Beltrán, on their own terms in a way that would help having them join the majority. Since both justices were not for full decriminalization, developing a ruling that would allow for abortion only in certain circumstances would sway them, but some of their concerns had to be addressed. With Vargas, this meant, as mentioned above, framing the discussion as a technical issue and working with Sierra Porto, with whom she had worked previously on some rulings. It also involved asking her to potentially join in as a co-drafter of a majority opinion. As the only woman justice, it could, strategists believed, encourage her to join in by taking partial ownership of a potentially landmark decision. Vargas, after all, had been deeply involved in rulings related to women's issues. Finally and most importantly, convincing Vargas involved accepting the inclusion of some of her priorities into a final ruling: an argument that the decriminalization of abortion was an issue of sexual and reproductive rights.

In the case of Beltrán, assuaging his concerns meant addressing his known position on the role of the judiciary in policymaking. In effect, Justice Beltrán was well known for expressing counter-majoritarian concerns and for advocating for judicial restraint. In this particular case, Beltrán had expressed the need for restraint given that Congress had recently reformed the criminal code. As someone from his chamber stated, "For the justice, the argument of [the need] not overstepping (*extralimitarse*) the role of the court was important. It is up to the legislator to make laws. We did not want to usurp the legislator's attributions."[78] The lead team in Justice Cepeda's office understood this position: "Beltrán was not for it [ruling on the issue] at the beginning. His position was clear, and he made it clear in the 2001 majority opinion [which he wrote]. The debate had been on whether the legislator had the right to criminalize. The debate was around whether Congress should decide. There were two visions: the judge or Congress. The idea was that Congress could potentially go beyond [what would be an acceptable limit]. We had to engage Beltrán's position."[79] As a result, Cepeda's team thought it important to argue that while it is up to Congress to make laws, the constitution limits the extent to which the legislator could punish behavior.[80]

The Political Context

Interviews with the actors behind the strategy that was just outlined point to a clear understanding of how the political context limited the extent to which abortion could be decriminalized. Three elements stand out. The first concerns public opinion. As you may recall, part of the strategy used by Mónica Roa and her team was to advocate for the liberalization of abortion through an active media campaign. Their strategy not only placed the issue on the national agenda, but their decision to frame the issue as a matter of public health—which disadvantages poor and marginalized women and girls—appears to have resonated with sectors of society. Part of this strategy was to tell stories of women and girls who had been raped and forced to carry their pregnancies to term—something that appears to have captured the public's imagination and shifted public opinion toward liberalization (Reterswärd et al. 2011). In effect, activists released public opinion polling suggesting that support for abortion, under certain circumstances, had increased (Kane 2008). *El Tiempo*, the newspaper in Colombia with the largest readership, endorsed the decriminalization of abortion under some conditions (Reuterswärd et al. 2011, 814). The perceived shift in public opinion was perhaps best captured by a justice during an interview: "It is important to note that Colombia is Catholic but a violent country. . . . Life can be contemptible (*despreciable*). . . . Gabriel García Márquez said 'Colombians kill each other craving to live,' but issues around life are complicated because of religion. We had to be careful. But society had changed, and we were conscious of that, we knew that it was ready for gradual decriminalization."[81]

Interviews also reveal that several actors at the court were cognizant of the importance of acting in a way that would not challenge the court's legitimacy in the eyes of the public. A justice and law clerk pointed to the need for an "impeccable" ruling so that they could avoid criticism. According to a justice, "We had to protect the court, and even for the conservatives . . . that was important—more important than one ruling. There is loyalty to the institution. It had to be a technical debate, not an ideological one, and that gave the ruling legitimacy."[82]

The second element was the perceived respect for the court's efforts to protect rights. While advancements in the area of reproductive rights had not been as steady or significant as in many other areas, especially socioeconomic rights, several interviewees noted that Colombian society had been widely accepting of a court that was active in the expansion of rights generally. According to a justice, "The court is known for its vision for protecting human rights. That is its reason for being. This is one area in which slow change had taken place; we could move in this area. It was a question of rights."[83] This perception is linked to the well-placed position of esteem that the CCC enjoys with Colombians (chapter 1).

The last and essential element was the possible reaction by *Uribismo*, the political movement led by the hard-liner President Uribe. As you may recall,

Uribe was elected in 2002 amid widespread disenchantment with the political system and, especially, its inability to deal with the country's armed conflict. Uribe capitalized on this situation, and his new political party, Colombia First (*Primero Colombia*), won the 2002 elections in the first round of voting (with 54.1 percent of cast votes). His first term was characterized by a *mano dura* (strong hand) approach in dealing with the country's security problems, which included organized crime and guerrillas (whom he categorized as "terrorists"). His approach yielded some apparent results, which made him one of the most popular presidents in decades: in effect, he won reelection in 2006 with a landslide in the first round: 62.4 percent of the vote. Uribe's first administration was also characterized by a tendency to overstep the power of the executive and challenge democratic practices, such as a reliance on presidential decrees to push through policies. This approach naturally put his administration in tension with the judiciary, and that included the CCC. In effect, in what has been labeled by an observer as the "first period of relations" between the executive and the court (Rubiano 2009, 111), the first two years of Uribe's administration saw unrelenting attacks on the CCC for striking down many of the president's initiatives as well as two (failed) attempts at carrying out constitutional reforms that would weaken its power and autonomy (Rodríguez-Raga 2011; Cepeda 2007). However, that tense relationship began to thaw in 2004. Uribe appears to have made peace with the prestigious and highly respected institution, and its relationship with the high court assumed a positive tone when the it upheld the president's bid to change the constitution allowing for his reelection. Indeed, upon the court's announcement of its decision on October 19, 2005, the president celebrated the court's "autonomy" and applauded its recognition of the "democratic rights of the people" (Rubiano 2009, 120).

Justices and law clerks appear to have recognized that a political opportunity existed at this time to push for a partial decriminalization of abortion. While Uribe was, as a devout Catholic, personally against abortion, interviews suggest that many at the court believed that possible retaliations from the executive were unlikely given the recent respect the president had shown to the court and the significant victory the president won with the reelection ruling in late 2005. To wit,

> The ruling is partially explained by the political context (*coyuntura política*). With the first [constitutional] challenge [in late 2005], there was a climate of tension, given the decision on reelection and other issues. We could not take it on. The court was divided. But things changed with the second challenge. We knew that there would be strong reactions

from society, but Uribe had just won big with the reelection ruling. . . . He could not turn on the court.[84]

The attorney general had come [out] for the partial decriminalization of abortion, and the Ministry of Social Protection as well. There was support for decriminalization . . . but it had to be gradual. Colombia was not ready for complete liberalization; they would attack the court . . . the government would.[85]

Their reading of the political landscape appears to have been spot on. Soon after the court handed down C-355, President Uribe declared that while he would join forces with the Catholic Church to strengthen respect for the right to life, he respected the court's decision (*Radio Caracol*, May 23, 2005).

Discussion and Voting

As the strategy to assemble a majority of votes was set and implemented, a two-stage process unfolded over the next several months until the justices voted on the case at a permanent session held on May 10, 2006, at 7:00 p.m. Justice Sierra Porto appears to have willingly accepted the role of leading the conversation once discussions stalled after Justice Araújo distributed his draft opinion calling for the complete decriminalization of abortion.[86] Sierra Porto does appear to have spearheaded this first part of the process. Indeed, at least three individuals who took part in these discussions referred to him as the "catalyzing actor" in distilling a consensus. This consensus began to crystallize in the lead-up to plenary sessions through informal conversations among the chambers of the five nonconservative justices, primarily through their law clerks. In this way, the various chambers got a sense of what the justices' positions were and whether they were shifting. Interviews reveal that the three conservative justices—Tafur, Monroy, and Escobar—were excluded from these informal discussions because their objections to the draft majority opinion were expected. Several interviewees tell a story of how pursuing partial decriminalization of abortion through the use of the proportionality test helped Justices Beltrán and Vargas become receptive to the idea.

The second part of the process involved the formal discussions that were held during five plenary sessions on May 3, 4, 5, 9, and 10. An analysis reveals the success of the strategy, developed by Justice Cepeda's team, to assemble a majority of votes through the deployment of strategic argumentation. In particular, it shows a softening of the position originally held by Justice Araújo, the convergence of the five nonconservative justice around the idea of decriminalizing abortion under three particular conditions, and the effectiveness of the "proportionality test" used by Justice Sierra Porto to reach a consensus among the five justices.

Records show that during three plenary sessions held on May 3, 4, and 5, the nine justices met and "matters related to recusals [on the case] were preliminarily resolved (*de manera previa*)."[87] According to the official reporting managed by the court, the bench held two additional plenary sessions on May 9 and 10, and the final vote took place in the evening of the latter.[88] A careful reading of these records uncovers the process that led to the C-355 ruling.

After Chief Justice Córdoba, who held the position at the time, left the room at approximately 9:15 a.m. on May 9 (due to his recusal from the case), Vice Chief Justice Escobar began to preside over the plenary session. After establishing the specifics of the case under discussion, Escobar yielded to Justice Araújo, the Justice Rapporteur, who opened with remarks summarizing the contributions made by the various intervenors and listing the demands for recusals and nullifications of the public action the court received at the beginning of the process. In an exposé that lasted about three hours, Araújo presented the contents of a *revised* draft opinion and made a case for striking down the challenged sections of the criminal code and arguing for the *partial* decriminalization of abortion. Indeed, the rigid justice kicked off the formal discussions with his peers from a more moderate position, alluding to the need to weigh competing rights and arguing for the decriminalization of abortion under three circumstances.

He began by arguing that his position on abortion was based on one essential premise: "citizens' freedom, a basic tenet of a liberal democratic state, conceived as a general freedom, manifests itself in various forms, among which include freedom of conscience, freedom of expression and opinion, and personal autonomy" (*Acta 17*, 7–9). Citing Kant, Araújo then connected democracy, freedom, and personal autonomy and argued that individuals in a democratic society enjoy a "personal sphere" of autonomy that cannot be "penetrated" by the state when making the most difficult decisions. Citing the various articles of the Colombian Constitution that grant women liberty and the right to the full development of their personality, he argued that this sphere applies in the case of reproductive decisions. The justice's known support for full liberties formed the basis for his formal argumentation.

Nevertheless, in the second part of his intervention, the Justice Araújo elaborated on what ought to be done when rights conflict. In this part, he sought to establish the legal status of "the product of conception" based on the discussions held by the Constituent Assembly of 1991, international treaties, and the constitution itself. Acknowledging the various "conceptions that exist around Life and the problems that exist around them," he argued that neither the Constituent Assembly nor international law had taken a clear position on abortion, nor can one "affirm that there is an enshrined (*consagrado*) absolute right to Life" (*Acta 17*, 7). In terms of the unborn, the justice argued that the rights of women were certain, and in the case of abortion, these rights came into conflict with those of a "being" that does not have a juridical personality but only "potentialities." A conflict arises thus, he stated. However, that "being" (the unborn) always needs the mother, whereas the mother is self-sufficient. While the unborn can become a person, that is not always the case, and if a right was to be conferred to it, it could not be the same as the rights conferred to the newborn. As a result, he summed up, one can only confer rights to a being that is "viable," which, according to the WHO, is only after the twenty-second week of pregnancy (*Acta 17*, 8). Before then, a woman should "be able to make the autonomous decision to terminate her pregnancy."

Finally, citing various rights women enjoy (individual freedom, equality, health, and human dignity), he argued that, regardless of what his personal beliefs were, the decision to obtain an abortion "is a moral decision in which the State should not intervene." From this logic, the justice concluded, discussions on the criminalization of abortion have to start from individual freedom; the complete criminalization of abortion violates freedom, personal autonomy, the free development of personality, and women's health; the decision to abort, while difficult, belongs to a "woman's freedom orbit," which the state cannot invade; and the decision to terminate pregnancy "should be allowed until the moment at which the unborn being is not viable; and, with more reason, in cases of rape, unconsented artificial insemination, a grave danger to life, and unvoluntary incest when kinship is unknown" (*Acta 17*, 8–9). The debate had shifted from the justice's original position.

In another (partially) surprising turn, the second intervenor, Justice Monroy, also took an expectedly rigid position, advancing two lines of argument. The first concerned precedent. Justice Monroy argued that in its 1994 ruling on abortion (C-133), the court had already pronounced itself on the dispute at issue. Thus, the issue had been settled (*cosa juzgada*) and could not be reopened. In support, the justice cited an expert (Jerôme Lejeune) who had also made this claim. The justice's second line of argumentation was, expectedly, around the unborn's right to life. Monroy argued that international treaties and the Colombian legal system had not explicitly addressed a constitutional right to abortion, and that science had demonstrated "thirty years ago that life starts at the moment of conception." As a result, since the Colombian state had the obligation to protect life, that included the unborn. Summarizing his own intervention, the justice argued that the *nasciturus* is a human being from the time of conception; that the unborn enjoys of rights to be protected and to be born; that one cannot infer from international human rights treaties which compel states to decriminalize abortion; that personal liberty has certain limits; and finally, that when one ponders women's rights with those "of the being to be born, those of the child prevail." While this line of argument is to be expected given the justice's conservative positions, in the last part of his intervention he stated that "in the case of an abortion placing in danger the death of the mother, there has to be an exoneration in penalties."

Justice Cepeda intervened after Monroy's exposé. Cepeda seems to have attempted to set the tone for the rest of the debate by framing the discussion around the need to balance competing rights. He first argued that there were two distinct and different positions on liberty and rights, and the best way to address them would be to establish that there is a "hierarchy of values that must be harmonized and, given the case, the right to decide has to take precedence" (*Acta 17*, 8–9). Cepeda, perhaps expectedly, stated that he did not agree with some of the premises presented by Araújo,[89] especially the broad conceptions of personal autonomy and liberty presented in the draft opinion, as well as the insufficient attention paid to the value that life carries. Cepeda then argued for the need to look at comparative law. He noted that various European constitutional tribunals had, despite differences in their lines of argumentation, confirmed that life begins at the moment of conception, and based on the ways they had dealt with the "collision of rights," one can find common elements. On abortion, there is a constitutional issue to be resolved by both the legislator and the judge, and none of those tribunals had ruled this to be an area solely under the jurisdiction of the former. The prohibition of abortion cannot be absolute (such as in the case of "therapeutic" abortion); the tribunals have not been indifferent to the fetus's life, hence the penalization of abortions after a certain window. Finally, a fetus's life is limited to guaranteeing the rights of women in extreme cases, such as when the life of the mother is in danger. In sum, he argued that his position was that "the Constitutional Court could not impose an extreme point of view of complete (*total*) criminalization but it cannot support decriminalization in all cases [either]" (*Acta 17*, 12). The justice clearly deployed arguments that would not antagonize his conservative peers (for instance, about the fetus's life), would address concerns expressed by Beltrán (counter-majoritarianism), and affirmed the need for a middle ground to win over votes (Beltrán and Vargas).

Justice Araújo intervened subsequently to rebut Monroy's point about the issue having been settled by the court. Araújo then argued that the (revised) draft opinion's position was not extreme on its point of departure (arguing for complete liberty and autonomy); rather, the opinion "advocates (*predica*) from an intermediate position . . . it tries to criticize extreme positions, thereby justifying its main position, which is the middle ground, which is the correct one, and should be the result" (*Acta 17*, 13). While the argumentative sparing between the two justices is, to the keen reader, expected given their personal dynamics and legal approaches, it becomes clear that, by this point in the plenary session, a consensus began to emerge.

The last justice to intervene on that day was Vargas. Vargas began by asking that the list of demands for nullification and their denials be listed in the final ruling. She then argued that the case had not been settled by the court since the challenges to the criminal code had been submitted from a "different optic" (*Acta 17*, 14). She added that she did not agree with striking down completely the challenged articles of the criminal code, as requested by the public action under discussion, without any "conditioning." The justice then argued that there are limits on the extent to which the legislator could penalize because it must "respect the limits that are imposed by constitutional principles and rights" (*Acta 17*, 12). The legislative scheme erred in assigning life an absolute weight (*valor absoluto*), she went on, thereby "privileging someone who has not yet been born, without taking into account a different consideration." The legislator had ignored other constitutional mandates that guarantee women's rights, including a woman's own right "to life, to liberty, personal autonomy, equality of opportunities, among others" (*Acta 17*, 12). Accordingly, Justice Vargas said that from her perspective, "the Court must look at those rights and in what measure some must prevail over others, as Cepeda Espinosa has also argued." The court cannot ignore the fact, she declared, that the constitution and international law call for the respect of human rights and sexual and reproductive rights. Before the session concluded, Justice Vargas said that, given all this, she agreed with the need to balance competing rights and called for the decriminalization of abortion under three circumstances: when the woman's life is in danger, when the product of conception results from rape, and when the pregnancy is unviable or the fetus is severely malformed. She ended her only intervention in the plenary sessions by declaring that she was ready to reach a consensus, but that the only thing she would reject was the "pure and simple" declaration of constitutionality since "Articles 122 and 124 have problems of unconstitutionality" (*Acta 17*, 15). The centrist judge and first woman justice at Colombia's highest constitutional tribunal had joined the growing majority to decriminalize abortion under three specific circumstances.

The justices were unable to finish their interventions on May 9, and a special plenary session was called for the next day at 9:15 a.m. [90] The first speaker in this final session on the file was Justice Sierra Porto. The justice began with a general observation that one cannot separate theoretical discussions from reality, and that in Colombia, this reality meant that criminalizing abortion causes many deaths because of the unsafe conditions at clandestine clinics. He then went on to say that the issues under discussion were the right to life, how to regulate abortion, and what decision should be taken. Before elaborating on his points, the justice declared that "the argumentative logic of the draft opinion was coherent and its conclusions valid" (*Acta 18*, 1). He then called on the court to "work on finding common ground (*puntos de aproximación*) to arrive at a decision of consensus and called on everyone to consider all arguments." He then argued that the point of departure had to be a woman's right to reproductive self-determination. An unwanted pregnancy, he argued, violates this idea of autonomy—we "must rescue this principle and it is key to the decision." At the same time, this idea comes into conflict with the idea of life, but it is not absolute. The legislator must therefore condition that right depending on circumstances. It follows, he proposed, that "it corresponds to the Constitutional Court to ensure that the Legislator's role be performed adequately and in tandem with the judges, to harmonize fundamental rights, for which the requirements of reasonableness and proportionality must be met" (*Acta 18*, 2). The application of these requirements, he argued, means, in practice, that the regulation of abortion must include conditions under which penalization does not apply: when a pregnant woman's health is in danger, when pregnancy has been "forced upon" the woman from rape, and for eugenic reasons. The application of the test of proportionality to his reasoning was as clear as water.

The next two interventions were by Justices Escobar and Tafur, in that order. Both justices voiced their disagreement with the draft opinion while nonetheless recognizing that the opinion represented a serious, judicious, and well-argued proposal. Justice Cepeda's plan not to antagonize the conservative wing of the bench worked. Escobar's main critique was that life begins at conception and, as such, must be protected by the state. He cited scientific evidence to make this point. He then argued that when the "inviolable" right to life enters into conflict with a woman's right to life, the decision had been made by the legislator and thus settled. The justice finished his intervention by admitting that his position "was also radical, equally based on principles, without being extreme and outside his personal convictions" (*Acta 18*, 6). On a scientific basis, "human life starts at conception, and, from that moment, the human being must be protected." However, he also stated that he "would not be opposed to a conditioning to foresee therapeutic abortion as a reason for [punitive] exoneration."

Tafur argued, in a rather short intervention, that the discussion had moved to a point where most justices were seeking consensus, but the main gap in the draft opinion was its lack of engagement with life and human dignity. Surprisingly, the justice did not engage any moral or religious arguments, nor did he reference canonical law. Instead, he argued that Colombia's constitutional framework (*bloque de constitucionalidad*) did not address abortion regulations. As such, it is up to the legislator to decide: "It is a matter for the Legislator to decide according to the Constitution and the weighing to be carried out over the protection of both the woman's rights and the protection of the gestation of the human being" (*Acta 18*, 6). It would appear, then, that even the most conservative justice on the bench had been persuaded to approach the issue through the lens of proportionality, though he ultimately deferred that exercise to Congress. Applauding the open-mindedness with which the discussion had evolved, he stated that while it would be ideal to reach a consensus, he was in favor of declaring the criminal code constitutional.

The last justice to intervene was Beltrán, who expressed satisfaction with how the discussion had unfolded, noting that positions had been presented with respect (*mucha altura*) and the desire to get it right (*acertar*)—something that made it easier to get to a decision. He argued that this was not a case of res judicata and proceeded to state that the main issue under discussion was a conflict between the right to life and the right to liberty. However, he went on, women had been granted specific constitutional rights that must be taken into account in this conflict. Under this lens, a woman cannot be considered simply a being to reproduce the human species but a person with the "fullness of rights, the first of which is the right to life . . . it is unconstitutional to demand that a woman to undertake the risk of dying for not practicing an abortion. . . . The criminalization of abortion constitutes an intromission of the State in the woman's private ambit, which violates her right to privacy, of her intimacy" (*Acta 18*, 7). Finally, the justice known for his countermajoritarian critiques of judicial activism, appeared to have settled his concerns. He stated "the Legislator's prerogative does not authorize him to penalize any conduct. They have to take into account the necessity principle to justify criminal penalties, that is to say, [the principle of] *ultima ratio . . .* in this case one must ask whether it is necessary to penalize abortion in an absolute manner" (*Acta 18*, 7). As a result, Beltrán expressed his support for the "direction" and conclusions of Justice Araújo's draft opinion. Finally, he urged to court to ensure that the state meet its obligations to provide health care and social security to women who decide to have an abortion.

At the conclusion of Beltrán's intervention, and as the general direction of the vote became clear, justices were invited to make some final remarks before the official vote. Justice Cepeda addressed the plenary session by summarizing the areas of agreement: to decriminalize abortion under the three circumstances. A brief exchange ensued, in which a discussion took place on the best way to draft the main component of the opinion and the conditions under which certain challenged elements of the criminal code were to be declared unconstitutional. After a fifteen-minute break used to decant the elements to be included in the main paragraph of the final draft opinion,[91] Vice Chief Justice Escobar called on Justice Sierra Porto to read the final draft, with some justices offering final wordsmithing suggestions. The justices then added the main argumentative elements that justified the decision, and a permanent session was called to order at exactly 7:00 p.m. The opinion was put to a vote. It was supported by Justices Araújo, Vargas, Cepeda, Sierra Porto, and Beltrán and opposed by Justices Tafur, Escobar, and Monroy. Justice Cepeda finally announced his intention to cast a concurring opinion. The session was declared concluded at 7:50 p.m. Abortion had been partially decriminalized in Colombia with the strokes of five pens.

The aforementioned process highlights several interesting issues. First and most importantly, a majority decision was possible because the revised version of the draft opinion presented for discussion in the plenary sessions moved from calling for a complete decriminalization of abortion to a conditional one. Justice Araújo, despite his original rigid position, moved to the center of the discussion because of pressure he felt about potentially being the missing vote for a majority. According to an interviewee from his chamber at the time: "His original position was not well received; it was not going to be accepted in the plenary session. The liberals were for partial decriminalization. He was of course worried about being blamed for the entire thing collapsing."[92] However, Araújo made sure that his own position was clear; he decided to add a concurrent opinion (to the majority one, which he co-drafted) in which he reiterated his original view on the decriminalization of abortion. For Justice Araújo, it was also seen as a victory to have his fellow justices agree to include a broader definition of health, which included psychological aspects, in the final draft of the ruling.

The reporting of the sessions shows that the introduction of the so-called proportionality test influenced the general tenor of the discussions and provided a technical and legal tool to facilitate compromise. Cepeda framed the discussion as a weighing of rights; Sierra Porto inserted the proportionality test; and most justices, including conservative ones, engaged with the concept. The proportionality paradigm allowed the liberal justices to address the importance of fetal life without antagonizing the three conservative justices. The reporting from the plenary sessions indicates there was a cordial dialogue; two conservative justices mentioned considering the exoneration of penalties in the case of a pregnancy that would endanger a woman's life, and two justices even expressed a desire to reach a consensus. And, importantly, the tone struck allowed for a logical way to weigh rights on a continuum where they collide. This paved the way for a discussion that primarily focused on where the court would place the conflict needle on that continuum. This allowed for thinking about a compromise and thus convincing the two vital centrist votes to join the majority. Interviews with justices and law clerks indicate that Justices Beltrán and Vargas would not have joined an opinion that called for the complete decriminalization of abortion. The idea of weighing rights, which led to a "conditioned" decriminalization, encouraged them to join the majority opinion. Finally, addressing Beltrán's counter-majoritarian debate by developing an argument around the need to place limits on the legislator's ability to punish behavior, and accepting Vargas's proposal to elaborate on sexual and reproductive rights, appears to have solidified those justices' votes. This is well captured by statements made by the justices and law clerks who were interviewed:[93]

The ruling was restrained because of the need to reach a consensus.

The idea of conditions helped to convince Vargas and Beltrán to join us.

The votes were not there (*no estaban dados*) at the beginning. The three conditions were key in reaching a consensus. . . . Sierra Porto was the catalyst. . . . He intervened and ensured a consensus around the idea to introduce the conditions. Without these, the math was not there (*las cuentas no daban*) because there wasn't a majority. This change helped convince Vargas.

Cepeda's plans built the consensus, and [he] was able to get Beltrán and Vargas on [his] side by urging Sierra Porto to introduce the [proportionality] test to weigh the woman's rights with those of the fetus. The main argument was the need to focus on the disproportion of the penalty—the excess of the penalty. That was the door to win votes. Vargas was undecipherable at the beginning, but in this case, she became a pivot. The argument on the probabilities of life between the two [mother and fetus] had a strong effect (*caló muchísimo*) on the undecided justices. At the beginning, there weren't five votes in favor of declaring the statute (*norma*) constitutional. We had to win those votes. Araújo's original position made the conservatives retrench. We had to win all five votes. The other three were already decided. . . . The introduction of the conditions turned (*dio un gran giro*) Beltrán's and Vargas's positions.

The introduction of the conditions was what was needed for the consensus. I had an issue with the complete decriminalization and [sought] to establish specific timelines to abort. The conditions were a way to have all the votes. Abortion cannot be whenever one wants. Let us restrain it (*acotémoslo*). Nobody was all too clear about total decrim-inalization. But we had to reach a consensus. The idea was to argue that we were not pushing for abortion, but rather to decriminalize [it] in extreme cases. This won votes. I knew that there would be repercussions.

Cepeda came from diplomatic circles. His father was a diplomat. He knew how to frame a negotiation. He was for consensus.

We had to convince Beltrán. He was conservative on some issues and liberal on others. The argument on health, on how many women die from clandestine abortions, helped to convince Vargas . . . [and] how this compares with the issue of a fetus's life.

The proportionality test helped to keep the debate technical. . . . It helped to align the stars.

Cepeda mounted the strategy that allowed for the consensus. Araújo was more institutional, and Cepeda more creative. I call him the "elastic man." He believed in respecting human rights (*era garantista*) but knew that it had to be through compromise and consensus. Cepeda pushed for the weighing of rights—the idea of using tests and the reasonable-ness of the court. The 2001 [C-647] decision was important. It talked about decriminalizing. It pointed to the fact that this issue could be weighed.

Vargas accepted the idea of weighing rights, but for her to vote in favor, we accepted [the need] to include the concretion of sexual and reproductive rights in the final ruling. It also helped that we asked her to co-draft it. It did not correspond to her because she was not next on the list [alphabetically]. We needed five votes, and that was a way to get hers. . . . It had to be a technical debate. . . . To argue that "I think" or "my opinion is" does not work. It is indefensible. Arguments have to be based on the constitution, based on principles, and through this, you [understand] how they conflict.

There is no doubt that I would have not voted for total decriminalization.

The Ruling

Once the votes were cast at the end of the May 10 plenary session, and after the court announced its decision, law clerks from the chambers of Justices Araújo and Vargas, with input from those in Sierra Porto's chamber, drafted the details of the ruling. The full decision was published on September 5, 2006. The rather large document (503 single-spaced pages) has both Araújo and Vargas as coauthors. Vargas had therefore been convinced to join in writing the decision, which unfolded across several opinions: there was a majority opinion signed by Araújo, Vargas, Sierra Porto, Cepeda, and Beltrán; two concurrent opinions from Araújo and Cepeda; and two dissenting opinions, one signed by Monroy and Escobar and the other by Tafur.

The historic majority opinion upheld Article 122 of the criminal code as constitutional but established that abortion was not a crime in three circumstances: when a woman's life or health is at risk, based on a condition to be certified by a physician; when serious fetal malformations make the pregnancy unviable, as certified by a medical doctor; and when pregnancy was the result of a criminal act, such as rape or incest, which were documented by a formal criminal report. The court also struck down the provisions of Article 123 that established that the consent of those age 14 and younger was not valid to authorize an abortion. The majority opinion also declared Article 124 unconstitutional. The opinion included Justice Beltrán's suggestion that the state and private providers deliver abortions in the three listed cases. Importantly, the final document includes Araújo's demand for a broader definition of health, which includes mental health. The importance of such an interpretation of a woman's health is worth citing fully:

> According to the constitutional right to integral health, [the procedure] can affect women from a mental viewpoint. This can include psychological anxiety to a woman that has been raped, the anxiety induced from socioeconomic conditions, or the psychological anxiety prompted by a medical opinion that the fetus may have suffered certain damage. This means that health is not only physical, but that it necessarily includes all the other components related to psychological, mental and psychosomatic well-being.

This was seen as a significant victory for the justice. According to one of his law clerks: "I stayed behind in the office working. . . . Sierra Porto's chamber was next to my office . . . [and] he dropped in and said, 'You won, and won well.' . . . The justice told me before he went home: 'I scored a major goal. . . . The WHO's definition of health is there, which includes mental health. That leaves open an immense field.'"[94] The opinion also addressed the issue of conscientious objection, declaring that it can only be claimed by individuals (*persona natural*) and not by state actors or health care institutions (*personas jurídicas*).[95] Finally, the document stated that the decision had immediate effect and that the rights it protects do not require further legislation or regulation to be enforced, while also indicating that state institutions had the prerogative to make policy based on the decision.

The ruling struck a balance between domestic and international law. The decision cited human rights treaties, interpretative decisions made by international bodies of those treaties, and elements in international conventions of human and women's rights. The opinion also argued that these mechanisms do not form part of Colombia's legal framework. This middle ground is clearly the result of the position some conservative justice held on the status of international law.

The decision presents two main arguments. The first, not surprisingly, regards life. The ruling held that while the Colombian Constitution protects life, the unborn is not a person and, as such, cannot be entitled to the constitutional right to life, although it can enjoy some constitutional protection (moving away from the distinction between the unborn and a person). The opinion then turns to women's rights. By deploying a gendered analysis, the opinion finds that women are uniquely affected by laws that regulate their bodies, sexuality, and reproduction. With a broad definition of health, the opinion identifies women's sexual and reproductive rights as human and constitutional rights. This finding clearly incorporates one of Justice Vargas's demands. The opinion further incorporates a dignity component. Directly derived from one of the constitution's guiding principles, it states that reproductive autonomy is an essential component of a woman's right to dignity. Finally, the opinion incorporates a socioeconomic perspective by alluding to the many obstacles that poor, rural, and Indigenous women face in accessing reproductive health care. This point was likely the result of Sierra Porto's comments on the gap between abstract legal arguments and their real-world applications in Colombian society. The opinion emphasizes the need to rely on the test of proportionality to weigh rights in an analysis that spans three detailed pages. The opinion holds that, when weighing the rights of a woman against those of the unborn, the complete criminalization of abortion is unconstitutional because it would make the life of the unborn the preeminent consideration and thus sacrifice the life of the pregnant woman.

The second line of argument engages the counter-majoritarian debate that was of so much interest to Justice Beltrán. It argues that the punitive exercise of the state, as expressed by the legislator, is subject to constitutional restrictions and limits regarding fundamental rights. Here, the ruling holds that a woman's right to dignity constrains the legislator. The ruling connects the right to dignity with the rights to health, integrity, and the free development of personality. It states that these rights place clear limits on the extent to which the legislator can use punitive measures. The points address Justice's Beltrán's main concerns. Finally, the ruling states that the legislator has the prerogative to decriminalize abortion in other cases.

Reflecting his desire to ensure his original position was clearly known, Justice Araújo adds a concurrent opinion to the main opinion he cowrote. In it, he argues that while he supports the compromise reached in the majority opinion, abortion should not be criminalized under *any* circumstance because it violates a woman's rights. He states that he disagrees with the premise that the unborn has a right to life: it is not a person, and as such, it has no rights. As a result, a weighing of rights is not sufficient. The focus must be on a pregnant woman's private autonomy. Citing philosopher Immanuel Kant, Araújo argues that individuals should guide their actions by their own reason, and society and the state should therefore protect that right as it is a fundamental freedom. Citing John Rawls, Araújo then connects his broad definition of freedom and democracy. As such, there is, for Araújo, no conflict in rights. Finally, Araújo's opinion underscores the importance of adopting a broad conception of rights.

It is perhaps not completely unexpected that Justice Cepeda would write a concurrent opinion, given the dynamics between the two justices overviewed in this analysis. Cepeda's opinion states that he agrees with the reasoning behind the majority opinion but adds one derived from an analysis of comparative law: if a country has a constitution with enumerated rights, the legislator cannot take "absolute positions." In the case of abortion, Congress cannot completely protect the right of the unborn or of the woman. His lengthy opinion (106 pages of text and 30 pages of annexes) includes the detailed comparative-law-on-abortion study he tasked his law clerk to develop (as you may recall, this law clerk was asked the "Fiji" question).

The (short) dissenting opinion signed by Justices Monroy and Escobar is straightforward. The justices reject the majority opinion's reasons and argue that the fetus's right to life takes precedence over a woman's right to liberty, health, and freedom to develop her personality. Life starts at the moment of conception, and since the right to life is an absolute right, it is the state's responsibility to protect it, and it cannot be subjected to any weighing of rights. Interestingly, the two justices, who during the plenary discussion had entertained allowing for one exception (when the woman's life is in danger), ultimately adopted a rigid position.

The dissenting opinion signed by Justice Tafur was surprising. Following the arguments he made during the plenary session, Tafur argued that it is not up to the court to decide on the matter but the legislator. And while it would be possible to consider some exceptions to the protection of the life of the fetus, this must be done within a broader health care policy that covers women's health, including contraception, the prevention of unwanted pregnancies, and the fight against infirmities that risk the life of the fetus—measures that are part of Colombia's Social Legal State. Abortion, he states, cannot be the only focus of policy.

Post-2006 Abortion Politics

The landmark C-355–06 decision introduced a model that allowed for access to abortion under three specific circumstances (*causales*): rape, serious fetal malformations, and risk to the pregnant woman's health/life. Taking on a gendered and intersectional approach, it further argued that racialized and poor women are disproportionately affected by unequal access to health care. The introduction of a health-based argument was hugely important. Six months later, the Ministry for Social Protection (subsequently named Health Ministry) established, by decree, that voluntary abortions under the new model should be covered by public health (Decreto 4444 2006). Despite the conditions C-355 introduced, which I describe in this book as having had moderate amplitude, the ruling was quite significant; it was the first judicial decision in the world to uphold abortion rights on equality grounds and the first one by a constitutional tribunal to review the constitutionality of abortion with a human rights framework (Ruibal 2014b). It was the pioneer during the First Wave of Abortion Decriminalization.

Similarly to what occurred in Argentina, Colombia experienced issues of implementation following the landmark ruling, and women's organizations were forced to judicialize cases of noncompliance challenging their constitutionality given the newly extended rights (González Vélez and Jaramillo Sierra 2021). Following the decision, activists began to present tutela cases before first-instance courts based on denied access to services. With the support of feminist organizations, several reported cases reached the court on the grounds that the rights C-355 had expanded were being violated. The court admitted and upheld several of those challenges and, through a series of rulings (T-988 2007, T-208 2008, T-946 2008, and T-388 2009), developed criteria for implementation. These rulings, for example, declared that placing obstacles to implementation was illegal and that the consent of any girl under age 14 was sufficient to access the procedure. It also established clear conditions under which conscientious objection could be exercised individually. These rulings set importance jurisprudence that clearly established how, based on C-355, access to abortion had to be provided to women and girls.

Unlike Argentina, however, the 2006 ruling sparked opposition to the ruling beyond noncompliance by health care providers, a backlash that included the systematic and active participation of state actors. While, as we know, President Uribe declared his acceptance of the ruling, powerful state actors refused to accept the decision and mounted an important campaign in order to sabotage C-355's reach. This campaign was led by the notoriously conservative Attorney General Alejandro Ordóñez, who began his administration three years after the ruling (2009–16). Using his office to lead the backlash, Ordóñez launched a series of activities in an effort to roll back sexual and reproductive rights, such as ordering (unsuccessfully) the closure of a reproductive rights clinic in Medellín and spreading misinformation (Ruibal 2014a). Importantly, Ordóñez judicialized his counterattack by challenging the constitutionality of the regulations elaborated by the Minister of Health (D-4444), arguing that they had to be approved by Congress. This effort was ultimately struck down by the Council of State in 2013 (González Vélez and Jaramillo Sierra 2021). Other attempts at annulling C-355 were rejected by the Constitutional Court.

Nevertheless, and surely to Ordóñez's disappointment, the court ruled on eighteen different occasions from 2006 to 2018 on the matter and reiterated its original position on abortion. Further, it summarized, rather clearly, its jurisprudence in a 2018 ruling (SU-096 2018): access to legal abortion is a fundamental right because it is about access to health care. It also clarified the modalities of access to the procedure under each condition (Jaramillo Sierra 2023).

This jurisprudence formed the basis for the 2022 ruling. In a historic (5–4) and highly anticipated decision, which followed significant mobilization, on February 21, 2022, Colombia's Constitutional Court decriminalized abortion within twenty-four weeks of pregnancy (C-055 2022). The court agreed with the constitutional challenge presented by the feminist coalition *Causa Justa*, which argued, in the main, that the existing model violated women's rights to health care established by the court itself as a fundamental right and that the state had failed to guarantee it. The ruling repealed provisions of the criminal code on abortion, thereby decriminalizing the practice up to week 24 of gestation and, thereafter, in cases of risk to health, rape, forced insemination, incest, or malformations that make the pregnancy inviable.

Given previous problems of implementation, the court made the decision immediately enforceable under the framework developed by the Ministry of Health and established through the court's jurisprudence since 2006. The majority decision relied on various main arguments to justify striking down the provisions in the criminal code. First, while the court had already decided on abortion and thus set precedent, it could partially revise precedent by reinterpreting the statue primarily because the social reality had changed. Specifically, it argued that a new interpretation was justified because when it released its previous decision (C-355), there were no arguments around the actual practice of abortion (it ruled in the abstract). Things had changed, it argued, because of evidence presented by the plaintiffs on obstacles to accessing abortions. This had not been part of the debate before. In the new context, issues such as gender violence had to be considered, especially in light of changes in comparative and international law.

The court also referenced the right to health. It argued that the court had itself established in a series of decisions dating back to 2006 that Colombians have the universal and inalienable right to health. It thus agreed with the plaintiffs that obstacles to access to abortion, as documented in the submitted challenge, violated this basic right. Reminiscent of the debates that took place on the bench in Argentina's Supreme Court leading up to the 2012 decision (chapter 3), the court also relied on the *ultima ratio* principle in its justification to declare itself on the case—that is, the idea that the criminal code should only be used as last resort in shaping citizen behavior. While, as we saw, justices at the Colombian Constitutional Court were weary of interfering in an assessment of the constitutionality of the criminal code during the C-355 discussions, given that it had recently been reformed by Congress (1999–2000), the court's attitude changed with a series of rulings after 2006, when it ruled directly on the criminal code (see, for example, T-388 2013). Relying on a proportionality test, the court this time argued that women's rights had to be balanced with the legislator's intentions because (a) Congress had not acted on abortion since 2006, and (b) there was inaction on the executive's part in facilitating access to abortion and providing support to women who could not raise children. It therefore concluded that women's rights were more pressing and that means of action, other than criminalization, should be employed.

The court also relied on the freedom of conscience debate and on equality rights in its majority reasoning. Regarding the first, the court picked up on the idea of dignity it had used in C-355 to justify the unconstitutionality of the challenged criminal code provisions. It argued that freedom of conscience is a right derived from a person's dignity. As such, forcing a woman to complete her pregnancy against her will violates her dignity. Being a mother is a highly personal decision linked to her life project, and it involves high personal, psychological, and emotional costs. Further, it argued that these decisions cannot be transferred to other individuals or the state. It essentially declared that women can be full citizens. Finally, the court used an equality frame in its justification. Building on its previous intersectionality reasoning and using data available until 2020, the court argued that racialized and poor women, as well as women in irregular migration conditions, were disproportionately affected by unequal access to health care, violating equality principles (Jaramillo Sierra 2023; Díez and Ruibal 2025).

Building on twenty-five years of precedent, Colombia's Constitutional Court reaffirmed its position that access to abortion is a fundamental right.

The 2006 ruling paved the way for the 2022 ruling.

Conclusion

The C-355 ruling was historic for its time. It was the first decision by a Latin American high court in the twenty-first century to partially decriminalize abortion using arguments framed around gender, equality, and human rights. This chapter has shown that the 5–3 majority decision came about because of the strategic deployment of arguments by a justice and law clerks who convinced two vital centrist justices to support partial decriminalization. Addressing their concerns derived from their legal approaches and the court's role in making policy, and the reliance on a proportionality test, were all critical in securing their votes: it facilitated the argumentative reasoning needed to reach a middle-ground consensus that allowed for the decriminalization of abortion under three specific conditions. Strategy seems to have been central to this outcome. Strikingly, the main actor behind the strategy, Justice Cepeda, shared similarities with Argentina's Justice Zaffaroni: both had an academic profile and were highly respected jurists.

Finally, just as in the Argentine case, the political context was key to assembling a majority of votes. This chapter has also shown that key actors in the court were aware of the extent to which the decriminalization of abortion was possible. They seized on a political opportunity that opened up in Colombia to push for broader rights, though in a moderate way.

Chapter 5

Mexico

Strategy through Procedural Argumentation

Introduction

This chapter analyzes the 2008 historic ruling by Mexico's Supreme Court (*Suprema Corte de Justicia de la Nación*, SCJN) in *Acción de Inconstitucionalidad 146/2007 y su Acumulada 147/2007* (AC 146–147/2007). In a majority ruling, the court upheld the constitutionality of Mexico City's 2006 reforms to the criminal code and health laws. The chapter shows that a group of strategic actors, made up of Justice José Ramón Cossío Díaz and his law clerks, took a moderate argumentative position to secure the largest majority of votes possible to uphold the constitutionality of laws decriminalizing abortion in Mexico City. Rather than pursuing a broader ruling that could have established expansive understandings of women's health and reproductive rights, these actors strategically argued for a procedural approach that centered on whether Mexico City had the constitutional jurisdiction to legislate on matters of criminal and health care policy. The successful deployment of a procedural argument was the result of strategic thinking by key actors vis-à-vis their colleagues on the court and external political conditions.

The 2008 Bench

The makeup of the 2008 bench, which handed down the abortion decision under analysis, is inherently connected to the process of political change in Mexico detailed in chapter 1—a process that accelerated in the late 1990s. Like Colombia, Mexico experienced increased political fragmentation at the turn of the century. In the Mexican case, the once-hegemonic Institutional Revolutionary Party (*Partido Revolucionario Institucional*, PRI) continued to bleed public support during the 1990s. This support instead went primarily to the two main political parties—the conservative National Action Party (*Partido Acción Nacional*, PAN) and the leftist Democratic Revolutionary Party (*Partido Revolucionario Democrático*, PRD)—as well as to a handful of smaller parties, such as the Workers Party (*Partido del Trabajo*, PT) and the Green Party (*Partido Verde Ecologísta de México*, PVEM). The protracted demise of the PRI manifested electorally in more municipalities and governorships being won by the two main opposition parties and, most significantly, the PRI losing a majority of seats in the Chamber of Deputies after the midterm elections of 1997 as well as the presidency in the historic 2000 elections.

The makeup of the Supreme Court was evidently affected by these changes in political party representation. As the attentive reader may recall from chapter 1, the 1994 reform allowed the Senate to confirm a candidate for a court vacancy based on a three-member list supplied by the president. The composition of the Senate has therefore been important in shaping the court's makeup. In 1985, the PRI held *all* (128) senatorial seats, but it held just 95 seats in 1994, 77 in 1997, 60 in 2000, and 56 in 2003. In the same time frame, the PAN increased its number of seats to 25, 33, 46, and 47, respectively, and the PRD saw its numbers change to 8, 16, 15, and 15, respectively.[1] Because a simple two-third majority is needed to confirm candidates to the Supreme Court, presidents have had to engage opposition parties to obtain support for their preferred candidates. However, given that the PAN has been the other major political party, most candidates were, until the late 2010s, the result of elite negotiations between the PRI and PAN (Elizondo Mayer-Serra and Magaloni 2010, 38–40). The makeup of the 2008 bench was therefore the result of negotiations President Ernesto Zedillo held with PAN during his administration, and of the ones President Vicente Fox (2000–2006) held with the opposition PRI during his (Sánchez et al. 2011). The first yielded seven ministers on the bench, and the second yielded four.

Before proceeding to an overview of each of the justices, it is important to underscore the challenges in positioning Mexican Supreme Court justices along a liberal-conservative ideological spectrum. The appointment of justices within the political context described earlier (chapter 1) means that, often, agreements on candidates are the result of political calculations around pressing public policy issues. This can obscure the ideological positions of various candidates (Elizondo Mayer-Serra and Magaloni 2010). Of the crises and reforms that Mexico experienced in the 1990s and 2000s, the most pressing policy issues were economic. There was a great deal of agreement between the two major parties on economic policy, as the PRI was mostly controlled by a neoliberal elite and PAN's positioning favored market-friendly economics.

One would therefore think that differences would lie in social policy issues. However, a peculiarity shared by both Presidents Zedillo and Fox was that their administrations were not characterized by conservative positions on moral issues. For example, the Zedillo administration was responsible for expanding health care for HIV-positive individuals and sexual minorities (Torres-Ruiz 2011). Fox, who many expected would become one of the most socially conservative presidents in contemporary times, pushed an important human-rights agenda that introduced reforms to combat discrimination against marginalized groups, including sexual minorities (Díez 2010).[2]

As has been pointed out (Cortez Salinas 2020, 41–42), in the case of Mexico, the main proxy used to position Supreme Court candidates in other contexts, the party of the nominating president, is not all that useful. For example, some of the most liberal-minded justices of the Ninth Era Court—Justices Juan Silva Meza (1995–2015) and Olga Sánchez Cordero (1995–2015)—were nominated by President Zedillo, who is considered by some to be conservative based on his economic policy. Yet Zedillo also appointed some of the most conservative justices the court has seen since the 1994 reform, including Sergio Salvador Aguirre Anguiano (1995–2012) and Guillermo Ortiz I. Mayagoitia (1995–2012).

The picture gets even blurrier when one considers the diversity of views that characterized the two main parties, especially the PRI. While the PRI's leadership moved toward market-friendly positions on economic matters in the 1980s and 1990s, the party's positions on moral issues were less consistent. The PRI assumed a rather ambivalent and changing position on moral policy issues and, after the 2000 elections, a deeply divided one. The electoral loss unleashed internal struggles among many of its factions as the technocratic wing of the party lost influence and the established left-leaning groups worked to restore the party's social democratic origins. These struggles provoked divisions around the party's official position on moral issues. While the leadership proclaimed support for a human-rights agenda at the national level, at the subnational level many PRI factions took on conservative positions as they competed electorally with the PAN (Díez 2015, 166). Candidate lists sent by presidents thus reflect internal and intraparty negotiations where the interests and positions of the groups and factions tend to be assuaged (Elizondo Mayer-Serra and Magaloni 2010, 40). Locating a justice's ideological positioning on moral issues based on the appointment process becomes challenging in the case of Mexico. Nevertheless, scholars have attempted this exercise. In what is, to my knowledge, the only study of its kind, a group of researchers gave ministers a score on a left-right spectrum based on the ministers' voting records in contested rulings (Sánchez et al. 2011). In that study, they analyze 161 divided votes cast between 1995 and 2007 (some 15 percent of the total) and code them depending on whether they fall on a left-right divide around economic and moral issues. Justices are then assigned a score from −2 to 2, from left to right. While helpful, these scores must be interpreted with caution because they have not always been accurate predictors on some contentious cases.

A second challenge in the study of judicial behavior in the Mexican Supreme Court refers to the difficulty in predicting judicial behavior based on the justices' legal preferences. While, as we saw in chapters 3 and 4 on Argentina and Colombia, respectively, one can identify (among some justices) a clear move away from legal positivism-formalism and into interpretivism, the change in Mexico, like its process of democratization, was less marked by the end of the 2000s. In Mexico, the weight of generations of judges trained in legal formalism has carried over for longer than in Argentina and Colombia. Part of the reason has been that, well into the twenty-first century, most federal judges in the country obtained training in the country's leading Faculty of Law (*Facultad de Derecho*) at Mexico's National Autonomous University (*Universidad Nacional Autónoma de México*, UNAM).[3] As Pablo Mijangos y González (2022, 157) argues, the "classic [legal] manuals" published until the 1980s and widely used at this Faculty of Law advanced an understanding of legal interpretation as rooted in the actual text of statute or legislation at issue. Often referred to as a "statist" and "minimalist" approach to the law (Cossío 1998b), this strict interpretation of the text preferred a narrow approach to interpreting human-rights guarantees in legal codes. The judges of the 1980s and 1990s tended to favor this minimalist approach to legal interpretation. As Ezequiel González-Ocantos notes (2016), relative to other Latin American countries, Mexico's Supreme Court had a pervasively "traditional legal culture" that lacked the "judicial imagination" shared by other jurists and judges in the region. As the author argues, despite the court's growing influence as a main political actor, the "Mexican judiciary in general and the Supreme Court in particular have lagged behind regional trends in terms of the development of doctrines that expand citizens' rights, using constitutional interpretation to define their content in progressive ways" (2016, 253). However, the mid-1990s ushered in important changes. The introduction of fixed fifteen-year terms for court justices in the 1994 reform (chapter 1) was in part meant to do away with a rigid system of constitutional interpretation through a faster turnover of justices (Mijangos y González 2022, 204), and a younger generation of jurists received training abroad and in new, innovative private and elite public law schools in Mexico City. As a result, neoconstitutionalism began to make some headway into court deliberations in Mexico's high court as a new generation of law clerks began to apply their legal preferences to the development of legal arguments (Cortez Salinas 2020).

Such changes prompted some scholars to divide judges into two camps: "interpretivists" and "formalists." Academics have, as a result, tried to place justices along a liberal-conservative around "judicial philosophies" between "interpretivists" and "legalists" (Sánchez et al. 2011).[4] Their work not only demonstrates that this division exists, but that it has grown over time. However, unlike the case of Colombia, and to a lesser extent Argentina, this categorization is a poor predictor of justices' voting behavior on moral issues. While in the other two cases, a justice's doctrinal approach could predict voting patterns, the same is not true in Mexico. Some justices on Mexico's top bench that have been placed on the formalist side, such as José Ramón Cossío Díaz (2003–18),[5] yet they have also been *garantistas* and have been key in pushing a human-rights agenda. Some justices have changed their position on legal approaches during their time at the court, such as Justice Sánchez Cordero, and became *garantistas* over time. While in the United States, the legal preferences of Supreme Court justices usually coincide with ideological positioning, this is not the case in Mexico. Supreme Court observers thus usually include more elements to explain and predict judicial behavior, such as justices' *criterios* (lines of argumentation), professional background (judicial career or not), closeness of their relationship with the sitting president, and even a desire to build prestige (Cortez Salinas 2020; Castagnola and López Noriega 2017). Importantly, it must be remembered (chapter 1) that the court's interest in engaging (and expanding) human rights grew in the 2010s, especially after the 2011 "human rights" reform. The period under study precedes this change.

With these caveats in mind, we can now turn to a detailed description of the 2008 bench. In general terms, the 2008 bench was made up of seven justices appointed and confirmed during the Zedillo administration and four during the Fox administration. The Ninth Era Court began operating on January 27, 1995, as the constitutional reform took effect. The eleven justices were nominated and appointed in the preceding weeks after Zedillo sent to the Senate a list of eighteen candidates. As in Colombia and Argentina, following economic and political crises, the sitting president had to balance fostering the court's legitimacy (which was one reason for Zedillo's 1994 constitutional reform) against the practical need to appoint justices who would not be too hostile to his main policy priorities. Moreover, while Zedillo's PRI had 74 percent of the seats in the Senate, and hence more than the two-thirds majority needed to confirm his preferred candidates, Zedillo's party had lost its two-thirds majority in the lower house. They therefore had to rely on other parties for support in any future constitutional reforms. The desire to foster legitimacy with practical reasons meant that Zedillo negotiated several of the justice candidacies with the main opposition party, the PAN. Seven out of the eleven justices were endorsed by PAN senators at confirmation.

The eleven new justices were confirmed by the Senate on January 26, 1995, and the new court began to operate on February 1. While confirmed at the same time, the constitutional reform included "transitional" provisions that set forced retirement dates for all justices to guarantee the staggered nature of the appointments: excluding potential resignations or deaths, two justices had to retire in 2003, two in 2006, two in 2009, two in 2012, and the rest in 2015. To achieve some continuity and historical memory, Zedillo proposed four candidates who had served in the previous court. Two candidates were rejected by the PAN. One of the other two, who served on the 2008 bench, was Justice Mariano Azuela Güitrion (1995–2009).[6]

Perhaps no other justice in the Ninth Era Court captures the conservative strain of old-guard *Priísmo* better than Justice Azuela.[7] A devout Catholic, Azuela was widely known in Mexico during the PRI hegemonic years for his judicial family lineage: his father was a PRI career politician who served as a senator as well as a judge in various state and federal courts, including the Supreme Court. Azuela, like most judges of his generation, graduated from UNAM's Faculty of Law, having written a thesis on papal doctrine. Specializing in constitutional, administrative, and tax law, he was confirmed to the court in 1983 after having served as a law clerk (*Secretario de Estudio y Cuenta*) a year after graduation and as a magistrate at the Federal Tax Court (*Tribunal Fiscal de la Federación*). Regarding his legal approach, Azuela not only captures the judicial legal formalism typical under PRI rule but also the formalism that has characterized justices who have had a judicial career before joining the Supreme Court. One of the most important predictors of whether a justice will adopt a narrow or interpretivist reading of the text is their background: those with a judicial career generally tend to be more formalist, whereas those closer to academia and the private sector tend to be more interpretivist (Suárez Ávila 2014, 347–49; Cortez Salinas 2020).

Unsurprisingly, according to the measurement developed by Sánchez et al. (2011, 142)—referred to hereafter as the SMM measurement or score—Azuela is placed on the "legalist" side of the ledger. Azuela's formalist approach manifested itself as a persistent reticence to side against the expansion of human-rights protection during his term at the court, which is a characteristic of legalistic justices. As Suárez Ávila (2014) has shown, those with a formalistic approach tend to be less supportive of reading into the constitution an ampler understanding of rights. Azuela's legal approach, combined with the social conservatism derived from his stern Catholic faith, made Azuela the second-most conservative justice in the Ninth Era Court (after Justice Aguirre) based on his voting record (according to the SMM ideological measurement). Indeed, Azuela was widely considered to belong to the conservative block at the court, along with Justices Aguirre and Ortiz Mayagoitia. In several landmark *amparo* cases regarding the dismissal of HIV-positive soldiers by the military handed down before the 2008 abortion ruling, Justice Azuela voted to support the decisions made by the armed forces.[8]

By far, the most conservative and traditional justice on the 2008 bench was Justice Aguirre. Also religious, Aguirre earned a law degree from the private and right-leaning Guadalajara University. Rather than entering the judiciary, he decided to run a public notary business upon graduation. Aguirre had close ties to the conservative PAN; he had been mayor of Guadalajara for the party after unsuccessfully running for a seat in the Chamber of Deputies in the early 1980s. As a result of the negotiations Zedillo had with the PAN, the justice's nomination received PAN's support during the senatorial confirmation.

Notorious for his extensive interventions during plenary sessions, which were famously sprinkled with unconventional and obscure language, Aguirre was one of the clearest cases of strict, formal, and traditional interpretation of the law. Aguirre took a textual approach to the law. Because he often referred to the "will" of constitutional drafters, his interpretive process was closest to US originalism. Widely respected by his peers for his historical and cultural knowledge, Aguirre was a critic of conventional control (*control de convencionalidad*).[9] He adopted a limited view of the extent to which a judge should rely on comparative law or international legal regimes.[10] He stated that the reliance on international law in judging "is virulent; it is caustic soda. It distorts (*violenta*) judicial certainty when international treaties are placed above the constitution. I disparage (*le tengo desprecio*) the so-called conventionality control. The constitution has primacy . . . you then have abortionists creating new rights. . . . Heck! (¡*Ay Caray!*) I do not think so (*pues fíjate que no*). It is a destructive argument."[11]

Justice Aguirre consistently voted against the expansion of rights during his time at the bench. He notedly cast dissenting opinions, along with Justice Azuela, on the HIV discrimination cases mentioned above. Indeed, on the SMM score, Aguirre is identified as the most conservative justice on the bench on the ideological continuum and clearly on the legalistic side on the judicial philosophy continuum. Aguirre's votes on salient cases were the most predictable on the bench. One justice expressed this view: "We did not see eye to eye on most things, not even on our tastes for shoes. But we knew where he was coming from, and there were no surprises with him. He was consistent in his argumentation, if overextended and flowery."[12] A generalized view at the court was that Aguirre's Catholic faith influenced his ideological positioning. Justice Aguirre is noted for having stated, rather paradoxically, "Religion does not drive my decisions. All religions have moral principles that give them support. Catholicism is like that. There are moral values, and then there are revealed truths, like those of Christ. Like 'Thou shall not kill.' Of course, I base my decisions on that. . . . About homosexuals [and same-sex marriage], all humans are free to live together (*convivir*) and be together (*juntarse*) with whomever they want (*con quién le plazca*), but that does not make it a human right."[13]

Also backed by PAN in negotiations with the Zedillo administration and generally identified with the conservative wing of the court, Justice José de Jesús Gudiño Pelayo (1995–2015) was the third member confirmed to the bench in 1995. Gudiño graduated with a law degree from the prestigious private and Jesuit *Universidad Iberoamericana* in the early 1970s, with an emphasis on constitutional and administrative law. He wrote his thesis on the relationship between collective property rights (*derecho ejidal*) and natural law. Like most Mexican justices, Gudiño arrived at the bench after a career in the judiciary: he started as a law clerk at the court in 1977 and then served as district and magistrate judge in several courts around the country. Identified by some interviewees, including a close law clerk, as being religious, Justice Gudiño was widely regarded as one of the most formalist justices on the bench. This trend is consistent among justices who come from within the judiciary. Indeed, by a stretch, the SMM measurement places him as *the* most legalistic justice. Gudiño made his approach to the law clear. In a 1999 landmark case (*Caso Temixco*) in which the court asserted its power to review the constitutionality of legislation based on procedures followed by a local government in boundary disputes, Gudiño cast a dissenting opinion, disagreeing with the majority opinion because, he argued, it had overstepped its authority and assumed that "the interpretation of the Constitution has no limits, or if that they exist, they can simply be ignored."[14] However, despite his legalist orientation, in the second part of his term Gudiño began to recruit more interpretivist junior clerks (colloquially known as *chiquis*) as the justice became more inclined to pay attention to discussions on human rights and constitutional interpretation (Cortez Salinas 2020). This change is reflected in the justice's shift to the left on the SMM ideological spectrum and the mixed nature of his voting record in landmark cases. For example, while he voted to curb freedom of expression in the Witz case,[15] he sided with the majority which declared that the dismissal of HIV-positive soldiers by the armed forces was discriminatory, in the cases cited above. As one of his law clerks stated:

In terms of whether he was a conservative or a liberal, it is difficult to categorize him; sometimes he was conservative, others not. There are several examples in which he voted with the conservatives. . . . There was a case of domestic violence. He favor[ed] that the victim provide proof (*cargas probatorias*), time, place, day, etc. . . . And I told him, "No, Justice, you cannot vote like that." And he said yes. It did not go well for him after that. They took it as proof of his conservatism. We would then discuss the case, and he would say, "Let's not talk about it anymore." . . . And there was the flag case [Witz case]. . . . The case came to be known as the "damn poet" (*poeta maldito*). My boss was the Justice Rapporteur (*Ministro Ponente*). He first proposed that it would not violate freedom of expression. There was a lot of criticism. The vote caused surprise. There was also the case of transexual rights.[16]

The fourth confirmed candidate, also backed by PAN, was Genaro David Góngora Pimentel (1995–2009). Before his confirmation, Góngora had a thirty-two-year career in the judiciary. He started as a law clerk at the court before going on to work at various district and federal courts; in addition, he held some administrative positions with the federal government. The justice, a northerner from Chihuahua State, fit the traditional norm of having studied law at UNAM's Faculty of Law. He specialized in constitutional and administrative law. He then, while serving as a judge, earned a doctorate at the same institution. Góngora is one of the justices to have had an academic profile. For almost forty years, he taught commercial, maritime, and amparo law at UNAM and Anáhuac University, and he was well known in legal and academic circles. His profile partly explains his smooth confirmation in the Senate. Justice Góngora is known for having been an active and innovative justice, especially during his term as chief justice (1999–2003). His term stood out for promoting institutional dialogue with the other branches of government, which resulted in a reform to the amparo law that expanded access to this judicial review mechanism by simplifying the processing and submission requirements. He also enhanced the financial autonomy of the court; he devoted resources to a newly created office intended to streamline the processing of constitutional actions and controversies.[17]

Justice Góngora's innovative approach to judicial administration and his belief in the power of the law as an agent of social change explain his disposition as a clear neoconstitutionalist. The SMM measurement consistently places him at the opposite pole from Justice Gudiño and identifies him as the most interpretivist of justices. A self-described liberal,[18] Justice Góngora ushered in important changes to the court's jurisprudence and judicial review powers. For example, in the 1999 Temixco case (referred to above), he assembled a majority of votes to affirm the court's constitutional authority to rule on the case, which resulted in an expansion of the court's ability to exercise judicial review of due process violations. He justified this position by arguing that constitutional actions had been established to resolve jurisdictional disputes and ultimately to guarantee "people's welfare." In another landmark case (58–2006), the court adopted a strict definition of standing and ruled that the administrative court of a state (Nuevo León) could not be a party in a constitutional controversy (in a dispute with the state's Council of the Judiciary). Góngora cast a dissenting opinion arguing that this limited view would harm people's lives by limiting the number of institutions that could access judicial review. Nevertheless, while Góngora is placed on the liberal side of the ideological spectrum according to the SMM calculation, his positions on socioeconomic issues and access to justices were clearer than on sexual rights, for example. To wit, while he voted for the expansion of rights in one of the two cases involving HIV-positive individuals (307–2007), in the other case (2146–2005), he sided with the two most conservative justices, Aguirre and Azuela, casting the dissenting opinion and having famously argued in the plenary session that "with the public interest in mind, we cannot allow these [HIV-positive] people to be instruments of countless infections to their peers or the public in general."

Justice Ortiz Mayagoitia was another of the four justices nominated by Zedillo in 1995. Despite this nomination, Justice Ortiz Mayagoitia did not receive confirmation support from the opposition in the Senate because of his close ties to the PRI and to Zedillo himself. Ortiz Mayagoitia earned a law degree from the Faculty of Law at the public Universidad Veracruzana in his home state of Veracruz before starting a long career in the judiciary. He served as a law clerk in the Supreme Court, a judge in various state and federal tribunals, and prior to his nomination to the court, a magistrate in the newly created Electoral Institute. Justice Ortiz Mayagoitia is generally associated with the conservative wing of the court: he is positioned on the right-side of the ledger according to the SMM measurement. Ortiz Mayagoitia frequently sided with Justices Aguirre and Azuela when casting his votes and was widely seen as being close, both personally and ideologically, to Azuela (he was a dissenting voice in the Temixco case). Ortiz Mayagoitia's ideological conservatism coincided with his strict approach to the law: he is the third most formalist justice, according to the SMM measurement. Frequently referring to the need to approach the law with "efficacy," Ortiz Mayagoitia could be easily categorized as the closest to a "textualist" when reading and interpreting constitutional provisions.

In a 7–3 vote on January 2, 2007, Ortiz Mayagoitia was elected chief justice by his peers in what was the first public election (with secret balloting) broadcast live on the Judicial Channel.[19] His ideological positioning and approach to the law were well captured by the reactions that ensued following his election as chief justice. PRI and PAN legislators, as well as socially conservative President Felipe Calderón Hinojosa (2006–12), warmly welcomed his election. PRD legislators decried it, given the justice's "judicial orthodoxy" and closeness to Justice Azuela (*Proceso*, January 3, 2007).

Another justice whose close ties to the PRI (and in her case, family ties to Zedillo himself) did not earn her support from PAN senators was Justice Sánchez Cordero.[20] Born in Mexico City to a wealthy and prominent family, Sánchez Cordero earned a law degree at UNAM's Faculty of Law (with an emphasis on contract law) before pursuing an MA in social and political science at Swansea University in the United Kingdom. Like Aguirre, Sánchez Cordero decided to become a notary public, following in her father's footsteps, rather than entering the judiciary upon graduation. Like Góngora, Sánchez

Cordero came to the bench with an academic background, having taught at various private institutes and at UNAM, where she also held administrative positions. She was elected as magistrate to Mexico City's Superior Tribunal two years before taking the bench. Justice Sánchez Cordero is the archetype of a judge whose ideological position and legal philosophy have changed over time. While early in her term she adopted a formalist approach to the law, by the end of her term she was widely considered a neoconstitutionalist. By the late 2000s, she notoriously declared that constitutional tribunals should "privilege an analysis and interpretation of rights enshrined in the constitution" and that a constitutional judge "must confront the challenge" of interpreting rights "from a substantial approach, without limiting themselves to countersigning (*refrendar*) what the Legislator decided."[21] She further argued that "law has to transform itself according to the needs of a changing and dynamic society, given that one of its functions is to contribute to diagnosing and solving social problems."[22]

The justice did indeed change over time. Sánchez Cordero is remembered in legal circles for having sided with conservative justices against an ample understanding of freedom of expression in the Witz case, having famously declared, "We think that if we allow [one] to write or express ideas against the national flag, despite how literal they are or could be, they really offend morality. It is not an unlimited right. It has those limits. The flag is a symbol of the pride of the Mexican people: any insult (*ultraje*) to it affects the stability and security of the nation" (*La Jornada*, October 6, 2005). And while she ruled with the majority on the liberalization of abortion in an early 2002 ruling (which is explored below), she framed her arguments around the idea that the constitution protected the right to life. By the end of her term, however, she joined Justice Silva as one of the most liberal justices in the court. Interviews suggest that Justice Sánchez Cordero's progressive liberalism and support for the expansion of human rights had become part of her judicial and public personae.[23] She consistently voted for rights protections, including in the two HIV cases mentioned above. Sánchez Cordero's evolution is reflected in the SMM measurements: her ideal points shifted on both continua during the 1995–2007 period under analysis, and on the ideological score, by 2007, she was the second-most liberal justice after Silva. In the words of one of her closest law clerks, "The justice was able to put her personal convictions aside, over time. She had problems with her family, which was very conservative, but she opened over time [on human rights]. It was a question of empathy, similar to the Catholic way of thinking. She was a woman with lots of empathy. She would listen. We had a lot of long discussions. I would share ideas with her, citing [Robert] Alexy and she was also influenced by thinkers such as [Miguel] Carbonell, committed *garantistas* (*garantistas de corazón*)."[24]

Unusual for a justice with a career in the judiciary, the last member of the 2008 bench confirmed during the Zedillo administration was Silva Meza, by far the most liberal justice on the bench. Silva Meza was the third justice with close ties to the PRI who did not receive opposition support for his confirmation in the Senate.[25] Also born in Mexico City, he graduated with a law degree from UNAM's Faculty of Law in the early 1970s, specializing in criminal law. Before his appointment to the court, Silva Meza worked as a judge and magistrate in various district courts in Oaxaca State and Mexico City and as a law clerk at the Supreme Court on two occasions (1974–77 and 1984–86). A self-described "republican" with a modest demeanor, Justice Silva Meza began his term with a low profile, having assembled a team of law clerks in his chamber (*ponencia*) who also had traditional training in law. However, as Josafat Cortez Salinas (2020) details, by the mid-2000s, Silva Meza— emulating Justice Cossío Díaz's innovative organizational strategy (overviewed below)—began to incorporate law clerks with nontraditional training and novel legal approaches. This contributed to a gradual change in his chamber's legal philosophy and analysis, which prudently moved toward a clear neoconstitutional, interpretivist position. This evolution is captured by a clear shift over the justice's first twelve years from legalist to interpretivist on the SMM legal philosophy measurement. Silva Meza was clear about his evolved approach to the law. According to him, constitutional interpretation must be "always" done in a "progressive and inclusive manner."[26] As a constitutional judge, Silva Meza believed in the "inherent relationship between the law and the social reality."[27] He consistently voted in favor of human rights. His progressive views were clear in cases like Witz, where he dissented from the conservative majority. Silva Meza was elected chief justice by his peers in 2011. His term was characterized by an unprecedented push for the expansion of human rights (Cortez Salinas 2020, 145). According to the SMM measurement, he is consistently ranked as the most liberal of all justices.

The other four justices on the 2008 bench were nominated and confirmed in a different political context: under the first non-PRI administration in over seven decades. However, political party fragmentation continued as no party had a majority of the seats in the Senate, let alone the two-thirds majority needed to unilaterally confirm candidates sent by the president. A great deal of negotiation took place among the three main political parties to fill the four vacancies. These candidates received the support of PRI, PAN, and PRD senators. One reason was the widely accepted respect for several of these candidates given their reputation and renown. According to Mónica Castillejos-Aragón (2013), these appointments resulted in a marked increase in the level of debates within the court given the justices' profiles.

The first among these four was Justice Cossío Díaz (2003–18), by far one of the most respected jurists the court has had. Justice Cossío was included on two lists sent by President Fox to the Senate to replace two justices who, according to the 1994 reform, had to retire in 2003.[28] Four of the six candidates on the list were women. Cossío was easily confirmed by the Senate, receiving 84 of the 92 votes cast and support from the three main political parties.[29] His smooth confirmation was largely due to his reputable academic background and knowledge of the law. Born in Mexico City, Cossío attended the public Colima University, where he specialized in constitutional law. He subsequently earned a master's degree in political science and constitutional law at the prestigious Center for Political and Constitutional Studies (*Centro de Estudios Políticos y Constitucionales*) in Madrid, a research center primarily funded by the Spanish state,[30] as well as a master's degree in law from UNAM and a PhD in law from Madrid's Complutense University. Justice Cossío arrived at the bench with a strong academic background, having been a full-time professor of law at the (private university) Instituto Tecnológico Autónomo de México (ITAM) since 1983 and the head of its Faculty of Law since 1995, as well as a lecturer at various other universities. He also taught full-time at the prestigious Institute for Judicial Research (*Instituto de Investigaciones Jurídicas*) at UNAM from 1985 to 1986 and from 1988 to 1999. His research has been devoted to the study of the evolution of constitutional theory in Mexico and the Supreme Court (see, for example, Cossío 1996, 1998c, 2001, 2002). He earned the rank of Level III (*Nivel III*) in the National System for Researchers (*Sistema Nacional de Investigadores*) two years after arriving at the court, which is the highest level in the country.

During his early career, after graduation, Cossío joined the Institute for Judicial Research as a teaching and research assistant. There, he interacted with some of the most established jurists in Mexico, such as Héctor Fix-Zamudio—jurists widely recognized for bringing a new interpretivist vision to constitutional law in Mexico. Cossío was heavily influenced by this new vision, one that moved away from a legalist-positivist approach to the law (known in Mexico as "judicial nationalism"), which viewed the constitution as a guiding document derived from a political pact reached by the revolutionaries to execute their political project. Instead, it viewed the constitution as a "legal norm" (*norma jurídica*)—a binding principle that structures and limits state power to the benefit of citizens.[31] Justice Cossío assumed the new vision at the court, with a clear focus on the expansion of human rights. As Cortez Salinas shows (2020), Cossío's chamber was responsible for spreading this new perspective to other chambers. In addition to his established academic record (he had published over 200 peer-reviewed pieces by the time he was confirmed), Justice Cossío also had prior experience at the court: he clerked for Justice Ulises Shmill and was private secretary to Justice Jorge Carpizo in the 1980s and early 1990s.

A clear neoconstitutionalist, Cossío's opinions were notorious for their innovative approach, reliance on sharp judicial technique, and engaging content. His interest in human-rights protection was clear, and he consistently sided with the liberal wing of the bench on human-rights cases. Two years after being sworn in as justice, he launched the court's Fundamental Rights Program,[32] and he was the justice who used the Hearing Prerogative (*Facultad de Atracción*) the most (Castillejos-Aragón 2013).[33] Interviews reveal that Cossío was highly respected by his peers and their law clerks and that his academic profile was an important part of his public persona. He also actively sought media exposure. Striking similarities between Justice Cossío's profile and those of Argentina's Raúl Zaffaroni (chapter 3) and Colombia's Manuel José Cepeda Espinosa (chapter 4) should be apparent to the reader: all are highly respected justices with established academic records, a neoconstitutional approach, and an interest in the expansion of human rights. As we shall see below, they also shared an additional characteristic: reliance on strategic thinking to assemble majority opinions.

The other justice confirmed from the two lists that Fox sent to the Senate was Margarita Beatriz Luna Ramos (2004–19). Unlike Cossío, her confirmation process was not a smooth one. Luna's name was submitted along with those of José Luis De la Peza and Elvia Díaz de León. The three candidates divided the senators. De la Peza, while serving as a magistrate at the Electoral Tribunal, voted to fine the PRI over a corruption scandal related to the 2000 presidential election.[34] PRI senators thus opposed his candidacy and supported Luna. PAN and PRD senators, however, voted for De la Peza, largely because of his apparent independence as magistrate.[35] None of the candidates received the required votes to be confirmed during two rounds of voting. As required, Senate leadership sent the list back to Fox, who submitted a "new" list that included, rather puzzlingly, Luna—the candidate opposed by PAN. Despite denunciations from some PAN senators, others voted for Luna the second time around. Supported by PRI and PRD senators, Luna barely earned enough votes (82) to be confirmed on February 19, 2004.[36] She joined Sánchez Cordero as the second woman on the bench.

From the southern state of Chiapas, Luna had a traditional judicial career. She earned her various degrees, including a doctorate, at UNAM's Faculty of Law, specializing in administrative and constitutional law. With no training abroad and limited teaching experience, Luna spent twenty-nine years in the judiciary, having served as judge in many federal district courts and as a law clerk at the Supreme Court for two years in the mid-1980s. Unsurprisingly given her traditional judicial career, Luna was a traditional and formalist justice. Her rulings were characterized by technical legal language that often avoided engaging in-depth discussions on substance and consistently relied on precedent. According to the SMM measurement, Luna's score on her legal approach is expectedly on the legalist side. In terms of her ideological leanings, Luna can be considered a centrist: she is placed in the middle of the ideological SMM spectrum. Her voting record was mixed. She sided with the liberal minority in the first controversial cases that reached the bench, such as the HIV cases mentioned previously, but she also sided with the most conservative justices (Aguirre and Azuela) on other cases.[37] While some of interviewees called her a "conservative," others would use the term "traditional" when discussing her profile. Someone at the court described Luna as "a formalist," and her approach "is about applying the law. It is about studying the issue directly. It is not about seeing the judiciary as having the role of doing politics. That is for the other branches and levels of government. That is because the process requires credibility. You must have jurisprudential consistency. Sometimes one changes their minds, but one must be consistent. It is not about judicial activism. There are, for example, issues with budgetary implications that do not concern the court."[38]

The second to the last justice confirmed to the 2008 bench was Sergio Valls Hernández (2004–19). Valls filled a vacancy that opened up after the passing of Justice Humberto Román Palacios in June 2004. As part of broader negotiations with the PRI after the 2003 midterm elections, in which no party held a majority in Congress (including the Senate), Fox sent a list of candidates with close links to the PRI.[39] As a former member of Congress (deputy in the lower chamber from 1985 to 1988), Valls had support from both PAN and PRI senators, so his confirmation was unproblematic, although some voiced a preference for one of the other candidates.[40] Also from Chiapas and with a law degree from UNAM, Valls earned no postgraduate degrees but had some teaching experience as an adjunct professor at UNAM. Rather unusually, his experience was mostly in the private sector, primarily in finance (with Bancomer Bank), in the judiciary (having served as a judge in Mexico City's Superior Court and the Judicial Council), and in public administration (as a legal adviser to various federal institutions).

Valls, who passed away in 2014, had a discreet demeanor and was cautious in the crafting of his arguments, especially in the televised plenary sessions. He can be considered a neoconstitutionalist, despite his educational and professional background; in fact, he ranks as the second-most interpretivist in the SMM score. Urging adherence to international treaties, Justice Valls was clear about his approach to the law, declaring that the Supreme Court as a constitutional tribunal could not limit itself. The court should be able "to solve the issues it receives, but also give substance (*proveer de contenido*) to fundamental rights enshrined in our constitution and international treaties, looking at the social reality and having the constitutional judge find solutions."[41] The justice usually expressed an interest in protecting the court's public image and legitimacy. Along with Justices Azuela and Cossío, who shared that interest, Valls created the Committee of Social Communication to foster a coherent public-relations strategy. While he is placed at the center of the SMM ideological score, Valls tended to side with the liberal wing of the bench on human-rights issues (in the HIV case and the Castañeda case, for example). He dissented in the Witz case, having famously dismissed the controversy by calling it a "pseudo-poem."

The last justice confirmed to the 2008 bench was José Fernando Franco González Salas (2006–21). After the retirement of Díaz Moreno in November 2006, Fox sent a list of candidates that included Franco, Rafael Estrada Sámano, and María Herrera Tello. While Herrera Tello had close ties with the Fox administration and with Fox personally,[42] Franco earned an easy majority of votes (92) partly because of his connections to the PRI,[43] in what was widely seen as a PAN-PRI agreement.[44] Born in Mexico City, Franco earned his law degree from an established law school (*Escuela Libre de Derecho*), specializing in constitutional, administrative, and labor law before undertaking a master's degree in political science and public administration at Warwick University in the United Kingdom. Franco had primarily a political background. Aside from serving as a judge at the Electoral Tribunal (1990–96),[45] he held many political appointments during the PRI's regime before 2000. Before his confirmation, he was appointed deputy minister of labor by Fox, a position he held for almost the entirety of that administration (2000–2005). Also known for his discreet demeanor, Justice Franco was widely regarded as a centrist, having sided with conservative justices in some cases (Witz and Castañeda) while at other times siding with justices who argued for the expansion of rights (HIV cases, for example). His arguments tended to favor delving deep into the content of a case, and he was often referred to as *garantista* in some interviews. Regarding his approach to the law, he is positioned on the interpretivist side on the SMM score, just after Justices Gudiño and Valls.

These detailed descriptions of the justices' profiles paint a picture of the 2008 bench with important general characteristics. First, there was a generational divide between the justices confirmed in 1995, when the Ninth Era Court began operating, and the justices who arrived at the court after PRI rule ended in 2000. While several of the 1995 justices had strong credentials when they were confirmed, important jurists such as Justices Valls and Cossío marked a clear change in terms of their knowledge levels and legal recognition. These were jurists of renown and credibility who, according to some authors, increased the level of discussion at the court (Castillejos-Aragón 2013; Cortez Salinas 2020). Because the nomination (and confirmation) of many of the 1995 justices resulted from grand political bargains between Zedillo and PAN during political and economic crises, this group of justices wanted to bolster their credibility to counter their perceived lack of legitimacy. As one of the four justices nominated by Fox stated: "I think that the justices that arrived in 1994 [and] 1995 suffered from a lack of legitimacy. . . . we had the idea of strengthening the court, and we launched many initiatives when we arrived, such as the new television channel, going to international fora . . . to send a message that, yes, we are a constitutional court."[46] While that may be true, the question of legitimacy is relative. Eight of the eleven justices on the 2008 bench were supported by at least the two largest political parties in the Senate. Indeed, within the larger context of political party fragmentation, the appointment process for Mexico's Supreme Court forces political compromise.

Beyond the question of legitimacy, however, a clear generational divide refers to the move toward neoconstitutionalism at the court. While some justices from the 1995 generation appeared to have gradually moved away from legal positivism, the bench remained divided, with the new generation leading the way toward interpretivism and an emphasis on human rights. As one of the formalist justices confirmed in 1995 put it:

> [On the approach to the law] there has been a seismic shift. There was [a] first phase in which they [the newly arrived justices] started to want to judge the law itself. This is very different. There are then no concrete parts. I am in total disagreement because there are no concrete parts in this movement (*corriente*). I am in defense of legality. When the law is judged in the abstract, it then comes down to what Pedro or Pablo say [it is]. There has been a revolution. There has been a mismatch (*desajuste*) in the way they compare. This is comparative law of another kind (*de otra índole*). They start to bring alien concepts into judging. Alien values and principles. The law then becomes contrary to constitutional formality. This has been a great step. We then start to separate the letter of the law from constitutionality. And then we had another phase with the idea of reasonableness. And everyone then wants to impose their own reasonableness. It is like marijuana. There then appears a "progressive" way of interpreting the actual plant.[47]

This so-called revolution divided the court in terms of the justices' approaches to the law. That division included schisms over the role that international law ought to play in deciding constitutional cases. While in a 1992 ruling (TP.C./1992) the court established that international treaties had a legal standing below the constitution, that position changed in subsequent rulings. A 1998 ruling (Amparo 1475/1998) held that international treaties carried the same legal authority as domestic constitutional law, and a 2007 ruling (P.IX/2007) held that international treaties superseded the constitution and national and subnational legislation. However, as Justice Aguirre's case shows, not all justices were convinced. As a justice suggested: "It is difficult to divide the justices between liberals and conservatives. A lot has to do with their positions on conventional control. The court was divided down the middle. . . . A lot has to do with the interpretation models used by the justices. We see new models, which change the meaning of sovereignty. In terms of diffuse [judicial] review, the court is divided between those who see these changes with sympathy because they reinterpret judicial positions and the traditionalists who exercise resistance."[48]

Finally, while it may be true that it is not always easy to categorize justices in Mexico along a liberal-conservative divide, there is no question that in some instances it can be done. Regarding the 2008 bench, one can safely say that there were clear conservative justices, such as Aguirre and Azuela, as well as some liberal ones, such as Silva and, over time, Sánchez Cordero. This is the bench that handed down the 2008 abortion ruling.

Decriminalizing Abortion: Strategy and Procedural Argumentation

The Regulation of Abortion in Mexico before 2007

The regulation of abortion in Mexico has historically been intertwined with the country's federal system of government. This system is characterized by two levels of criminal-law regulation: the federal criminal code, for crimes committed in areas of federal jurisdiction (such as public federal hospitals), and subnational criminal codes enacted and administered by the thirty-one states and, since 1997, Mexico City. Unlike Argentina and Colombia, the politics of abortion in Mexico have played out differently because of this jurisdictional framework. The first piece of legislation to prohibit abortion was the 1871 federal criminal code, also called the *Juárez Code*, named after Liberal Party President Benito Juárez (1858–72). This code (which served as a template for all the states that criminalized abortion) differentiated between homicide and abortion and applied more lenient penalties to the former (Ruibal 2014b, 52). One of the least stringent criminal codes in Latin America, it established exceptions based on the risk to the pregnant person's life or as a result of a woman's "negligence." The federal code served as a model for all subnational jurisdictions that criminalized abortion. In 1931, a new federal criminal code was enacted and has been in force since then, and it applies to Mexico City (known as the Federal District until 2015). The code made abortion punishable by one to six years of imprisonment but allowed for general exceptions in cases of rape, when a woman's life is in danger, and for accidental abortions. While the federal code was only applicable in federal jurisdictions, all subnational states again used it as a model and criminalized the practice for both the women who undergo the procedure and the health practitioners who perform it. Largely because of women's mobilization during Mexico's second-wave feminist movement, some liberalization occurred in many Mexican states, primarily in cases of fetal malformation and health risks (Kulczycki 2007).[49]

Mexico City adopted its own criminal code in the mid-1990s. Within the broader push for decentralization in the 1990s in many countries, and similar to what happened with Buenos Aires, reforms granted the city significant autonomy. Citizens were able to elect the mayor (Chief of Government, *Jefe de Gobierno*) and a Legislative Assembly (*Asamblea Legislativa del Distrito Federal*),[50] as well as enact their own legislation, which included a criminal code. The city at first replicated, almost word for word, the provisions from the federal code regarding abortion.[51] By 2000, Mexico City was the only jurisdiction in the country that had not liberalized access to abortion since 1931.

The situation began to change that year. Under the interim government of PRD mayor Rosario Robles,[52] whose party enjoyed a legislative majority, the Legislative Assembly passed a reform to the criminal code in August 2000 that added three exceptions to the criminalization of abortion: congenital fetal malformation, the risk to a woman's health, and unconsented artificial insemination. On September 25, the reform, colloquially dubbed the Robles Law (*La Ley Robles*), was challenged by twenty-two PAN and Green Party legislators through a constitutional action (AI 10/2000) because it violated the fetus's constitutional right to life as enshrined in the 1917 constitution. This was the first time in the court's history that an abortion case had reached its docket. The constitutional challenge expectedly provoked a great deal of national debate and social mobilization.[53]

As with all cases that arrive at the court, the case was assigned to one of the justices according to a preestablished (yet not publicly known) sequential list. Like in Colombia, this justice becomes the Justice Rapporteur. The justice then takes charge of administering the case and, based on their assessment, develops a draft opinion (*Proyecto de sentencia*) to be discussed by their peers. The other ten justices then vote on the draft opinion.[54] Importantly, the 1994 reform established that a supermajority of eight out of the eleven justices is required to strike down as unconstitutional any challenged legislation. This case was assigned to Justice Sánchez Cordero, who was then the only woman justice. After deciding to hear the case,[55] the Justice Rapporteur invited the parties to present their arguments.

The dispute in this case revolved around whether the law violated the constitutional right to life. Defending the Robles Law, the representative of the Legislative Assembly and the Office of the Mayor argued that the reform did not violate the constitutional right to life because no living being exists until several weeks after conception. Rather, the legislation protected life by safeguarding women who seek unsafe clandestine abortions and may die from these procedures. The attorney general, representing the "interest of the nation," agreed with the constitutional challenge. He argued that life does in fact begin at conception. After hearing from the parties, Sánchez Cordero released her draft opinion to be discussed with her peers on October 25. In the document, the justice agreed that the constitution protected the right to life from conception and argued that the reform to Mexico City's criminal code did not violate this right. This was because the legislation maintained the criminalization of abortion and merely empowered the legislators to waive the application of criminal sanctions in some circumstances: "The Federal Constitution protects human life and equally protects the product of conception as a manifestation of human life regardless of its biological state," but the reform "does not authorize the deprivation of life of the product of conception. It establishes a possibility of not applying the sanction" (AI 10/2000). Given the salience of the issue, the justices, rather unusually, held a series of private meetings to study the case before the two public sessions that took place on January 29 and 30, 2000. In those sessions, the justices advanced various arguments in favor of and against the draft opinion. Seven justices voted to uphold Mexico City's reform, and four voted to strike it down.[56] The court's decision, while historic, nonetheless maintained the criminalization of abortion. As Marta Lamas has argued, women continued to be the subjects of a "legal pardon" by the state (Lamas 2017, 35), which essentially deprived them of full citizenship.

This status changed in 2004. In a peculiar turn of events, the Legislative Assembly, under socially conservative PRD Andrés Manuel López Obrador, undertook reforms in 2003 to the criminal code and the city's health law that further liberalized abortion. However, this time the reforms, rather puzzlingly, generated little public debate and were not challenged before the Supreme Court. The legal changes, which went into effect in early 2004, established that abortion was not a crime where penalties had been waived. The reforms also incorporated a key demand from conservative groups for the first time in the country: exceptions for conscientious objectors by practicing health care providers. Additionally, the reforms mandated the municipal health system to provide free access to legal abortion services, making Mexico City the most advanced jurisdiction in the country in providing abortion access. The reforms also reinforced penalties for individuals who perform abortions without the consent of the birthing patient. As Alba María Ruibal points out (2014b, 70), proponents of liberalization framed the debate around the argument that rights and freedoms are not absolute and must be balanced against competing rights.

The Judicial Road to the AC 146/147 Decision

The 2000 and 2004 reforms were the prelude to what became, by far, the most ambitious step toward the decriminalization of abortion by any Latin American jurisdiction during the First Wave of Abortion Decriminalization. Within the context of what became one of the most progressive administrations in the country under Mayor Marcelo Ebrard (2006–12), Mexico City approved reforms to its criminal code and health law that allowed unrestricted access to abortion during the first twelve weeks of pregnancy.[57] After intense public debate encouraged by the mayor's office and organized by the assembly through public forums starting in March 2015, a majority of legislators approved the reforms on April 24, and Ebrard signed them into law two days later.[58] The reforms legalized the "termination of pregnancy" on demand during the first twelve weeks and—importantly for a country with high levels of poverty, inequality, and unequal access to health care services—mandated its provision for free by public hospitals in Mexico City regardless of individuals' social-benefit status. The reforms to the city's health law also established that sexual and reproductive health were a public policy priority and required the government to develop programs to provide comprehensive information and orientation on reproductive health, as well as contraceptive services.

The significance of these reforms cannot be underestimated, especially considering the decriminalization of abortion in Argentina and Colombia analyzed in the previous chapters. First, Mexico City, in line with Mayor Ebrard's idea of expanding full citizenship,[59] decriminalized abortion in the first twelve weeks of pregnancy, affording women full agency as citizens for the first time. The reforms do away with Lamas's "legal pardon," since women need not justify their decisions before any state actor: they have earned the full democratic right to bodily autonomy.[60] Second, unlike the two previous reforms, these reforms made the state responsible for providing free abortions on request through public hospitals. In a part of the world where poor girls and women have been disproportionately affected because only unsafe abortions in clandestine clinics are available to them, the provision of safe abortions in public hospitals represents a significant public policy change. The reform's impacts were dramatic: hospitals began providing abortions the day after the reforms came into effect, and the mortality rate for the first 65,000 girls and women who underwent the procedure was zero (Ruibal 2014b, note 273). Finally, mostly because of the influence of women's groups, especially the leading nongovernmental organization GIRE (Information Group on Reproductive Choice, *Grupo de Información sobre Reproducción Elegida*), the debate, building on previous reforms, emphasized the need to balance competing rights and was framed as such by proponents of decriminalization (Ruibal 2014b).

The debate, however, did not stop there. On May 24, 2007, rather paradoxically, the then-president of the National Human Rights Commission, José Luis Soberanes Fernández, a conservative and Opus Dei member, filed a constitutional action to challenge the constitutionality of the reforms before the Supreme Court without even consulting the commission's consultative council. The next day, President Calderón's attorney general, Eduardo Medina-Mora Icaza , followed suit with his own constitutional action challenging the changes made to various articles of Mexico City's criminal code and health law (Articles 144, 145, 146, and 147, 16Bis 6 and Bis 8). Both actions argued that the legislation's definitions of pregnancy and abortion violated the constitutional right to life of the "product of conception." However, the attorney general argued that the reforms violated the precedent set by the court's decision on the Robles Law, whereas Soberanes focused on the jurisdictional conflict and argued that health care policy was a matter of federal jurisdiction beyond the scope of Mexico City's constitutional authority. The process then moved on to the chambers and the halls of the Supreme Court.

The Abortion Debate Begins at the Supreme Court

Upon receipt of the two files, the Office of the Chief Justice (*Presidencia*) sent the file submitted by Soberanes to the justice next on the preestablished list to be Justice Rapporteur—in this case, Justice Aguirre. Justice Aguirre declared both files (*expedientes*) admissible on May 25 and 28, 2007; assigned them their now-famous numbers AC 146/2007 and AC 147/2007; and instructed the addition (*acumulación*) of the second file to the case. On May 28, the justice affirmed the legal standing (*personalidad*) of the plaintiffs and, as required, instructed Mexico City's Legislative Assembly and the Office of the Mayor to file their positions before the court (*informes*).

It would be difficult to provide a robust analysis of the process that led to the 2008 ruling on abortion without highlighting some particularities of judicial decision-making at the Mexican Supreme Court.[61] Most important, the debate among justices predominantly occurs during public plenary meetings, which have been televised live since 1996.[62] While private sessions are not uncommon, interviews reveal that justices have limited interaction among themselves and do not know what arguments their peers will present. Justices and their law clerks can have an idea of what stance a justice will take on an issue based on their ideological leaning, voting patterns, and the positions they have taken in the past on various issues (*criterios*). Accordingly, people at the court tend to speak in terms of "probabilities." Justices can, for example, get a sense of what other justices are thinking about a case during the famous "Tuesday breakfasts" the justices hold weekly while the court is in session. As one justice mentioned: "[Justice] Aguirre used to say that the Tuesday breakfast is not to be missed. Discussions unfold *a navaja limpia* (with a clear shaving blade)."[63] Informal discussions may also take place between justices who have close personal relationships. As a justice indicated: "No. We rarely speak with one another. It is a type of an informal tradition not to do so. It can be frowned upon because we are expected to convince others with our arguments. We rarely speak with others. I may have spoken with Góngora [about this case], and it is probable that Sánchez Cordero may have spoken with Silva because they got along well, and Aguirre with Azuela. But that is it. Convincing your peers (*el convencimiento*) takes place in the plenary discussions."[64]

According to another justice, "There is very little negotiation before the plenary sessions. Justices may talk, but they talk with like-minded justices whom they do not need to convince. Like Góngora says, 'It is a debate among saints (*es un debate de santos*).' It is rare [to try to influence others]. You sense where the direction of the vote (*el sentido del voto*) is going. It is not the same with administrative negotiations, such as the election of the chief justice, or the *Salas*: there is definitely pre-negotiation there."[65]

There also appears to be little communication among law clerks before plenary sessions. This applies even when clerks have close personal relationships, oftentimes since law school. According to one law clerk:

There is no antechamber. You present arguments *a navaja limpia* and try to convince justices during the plenary sessions. One knows [the probability of] how a given justice will vote, given their *criterios*. You may speak once in a while with other law clerks, but there is no lobbying. Nor among the justices. We have a very [courteous] way of operating. We do not try to influence directly other justices. I, for example, am in charge of developing charts on how the ministers have voted. In momentous cases (*casos trascendentales*), I put up a blackboard on this wall [pointing at the wall] to track how justices have voted on similar cases, while making sure that [my] justice is consistent given his jurisprudential line. But, no, we do not talk.[66]

According to another law clerk, "There may be antechamber discussions, but only with [those with] whom you may be able to talk, but there is no intention to convince or change minds. People tend to have an idea of how a vote is coming (*cómo viene el sentido del voto*), and that is even the case with the[ir] justice, and he gets along with everyone."[67]

The implications of this process should be apparent, especially when compared with the Argentine and Colombian cases. Whereas in those two high courts much of the convincing took place before plenary discussions, the persuasive process at the Mexican Supreme Court takes place through the exchange of arguments during plenary sessions. Regarding strategic decision-making, then, the justices and law clerks of the Mexican Supreme Court can try to influence other justices' votes through collective discussions, without knowing for certain how many votes each justice has on their side. This explains why justices and law clerks speak about the probability of votes during interviews and about the "likelihood" that an argument may influence another justice. As a result, and contrary to other courts, the process does not begin by seeking a consensus in the development of a majority opinion supported by one justice. Instead, the process begins with the justices presenting arguments while simultaneously calculating the probabilities that other justices will support each argument. In the Argentine and Colombian cases, a handful of justices and law clerks began to build a consensus by seeking votes through the strategic development of arguments, persuading one justice at a time. In the Mexican case, one result of the particularities of the court's decision-making process is that rulings are often divided decisions with multiple concurrent and dissenting individual opinions. AC146–147/2007 is a case in point, as we shall see.

Another important influence on decision-making at Mexico's Supreme Court is the role of law clerks. Similar to the Argentine and Colombian cases, law clerks play a key role researching and developing arguments for justices to advance when deciding cases, in part because of the significant workload the eleven chambers undertake.[68] On average, each chamber tends to have eight to ten law clerks with expertise in various fields of the law. The clerks tend to work as a team. As in Argentina and Colombia, there exists a great deal of variance in the way these teams operate in each chamber. According to two justices from Mexico's Supreme Court:

We depend a lot on our teams, given our workload. We ask them to elaborate arguments, giving them direction.[69]

One starts to depend a lot on our teams. The workload is very high, and it is impossible for us to do it all. During the first year, I had to deal with 7,200 cases; last year it was 18,500. One is influenced a lot by these teams. And these have their own logic (*dinámica*), their own personalities, their own prestige (*prestigios*).[70]

Another important characteristic of decision-making at Mexico's top court concerns the practices around standing. As we now know, only certain state actors have standing to initiate judicial review challenges. Only the actors involved can respond to these challenges, and they must be invited to do so by the Justice Rapporteur. But this rigidity has sometimes been diluted by three informal practices. The first refers to asking for expert opinions and *amicus curiae* briefs on relevant topics. This practice began informally in 2005, when Justice Cossío reached out to medical experts seeking clarity on the implications of being HIV-positive while serving in the military (AR 2146/2005). The practice has become fairly established ever since, and justices, when serving as Justice Rapporteurs, have tended to rely on it when necessary. The second practice stems from the decision, also initiated by Cossío during the AC 146–147/2007 process, to hold public consultations. Through these consultations, a variety of state and nonstate actors are able to insert their opinions and arguments into the judicial decision-making process. The third practice, which some authors correctly deem problematic (Elizondo Mayer-Serra and Magaloni 2010, 54–56), involves private meetings between justices and stakeholders in cases. These meetings are often held in the justices' chambers. Colloquially known as *alegato de oreja*, or ear-argumentation, this practice, which appears to have decreased significantly over time, has allowed various state and nonstate actors to meet in private with justices to advance their positions on cases.

One last characteristic of decision-making at the Supreme Court is the so-called *engrose*: the drafting of the final decision after votes are taken in plenary sessions. The term takes its meaning from the word *engrosar*, "to thicken." Literally (and roughly) translated, *engrose* means "the thickened item," referring to the detailed drafting of the arguments of the final ruling once the votes have been taken in the plenary session. When a Justice Rapporteur's draft opinion is supported by the majority of their peers, that same justice is tasked, at the instruction of the chief justice, with drafting the final ruling. This ruling includes any dissenting and concurring opinions from other justices (these justices will draft their own and forward them to the Justice Rapporteur). If a draft opinion is defeated by a majority of votes, a justice within that majority is tasked with drafting the final ruling at the discretion of the chief justice.

The decision-making process at the court is then divided into four main stages: case assignment (chief justice) and admission (Justice Rapporteur); Justice Rapporteur's presentation of a draft opinion; discussion of draft opinion and vote in public plenary sessions; and drafting of the *engrose* and its publication. With this process in mind, let us return to the analysis of the process once the AC 146–147/2007 case was admitted.

An intense public debate ensued following the admission of the case by Justice Aguirre. At the local level, some jurists and Mexico City legislators reacted negatively to the assignment of the case to Aguirre. Aguirre's close ties to social conservative groups and his devoutness as a Catholic caused some to doubt that he would adjudicate the case fairly.[71] The justice attempted to assuage these fears by meeting with legislators and promising to leave his personal convictions aside and to study the issue in depth (*Cimacnoticias*, June 15, 2007). On a broader social level, the country was plunged into a national debate about abortion, largely because of the implications the ruling could have on the abortion laws in the thirty-one Mexican states. The case had national import. Indeed, the debate around abortion was placed atop the national public agenda until the court voted on the case on August 28, 2008.

Those who wanted to uphold the Mexico City reforms coalesced around the leadership of a pro-choice organization, the National Alliance for the Right to Decide (*Alianza Nacional por el Derecho a Decidir*). This organization brought together a network of academics, jurists, and activists who presented a variety of reports and press releases, organized public discussion sessions at various universities, and submitted amicus curiae briefs to the court. Many of the network's activities were supported by private and public universities, such as UNAM's prestigious Institute for Judicial Research, as well as institutions that supported and funded the publication of important academic works on abortion.[72]

The opposition crystallized when the debate began in Mexico City's Legislative Assembly earlier. The opposition challenging the constitutionality of the reforms was led by the National Pro-Life Committee, *Provida*. Founded in 1989, the committee, made up of over 140 organizations, had close links to the Catholic Church leadership and PAN. Well-funded and organized, the network also organized a variety of discussion forums and activities with financial support from international organizations, such as Human Rights International and wealthy Mexican businessmen (González Ruiz and Infante 2004).

As the national debate gathered strength outside the court, the case began its course inside the court. As required, Justice Aguirre asked the actors behind the challenged reform (the mayor's office and the assembly's leadership) to defend the legislation. The mayor's office, led by its legal adviser (*Consejera Jurídica*), Leticia Bonifaz, assembled an ad hoc advisory council made up of academics and medical experts tasked with developing arguments to defend the reform.[73] The result was a 184-page document, submitted to the court on June 19, 2007. Signed by the mayor, the document addressed all the arguments presented but primarily focused on the jurisdictional question and the constitutional right to life. On the jurisdictional question, it argued that the National Human Rights Commission was acting beyond its authority in bringing the constitutional challenge. The council argued that the commission only had the authority to initiate constitutional actions when laws violated human rights, which the council argued was not at issue on the facts of the case. Moreover, the council argued that Mexico City had the power to legislate on health care matters in its jurisdiction and that a politically sensitive case was not the proper forum to deal with jurisdictional issues. It further argued that the constitutional reforms of the 1990s had devolved authority to Mexico City to legislate on health care matters in its jurisdiction. The council also questioned the decision by the commission's president to act without support from its own consultative council, stating that Soberanes's was "motivated by personal convictions."[74] Regarding the fetus's right to life, a central element in both challenges, the council noted that this position was not supported by international law. Not a single international treaty existed that considered the embryo a person, and the reform had not "tacitly or explicitly ignored the right to life." Finally, the council argued that the primary objective of the reform was to afford women dignity and to guarantee respect for their decisions.

The following day, leaders of the group that initiated the reforms in the city's assembly, led by legislators Leticia Quezada Contreras and Víctor Hugo Círigo Vázquez, submitted their own report with supporting arguments. The 312-page document was prepared with the support of various renowned Mexican jurists and political scientists.[75] The document contained arguments similar to the ones submitted by the mayor's office but added that nowhere in the constitution is there a reference to rights awarded to "the product of conception," and that the constitutional's sole reference to pregnancy addressed a pregnant woman's rights under labor law. The document also emphasized women's rights to self-determination, as stipulated in various constitutional articles (Articles 1, 4, 5, 11, 14, and 16).[76]

The next step was the solicitation of expert opinion. While Justice Aguirre had opposed Cossío's initiative to start consulting experts during the processing of the 2146/2005 case concerning HIV-positive individuals in the military,[77] he changed his mind as the Justice Rapporteur in this instance. The decision was the result of strategic thinking between two key players: Justice Aguirre and Justice Cossío. According to Cossío, even if he opposed the idea, Aguirre was in a way forced to seek expert opinion so that he would be able to oversee the process. Aguirre knew that if he did not enlist experts, then Cossío would. As Cossío stated: "He [Aguirre] knew that if he did not bring them [scientists], I could do it myself, and if I brought them myself . . . I would give him a good beating (*paliza*)" (as quoted by Cortez Salinas 2020, 63). Aguirre's intention to manage and control the solicitation of expert opinions became clear, given the biased nature of the questionnaire he developed for experts. The questionnaire, sent to four experts on August 1, 2007, consisted of forty questions that probed the idea of when life begins during pregnancy, clearly reflecting the justice's position in the debate.[78] As the most conservative justice is known to have stated:

> My position has always been clear. Life starts at conception, and I defend life. Humans are primates, and various studies show experimentally that the zygote is a gestating human being. It is like an egg; if you pinch it, it retracts. The zygote does the same. There is no debate around that. I cannot accept it. The abortionist argument is destructive. . . . Abortionists are influenced by people such as Dr. [Ricardo] Tapia [Ibargüengoytia]. . . . It of course is a question of principles and morality. . . . Cossío is essentially an amoral person. I respect him. But he is not guided by morality. And this has nothing to do with my religion. It is a stupidity to say that I am guided by religion. It is a *sambenito*.[79]

The same day the questionnaire was sent out, the justice also asked federal and subnational institutions for information regarding mortality rates of women who had sought abortions since 1993.

As Aguirre shepherded the process inside the court, justices and law clerks in neighboring chambers began working on their analyses of the case. While the formal discussion among justices would not start for another year, interviews reveal that most people at the court expected that Aguirre's draft opinion would declare the reform unconstitutional. Given Aguirre's personal views, his consistent voting behavior, and the arguments he advanced in the AI 10/2000 case, many suspected that his conclusion would be based on the fetus's constitutional right to life. It seems that, even before the justice released his draft opinion, the debate had already been framed. The justices and law clerks began to work accordingly. As stated by several actors interviewed:

> Aguirre would set the tone of the debate. It took me a while to learn the dynamic of the discussion. When I first arrived, they would manipulate me. They would use me like a hunting dog: you let the dog go get the duck, but you shoot the duck after the dog leaves. Aguirre and Azuela used to do that. They did it a lot from the beginning. They would tease me (*me picaban*) so that I would react, and then I would answer a particular question, asked in a particular way. I realized soon enough how it worked. When the abortion case arrived at the court, I knew how it was going to unfold. Aguirre was consistent, and he was going to set the tone. And there are certain dynamics that become predictable given

certain personal dynamics. There are rivalries inside the court. There are internal disputes. There are a lot of egos. For example, between Aguirre and Góngora: if one says A, the other says B. If one says one thing, the other says something else, and, well, that is how they vote. And we knew what Aguirre would say on this one.[80]

Aguirre and Azuela were very religious. Aguirre was going to be a priest. He represented the interest of the [Catholic] Church, and his argument was going to be around the right to life. Those were his constituents. It was as clear as water.[81]

Aguirre was a guide (*referente*). He would center the debate. And not only because of his personality, but he was respected. We knew what was coming. There would be no surprises.[82]

As the perception of how the debate would be framed set in, justices and their law clerks began to study the case and consider possible lines of argumentation. Importantly, and unlike the Argentine and Colombian cases covered in the previous chapters (where a group of law clerks from a couple of chambers worked together in the development of arguments), law clerks at the Mexican Supreme Court worked independently, and their work varied across chambers depending on the working styles of the justices and their positions on the issue. Where a justice's position was clear from the beginning, law clerks were tasked with developing arguments with very clear directions. For example, according to one of the three conservative justices:

My position was clear to everyone. I base my thinking on just naturalism (*jus naturalista* or natural law). This goes against neo-positivists [whose thinking is] based on human rights. They are based on international discussions that are not based on just naturalism. Yes, it is difficult for them to convince us given our visions and our convictions. We have firm positions. Life starts at the moment of fertilization, which produces men and women. And this is enshrined (*plasmado*) in the constitution, the right to life. Article 14 defends it. There are religious truths that can coincide with the truths of nature: a lot of religions defend the right to life. My position was clear, and my team knew it. I asked them to draft arguments based on this. I had already advanced my arguments in the previous case. It was clear.[83]

Where a justice's position was not clear, different directions were issued. To wit:

We knew how the issue was going to unfold (*se veía venir*) from the challenge (*impugnación*). We developed a team, and [the justice] gave us instructions to carry out research, each one focusing on one area [of the law]: comparative, penal, et cetera. There were many aspects (*aristas*). We each had a topic. He tasked us to the various topics. He asked us for possible responses—to respond with arguments. We devoted ourselves to it. He debated with us. We did not know how he was going to vote. He matured the issue on his own. He reflected on it by himself. It was a sort of training. He had friends in many media outlets. Many friends. He would talk to them. He was nurturing himself. He also had Catholic friends. He listened to everyone, technical arguments, philosophical arguments.[84]

It was a slow process. The justice was not very clear at the beginning. He asked us for various possible arguments. He was very relaxed. He gave us latitude and supported us. He wanted to learn. And wanted to do it on his own. His wife even told him that he had to vote against, and he responded: "I don't meddle with the administration of the household; don't meddle with my issues." He wanted to do it by himself. It helped us to have Aguirre there because he would force us to counter his arguments.[85]

It is impossible to determine how all the justices leaned on the issue, and information collected from interviews varies. However, interviewees suggest that most people in the halls of the court anticipated that Justices Aguirre, Azuela, and Ortiz Mayagoitia would find Mexico City's reforms unconstitutional; that Justices Sánchez Cordero, Silva, and Cossío would uphold the reforms as constitutional; and that the rest of the justices were undecided or their positions were unclear.

As the process began inside the court, lobbyists from various groups attempted to influence deliberations. You may recall that it is an accepted practice to hold private meetings between stakeholders and justices in Mexico's Supreme Court. Interviews reveal that this type of contact began early in the process and continued until the day the court decided the case in late August 2008. According to one justice, "All sorts of groups came to see us, [such as] Serrano Limón. They sent us thousands of cards by mail. . . . Litigants are very astute, and they observe us very well. They develop individual arguments for each justice to try to convince them. At the beginning [when the case arrived], they would send young women (*chamacas*) with plastic fetus poppets to try to convince us. It is about trying to win the vote (*atraer el voto*). We realized that this was an intense issue (*un tema muy fuerte*)."[86]

The Strategic Development of Arguments

It is within this context of intense national debate on abortion and the lobbying of individual justices that Justice Cossío's chamber took center stage and developed a multilayered strategy to uphold Mexico City's reforms. Justice Cossío's position was clear from the start: he was for the decriminalization of abortion as a known *garantista*, and his team knew it. First, as part of the justice's desire to generate greater discussion by introducing innovative legal thinking at the court (Cortez Salinas 2020, 167), he established the Fundamental Rights Program (mentioned above) that allowed for the receipt of amicus curiae briefs from relevant experts. The first amicus curiae was received by the court in 2007 during a heated debate on the constitutionality of telecommunications reform (AC 26/2006). Justice Cossío, with the endorsement of the chief justice, put out a call in early 2008 soliciting amicus curiae from national and international organizations. The idea was to try to open the debate and allow for the introduction of arguments that had been successful in the decriminalization of abortion elsewhere. According to a law clerk in Cossío's chamber, "We were asked to carry out research on abortion comparative law in the development of arguments . . . [which] was also what the amicus [curiae] were for: to expose justices to arguments used in North America and Europe by human-rights groups in support of decriminalizing abortion."[87] In what became a watershed moment for the court, by the end of the process, over fifty amicus curiae were submitted, the largest in its history. The amicus briefs were penned by members of national and international organizations, both for and against abortion, and included well-known figures in abortion litigation circles in Latin America, such as Rebecca Cook, a professor of law and then-director the International Reproductive and Sexual Health Law Program at the University of Toronto.

The second part of Cossío's strategy was to allow for the "airing" of the debate and the introduction of various perspectives and viewpoints based on scientific evidence and sound legal arguments. This could be done, the justice thought, by holding public consultations with civil-society organizations. In early 2008, Justice Cossío approached Chief Justice Ortiz Mayagoitia and asked that the court hold public hearings on the issue that could be broadcast live through the court's television channel. As someone in his chamber stated, "We realized that the antiabortionists were many and well organized. We had to open the debate. We asked Ortiz Mayagoitia to hold public hearings (*audiencias*)."[88] The chief justice agreed. According to someone in the chief justice's chamber, "Cossío personally asked for the public hearings because the issue was a heated one (*candente*), in order to channel (*encauzar*) the proposals and everyone's viewpoints. There was a practical element as well: it allowed for an easier way to interact with everyone—easier than having to see all of them individually. The proposal was accepted, and everyone in the court was asked, and all accepted. The idea was to listen to everyone in an organized way."[89] On March 10, 2008, the court issued a "general agreement" (*Acuerdo General* 2/2008) announcing that public hearings would be held.

In what became a historic step, the court held the first public hearings, inviting individuals and civil-society organizations to present their views. Held in the plenary room of the court's "auxiliary" (and beautiful) building in the southern part of Mexico City, six hearings were organized, each attended by all eleven justices. The hearings were organized based on whether attendees defended or rejected the constitutionality of Mexico City's reforms for decriminalizing abortion. Three sessions—on April 11, May 23, and June 13, 2008—heard arguments for the unconstitutionality of the reforms. Three other sessions on April 23, May 30, and June 27 heard arguments for the constitutionality of the reforms. Leading the debate on the unconstitutionality of the reforms, the two main plaintiffs, Soberanes and Medina-Mora, opened up the sessions. Defending the reforms were Bonifaz and Círigo. The hearings were attended by eighty individuals in total, forty representing each side. This was the broadest public debate Mexico's Supreme Court had encouraged in its history. The court also published, for the first time, a website that contained all the documentation related to the case and recordings of the hearings upon completion.

Interviews reveal that there were two main objectives for holding public hearings. The first was to establish where the justices stood on the issue. This could be assessed through the justices' interactions with presenters and through the interviews they might have with media outlets. While the positions of some justices were clear, others were not. The thinking was that the hearings would generate debate, which could bring the justices into the discussion and encourage them to disclose their positions.

The second objective was to develop an argument based on a proportionality test that would weigh two competing rights: the right of the unborn versus the right of the mother. The public hearings would, the thinking went, show there were many views on abortion and little consensus, and that the way to resolve competing views was to apply a proportionality test. According to someone in Cossío's chamber, "When [Cossío] taught at ITAM, [he] worked with Alma [Beltrán] on the Ley Robles case. Alma was writing a thesis, and worked at GIRE, and helped in the development of arguments. Her thesis identified the main arguments against and for abortion. This helped in the development of a strategy, and proportionality was key."[90]

Justice Cossío instructed two of his law clerks, who identify themselves as neoconstitutionalists, to develop lines of argumentation around the use of a proportionality test. According to one of these two law clerks, they "worked very hard on comparative law that had used proportionality and balancing."[91] The results were captured in a document developed by the two law clerks titled "Strategy: Chamber of Justice José Ramón Cossío Díaz."[92] It detailed, in nine steps, the main arguments the justice should use to convince hesitant justices to uphold the reforms through the application of a proportionality test. These arguments were as follows: (1) to remind justices that the discussion should not be about the sacred value of life, to take seriously the "virtues of judicial independence," and to remind them of the importance of judicial impartiality; (2) to depart from the premise that before twelve weeks of pregnancy one talks about the idea of life as a [moral] "good"; (3) to establish that life does not have an absolute value (with examples and references to various constitutional provisions); (4) to accept that the above "leads one to conclude that, even when one recognizes life as a good [and worthy of constitutional protection], that this recognition cannot be interpreted to bar legislators from regulating matters related to life"; (5) to declare that the regulation of abortion falls under states' jurisdiction, and that Mexico City was within its authority to decriminalize abortion in its jurisdiction; (6) to find that the legislator had the jurisdictional authority (*potestad*) to criminalize activities where constitutional standards were respected; (7) to find the objective of the reforms was to guarantee women's rights as established in Articles 1 and 4 of the Constitution; (8) to find that a proportionality test was necessary to assess whether the legislation appropriately balanced competing rights; and (9) to find that the twelve-week limit adhered to the above standards and, "as a result, the validity of the challenged statue must be recognized."

Nevertheless, in one of the most fascinating twists to this story, this strategy changed. Interviews reveal that there was a perception within the chamber that arguments that overtly engaged with women's rights would convey the image of the court overstepping its role and being activist; this approach, it was believed, would not be enough to assemble a strong majority asserting the constitutionality of the reforms. A clear strategic calculation took place about the limits, both outside and within the court, of pursuing a robust human-rights ruling. As someone in Cossío's chamber noted: "There was a lot of pressure. We realized, especially during the public hearings, that the antiabortionist groups were bigger in number and better organized. There were some 150 groups on the right, and some 30 on the left."

It was at this moment, interviews reveal, that the decision was made to shift the debate away from when life begins and from arguments about women's rights and instead to advance a more technical argument. Justice Cossío decided to pursue a line of argumentation on whether Mexico City had the jurisdictional authority to decriminalize abortion. As someone in the Justice's chamber stated:

We decided to elaborate a strategy inside the chamber not to present an argument as one of life or death. That is what conservatives wanted. And would not win. We disguised (*disfrazamos*) the argument and we steered it toward a technical area (*campo técnico*). We did not take it toward where the conservatives wanted us to take it. It had to be a jurisdictional argument (*argumento competencial*), to take the argument to a technical area . . . and they were fooled . . . (*se fueron con la finta*). They thought that the argument was going to go there [around life], and no. . . . . Little by little we were framing (*derivando*) the issue as a jurisdictional one.[93]

Interestingly, the decision to change argumentative tracks caused significant friction among law clerks. As Cortez Salinas detailed in his masterful work (2020), Cossío, with his intention to bring new perspectives to the bench, assembled a team of law clerks with different perspectives. Some clerks had a neoconstitutional orientation while others had a more formalist, positivist approach to the law. The decision to change lines of argumentation meant assigning the task of elaboration of new arguments primarily to one law clerk who self-labeled as a "positivist." As one law clerk explained:

We had worked very hard on applying the proportionality test, but Cossío discarded the idea and gave the file to [name withheld], who argued in favor of a jurisdictional argument. He worked with two other law clerks. And that was a watershed moment, and we felt it as a betrayal. [Name withheld] leaves the chamber a year later because of that, and I tried to leave as well, but Cossío said no. We called the three law clerks the "triumvirate of evil." They displaced us and used an argument around jurisdictional questions. They took us out—better not to talk about abortion.[94]

As one of the three law clerks assigned to developing a jurisdictional argument explained in two candid and extensive interviews:

What we tried to do was to make it [the argument] as jurisdictional (*competencial*) as possible. It was 100 percent strategic because if not, it would not have worked (*no hubiera pasado*). It would be difficult to resolve. . . . The plan was not to enter into the culture wars—to make it the least ideological [as] possible. Because that way, it would work. We decided not to meddle with the right to life. Though at the end. I could not get it out of the discussion. There was no consensus. . . . But we decided not to debate it and steer the discussion to the jurisdictional argument. A great advantage of this ruling was that the issue came with great democratic legitimacy through the votes of the [Mexico City Legislative] Assembly. It is different than with an amparo. With concrete-review cases . . . we are positivists. Formalists. They call us neo-formalists. When they asked us to go elsewhere [with other arguments], I said "no way" (*ni madres*), we are formalists. That was our training. The question of proportionality becomes whatever you want it to become. Arguments around [human] rights become whatever you want them to become. . . . We are careful not to touch issues on their substance (*en lo substancial*) because we lose the debate. We know that in some cases, these strategies change votes.[95]

Three important observations can be made so far. First, interviews with members of Cossío's chamber reveal the importance the law clerks play in the crafting of arguments. Second, they reveal, in this case, a sense that Justice Cossío's team had the ability not only to frame the debate but to sway justices with their arguments and win votes. They point to the important influence and role the justice played on the bench. And this is a striking similarity with the Argentine and Colombian cases I have covered in this book: a highly respected justice playing a central role in the crafting off arguments. Finally, the interviews suggest that key players are keenly attuned to dynamics internally and externally when thinking about how to develop arguments and win votes. Here, they sensed how other justices would vote *even though* there seemed to be little communication between justices and law clerks. For example, the law clerks knew that Aguirre, the Justice Rapporteur, would advance an argument based on the right to life. Externally, the law clerks seemed aware of the limits of how far the court could go in expanding the interpretation of rights. In other words, the law clerks were aware of the political opportunities available to push the law in a certain direction. As one of Cossío's law clerks suggested: "Before this decision, the justice had been opening up on the issue of human rights, from 2004 to 2008 . . . but he was afraid [in this case]. He had not attempted to collect votes. They told him that he could not wink to feminists. He chose to adopt a restricted, Kelsenian approach. . . . His calculation was that he would not win that way, but the terrain had been laid since the HIV issue, [so] we could have won. But he decided not to. He thought that there were constraints."[96]

The issue of "winking" to feminists was also brought up by another law clerk in Cossío's chamber: "We of course had been working with feminists ideologically, but we could not come across as being seen that they had lobbied us, and we also needed to strike a balance with conservatives. Remember that the justice was appointed by the PAN. We could not be seen as throwing a bone to feminists. We are not political actors. Ideologizing positions do not work. It does not work that way (*por ahí no va*). These debates are not won when minorities, women, feminists, make them about rights."[97]

An important constraint on the justices' ability to pursue their policy preferences is captured by the idea of "constituents," which was brought up by a justice in another candid interview. When asked how justices make decisions, the justice replied:

> The first [element that goes into judging] is ideology. The one we bring with us to the court. And then [it] is the law. But then there are the constituents one has. In my case, it was the group that appointed me. You want to be brought into that group, and you want to return the favor. One acts according to that belonging. For some, it could be religious groups. One traces and does what one does depending on this, because we are part of these social and political groups. One wants to be accepted. One has a feeling of acceptance and belonging, and you have to act accordingly when judging. That is how the game is played. These are the constituents: it refers to who reads what you write, who understands you. In my case, I earned ample support at the Senate—something that gave me some liberty of action—but a group nominated me. I have worked with some Senate leaders. It is not accountability. It is about with whom you talk. How one wants to be remembered. I carved up a space. It is not about getting where you want to go, but how you get there. But there is some latitude. You cannot arrive tied up, like conservatives. They wanted to speak with me, but I did not go to baptisms [or] weddings. Justice Franco comes from [Carlos] Abascal, [President] Calderón. They have to show an interest in the family; he comes from the Libre de Derecho. And this is of course tied to personality. The psychology of personality. You have to create a personality, and you start to become trapped by the image of yourself [that] you created. And that personality is linked to the people that appointed you. The character you create starts to trap you. It is a type of ideological entrapment. The religious [justices] feel that they represent their base. It is a type of radicalization . . . one starts to act on semiautomatic. It is personality cultivation.[98]

In this particular case, members of the Cossío's team were well aware of these contours. As one of them suggested: "We knew that there would be backlash in arguing for the constitutionality of the reforms. Especially with some groups, and in the presidency. The jurisdictional argument was a way to cover us. The reforms had democratic legitimacy, and we knew that most Mexicans do not agree [with abortion], but Mexico City is different, and it is dominated by the left. Conservatives controlled many states. For them, it would be a partial setback."[99]

Armed with an argument constrained by the given political opportunities and certain to win several votes, members of the strategic chamber moved on to the next step of the process: debating the draft opinion released by the Justice Rapporteur.

Draft Opinion

Justice Aguirre released the draft opinion—a 610-page document—on August 15, 2008. As expected, and, literally, in his opinion, the main part of the Mexico City reforms, the decriminalization of abortion during the first twelve weeks of pregnancy, was unconstitutional.[100] Starting from the premise that there is no consensus on when life begins, the document advanced the argument that it was up to the Supreme Court to determine whether the constitutional protection of life began at conception. If so, it suggested, then Mexico City did not have the jurisdictional authority to bring about reforms that affected that right: only the constitutional assembly had this authority. The document therefore addressed the substantive issue before looking at the jurisdictional issue. The main argument for striking down the reform was that the right to life was implicitly protected in three articles of the constitution (Articles 1, 4, and 12). The next step, the document went on, was to determine whether the right to life was absolute. The justice argued that it was, relying on Article 22, which prohibited the death penalty, and Article 14, which outlawed "the depravation of life." There are, the justice stated, "no limitations or restrictions" to those constitutional provisions. The document then proceeded to discuss when life begins. Based on a broad interpretation of labor protections for pregnant women (Articles 4 and 123) and surprisingly coming from someone who "disparaged" conventional control, the opinion cited international agreements (with an emphasis on the Convention on the Rights of the Child) to argue that life starts at conception. With this reasoning, Aguirre held that the main provisions of the reforms were unconstitutional and must be struck down (declared null). The draft opinion also presented a series of secondary arguments, including one based on gender discrimination (i.e., men are discriminated against when a woman carries out an abortion without the man's knowledge). The main argument, though, was based on three parts: the right to life was enshrined in the constitution; the protection of human life spanned from conception to death; this protection was absolute and could not be limited or restricted.

The release of the draft opinion reignited the national debate on abortion, as it came with the announcement that the first public session to discuss the draft proposal was scheduled to take place ten days later. The issue consumed many discussions in media outlets, and several protests took place in cities across the country. Rather dramatically, just as the televised plenary discussions were about to begin, antiabortionist activists blanketed Latin America's largest main square, the *Zócalo*, which the majestic Supreme Court building overlooks, with hundreds of small white crosses symbolizing dead fetuses.

The eleven justices debated the draft opinion for four days. The first session began at 3:11 p.m. on August 25, 2008. After the chief justice opened the televised session, Justice Aguirre, in a defensive tone and using characteristically elaborate language, prefaced his presentation by saying that, contrary to the many criticisms his document had received, his arguments were not based on morality. He also took offense at references to the existence of conservative "blocks" on the bench. He then said that the court's duty should not be influenced by public opinion ("it is not a pollster") and, taking an originalist position, referred to ideas about liberty captured by the constitutional drafters of the 1857 Constitution. Aguirre argued that his draft opinion rested on four issues: whether Mexico City had the jurisdictional power to limit the right to life as protected by the constitution; whether Mexico had international commitments to respect life; the judicial "uncertainty" that the new definition of abortion (beyond twelve weeks) created; and that the conclusion was about protecting the life of the unborn, not about criminalizing women.

Aguirre's presentation was followed by what usually characterizes the beginning of plenary sessions in Mexico's Supreme Court: suspense. Everyone, including the justices themselves, waits to see how the justices will position themselves before voting as they decant their own arguments. Recall that little communication takes place between chambers before the public plenary sessions. As with most academic committee meetings, which the reader is likely familiar with, the floor is open to whomever wants to speak during plenary sessions, as participants raise their hands in no predetermined order. Expectedly, Justice Góngora, who had a personal rivalry with Aguirre, took the floor and, in a lengthy intervention, criticized many parts of Aguirre's arguments with references to women's rights, procedural technicalities, and philosophical ideas about freedom. His intention had been to ensure that every argument was addressed. As one of his law clerks stated, "He wanted to speak for as long as possible destroying his [Aguirre's] arguments. One by one. He asked his law clerk [name withheld] to compile arguments in favor of abortion from the international level and comparative law to destroy his arguments. His intention was to give him a beating. He asked us to attack that proposal. He said to me: 'Find all the arguments necessary and destroy them.'"[101]

In what was undoubtedly the most important part of the discussion, Justice Cossío took the floor next to frame the entire debate, as he and his team had strategically planned. In a short intervention, the justice argued that the fifth part (*Considerando*) of the draft opinion, the section addressing whether Mexico City's Legislative Assembly had the jurisdictional authority to legislate on the issue, could be discussed prior (*de manera preliminar*) to debating other substantive aspects of the opinion. He then proposed that the bench do so during the next session, which was to be held the following day. Heeding the justice's advice, the chief justice asked his peers whether, as Justice Cossío had suggested, they should analyze "in a preferential manner" the "formal jurisdictional powers" of Mexico City's Legislative Assembly. Except for Aguirre, the other ten justices agreed with the proposal and voted in favor. Ortiz Mayagoitia, the chief justice, then concluded: "Good, then tomorrow we will start the preliminary discussion to the in-depth issues with this matter dealing with [Mexico City's] formal jurisdiction" (SCJN 2008a, 63). In an interesting twist, Justice Aguirre surprised the room by declaring that "with my dissenting vote" (discussing the jurisdictional part first), "tomorrow the ministers will have a full study on the matter" (SCJN 2008a, 64). The justice said that he had "a study" ready and only had to print it, to which the chief justice responded: "Let's hope you can get it to us tonight, Justice! If it is already done, let's hope you can get it to us tonight" (SCJN 2008a, 64). Aguirre assured his peers: "Just what it takes me to print it" (SCJN 2008a, 64).

It is unclear from interviews whether Justice Aguirre knew that Cossío's chamber had planned to steer the debate toward the jurisdictional argument. At various points during the plenary session, Aguirre referred to the "multiple" additional studies he had tasked his team to prepare for the plenary discussions. But the inclusion of those studies into the process contributed to framing of the debate around the issue of jurisdiction.

After Ortiz Mayagoitia opened the next session in the morning of August 26, 2008, Justice Aguirre took the floor and referred to the study he had sent to his peers the night before. Relying on the study, Aguirre argued that Mexico City did not have the jurisdictional authority to legislate on matters of health care policy or on the "spirit to protect health and the life that derives from it" (SCJN 2008b, 6).

Justice Cossío took the floor next to cement the debate around the jurisdictional angle. Captivating his peers, who stared directly at him (including Justice Aguirre, who uncomfortably sat to his immediate left on the U-shaped bench), Cossío argued that he wanted to present his position on the matter and that the justices had to approach the issue "strictly from the jurisdictional powers of the Legislative Assembly" (SCJN 2008b, 6). The justice argued that the main arguments against the constitutionality of the reforms as submitted by the plaintiffs were synthesized in the draft opinion in this manner and that was the "core issue that concerns us" (SCJN 2008b, 6-7). He argued, "This is not a matter to be analyzed in material terms. That is to say, we cannot see pregnancy as a material phenomenon. We have to see pregnancy as a jurisdictional matter" (SCJN 2008b, 10). As his peers stared at him while he slowly flipped through the pages of his prepared document, the justice went on to say that the constitution was very clear that the levels of government shared responsibilities over health policy and, as such, the reforms undertaken by Mexico City were constitutional. "For these reasons, Chief Justice," Cossío argued, "it seems to me that the Legislative Assembly clearly has the jurisdictional power to establish the definition of pregnancy, [of the] conditions surrounding abortion, given that it is in charge of the jurisdictional power of maternal and child policy, on one hand, and, on the other, and as clearly detailed by Article 122 [of the Constitution], to establish a criminal code, and, as such, its definitions and penalties. For this reason, I am in favor [of] the jurisdictional power of the Assembly to define these matters. *Muchas gracias*" (SCJN 2008b, 15–16). The debate was framed.

As each of the other justices took the floor after Cossío's intervention, they directly responded to the jurisdictional question as the justice had posed it. Because responses had to be given in a binary way, the justices elaborated on their reasons for weighing whether Mexico City had jurisdiction over health policy and criminal behavior before answering with a yes or a no. Astoundingly, except for Aguirre, all the justices, including conservative Justices Azuela and Ortiz Mayagoitia, agreed that the capital city had the constitutional authority to legislate on both health policy and criminal policy. Justice Azuela objected to including Aguirre's document in the debate and lamented that the discussion had moved into the realm of jurisdiction. He declared that the answer to the posed question was "easily" answered in the affirmative. Ortiz Mayagoitia, for his part, declared that he agreed with the questioned jurisdictional policymaking power of Mexico City but declared that he was nonetheless in favor of the draft opinion. It became apparent to some that, with the question posed and the answers given, the eight-vote majority support for the reforms had crystallized. The Supreme Court had therefore upheld the decriminalization of abortion.

As people in the room began to realize what had happened, Justice Aguirre took the floor. In a tense room, the justice provoked great laughter by declaring that, after all his years at the court, he "had never been able to achieve unanimity" among his colleagues (SCJN 2008b, 64). He declared himself surprised by how the discussion had gone and announced that he had not included the study about Mexico City's lack of jurisdiction in his draft opinion because he thought the issue was "trivial and vacuous." The real debate went beyond the issue of jurisdiction. Aguirre then volunteered to withdraw the study he had shared and to move on to the next part of his draft proposal. Justice Cossío disagreed and urged his colleagues to include the study, proposing that it become part of a new draft opinion. He offered to draft this section of the opinion himself. His colleagues agreed.

The discussion took an important turn at this point of the debate. The chief justice, realizing that the proposal had unanimous support, declared that Mexico City had the constitutional authority to legislate on abortion and health policy and, as a result, on abortion. He then suggested that Aguirre's study be included.

Ortiz Mayagoitia suggested that the justices' positions on other aspects of the draft opinion would have to be of a "personal nature" to be advanced individually by each justice. Justice Azuela, from the conservative wing of the court, agreed with the idea and, based on how the discussion had unfolded so far, captured where the direction of the votes was going: "This will be a majority." The chief justice then took a vote: except for Aguirre, all the justices agreed. The plenary clerk (*Secretario General de Acuerdos*), who sits in front of all the justices, declared: "Mr. Chief Justice, there is a majority of votes in the direction that the study of formal jurisdiction be included in a final opinion, and that the Legislative Assembly does have jurisdiction" (SCJN 2008b, 77). As is his prerogative, Ortiz Mayagoitia appointed a justice to draft the final opinion. Expectedly, he tasked Cossío with writing the jurisdictional part of the final opinion.

The plenary session was suspended for a break at 13:05 p.m. As the sound of the chief justice's gavel pounding on his desk was heard, it became clear that Cossío's strategy had proved successful: there would be enough votes to uphold the constitutionality of reforms undertaken by Mexico City if the jurisdictional question was the one to be answered.

The tone of the discussion had changed. As a law clerk for Justice Gudiño stated:

> The arguments about jurisdiction were technical. The issue really lightened the discussion and made things easier. It depressurized . . . everything. It is difficult for a judge to decide on how far legislators can go in bringing in penalties. This was a different discussion. It is easier to decide. It is more difficult to discuss penalties (*tipificar*). Ortiz Mayagoitia started to talk about natural rights. That is a lot more difficult to discuss. The debate would not have been the same had it gone that way. It [is] like when we received a challenge around [penalizing those who steal] turtle eggs. Is it up to us to set penalties? In terms of women's rights, of where life starts, that is a lot more complicated.[102]

As a law clerk for Justice Silva also recounted: "The debate changed [during the plenary discussions]. Cossío cast a spell on the justices and the debate (*los engatusó*). That was a smart exit [for him] that would not bring [him] problems in the future. He decided to advance a formal argument. And it worked. Let's remember that Cossío was appointed by a conservative president, and that we still had a conservative president. The mechanics of the issue makes it easier to uphold a given statue. It was the case here. Cossío won the debate."

And the debate had indeed been won. Upon the resumption of the session, Justice Azuela took the floor to suggest to his colleagues that they keep their interventions on substantive issues succinct, alluding to the fact that the matter had essentially been settled. Over the next day and a half, the justices presented their arguments on substantive parts of the draft opinion. However, they did so based on the already implicit understanding that the reforms undertaken by Mexico City were constitutional, given that the jurisdictional issue had become the center of discussion. In prepared statements, the justices discussed various parts of the draft opinion, infusing the discussion with their own positions in mostly expected ways.

Justice Luna's intervention, for example, was delivered like an academic lecture on legal technicalities, whereas Justice Góngora's lengthy intervention that lasted an hour and a half surveyed, again, all aspects of the draft opinion. Perhaps the highlight of the discussion was a gripping intervention delivered by Sánchez Cordero, who firmly and eloquently challenged the idea that men could understand the debate around the need to seek an abortion. Silva, the most liberal justice on the bench, took a clear interpretivist approach. He reminded his colleagues of the "social character" of the constitution and argued that the Supreme Court's role was to understand the "social reality" to make sure that constitutional rights be guaranteed (SCJN 2008c, 24). For him, the draft opinion was flawed because it only looked at one side of the debate (the unborn's right to life) and not women's rights. There were, he argued, two conflicting sides, and for him, the legislator had struck the right balance with the reforms. With a nostalgic tone and reminiscing about when people took "liberty" seriously, Azuela implicitly suggested that abortion could be abused as a family-planning mechanism. The justice grounded his argument on when life begins and argued that it began at the moment of conception. When asking rhetorically about women's rights, Azuela suggested that women could give their children up for adoption. For him, that would be the ideal response (SCJN 2008c, 61).

Perhaps the most surprising intervention in this second phase of the discussion was Cossío's. The justice argued that a proportionality test would not be an appropriate way to analyze the issues. While, he argued, women's rights are enshrined in the constitution, the unborn's right to life is not. As such, it could not be weighed against the former's. After an eloquent intervention, the justice concluded: "[Given the above], I do not understand how we could weigh, on one hand, women's rights, which in this case are concrete, which are recognized, against a constitutional right that is not protected, that it is not a fundamental right, because I am still unable to find it in the Constitution or International Law, and, of course, I continue not to believe that this is implicitly or logically included. For these reasons I am in favor of the challenged precepts. Thank you, Chief Justice" (SCJN 2008d, 23).[103]

The justice thus buried the original strategy that three of his clerks had proposed he take in the debate to win votes.

The debate over abortion that had consumed Mexico for almost two years reached its climax. Outside the court, amidst heated debate, Mexico's cardinal, through a statement released by his bishops at a press conference, declared that it caused the Catholic Church "profound pain" that a majority of justices had decided to support the decriminalization of abortion in Mexico City (*La Jornada*, August 28, 2008). Inside the court, the last session of the debate began on the morning of August 28. After the chief justice's gavel marked the opening of this last session, Aguirre, knowing that his draft proposal had not garnered the eight votes required, repeated his position saying: "I reaffirm my conviction that the Constitution textually enshrines the right to life, even more because it explicitly interprets it as a necessary condition for the exercise of all other rights. . . . We cannot prefer ceasing to be. . . . We must defend life" (SCJN 2008d, 64). The debate then turned to a discussion of some remaining issues, such as whether the changes to penalties associated with the new definition of abortion (past twelve weeks) were properly drafted and constitutionally valid.[104] As often occurs during these public sessions, a period of confusion ensued. The chief justice asked his peers whether they wanted to discuss other parts of the draft opinion, flipping quicky through the pages and listing a variety of issues. However, the debate had clearly been exhausted, and no justice asked to take the floor. Ortiz Mayagoitia then suggested that a vote be taken on the components of the draft opinion, to which Justice Azuela responded that there was no point because the decision on the constitutionality of the reforms had already been made. The chief justice thus called for a vote.

After the vote, Aguirre stated that he would prepare a dissenting opinion. Given the discussion, Justices Azuela and Ortiz Mayagoitia declared that they would join the dissenting opinion, as they both believed that the constitution protected the right to life from the time of conception. The other justices, including Justice Cossío, who Ortiz Mayagoitia tasked with drafting the final draft opinion through the *engrose*, announced their intention to cast concurrent opinions. The first push to decriminalize abortion in Latin America with no conditions had thus been upheld as being constitutional. Before ending the session, Chief Justice Ortiz Mayagoitia solemnly declared:

> The Supreme Court's decision does not criminalize or decriminalize abortion. It is not within the power of this constitutional tribunal to

establish crimes or penalties. We have only established the constitutionality of a statute approved by the respective institution, and, in this case
in particular, we have taken part in the definition of an issue of national
transcendence. In every nation where abortion has been debated by
constitutional tribunals, there is a before-and-after moment. Based on
the decision taken here, the after [moment] begins in the Mexican case.
The judicial and social effects of a decision taken by this entity are
undeniable. (SCJN 2008d, 78)

The "after" moment was the result of the strategic deployment of technical arguments by Justice Cossío and his team. As mentioned earlier, it is difficult to establish the exact number of justices who would have voted to uphold
the reforms had the jurisdictional argument not been deployed. Counterfac-
tuals are impossible to test. What is certain, however, is that several justices
were undecided at the beginning of the process and that they were won over
with the jurisdictional argument.

To wit, various interviewees offered these comments:

I am against [abortion] personally. But the issue is whether it is constitutional to send women to jail. It is not. This is about respecting federalism, and the legislator should decide given the political, social, and
economic context. The personal cannot take precedence. Personal
opinions should not be at play. I developed my own analysis. This is for
subnational governments (*gobiernos locales*) to decide. If the question is
whether the debate had been different, had it been about life? [Inter-
viewee makes emphatic gestures.] Completely different! One cannot take
into consideration our philias and phobias. They were never part of my
decision. I do not believe in judicial activism. I would not have voted in
favor [of the constitutionality of the reforms] without the jurisdictional
discussion. Absolutely not.[105]

[Justice] Gudiño did not have a predetermined idea. We worked with
him (*lo acompañamos*) in the process with information. He debated with
us. He did not share with us what his vote would be. The technical slant
enlightened everything.[106]

For justices like Valls and Franco, the jurisdictional argument
weighed a lot. Their positions were not clear. And their positions, like
Cordero's, changed over time. Silva also opened up over the years.[107]

Importantly, even some liberal justices' votes were not as clear as assumed.
This was the case for Justice Silva, the most liberal justice on the bench, as
recounted by a key law clerk in his chamber: "The justice was undecided. We
presented to him all the arguments. Silva was a liberal, but a 'state lawyer.'

He liked the jurisdictional argument. It worked because of the argument. He was open-minded. Respectful. He would bounce back arguments. We held various discussions. There were six men and two women in the chamber. We discussed various issues. We held four months of discussions. Our report was 150 pages long. The right to abortion was part of the discussions. We studied other cases, such as Germany."[108]

Further, it must be underlined that even Justice Cossío's vote, the one from the strategic justice, might not have been cast in favor of decriminalizing abortion if not for the jurisdictional argument. As one justice stated, "[Cossío] made clear to us that it would not work (*no salía*) without the jurisdictional angle (*lo competencial*)."[109]

The Final Draft Opinion

The last stage in the elaboration of the ruling, the *engrose*, appears to have been a complex one. The final ruling, issued on February 26, 2009, was highly controversial. When the justices decided to vote during the last session of the public discussions, they voted in the abstract and without a new, formal draft opinion that garnered support from a majority of justices. As a result, Justice Cossío, who had been tasked with preparing the final document, had to collect the arguments advanced by the justices to produce the court's final position. But that did not happen. In the months following the plenary sessions, law clerks from the eight chambers that would contribute to a majority opinion held a series of meetings. Interviews reveal that these meetings were difficult and did not produce a consensus. The core of the problem was that Justice Cossío, following his strategy, wanted to center the jurisdictional argument. The other justices disagreed. Recall that, while they had agreed to support that argument, they also advanced a series of sub-arguments during the deliberations, such as the importance of women's rights. All seven of the justices wanted to include these sub-arguments in the final document. Justice Cossío disagreed and insisted on keeping the jurisdictional argument central. The result was a final opinion that focused on Cossío's jurisdictional argument as the guiding one, with seven concurrent opinions. As recounted by several individuals at the court:

> We held some five to ten sessions after the plenary sessions. But there were a lot of bashings (*madrazos*). We would tell them [Cossío's chamber], we did not write that, and we wrote that, and you are not including it. Very few people talk about the last stage of the process, the *engrose*. Procedurally it was a total aberration. The meetings were intense. There

were blows. Bashings. The system is actually quite baroque. It has an impact on the rulings because it weakens their reach. It was a very complicated process, and Cossío's chamber would not back down.[110]

The *engrose* was a nightmare. It was very complicated. They underestimated all of us. I remember telling [one of Cossío's law clerks], "No way (*no manches*)." It was very difficult until the justice [Gudiño] instructed me to tell them that enough was enough. There was no congruence until we said, "Fine, have it your way." The document does not reflect everyone's opinions. We had a Frankenstein. And we understood that it was the only way to do it. There were many ways of doing it. It was very uncomfortable. [Name withheld] said, "I will leave it as is because of the votes." It is clear that the result [would have] been different had another law clerk been in charge. He depurated the document and relied on formalism. We held various meetings, and nobody was happy. We told him that he could not put words in other people's mouths, and he said that it had to be technically tidy. It was difficult to know who in that chamber was leading the discussion: Cossío or the law clerk. He said something that hurt us a lot: "We cannot throw a bone to women." If I had overseen the process, it would not have been the same. But at the beginning, we agreed that they should be in charge of the process because they were highly respected, and they were technically very good. But we felt betrayed.[111]

The intense meetings subsequently came to a head. Members of Cossío's chamber held an emergency meeting with the chief justice asking him to bring the process to an end, as there would be no consensus. As Justice Cossío's is known to have said: "They asked me to put this or that there or that they would present a concurrent opinion. It was a difficult process. I told [Chief Justice] Ortiz Mayagoitia that it would not work. I had to do a sort of emendation (*enmendado*)."[112] Cossío insisted on keeping the jurisdictional argument as the basis of the final opinion, even as the process was called to a close by the chief justice. The result was a majority opinion of one vote with seven concurrent opinions. The seven justices presented some of the subsidiary arguments they had advanced during the plenary sessions, beyond Cossío jurisdictional argument. Interviews reveal that the process was divisive. In fact, one of Cossío's law clerks, now a well-known professor of law in Mexico, quit because of how the process unfolded.

The final majority opinion, in keeping with Cossío's strategy, was short and rather barren. It presented three bases to uphold the constitutionality of the reforms: that Mexico City had the jurisdictional power to legislate on health and criminal policy; that there was no absolute right to life enshrined in the constitution; and that the penalties for abortions after twelve weeks were appropriate. Importantly, there are no references at all to women's rights—the issue that had generated intense responses from some justices. Women's voices were suppressed in the final document, despite the protracted nature of the process, which involved the largest number of public consultations the court had ever held and input from numerous women's groups. Anecdotally, a law clerk for Justice Valls recounted: "I entered the elevator after we held one of our final meetings. Justice Sánchez Cordero entered after me. She told me: 'We lost. Women lost. They won.'"[113] Even after the constitutionality of the reforms had been confirmed, Justice Cossío and his team decided to keep the argument on a jurisdictional dimension, framed around the concept of the "freedom of legislative configuration" (*La libre configuración legislativa*): the freedom of subnational governments to criminalize behavior. According to a member of Cossío's chamber, "We did it [draft the *engrose*] as a courtesy, but also because we wanted to maintain a balance. We had [Walter F.] Murphy's work in mind. We tried to maintain a balance but had in mind that we could not come across as having been influenced by women's movements. It is difficult at times because you cannot create too much fragmentation. You will need their votes later. We were constrained during the entire process and that included the *engrose*."[114]

Interestingly, all seven of the concurrent opinions explicitly stated that they disagreed with the *engrose*, indicating that it did not capture the spirit of the discussions the justices held during the plenary sessions. They then asserted a variety of alternative bases, beyond jurisdiction, to uphold Mexico City's reforms as constitutional.[115]

Justices Aguirre, Azuela, and Ortiz Mayagoitia presented a dissenting opinion that captured the main arguments presented by Aguirre in the first draft opinion. The dissenting opinion held that the reforms were unconstitutional because they violated the right to life as implicitly recognized in the constitution. The opinion asserted that the right to life was absolute and included life from the time of conception. It further held that the legislator could not place limits on life.

The ruling thus made Mexico City one of the first jurisdictions in Latin America to decriminalize abortion during the first twelve weeks of pregnancy. A historic event, to be sure. However, the battle for, and against, the criminalization of abortion in Mexico continued after February 29, 2009.

Post-2009 Abortion Politics

Perhaps expectedly, and similarly to the Argentine and Colombian cases, the 2008 landmark ruling by the Mexican Supreme Court sparked a backlash by conservative forces. Given the particularities of Mexican federalism, the backlash played out along jurisdictional lines. Following the ruling, sixteen Mexican states reformed their constitutions to enshrine the right to life since conception (Chihuahua had done so in 1994). In many instances, the reforms extended explicit rights to the embryo until birth. Nevertheless, two of these reforms were subsequently challenged. In January 2009, the president of the Human Rights Commission of Baja California submitted an action of constitutionality against the state's reform to the Supreme Court (AI 11–2009). Nine months later, the opposition legislative minority of the state of San Luis Potosí submitted a similar challenge (AI 62–2009).

Remarkably, José Franco, a justice who, we may recall, was one of the wavering justices during the discussions around the 2008 decision, developed two separate draft decisions declaring the unconstitutionality of the reforms. More remarkably, Franco penned the draft decisions that moved away from a jurisdictional logic and developed arguments based on women's rights. Franco relied on a proportionality test to balance the rights of women with those of the unborn. It argued that the rights of the unborn were not absolute and had to be balanced with women's rights to dignity, health, and reproductive freedom. Finally, it argued that subnational legislatures had the jurisdictional prerogative to extend rights already established in the national constitutional, but not the authority to create new rights.

Nevertheless, going against tradition, Justice Franco decided not to hear the two cases together in what appears to have been an effort to gain a majority of votes in at least one case in an attempt to establish jurisprudence on abortion beyond jurisdictional issues. Strategically, Justice Franco argued that there was an important difference between the two reforms; consequently, they had to be analyzed separately: whereas reforms in one state (Baja California) did not establish an absolute prohibition of abortion, the other state (San Luis Potosí) did. During the live discussion around the latter case, Justice Franco argued that the absolute prohibition of abortion (Article 16 of the state's constitution) annulled the ability of the state's legislators to discharge its lawmaking duties freely, thereby violating the constitution. Interviews with justices and law clerks suggest that the last line of argumentation was intended to win the votes of justices, such as Margarita Luna, who, as you may recall, supported upholding the constitutionality of the Mexico City reforms on similar grounds.

The two draft decisions did not reach the necessary eight-vote majority to declare the reforms unconstitutional. In both cases, four justices voted against Justice Franco's draft proposals and seven for them. Compared to the discussions leading up to the 2008 ruling, noteworthy are Franco's and Luna's positions. In 2008, both justices appear to have been swayed to vote for the constitutionality of the Mexico City reforms on jurisdictional grounds. This time around, Justice Franco decided to go beyond and embrace more substantive arguments based on human rights. It speaks to the change in policy preferences that some justices undergo while on the bench, as we have observed in this book. As for Luna, it appears that the jurisdictional argument deployed by Franco on the San Luis Potosí case may have been convincing, but she could not agree with the more substantive aspects of the ruling. In terms of the other justices who remained on the bench in 2011, they voted in the same direction as in 2008 (Aguilar, Cossío, Valls, Sánchez Cordero, Silva, Aguirre, and Ortiz Mayagoitia). In this case, one vote made the difference in restricting access to abortion at the subnational level in some jurisdictions.

The story, however, did not end there. The court decided to rule on additional cases concerning federal issues. In 2018, the court handed down two important rulings, also drafted by Justice Franco, that continued to set precedents on abortion. In two unanimous votes by the Second Chamber (which deals with administrative law), the court ruled that the delay and denial of access to abortion for a teenage girl and a young woman who had been victims of rape were unconstitutional. In the first case (AR 601–2017), the legal representatives of a teenage girl submitted an amparo in 2017 arguing that her constitutional right to an abortion, as established by the criminal code of Morelos State, had been violated. The girl sought the procedure at Cuernavaca's General Hospital. The institution's bioethics committee denied the procedure on the grounds that there were no indications that the girl's life was in danger, which was one of the conditions for an abortion to be permitted as set by the state's code. The court's Second Chamber ruled in April 2018 that the denial of abortion constituted a "grave violation" of human rights, given that the decision prolonged suffering resulting from the physical and emotional damage inherent in sexual violence. Interestingly, in this case, the court argued not only that the state's exceptions to abortion, as established by Article 119 of its criminal code, violated Article 1 of the federal constitution, which guarantees access to health, but it also declared the plaintiff to be a victim and, as such, subject to remedies as established by the federal Victims Law (*Ley General de Víctimas*).

In the second and similar case, a woman from the state of Oaxaca sought an abortion at Dr. Aurelio Valdivieso Hospital on the grounds that the state's legislation allowed for the procedure when the pregnancy is the result of rape. The hospital's administration denied the woman, Lizzet Frida Cruz Cruz, medical attention because the hospital staff was on strike, and it could only deal with emergencies. It declared that her case was not an emergency. Cruz Cruz submitted an amparo to a first-instance court in October 2016. That court subsequently asked the Supreme Court to hear the case (*Amparo en*

Revisión). The court acceded to the request and, on April 18, 2018, the Second Chamber handed down a similar ruling arguing that the denial of the procedure constituted a grave violation of human rights. It argued that abortion in her case was indeed an emergency; as such, it should have been prioritized with the hospital's staff strike. It further argued that delays in the provision of the service affected the victim's psychological and physical health and her personal and mental integrity. Similar to the other case, the Second Chamber ruled that the denial of the procedure made the plaintiff a victim and, as such, entitled to remedies established by the federal Victims Law.

Noteworthy in both cases is that the unanimous rulings not only declared violations of state legislation but also a violation of the right to health as established by Article 1 of the federal constitution. The rulings therefore began to set jurisprudence on abortion beyond jurisdictional delineations, thereby opening the door for more substantive rulings.[116]

While these two rulings left the door ajar, an important 2019 ruling by the court opened that door widely. The highly anticipated case took over five years to resolve. On September 23, 2013, a woman identified only by her first name, "Marissa," was informed by Mexico City's National Health Center (*Centro Médico Nacional*) that she was pregnant and that her pregnancy was high risk. She was later also informed that the fetus exhibited signs of Klinefelter syndrome (a condition that prevents individuals from fully developing genital organs during puberty). On November 6, Marissa formally requested an abortion, which was denied on the grounds that the fetus could become self-sufficient upon birth, despite the syndrome. The hospital further argued that access to abortion was not established by federal legislation and that, because the hospital belonged to the federal health system, it could not be performed. Marissa submitted an amparo to a federal court of first instance arguing that the denial of the procedure violated her right to achieve physical, mental, and integral health, as established by Article 1 of the constitution. The case worked itself through the system and, in November 2015, the Supreme Cort decided to hear the case.

The court's First Chamber ruled on the case over five years later (AR 1388/2015). In an important and unanimous ruling on May 15, 2019, the chamber handed down a decision that built on the reference made in the two previous cases to the constitutional right to health and, for the first time, included a gender perspective. The court ruled that the denial of abortion in this case violated the constitutional right to health. It argued that in making decisions, federal institutions must guarantee and prioritize individuals' right to the highest attainable health standards possible, and that included various aspects of health, such as physical, mental, and emotional health, as well as social well-being. Further, the court ruled that the restricted nature of statutes can complicate women's access to justice in abortion cases and that decision-makers must consider a gender perspective in investigating and adjudicating cases to avoid the historic discrimination women have suffered. It thus argued that the denial of such procedures, given that they only affect women, is intrinsically discriminatory. The ruling then clearly established for the first time that the denial of abortion when an individual's health is at risk is unconstitutional in Mexico.

The court built on its initial incursion into the application of a gender perspective in abortion cases in subsequent ones. On July 7, 2021, the First Chamber decided on another, similar case (438–2020). The parents of a disabled teenager in the state of Chiapas sought an abortion after the girl became pregnant after being raped. The hospital (*Hospital General de Tapachula*) refused the procedure because the girl was 23.4 weeks pregnant, and the state code allowed victims of sexual assault access to abortion only within 90 days. Upon the denial, the girl's parents challenged the decision by submitting an amparo to a court of first instance. Similar to the other case, this one worked its way through the system, and the Supreme Court decided to hear it. In its unanimous ruling, the court not only determined that the denial of the procedure was unconstitutional because it amounted to gender violence against the plaintiff, but it also began to apply an intersectional perspective, arguing that the plaintiff's socioeconomic status must also be considered. Importantly, it declared unconstitutional the 90-day provision of the Chiapas criminal code: "The temporal limitation on legal abortions resulting from rape constitute[s] an act of violence against women which violate[s] her rights to the free development of personality and mental health" (438–2020). The ruling picked up on its previous reasoning and argued that the historical disadvantages that women have suffered must be considered.

This jurisprudence set the stage for the more recent rulings on abortion by Mexico's Supreme Court. In 2021, the court became the first court in Latin America to declare that the criminalization of abortion at any point of a pregnancy is unconstitutional (148–2017). The ruling was the response to a constitutional challenge to the provisions in the recently reformed criminal code of Coahuila.

The challenge was submitted to the court on November 27, 2017, by Mexico's attorney general. The court agreed to hear the case two days later. The challenge argued that three provisions of the new code were unconstitutional. First, it included an aspect of criminal law that was only under the jurisdiction of the National Congress.[117] Second, the reforms to two articles (195 and 196) prohibiting abortions during the first trimester violated a woman's right to personal autonomy and reproductive health. Finally, the application of different penalties to those found guilty of committing sexual assault, whether inside or outside a relationship, violated the right to sexual integrity.

The court took over two years to decide the challenge. The draft decision was penned by Justice Luis María Aguilar, who succinctly proposed a simple question to his colleagues: Was it constitutional to apply a jail sentence to a woman who decides to terminate her pregnancy (and, should it be the case, the person that performs the procedure with her consent)? The question, he argued, was whether Articles 195 and 196 of the state's criminal code were unconstitutional, as the attorney general's challenge had argued.

The highly anticipated case was debated by the full bench over two days, September 6 and September 7, 2021. On the second day, the court decided *unanimously* that Article 196 of Coahuila state's criminal code was unconstitutional.[118] It argued that three main activities were constitutional: obtaining an abortion procedure; its support by specialists; and an abortion as a result of rape beyond twelve weeks of pregnancy.

The court argued that "the product of gestation" warrants protection and that such protection increases over time. However, it argued that it cannot ignore the right to reproductive freedom that women and gestating persons have. Importantly, in their discussions, the justices decided to extend their analysis and assess the constitutionality of articles that had not been challenged by the attorney general. They discussed Article 198, which penalized medical staff who practiced the procedure, and Article 199, which limited the application of exemptions (rape and forced insemination) to twelve weeks of pregnancy. The court struck down both articles. It also declared that the invalidity of these provisions was retroactive to the day the reforms were approved. Importantly, because the decision surpassed the necessary qualified majority of eight votes (see chapter 1), it has *erga omnes* effects across the Mexican judiciary; it forces all Mexican judges, federal and subnational, to follow the court's ruling. Based on that decision, judges across the country must consider unconstitutional provisions of any subnational criminal code that prohibits abortions completely.

The court's main argument was based on the right of gestating individuals to decide. Picking up on the need to weigh rights, it argued, rather precisely, that the right to decide does not nullify the right to life. Both have to be protected in a balanced way. Also building on the introduction of a gender lens, it further argued that discussions on the interruption of pregnancy must draw on a gender-identity perspective to include pregnant individuals beyond women and girls. Arguing that dignity is a necessary condition for the enjoyment of other rights, it declared that gestating individuals must enjoy the right to bodily autonomy and must be able to build their identity autonomously.

It is important, the court argued, for gestating people to build their life projects based on individual decisions. According to the court, the state cannot decide when it is right to stop a pregnancy because that invades personal privacy. Further, the ruling drew on its previous antidiscrimination perspective to argue that the state should eliminate discrimination and stereotypes that force people to reproduce.

The court built on the jurisprudence regarding the right to health and established that the state must provide all conditions for its full exercise. The decision draws on the 2007 ruling to argue that limits on abortions must be reasonable. Building on the proportionality test used in a previous ruling (438–2020), it made it applicable to the entire federal judiciary. The court also argued, relying on available official statistics, that the social context must be considered and established necessary conditions to guarantee sexual and reproductive health. It included an intersectional perspective to argue that rights protections must consider the social marginalization of gestating individuals.

At the end of the September 7 session, streamed live and followed by millions of Mexicans, Justice Aguilar summarized the various arguments that had been advanced by the bench and were to be included in the *engrose*. Before dismissing the session, Chief Justice Arturo Zaldívar, concluded the discussion by stating:

> And in this way, the matter is resolved definitively. Justices, today is a historic day for all Mexican women and gestating individuals. Today is a historic watershed moment for the rights of all Mexican women, especially for the most vulnerable. With this unanimous decision by the constitutional tribunal, we do not only invalidate the statues under discussion, but we establish a mandatory instruction (*criterio*) to all judges across the country. . . . From now, a new path starts, of liberty, of clarity, of dignity and respect to all gestating individuals, but especially women. Today is another step in their struggle for equality, for their dignity and for the full exercise of their rights (SCJN 2021, 67).

And in that way, the chief justice adjourned the meeting with a clear bang of his gavel, definitively settling the issue of abortion in Mexico. Nevertheless, while the ruling struck down Coahuila's criminal code and extended its reach to every subnational jurisdiction, activists decided not to wait until all Mexican states reformed their criminal codes to repeal provisions criminalizing abortion, even if they are a dead letter for all intents and purposes. Moreover, as the reader may recall, the federal criminal code also contained provisions criminalizing the procedure even if they were no longer enforceable. Following the 148–2017 ruling, feminist activists from the organization GIRE, in coordination with other organizations, mounted a strategic litigation campaign to ensure that all of these provisions, at the state and federal levels, be repealed. They began to submit amparos to challenge each of these codes using the exact same arguments that Justice Franco developed in 148–2017.

The court began to decide on these challenges in 2023. On August 30, 2023, the court's First Chamber struck down the criminal code of Aguascalientes State on the exact same grounds used in the Coahuila case and ordered Aguascalientes to repeal those provisions (AR 79–2023). It also explicitly ordered all state administrative and health authorities not to enforce the existing criminal code provisions. Less than two weeks later, on September 11, the chamber struck down the provisions of the federal criminal code (Articles 329 to 334) that prohibited the practice (267–2023). The court justified its decisions using the exact same argumentation: the criminalization of abortion is contrary to the right to reproductive freedom and individuals' right to decide. It relied on more than two decades of its own jurisprudence to justify these decisions.

The landmark 2008 ruling was a foundational pillar of this process.

Conclusion

The 2008 ruling marked a historic moment for reproductive rights in Mexico. It made Mexico City the first jurisdiction to decriminalize access to first-trimester abortions with no restrictions. Women in Mexico City earned the right to become full citizens as the historic "legal penalty" that (mostly) men had applied to women for exercising full bodily autonomy was finally removed. As this chapter has shown, the ruling resulted from the strategic deployment of a procedural argument that helped convince undecided justices to uphold the constitutionality of the Mexico City reforms. As shown, a group made up of one justice and a handful of law clerks accurately assessed that a jurisdictional argument would be the safest way to assemble the largest number of votes. The group assembled these votes by being keenly aware of the internal dynamics on the bench and the external dynamics of the political context. These constraints convinced the strategic actors to pursue a narrow line of argumentation that did not push for a broader expansion of sexual and reproductive rights but nonetheless reasserted women's rights, as enshrined in the constitution.

Chapter 6

Costa Rica

Absence of Strategy and Policy Stasis

Introduction

This chapter shows that the 2007 *A.N.* decision (2000–07958, *V.N.R. v. Hospital México*) by the Costa Rican Constitutional Chamber (*Sala Constitucional*, CRCC) to reject the constitutional challenge (*amparo*) on access to abortion was primarily the result of stern opposition expressed by some men justices on the bench, particularly Justice Fernando Cruz Castro. As the case of the pregnant teenager whose therapeutic abortion had been denied reached the chamber, Castro argued that the right to life was enshrined in the Costa Rican constitution—and that included the unborn. While acknowledging the potential health risks the pregnancy posed to the girl, the majority of justices (five) agreed that the chamber could not even hear the case because the backlash, they argued, especially from deputies in the Legislative Assembly, would be too strong. As Castro declared, the chamber "could not be seen as pro-abortion" (*abortista*). The two women justices, Ana Virginia Calzada Miranda and Rosa María Abdelnour Granados, dissented. In their minority opinion, the justices argued that the chamber should require additional information before deciding not to hear that case. The analysis in this chapter demonstrates the impossibility of Calzada and Abdelnour to act strategically given the opposition they faced on the bench. Calzada, who penned the minority opinion, could have forced a discussion as only one vote is necessary to hear a case. However, she decided not to because the political costs could have been too high had she acted alone.

The chapter has two sections. The first one looks at the composition of the 2007 bench that decided the judicial decision under study. Unlike the other three cases in this book, the analysis reveals the absence of strategic leadership willing to push for the expansion of reproductive rights. The second section analyzes the process that led to the nondecision.

The Appointment Process and the 2007 Bench

The Legislative Assembly and the Appointment Process

Unlike most presidential systems, as detailed in chapter 1, in Costa Rica, the National Assembly is solely responsible for nominating the seven permanent justices of the CRCC. The executive can attempt to have a preferred candidate selected through party deputies in the legislature, but it does not play a direct role in the process. Permanent justices are confirmed for renewable eight-year terms with a two-thirds majority of the fifty-seven deputies (since 2003). The appointment process in Costa Rica is therefore squarely political. A 1999 reform to the assembly's internal regulations established a permanent commission in charge of appointments (*Comisión Permanente Especial de Nombramientos*, CPEN) to professionalize the process. The commission must issue a call for application submissions in the country's main national newspapers and then select candidates for a short list, which is then presented to the assembly's plenary for voting.[1] Through a rather elaborate system, candidates are eliminated in six rounds of voting until one candidate obtains the required thirty-eight votes to be confirmed. Substitute justices are nominated by the Supreme Court. It proposes two candidates for each vacancy.

As in the other cases we have covered, the appointment system can shape the profiles of justices confirmed to the constitutional tribunal as well as their behavior. In the case of Costa Rica, the confirmation of justices was, until the early 2000s, essentially controlled by the two main parties that governed the country for decades: the dominant (center-left) National Liberation Party (*Partido de Liberación Nacional*, PLN) and an opposition party, which since 1983 became the (center-right) Social Christian Unity Party (*Partido Unidad Social Cristiana*, PUSC). However, adhering to a regional pattern, Costa Rica's stable two-party system came to an end in the late 1990s as a result of a broad process of political realignment and fragmentation. In the context of the global shift to market-friendly economics, the PLN shifted from its historic social-democratic position to a more economically liberal stance during the early 1980s and early 1990s (Raventós Vorst and Ramírez Moreira 2006). The party's rightward slide left a void on the left of the spectrum, thereby providing an opportunity for the emergence of new leftist parties. It also blurred the ideological lines between the PLN and the PUSC, weakening the latter. The space vacated by the PLN was progressively occupied by a new party, the Citizens' Action Party (*Partido Acción Ciudadana*, PAC). This ideological reorganization induced a realignment of the electorate, with some voters withdrawing support from the two traditionally dominant parties and redirecting it to smaller ones (Carreras 2012). The process accelerated as support for these parties continued to decrease. The PUSC saw its support evaporate as two former presidents from the party were convicted of corrupt dealings, damaging the party irreversibly (Booth 2020). For its part, the PLN's continued commitment to economic liberalism, exemplified by its push for a free trade agreement with the United States and Central America, cost it support, much of which shifted to PAC, which strengthened considerably: it came within 1.1 percent of winning the presidency in the second round of the 2006 elections. Costa Rica's partisan duopoly thus unraveled as both parties' combined share of the vote decreased steadily: from 97.4 percent in 1994 for presidential elections, to 80.6 percent in 2002 and 60.3 percent in 2014; and from 92.98 percent for the legislative elections in 1994 to 63.16 percent and 49.19 percent, respectively (Cascante Matamoros and Lara Escalante 2021).

The other element is political fragmentation. While the electorate has exhibited some disaffection with politics, it did not result in political dealignment, as abstentionism did not see a significant decline.[2] Rather, voters have shifted their support to smaller parties as they have maintained electoral engagement. The number of political parties has thus progressively increased, and the duopoly that the two main parties had in the Legislative Assembly effectively ended in 1998, when neither party won a majority of votes. The two main parties' legislative representation decreased further in 2002 with the incursion of PAC and an increase in seats for the Liberty Movement (*Partido Movimiento Libertario*), which elected a combined number of twenty-two seats.

These changes have influenced the appointment process and seem to have affected judicial behavior in complex and unpredictable ways. Prior to the end of the two-party rule, the two main parties engaged in negotiations to support candidates to fill vacancies in the CRCC (Muñoz Portillo 2014, 17–18) through what a justice described as a kind of informal quota system whereby the two parties took turns confirming their preferred candidates for the Supreme Court.[3] In effect, during the first decade of the CRCC's functioning, most justices could be easily identified with one of the two main political parties. The end of the two-party system, along with the required two-thirds majority vote for confirmation, meant that negotiations among parties broadened to include the preferences of smaller parties, especially PAC. Indeed, the time to confirm justices began to increase in the mid-2000s (Muñoz Portillo 2014). One of the effects has been that newly confirmed justices began to exhibit stronger judicial and professional credentials as more qualified candidates are more likely to obtain multiparty support (*Estado de la Nación* 2015; Cascante Matamoros and Camacho Sánchez 2019). A more fragmented parliament has also meant that voting patterns at the CRCC have become less unanimous. Because justices tend to adopt a deferential position toward the assembly (chapter 1), a more fractured parliament appears to have applied pressure to split votes as justices seem to respond to an increased plurality of political positions in the legislature. Indeed, research on voting patterns on constitutional challenges (*Acciones de Inconstitucionalidad*, AI) at the CRCC shows some clear trends: from 2005 to 2015,[4] the number of unanimous votes

(7–0) on admitted cases decreased from 80 percent to 48 percent (*Estado de la Nación* 2015, 211–12).

While one would expect that increased dissension on the bench would be associated with wider and clearer ideological divides, that does not seem the case. The data presented by the same study do not appear to allow one to discern clear ideological profiles among the justices. In general terms, the analysis suggests that there are areas where there tends to be more agreement among the justices. For example, unanimous voting tends to be higher in taxation cases (79 percent), environmental cases (64 percent), and criminal cases (65 percent). A more divided bench appears to emerge in areas related to collective bargaining and electoral issues. One of the main conclusions from a study on judicial behavior is that "there do not exist coalitions [among justices] that would go beyond particular cases and that would allow [one] to predict voting based on recognizable political and judicial philosophies" (*Estado de la Nación* 2015, 223). In terms of social issues, specifically those related to "religious" issues in Costa Rica (which include sexual and reproductive rights), there seem to be some divisions—although the bench appears to lean generally toward the conservative side. What we have, then, is a constitutional tribunal in which there seems to be a consensus in some areas, such as voting in favor of amparos on socioeconomic issues (i.e., medicines), and high levels of agreement on other issues, such as taxation, the environment, and "religious" issues. Ideologically, it would be fair to say that it leans to the progressive side on some issues (the environment) and to the conservative side on others (moral issues). Based on 100 salient rulings during the 2000s, an analyst captured voting at the CRCC rather well: "If the Constitutional Chamber was a person, it would reason conservatively in debates that involve religion, it would endorse free trade, it would have its eyes attentive to assess collective agreement cases, and it would have changed its mind on presidential re-election. On the environment, it would show a marked inclination toward the protection of ecosystems, but, at least in the cases it has dealt with, its recent reasoning endorsing mining [in the *Crucitas* case], it would make it lose some of the green image it had. It would even cause surprise" (Fernández Sanabría 2010, 5).

The CRCC's multiple personae (mostly independent and active in some areas, yet timid and socially conservative in others) appear to heighten in relation to sexual and reproductive rights. When asked why the chamber tends to lean conservative on moral issues, justices and law clerks responded this way:

It has changed. It has been a process. During the 1990s, after justices were well placed, justices had been very conservative, but things start to change with justices with more autonomy, such as [Justice Luis Paulino] Mora Mora. The chamber gains some autonomy. That is very traumatic for the system. It is a *chichicaste*. This awakens the political class, and they logically decide, "We have to get our hands in there." From then on, in 1999, the appointment process is guided by one intention: do not touch those issues. They are to be dealt with by the assembly. And there is of course the religious component—it plays a role. Yes, there is a consensus that we are in favor of social rights, but there is also a consensus against sexual and reproductive rights. That is up to the assembly to decide.[5]

Yes, the chamber is conservative on those issues. It is the white elephant in meetings. It has never been mentioned, but it is always present. We are not robots. We decide according to our life experiences. We know not to go there. The backlash from parliament would be too strong. We agree not to go there.[6]

There exists a consensus beyond partisanship (*partidismo*) that we do not touch those issues (*no se tratan*). It is a reflection of a sanctimonious society (*sociedad mojigata*). Those are taboo topics. The court responds to society. Justices are extremely cautious with subjects that are not politically accepted.[7]

With these general traits, patterns, and insights in mind, we can now turn to the individual profiles of the justices who decided the *A.N.* case.

The 2007 Bench

Out of the four case studies I cover in this book, Costa Rica's constitutional tribunal is the only one in which substitute justices can sit on the bench when a permanent justice is unable to attend a voting session. This institutional feature adds specificity to the bench and forces researchers to approach analyses of judicial behavior with caution, especially in a ruling such as *A.N.* The case appears to be unusual because, generally, landmark cases in Costa Rica's Constitutional Chamber tend to be decided by the full bench of permanent justices. While there have been times in which landmark decisions are decided by a bench that included one substitute justice, the *A.N.* amparo decision was made by an unusually high number of substitute justices: three. One of the challenges in studying substitute justices is developing profiles based on voting patterns, given that their interventions are irregular. However, interviews with justices (both permanent and substitute) suggest that the substitute justices are deferential to the permanent ones. As stated:

> Substitute justices cannot change the direction of the vote. If one tries, they can move the session to another day. They are there to support what

is decided. They are very vulnerable because they are reelected every four years. There is actually only one of them right now with expertise in constitutional law. . . . Substitute justices are threatened with a scandal should they not vote with the majority.[8]

We are told how to vote. We have to go with the majority. We are subject to political pressure from the assembly and the court because we have to be reelected every four years, and we want to be reappointed. We come in when we are called in. Many of the decisions are already written up when we come to vote. Most substitute justices just go with it. The system is pyramidal. We are essentially told how to vote, and law clerks are nobodies.[9]

We [substitute justices] do not have much latitude in deciding. We are told how to vote. There is a lot of pressure from the assembly because we are reelected every four years. We are subject to political pressure. We only come in when called, given our turn on the list, and we have to go with the majority. It really is rare that we vote against. The system is very pyramidal. We go with the flow.[10]

This all suggests that the analysis of the decision behind *A.N.* must center mostly around the four permanent justices present.

One of these four permanent justices was the most senior member on the 2007 bench: Luis Paulino Mora Mora (1989–2013). Mora Mora was appointed to the CRCC's first bench upon its establishment in 1989 (and reelected in 1997 and 2005). Mora Mora was a well-known jurist, academic, and politician in Costa Rica. As with many prominent lawyers, including the other three permanent justices on the 2007 bench, he gained his law degree from the prestigious University of Costa Rica (*Universidad de Costa Rica*), in the country's capital, San José, specializing in criminal law. He subsequently pursued a doctorate in law from Madrid's Complutense University. After having served as a judge in criminal tribunals in various parts of the country, Mora Mora was confirmed to the Third Chamber of the Supreme Court in 1983 before serving as minister of justice during the first administration of Óscar Arias Sánchez, from 1986 until 1989. He therefore had direct links with the PLN. Interviews at the CRCC paint a picture of a hardworking, formalist justice who was difficult to classify ideologically. While he served for Arias and his candidacy to the CRCC was supported by the PLN leadership, he maintained an important degree of autonomy, having voted against the presidential reelection in 2001 and 2003 (even though Arias had been behind the movement). Based on his voting record, Mora Mora, a self-professed Catholic, can be identified as having been conservative on moral issues and more progressive on others, such as criminal cases and free trade. For example, he joined the majority in a case (2007–09469) declaring the Central American Free Trade Agreement (CAFTA) between Central American countries, the Dominican Republic, and the United States constitutional, yet he also joined the majority in the case (2000–02306) concerning in vitro fertilization (IVF).[11]

This IVF case is an important one for our purposes. After five years of deliberations, the CRCC declared a decree passed in 1995 by the Ministry of Health that allowed and regulated IVF to be unconstitutional. The decision was in response to an AI submitted by the legal counsel for the country's Catholic Bishop Conference, Hermes Navarro del Valle. He argued before the chamber that the decree violated the right to life of embryos discarded during the procedure. The CRCC, in a 5–2 ruling, agreed with the challenge and declared that life begins at conception, that the embryo has "personhood" status (subject of rights), that it is a human right according to Costa Rica's constitution, and that any surplus of embryos from IVF procedures violated life. This ruling marked a roadmap for discussions on sexual and reproductive rights in subsequent years, as we shall see below.[12] Justice Mora Mora consistently adopted a conservative position on these cases: he voted against IVF and voted conservatively on the first decision on abortion (2004–2792) to reach the chamber (discussed below), as well as on other "religious" cases, such as the 2004–8763 decision.[13] They clearly placed him on the conservative side of the bench. In terms of legislative-judicial relations, Mora Mora had a mixed position. While he sided with the majority's position that the chamber had the prerogative to decide on collective-bargaining cases, he also declared, "I recognize that the Chamber has too many prerogatives, especially in relation to the Assembly, where oftentimes justices have to get involved in political issues that should not be in their action field" (cited in Cascante Segura 2017, 45).

The second justice belonging to the 2007 bench, and the chamber's acting chief justice (*Presidenta*) at the time,[14] was Ana Virginia Calzada Miranda (1993–2013). Justice Calzada was the first woman appointed to the CRCC in 1993. She was reelected in 2001. Calzada, from a well-heeled family in Costa Rica, had clear connections to the PUSC. Her candidacy was strongly endorsed by the party, and her ex-husband (Bernardo Aragón) was a deputy in the assembly. As with the majority of justices, Calzada earned a degree in law from the University of Costa Rica, specializing in family law. She then pursued a doctorate in law at Alicante University in Spain. The justice worked in many lower courts and provincial tribunals before her confirmation by the assembly. She also taught law part-time at several universities. An evangelical, Calzada was often identified by her peers in interviews as being religious and conservative, at times referencing the Bible. On moral policy issues, Calzada publicly made it clear that, given the divisiveness in society, she believed in judicial restraint and preferred that the legislature make those decisions (*Semanario Universidad*, May 30, 2012). Nevertheless, despite her partisan links to the PUSC and her perceived ideological position within the CRCC, Calzada's profile is also difficult to categorize ideologically based on her voting record during the 2000s. In terms of free trade, for example, Calzada voted in favor of CAFTA, but she also voted against some of its implementation statutes, citing procedural anomalies. On the environmental front, Justice Calzada voted regularly with the majority in favor of environmental protection but also supported the constitutionality of the Crucitas case. Unlike Mora Mora, Justice Calzada deferred to the legislature on collective bargaining, arguing that it was not up to the chamber to decide in the area. Yet, she also voted against the presidential reelection in 2000 and 2003 on the grounds that the legislature could not take away basic rights enshrined in the constitution, as it did in the 1969 reform, and that such change would require broader constitutional reform. Calzada took a clear position in both cases despite the potential political backlash from PLN leadership in particular. In effect, her votes on both occasions made it harder for her to be automatically reconfirmed in 2009 (Muñoz Portillo 2014, 54).

Justice Calzada's views on religious issues were somewhat clearer, having adopted a dissenting position in some cases that diverged from the conservative majority. She showed support for gender equality before the debates on abortion reached the CRCC. In an important yet somewhat unknown ruling (0716–1998), she penned a decision, ultimately joined by her all-men colleagues, in which she agreed with an amparo submitted by a woman deputy who had argued discrimination by the other two branches of government for not having appointed any women to the board of directors of Costa Rica's Public Administration Regulator (*Autoridad Reguladora de los Servicios Públicos*). In a clearly crafted decision, Justice Calzada agreed that the designation of an all-men board violated the principles of equality and nondiscrimination found in the constitution and statutes. While arguing for institutional stability, the ruling did not order a new makeup for the board; instead, it ordered remedies and compensation to the plaintiff. In the landmark IVF case, Calzada led the minority (2–5) in arguing for the constitutionality of the procedure. While taking a somewhat conservative tack to her logic based on the principle of "life," Justice Calzada argued that the right to life is protected when proper measures are adopted and that IVF does not violate "the right to life or human dignity, but, on the contrary, it is a tool that science has placed in the hands of people so that they exercise their reproductive rights and the rights to establish a family, values that are protected in our

Democratic Legal State." Calzada also led the 2–5 minority in the 2004–08763 decision on the automatic legal recognition of marriages performed by Catholic priests. On abortion, Calzada was absent for the first abortion decision (2004–2792) and, as we shall see in the following section, took a timid minority position on the *A.N.* case.

The third permanent member of the bench was Gilbert Armijo Sancho (2002–15). As with the previous two justices, Armijo earned his law degree from the University of Costa Rica, specializing in criminal law, and a doctoral degree at Carlos III University in Spain. Armijo was the justice with the lowest political profile. While interviews reveal that he had ties to the PLN, he did not occupy any political positions before his confirmation; his trajectory was solely in the judiciary. Justice Armijo is also recognized in legal circles in Costa Rica for his esteemed profile as a jurist and academic. He taught law at the University of Costa Rica and received prestigious awards for his publications.[15] Having served in various positions within the judiciary across the country, Armijo was confirmed as a substitute justice at the Supreme Court before his confirmation in 2002 as a justice at the CRCC. Replacing a highly conservative justice (Rodolfo Piza Escalante), Armijo was seen as the first consensual candidate within the context of political party fragmentation described earlier. He was the first candidate recommended unanimously by the CPEN (out of eighteen) to the assembly's plenary, and his confirmation obtained multiparty support on the floor. The strong support was widely seen as being due to his apolitical trajectory (*La Nación*, April 4, 2002), a sentiment captured in a support letter his candidacy received from the National Union of Judicial Employees (*Asociación Nacional de Empleados Judiciales*). A Catholic who belongs to the conservative Opus Dei, Justice Armijo can be described as mostly leaning to the conservative side. Yet his voting record on landmark decisions is mixed at best.

As the most active opinion writer on the bench, Justice Armijo was a consistent dissenter on certain issues with Justice Cruz Castro (2004–23). According to the study cited previously (Cascante Segura 2017, 21), both justices joined forces on the 2007 bench more than any others: 76.2 percent of the time. On environmental issues, the justice was often referred to by interviewees as the "greenest" justice at the chamber. In the Crucitas case, he was the only dissenting voice, agreeing with all the main arguments presented by the plaintiffs, and in a dissenting opinion, he ruled that the mining project was unconstitutional. Justice Armijo regularly joined Cruz Castro on economic issues; they both cast minority opinions arguing for the unconstitutionality of CAFTA based on content and process. In terms of the appropriate role of the CRCC, Armijo joined colleagues who believed that the chamber should not get involved in deciding collective-bargaining cases. Armijo also belonged to the conservative majority on religious issues: while he was not yet at the chamber during the IVF case, he voted with the majority on the first abortion case and on the case related to marriages officiated by Catholic priests.

The fourth member of the bench that decided the amparo case on abortion was Cruz Castro, perhaps the most easily recognizable high-court justice in Costa Rica. Cruz Castro, like the other three permanent justices, earned his law degree from the University of Costa Rica, specializing in criminal law, after completing a bachelor's degree in political science. He subsequently earned a Doctor of Law at Madrid's Complutense University. Like Mora Mora, Justice Cruz Castro had a long career in both the judiciary and politics. Cruz Castro served as a judge in various courts (mostly criminal) and as a public prosecutor before his confirmation in 2004. He also had a distinguished career in academia, having published a substantial body of award-winning scholarly work.[16] As a member of the PLN, Cruz Castro also served as a politician during the 1980s in various positions, including in the Office of the Public Prosecutor (*Ministerio Público*) and on investigative parliamentary committees. Cruz Castro's candidacy for the CRCC was supported by the PLN leadership, especially by then-deputy Laura Chinchilla.[17] He also obtained multiparty support. Part of the more vocal student movement in Costa Rica during the late 1960s, Cruz Castro has identified himself politically as belonging to a "Christian" and "Social Democratic" left-of-center vein (*Delfino*, March 13, 2018) and was generally perceived in the halls of the chamber as the most liberal justice on the bench.

An affable person well-liked by his peers, Cruz Castro's self-proclaimed liberalism does not appear to have always influenced his votes. As mentioned, Cruz Castro often sided with Justice Armijo on the 2007 bench, and they both adopted positions that were pro-environment and against free trade. However, in the Crucitas case, Cruz Castro voted with the majority in allowing the project to continue, but he cast a dissenting opinion expressing concerns about potential environmental damage. On trade, he joined Armijo in the 2–5 minority on the CAFTA case, arguing that the process contained numerous problems, and he was against the constitutionality of the treaty. The justice was not at the chamber during the two reelection decisions. In terms of judicial-legislative relations, Cruz Castro consistently argued for the court to get involved in collective-bargaining issues. On religious issues, Cruz Castro had not arrived at the court when the IVF and the first abortion case were decided, but he voted in favor of the constitutionality of the case on Catholic marriages and subsequently voted consistently against same-sex relationship rights.

The three other permanent justices who belonged to the CRCC in 2007 were Luis Fernando Solano Carrera (1997–2008), Ernesto Jinesta Lobo (2002–18), and Adrián Vargas Benavides (1996–2010). As mentioned, the three justices did not participate in the *A.N.* decision. In their places, the three substitute justices were Rosa María Mayela de los Angeles Abdlenour Granados (2003–17), Max Alberto Esquivel Faerrón (2005–7), and Jorge Arturo de Jesús Araya García (2005–13). Also as mentioned, it is difficult to establish a profile of substitute justices given their irregular voting patterns (as they are called in to vote only when permanent justices are unable to do so) and limited available information. Indeed, studies on voting patterns at the CRCC tend to exclude substitute justices (Cascante Segura 2017). However, based on available information and several interviews, it appears that Justice Abdelnour was on the conservative side of economic and social issues. As with most substitute justices nominated by the Supreme Court, Abdelnour had a more traditionalist approach to the law, reflecting her career in the judiciary. She, like most of her peers, graduated with a law degree from the University of Costa Rica, specializing in commercial and public law. She then earned a master's degree in education from a Mexican university (*Universidad Tecnológica de México*) and a doctorate in law from Navarra University in Spain. Before her confirmation as a substitute justice by the Legislative Assembly in 2003, Justice Abdelnour had extensive experience in the Costa Rican judiciary and academia, having first served as legal counsel for the Office of the Attorney General (*Ministerio Público*) in 1986. Interviews revealed that she had close ties to the PUSC and would take pro-life positions.

The second substitute justice was Esquivel. Confirmed to the bench in 2005, he only remained in the position for two years before being confirmed as permanent justice to the country's important Electoral Tribunal. Esquivel earned a law degree from the University of Costa Rica, specializing in administrative and public law, and subsequently a bachelor of arts in political science from the same institution. Known to be religious, though with ties to the PLN, Esquivel also leaned toward conservative views on social issues. Before his nomination by the Supreme Court, Justice Esquivel had held positions in the judiciary and academia: he held various positions at the University of Costa Rica, in the Faculty of Law and the Department of Political Science, and in the judiciary, mostly in the country's Ombudsman's Office (*Defensoría de los Habitantes de la República*).

The third substitute justice to have decided the case under analysis was Araya. Based on interviews, Justice Araya appears to have been ideologically the most conservative of the three substitute justices, and likely the most conservative of the 2007 bench, even if he had close ties to the PLN.[18] Justices and law clerks at the chamber would refer to Araya as being "very conservative," "strategic," and "reserved," with a tendency of keeping a "low profile." After earning a degree in journalism from the private conservative-leaning

Autonomous University of Central America (*Universidad Autónoma de Centro América*), Araya pursued law at the same institution. He then undertook a "specialization" (*certificate*) in constitutional law at the prestigious Center for Constitutional Studies (*Centro de Estudios Constitucionales*) in Madrid, before earning a Doctor of Law at one of Costa Rica's main and traditional law schools (*Universidad Escuela Libre de Derecho*). Before being confirmed by the assembly in 2005, Araya had a career in the judiciary, academia, and as a private litigator; he also held various political posts during PLN governments in the 1990s. He was a rarity among substitute justices in that he had received training in constitutional law. Despite his closeness with the PLN, his position on abortion was clear. When asked in an interview about it, he said: "What one does is to defend the Constitution and the international agreements that are very clear in not allowing abortion in an open or generalized manner, but only in the exceptions of therapeutic abortions" (*La Nación*, March 21, 2009).

Before proceeding with the analysis of the 2007 decision, it is worth highlighting two important aspects of the substitute justices and the 2007 bench. Among the substitute justices, interviews reveal a clear predisposition to defer to the permanent justices when voting. The second point is that there was no discernible strategic leader on the bench in the case of Costa Rica, whereas in the cases of Argentina, Colombia, and Mexico, also covered in this book, interviews revealed an important degree of admiration and deference to one particular justice (Justices Zaffaroni, Cepeda, and Cossío, respectively). As the next section details, Justices Mora Mora and Cruz Castro dominated the discussion of the case; however, justices (both permanent and substitute) and law clerks did not identify one member of the bench whose expertise or persona stood out from the others—reflecting, in a way, Costa Rica's egalitarian political culture. As explained by one substitute justice interviewed, "There is an ambience of community at the Constitutional Chamber, a desire to seek consensus, and there was no intellectual egotism or personal protagonism. [It is] very difficult for anyone on the bench to try to impose their ideas on others. It was a community."[19]

Deciding on Abortion: Absence of Strategy and Stasis

The Regulation of Abortion in Costa Rica

Abortion in post-1949 Costa Rica has been expressly regulated since reforms were made to the country's Criminal Code of 1970 (Articles 118 and 121). The code criminalized abortion as a "crime against life" except in cases called therapeutic abortions when the mother's life or health is in danger. Penalties range from six months to ten years in prison, depending on a combination of two factors: whether there was explicit consent by the woman or the individual who carries out the procedure (*aborto procurado*); and the "gestational life of the fetus or embryo" (Article 118). The code contains some rather obscure additional stipulations. It establishes that penalties can be lowered (to three months to two years) when the abortion is performed to "hide the dishonor of the woman" (Article 120) and allows for a "judicial pardon" when the abortion is performed when the pregnancy is the product of a consanguineous relationship (Article 93).

The regulation of abortion in Costa Rica has intersected in judicial debates with two other important provisions. The first is the concept of the "inviolability of life" established by Article 75 of the constitution. The second concept is personhood, which refers to a person with rights under the law. The civil code establishes that "the existence of a physical person begins at birth, and it is declared as being born (*se reputa nacida*) for all purposes that benefit it from 300 days before its birth" (Article 31). That is, the recognition of legal personhood is applied retroactively, going back to a point in time before pregnancy begins.

Nevertheless, while therapeutic abortions may be legal, observers have found a regular pattern of medical providers denying them (Morgan 2018). In the years leading up to the *A.N.* decision, there seems to have been a clear gap between the legal framework and reality on the ground. Between 2002 and 2006, a total of twenty-six legal abortions were performed, yet 10,000 women and girls seek an abortion every year in Costa Rica. Further, during the same period, 379 deaths were reported because of fetal malformations at birth (*La Nación*, June 16, 2011). These data point to limited access to abortion, despite the somewhat permissible legal framework.

One of the first challenges to the regulation of abortion came with the 1995 presidential decree on IVF. As we have seen, the decree temporarily altered the "inviolability" of life established in the constitution. It was restored by the 2000 ruling.

The second challenge came with the first decision (02792) on abortion to reach the chamber in 2004. In that case, a citizen brought an AI to the CRCC arguing that several articles in the criminal and civil codes were unconstitutional because they violated the principles of equality and the right to life enshrined in the constitution. The plaintiff developed an argument from a conservative angle around the inviolability of life established by the IVF ruling. He argued that the application of differentiated penalties to homicides and abortions violated principles of equality because in both cases life was affected in the same manner, given that the lives of the unborn and individuals had the same value. He further argued that the penalties should therefore be the same. The CRCC disagreed with the AI and declared the differentiated treatment of penalties in these cases to be constitutional. Importantly, like some of the debates that unfolded in the other three cases I have explored, the CRCC relied on the concepts of proportionality and reasonableness to develop its argumentation. In a decision penned by Justice Mora Mora, who was joined by five of his colleagues (including Justice Armijo and Justice Solano dissenting), the chamber argued that the challenged statutes were constitutional because, according to the civil code, the unborn is recognized as a person. However, the chamber also argued that it is completely feasible that, when dealing with life as a legally protected good (*bien jurídico*), circumstances may be considered to set penalties that can be applied proportionally, depending on the effect the crime has on society. It went on to suggest that it is constitutional to "differentiate between a born human being and a human being not yet born" because, even when in both cases we are dealing with human beings, they are in "clearly differentiated stages of life," both socially and medically. In addition, it goes on, there exists a situation of dependence between the unborn person and the mother's basic rights that must be taken into account (which is not the same as cases of homicide). Further, the differentiation of penalties must respond to the cultural environment, as established by Latin American and European norms. It also argued, citing its own jurisprudence (10543–2001), that it is up to the legislator to establish criminal policy, including appropriate penalties.

This ruling was extremely important for three central reasons. First, it upheld the chamber's jurisprudence on the constitutional right to life and the unborn's legal personhood from the moment of conception, an expressly conservative position. Second, it relied on the notion of "proportionality" to justify the differentiated application of penalties. As we have seen in the preceding chapters, the adoption of proportionality reasoning has been used by some justices in other constitutional tribunals to expand women's rights and to further liberalize abortion beyond the case at hand. This ruling provided an opportunity for justices in subsequent cases to use this newly opened door to liberalize abortion beyond what the legal framework permits, as was the case with Argentina's FAL decision. Finally, and continuing with the long tradition I sketched out in chapter 1, it included a clear deference to the legislator in the making of criminal policy. These points would be addressed three years later by the CRCC.

The A.N. (Non)Decision

The second case on abortion arrived at the CRCC on June 5, 2007. It refers to an amparo recourse submitted by M. R. C. on behalf of her daughter Ana (identified as V.N.R in the submitted form) against one of the three main public hospitals in San José, the country's capital city, the Hospital México, for having denied her a therapeutic abortion.

Ana had been suffering from recurring vomiting and bleeding episodes and sought medical help. During medical exams, an ultrasound revealed that she was six weeks pregnant. The fetus was diagnosed with occipital encephalocele, a medical condition that makes life outside the womb unviable. The fetus's condition was confirmed by subsequent testing, and the pregnancy was declared "high risk." The diagnosis caused Ana to develop severe depression. She sought a therapeutic abortion several times but was repeatedly denied it. Ana's condition deteriorated progressively until she had to be hospitalized three months later. Her depression was medically confirmed. She sought a therapeutic abortion one last time at the Hospital México, which was again denied, and the hospital released her on May 28, 2007, on the advice of lawyers representing the National Social Security System (*Caja Costarricense de Seguro Social*). Throughout the process, Ana and her mother are said to have been treated in a hostile manner by medical staff (Arroyo Navarrete 2018, 45).

Ana's mother submitted the amparo claiming that the denial of abortion was based not on medical grounds but on other criteria. The amparo argued that the unviability of the pregnancy had been medically established, but the denial was being based on other grounds—namely, fear of social backlash and criminal repercussions if the abortion was carried out. It therefore argued that Ana's right to health and life, as established by Article 21 of the constitution, had been violated because she had developed suicidal tendencies.

The chamber's decision in the *A.N.* case was made in a remarkably fast forty-eight hours. After Ana's mother submitted the file on June 5, 2007, and conforming to the rules, the case was accepted by the Chamber Secretariat (*Secretaría de la Sala*). As stipulated by the Judiciary Act, files are then assessed by a triaging office (*mesa de direccionamiento*), which is made up of seven law clerks, one from each justice's chamber (*vocalías*). This office produces an original assessment (*análisis jurídico*) to gauge whether the case relates to a constitutional issue. If the assessment suggests that it does not, it is then declared rejected (*rechazado*) and taken to a vote. If it is considered admissible because it raises a constitutional matter, then the law clerks prepare a report indicating which constitutional rights have allegedly been violated. Files are assigned a file number. In this case, the file (number 07–007740–0007-CO) was assessed and then referred to the Office of the Chief Justice (*Presidente*), which, at that time, was occupied by Justice Calzada (she was acting chief justice). Importantly, for our purposes, the chief justice has the prerogative to accept the file for discussion (*darle curso*).

Justice Calzada's chamber (*vocalía*) did not decide, at this point, whether the case should be admitted (*darle admisibilidad*) for discussion; rather, it turned it over to Justice Cruz Castro's chamber, which was next in line to study the file, as files are allocated in turns to the other six chambers. Just as in the three other cases we have covered, the salience of the topic appears to have forced an irregular treatment of the file. Interviews reveal that given the high workload of amparo files that the CRCC receives, these cases are customarily distributed to informal antechambers (*mini-salas*) made up of law clerks from three justice chambers. They make decisions that are then briefly reviewed by law clerks from the remaining chambers. The issue can be discussed by the entire bench should any law clerk request it.

Importantly, the fact that the file was given a file number with a "CO" at the end means that the "admissibility law clerks" (*los letrados de admisibilidad*) concluded that it dealt with a constitutional matter and should be admitted. It appears that the file was not seen by an informal antechamber but was discussed by the seven justices on June 6, 2007, which was a Wednesday. Interviewees revealed that "important" cases are discussed on that day of the week. The file was the first one discussed on that day, and what followed was a short and intense meeting in the "voting room" (*Sala de votaciones*) where only justices are present. As a law clerk put it, "Decisions are made in the voting room, where there is no one else except for the justices. There are no law clerks present."[20]

According to the recollection of some of those present, positions were clear from the very beginning from two justices: Cruz Castro and Mora Mora, who began the debate and appear to have dominated the discussion. As someone present in the voting room that day recounted:

I remember that meeting very well. The file was circulated ahead of time. Back then, it was all paper. There were no preliminary discussions to that case. They decided to discuss it right away. . . . I was sitting across [from] Cruz Castro. . . . Calzada was acting chief justice at the time, and she was sitting to my left. Mora Mora was the Justice Rapporteur (*Magistrado Instructor*). It was clear that he had spoken to [Cruz] Castro. Castro and Armijo voted together, from what I remember, but Castro and Mora Mora took over the discussion. . . . I remember it very well . . . Mora Mora explained that we could not even discuss the file, that it would be a scandal. He said that we had to dismiss it (*rechazarlo*). We cannot decide here about life or death. Justice Castro then intervened and said something to the effect that "it exceeds the reason for which we are here" (*excede la razón por la que estamos acá*). . . . Justice Calzada then spoke. . . . She asked that we should all put ourselves in the woman's shoes. . . . She suggested that we should at least ask for more information, to ask the hospital for additional information on the woman's health. But Castro was very clear. We could not touch the issue. [Justice] Abdelnour agreed [with Justice Calzada]; she said that we needed more information . . . that if the woman had suicidal thoughts, her life could be in danger. The justices [Cruz Castro and Mora Mora] did not budge.[21]

A careful review of the file processing reveals that the file was indeed sent to Justice Cruz Castro's chamber and that he would have been the Justice Rapporteur for the case, not Justice Mora Mora. The recollection of the justice just quoted may therefore be faulty. However, their recollection suggests that Justices Cruz Castro and Mora Mora did indeed set the tone for the discussion and dominated it, something that was corroborated by other interviewees. The two justices appear to have decided that the case should be rejected and not accepted for substantive discussion. It also appears that the majority of those present agreed with the position advanced by the two justices. As a justice who sided with the position stated in an interview: "There wasn't much to discuss then. The IVF case had given us a clear directive on reproductive rights. . . . There was a consensus that this was an issue of life (*cuestión de vida*). I agreed and did not say much. It was clear to me that it was an issue of life."[22]

When asked to explain the reasons behind the position, justices present in the voting room said the following:

There is a dominant view from the San José Pact that life starts at conception. And there is a religious component as well. Sometimes we know much about what is not talked about. There is silence on those issues. There is a desire to have consensus, and in that area [abortion] that is the case. I personally do not have an issue with abortion. But we could not engage the issue. By simply admitting the case, the newspapers would start saying that we were discussing abortion! That is not what we are here for. That is not our role. It is up to the legislator to decide those issues, to the assembly.[23]

It was the first case we discussed that day. For Castro, it was inconceivable that we would admit it. It was clear that there would not be a majority, and he was not get[ting] involved. It was clear that it would not move. Divorce is as far as we can go. We are comfortable there. It is one of those central issues (*temas medulares*) where we can go, but not the rest. The 2007 case reflects a general feeling of society. The decision reflects social attitudes toward the issue. The chamber has been driven by a hard line on that issue, and they would not want to take on the political costs, to create enemies in the assembly. Of course, reelection matters and enters the calculation when making decisions. The justices want to ensure that there [will] be stability, to foster confidence in the chamber by the general public, influenced by a national feel (*sentir nacional*). If we move too much to one side, we will all fall. Castro, the liberal, would not move us that way.[24]

Law clerks who were familiar with the case were also asked to explain the position taken by these justices; they stated:

The chamber was not going to engage that issue [abortion]. Mora Mora was clear about that. He mentioned that in those complicated cases, to admit an amparo would have had a media impact. It sends a message to society that we are debating it—that we are considering options. They [justices] are very careful about those issues. In this case, asking for a medical report would have sent a signal that they were open to considering it (*señal de apertura*). . . . It could have turned into a political invoice (*factura política*). . . . People would have thought that the chamber had started to get its hands on the issue (*metiendo la mano*). It is taking a position.[25]

In this case, rejecting the file, the long justification for not accepting it was done precisely out of caution (*para cuidarse*). They [the justices] are completely immersed in politics. There is a direct influence in those cases.[26]

On religious issues, on abortion, the chamber was not characterized by liberal votes. The personal ideology of the justices plays a role, [and] the weight of religion . . . There was a bit of a religious foul smell (*olor tufo*) flowing through the chamber. . . . It was unthinkable for Fernando Cruz to discuss it. He said that if the media learned that it [abortion] was being discussed, we would been called an abortionist chamber. They were worried about society's reaction. That was important at the time. Some rulings, such as on free trade, really hit the chamber with an image problem, and there was worry . . . the religious component was present. . . . It was the only instance when religion was mentioned: "We cannot take on God's role because we are not going to decide between life and death." . . . Religion was present.[27]

Faced with such strong positioning, the two women justices, Calzada and Abdelnour, suggested that the chamber request additional information to determine whether the suicidal thoughts Ana had entertained and that had allegedly been documented in the amparo posed a real threat to her health and life. As one of the two justices recounted:

> [Name withheld] and I were the only ones that who agreed [that more information be collected]. The other ones did not because of religion, because they did not want to be seen as an "abortionist chamber," and because of the reaction in the media. We had to separate our personal views from the case at hand. That was certainly true for me. The others could not. I engaged in a minimal discussion with them because their positions were firmly decided. . . . [Justice] Fernando [Cruz] is liberal in some respects but not on this. . . . He said something like, "Who are we to tell the entire populous (*el pueblo entero*) what to think?" The men at the chamber did not see certain things in the same way. In some instances, they would listen to me but not in others. . . . There are some informal practices at the chamber. It was clear that the idea of admitting the case for discussion was not going to be accepted. . . . If I had insisted, a scandal would have occurred (*se hubiera armado un San Quintín*) . . . something radical would have happened (*se te da vuelta la tortilla*). . . . It was clear to me that we should have discussed it.[28]

It is important to note that, as acting chief justice at the time, Justice Calzada could have forced her colleagues to discuss the case substantively because that is one of the prerogatives that the chamber has. Once the case was admitted, the defendant in the case (Hospital México) would have automatically been informed of the constitutional challenge and been asked to provide the information required to defend their case. Justice Calzada could then have asked for any additional information. She chose not to do so. As a law clerk familiar with the case mentioned: "Calzada forced the debate on admissibility. Yes, as the chief justice at the time, she could have made sure the case [was] admitted (*darle curso*) and discuss[ed] substantively. . . . There was no precedent for the case, and so, technically, they should have admitted it and discussed it. Because it was a new issue, it warranted an ampler discussion. It should have been admitted (*haberse cursado*)."[29]

The above excerpts from the various interviews reveal several key points. First, the justices who decided the case were keenly aware of the potential societal repercussions that admitting and discussing the case would have. That includes the two women justices who argued for requesting additional information from the hospital. They seemed to believe that society would not accept the chamber taking on the issue and were aware of the limits of their "field of action" and the national consensus mentioned earlier (chapter 1). In other words, they did not sense that a political opportunity existed at all to push beyond those boundaries. Second, as expressed by a justice, they believed that it was not the chamber's role to decide the issue; that responsibility belonged to parliament. The tradition of deferring to the Legislative Assembly on divisive issues appears to have played an important role in the justices' calculations. Importantly, the justices also appeared to be attuned to public opinion: a vast majority of Costa Ricans have expressed opposition to the CRCC getting involved in deciding cases on sexual and reproductive rights.[30] Third, the opposition from five justices appears to have been so strong that even Justice Calzada, who wanted to explore the possibility of studying the issue further, backed down, even though she had the power to accept the case and discuss it.

Further, unlike the other cases we have seen, the minority (in this case, the two women justices) who were open to discussing the issue did not rely on alternative arguments to persuade their colleagues. This is an important point. Let us recall that abortions are legally permitted in Costa Rica when the health or the life of the pregnant woman was in danger. Based on the information submitted in the amparo, this was certainly the case here. Whereas in other cases arguments based on women's rights were advanced to initiate a conversation and try to reach a compromise, this situation differed. Interviews suggest that there was no room for compromise and that deploying alternative arguments beyond those based on life would have been futile. Finally, in contrast to the other three cases, it appears that law clerks did not play any role in discussions and decision-making. As we saw in the previous three chapters, law clerks were key players in the processes that led to the liberalization of abortion. This was not true in the *A.N.* case. This seems to be due to two main factors: the subordinate institutional position of law clerks at the CRCC and the limited interaction and exposure that law clerks have to ideas from outside the chamber (which includes education and training outside Costa Rica). As explained by various law clerks who were interviewed:

The system is very pyramidal. They are positions based on trust (*puestos de confianza*). Justices appoint them and fire them at will. Even permanent law clerks (*letrados proprietarios*), who work for the judiciary, can be moved to a different office. Generally, we are all not that well respected. Clerks may change the format of an opinion, but we do not try to change the content or try to challenge it because we know how they are going to vote. Law clerks do not try to change justices' minds. . . . [In terms of training and expertise] there are no law clerks with expertise in constitutional law. Most are not all that qualified. Many of them enter as junior law clerks (*meritorios*), and so they do not have much expertise.[31]

Yes, they are positions based on trust and loyalty. We have no autonomy, unlike other constitutional tribunals, such as Spain's. We are not really encouraged to attend conferences. . . . We are essentially banned, and why learn if it is useless? We are not allowed to take any positions. We are support staff. It has been a while since I spoke to a justice on a personal level. Everything comes from above, and every chamber is an island. In controversial cases, the justices take on the files, and that is that.[32]

It is a bit of a loop. . . . Law clerks move from one office to another, and we do not really interact with the outside world. I think this has an effect on judicial innovation and creative argumentation. There are very few of us with doctoral degrees, plus we are overwhelmed with so many cases. It is mechanical. We used to travel before, at the beginning. I started in 1992. We could travel abroad, but that changed. That has been closing. The political cost is heavy. There is no money for traveling. It is not well regarded in the country. We have abandoned foreign influences. We do not let ourselves be influenced by external ideas.[33]

I am an exception. I studied constitutional law at [a US] university. We are literal clerks (*escribanos*). There was excitement in the 1990s, but people who came in with new ideas ran into a wall, into resistance.[34]

The work we do is essentially writing (*escribentes*). There is a great deal of ideological alignment with the justice. Those who are not comfortable are moved to a different office. We function in a [routine] manner. The most controversial issues are taken over by the justices themselves. There is a certain institutional culture that requires loyalty. There is fear to advance ideas. One ends up feeling alienated. If we know how the justice will decide, why discuss it? I believe that I changed a justice's mind one percent of the time since I have been here. There is no funding to study abroad. I believe there are two scholarships for judges to study abroad in the entire country. . . . In terms of argumentative innovation, it really depends on the law clerk, but we are very fragmented. We do not discuss things among ourselves. There is no leadership among the law clerks. There is some communication, but it is on a personal level. Justices have their set ideas, and we are intimidated to change their minds. In controversial cases, it would never occur to me to change a justice's mind.[35]

After the vote was taken, likely on June 6, 2007, the CRCC released its decision at 10:30 a.m. the following day: the amparo was dismissed because it "exceeds the competencies (*ámbito de acción*) of this Chamber." The document is unusually long for a dismissed case; these decisions generally provide only a few lines outlining the procedural reasons for the case's inadmissibility. The majority decision, which spans six of the eight pages, is signed by Justices Mora Mora, Armijo, Cruz Castro, Jorge Araya, and Alberto Esquivel. It argues, in bold, that "it is about a case of extreme doubt regarding the protection of life, which, given the uncertainty, and based on a medical opinion, this jurisdiction cannot make a decision that inevitably weighs on a value of great importance such as the inviolability of human life."

As a way of concluding, it clearly refers to the idea of parliamentary supremacy in a convoluted passage:

> As indicated, the Legislator, in Article 121 of the Criminal Code decided in which cases a violation to life can go unpunished in our system, a violation that it is reasonable to this Chamber given the collision of rights that it represents, between the life of the mother and the fruit of her conception, the only case in which the suspension of pregnancy is valid in our system, this Chamber not having the power to supplant the will of the Legislator and to add one more cause for impunity in the matter.

The majority opinion, drafted by Justice Cruz Castro, rests primarily on the importance of protecting life. In the argumentative section (*Considerando*), the opinion argues that the chamber is obligated to protect life; international and domestic law has established that life begins at conception; life is not absolute and can have limits, but those limits can only be determined by the legislator and not by the chamber through a legal ruling; and the valid exceptions for therapeutic abortions do not apply in this case because the health of the mother was not threatened by the pregnancy but by "suicidal tendencies." Finally, it argues that even though termination of the pregnancy was recommended by a psychiatrist, the medical staff at CCSS "feared criminal reprisals," which indicates that they did not believe the requirements for a therapeutic abortion were met. The five men justices, as a result (*por tanto*), decided that the case be *rechazado de plano* (dismissed).

Justices Calzada and Abdelnour, the two women justices, in a brief minority opinion, argued that the case should be studied further and admitted because of the possibility that it met the requirements for a therapeutic abortion considering the suicidal thoughts that Ana had exhibited. Drafted by Justice Calzada, the opinion indicates that the two justices agree with the majority that the constitutional drafters of 1949 provided ample protection for human life, which must be upheld by the "modern rule of law" (*Estado Moderno de Derecho*). However, they argue that further information is needed to determine whether there was a connection between the pregnancy and Ana's psychiatric medical condition.

And, with that nondecision, policy stasis regarding the criminalization of abortion was set in Costa Rica.

Ana gave birth thirty days after the submission of the amparo after a complicated seven-hour procedure. She had a stillborn baby.

Post-2007 Abortion Politics

The puzzling case of Costa Rica's Constitutional Chamber in the regulation of abortion continued in a similar trajectory after the 2007 decision. The country's landscape of sexual and reproductive rights was not altered until international organizations became part of the story. One of the most active and progressive tribunals in Latin America in the socioeconomic rights area continued to refuse to alter the regulation of abortion in Costa Rica.

After Costa Rica's Constitutional Chamber refused to hear the amparo submitted by Ana in 2007 in the *A.N.* ruling, it came to a similar decision in 2013. In this instance, Aurora, a married thirty-two-year-old woman became pregnant after years of trying. On August 9, 2012, Aurora underwent ultrasound tests at Rafael Angel Calderón Guardia Hospital in San José, which revealed that her fetus had abdominal wall syndrome and several other malformations. These conditions were confirmed in subsequent testing, suggesting that they were incompatible with extrauterine life. Aurora's case is familiar to observers of similar situations in Latin America. As her pregnancy progressed, she began to experience multiple health issues all while her file was caught up in administrative delays in the hospital as medical staff suggested she undergo additional testing, which prolonged her situation. Aurora formally requested an abortion in November of the same year, but medical staff denied the request, justifying their decision by stating that the procedure was only permissible when the pregnancy poses a risk to the mother's health according to the country's criminal code (Arroyo Navarrete 2018).

Aurora submitted an amparo to the Constitutional Chamber on December 17, 2012, arguing that it was the hospital administration's "duty to guarantee access to legal medical procedures without discrimination such as the therapeutic interruption of pregnancy." She further argued that forcing her to continue with her pregnancy was having severe physical and mental health consequences. In early 2013, while awaiting a decision by the chamber, Aurora gave birth to a baby that lived for five minutes after delivery. While in this instance the chamber did hear the case, it ruled (R 2013002331) in a decision made on February 22, 2013, and sent to the plaintiff by email four days later, that her case had become moot, losing standing (Valverde Díaz 2018). Unlike the 2007 decision, which took the chamber forty-eight hours to process, this time the chamber took over six weeks to rule on the case.

As in the 2007 nondecision, the chamber decided to maintain the status quo and not expand access to abortion, unlike what we have seen in the other three cases. The mootness of the second case stands out because of what transpired in the 2012 FAL case in Argentina, when the Supreme Court not only admitted the case despite its mootness but also used it to hand down a landmark ruling with far-reaching implications.

Costa Rica's story took an important turn *after* the Aurora case was decided. Represented by Costa Rican feminist and activist Larissa Arroyo Navarrete, Ana and Aurora took their cases to the Inter-American Commission on Human Rights (IAHR) arguing that Costa Rica's Constitutional Chamber had violated a series of rights enshrined in the country's constitution and the Inter-American Convention on Human Rights.

On May 5, 2015, Costa Rica's Foreign Affairs Ministry proposed to the IAHR that the parties involved (the plaintiffs, the Costa Rican state, and the IAHR) reach an agreement and to commit themselves to developing clear guidelines on how access to therapeutic abortions should be carried out (*La Nación*, June 7, 2015). Specifically, the ministry committed Costa Rica to develop a protocol regulating access. Despite pressure from the victims, their legal representatives, and activists, it took over four years for Costa Rica to publish the protocol. In late 2019, the government of Carlos Alvarado (2018–22), after having won a contested election in which moral issues figured prominently in the campaign, published the regulation through a presidential decree with the Ministry of Health. The decree (Decreto 42113-S) established that the Health Ministry and the Social Security System would detail the implementation protocols, which were published in late 2020.[36] It thus took thirteen years after Ana had her stillborn baby for the Costa Rican state to implement Article 121 of the country's criminal code properly, and it did so only after her case was taken to an international institution.

Another important development was the decision (12,361) by the Inter-American Court of Human Rights regarding Costa Rica's policy on IVF. As the attentive reader may recall, in early 2000, the Constitutional Chamber struck down, in a 5–2 decision (2000–02306), a decree from 1995 that regulated the practice. The majority ruling argued that the Costa Rican constitution protected life from conception and that the right to life was thus enshrined. Importantly, it also referred to the right to life as interpreted by justices in their reading of the American Convention on Human Rights. In early 2001, an individual petition was filed with the Inter-American Commission of Human Rights against the Costa Rican state on behalf of nine infertile couples whose lives had been affected by the decision. The commission heard the case (25/2004) and recommended it to the Inter-American Court of Human Rights. The court handed down its opinion on November 12, 2012, in the *Artavia Murillo* case. In a majority opinion (5–1), the court held that the Costa Rican state had to annul its prohibition of IVF because it violated the rights to privacy, family, personal liberty, and integrity. Importantly, using various modes of interpretation, the court argued that "an embryo" could not be considered a person under Article 4(1) of the American Convention. The convention's right to life, it argued, could not be extended to an embryo before implantation. It therefore challenged the idea that life begins at conception.[37] It ordered reparations for the victims. By 2019, the Costa Rican state had complied fully with the ruling by annulling the prohibition of IVF, providing its judiciary with training on reproductive rights, and developing guidelines for compliance by the Social Security System (Serrano Guzmán 2024). The ruling was important because it clarified that, under the inter-American system, embryos cannot be considered judicial persons and that the rights of embryos cannot take precedence over the rights of women (Lemaitre and Sieder 2017).

In the non-case of Costa Rica, then, it took pressure from the inter-American system to expand reproductive rights with a rather passive constitutional tribunal. However, the politics of abortion in the country took an uncertain turn in early 2025. On January 29, the government of populist Rodrigo Chaves Robles (2022–), in what appears to have been an attempt to reward conservative forces in the National Assembly for their previous support and with the 2026 elections in mind, announced it was submitting a bill to the legislature to increase penalties for abortions performed in the country, stating: "Human Life is inviolable, that is what our Constitution states and in this Administration we will defend babies that have not yet been born" (CP-007–2025). The bill intends to reform the criminal code by introducing increased penalties.

Conclusion

The landmark *A.N.* ruling starkly contrasts the three others I have covered in this book. Those rulings in Argentina, Colombia, and Mexico were historic because, to varying degrees, they decriminalized abortion under certain circumstances within the First Wave of Abortion Decriminalization. In Costa Rica, that was not the case, even though the plaintiff had indeed the right, as set out by the 1970 criminal code, to seek a therapeutic abortion. The country's highest constitutional tribunal decided to keep the status quo. The factors that I have identified as explanatory for the liberalization of abortion in the other three cases are not present in the Costa Rica case. First, strategic actors were absent from the bench who could have developed an argumentative plan to convince other justices to join in their desire to enter a discussion. In this case, Justices Calzada and Abdelnour encountered such fierce resistance that dialogue was not in the cards; they could not even convince their men counterparts to seek more information on the case. Their inability to begin a discussion appears to be connected to two elements that I identified in the other three cases that are missing here: the lack of discernible leadership (which in the other cases was related to a significant role a justice played on the bench because of their academic or professional personae) and the interpretivist turn some justices *and law clerks* took in the adjudication of cases.

The other important factor relates to the political climate. In the case of Costa Rica, the majority's resistance to even start a debate appears to be a direct function of what justices believe is the appropriate role the CRCC must play in the country's politics. As some of the polling data I presented in this chapter show, justices seem to be rather attuned to public opinion: even eleven years after the ruling, most Costa Ricans do not think the CRCC should engage sexual and reproductive rights. Largely linked to the country's judicial tradition, justices refused to open the debate for fear of a backlash from the Legislative Assembly, a legislature that has traditionally enjoyed what amounts to parliamentary supremacy. The political climate that I identified in the other cases was not present here.

Conclusion

The Changing Landscape of Abortion Rights

Social scientists are often confronted with the challenge of studying moving targets. The phenomena we study and puzzles we seek to solve can change, and quickly, from the time we design a plan of investigation to the time we publish our findings. That is why it is often and rather accurately said that research results provide but a snapshot of social phenomena because social and political landscapes can turn on a dime. However, even with this in mind, one can only be amazed by how quickly Latin American sexual and reproductive rights have changed over the last quarter of a century. Indeed, it is difficult to think about another aspect of politics in which there has been such stark change. From antidiscrimination legislation to same-sex marriage to gender-identity rights, the expansion of rights has been rather remarkable.

It has also included abortion policy (in some countries). As you may recall, Latin America had, by the turn of the century, one of the strictest regulatory systems of access to abortion in the democratic world and, despite the Third Wave of Democratization and strong women's mobilization (chapter 1), no change crystallized. Political scientists consequently labored to explain policy stasis.

Alas, how things change. Few would have predicted the current state of abortion regulation in the Americas. Armed with stereotypical lenses unable to pierce past stereotypes (and invariably referring to Latin America as a deeply conservative and religious region), international observers have been seemingly, and genuinely, astonished by the recent liberalization of access to abortion in Argentina (2020), Colombia (2022) and Mexico (2021, 2023). Such astonishment has likely been reinforced by the extraordinary changes that have taken place in the United States with the 2022 overturning of the historic *Roe v. Wade* decision by the US Supreme Court (SCOTUS). No one would have bet, scarcely five years ago, that some Latin American countries would become more liberal on access to abortion than one of the first democratic countries to establish the constitutional right to abortion over a half-century ago.

What happened?

The most recent changes to abortion regulations in some Latin American countries are a culmination of a process that began at the turn of the twentieth century, which I have termed in this book the First Wave of Abortion

Decriminalization in Latin America. In recent years, state and nonstate actors have largely built on arguments crafted and deployed by the courts during that time to further liberalize abortion. Indeed, the more recent wave has built on the judicialization of abortion politics that occurred during the First Wave. It is therefore impossible to understand the recent changes without knowing what happened before, when the story first started to take a turn. While scholarship on abortion politics in Latin America has greatly contributed to our understanding of abortion policy change during the First Wave (Blofield and Ewig 2017; Marcus-Delgado 2020), a missing part of the puzzle concerns explanations for policy stasis and change through the courts as part of Latin America's judicialization of politics. Studies on abortion policy have thus far focused only on policymaking through legislatures.

That is exactly what this book has endeavored to do: to fill that gap and explain abortion policy stasis/change through the judiciary during the First Wave of Abortion Decriminalization in Latin America. As part of the judicialization of politics in Latin America, courts began to assume augmented policymaking powers through the assertion of constitutional review prerogatives, thereby becoming important political players. Latin American high courts have been key players in this process; they began to decide on a variety of policy areas by delivering highly political and consequential decisions, which included abortion. And while abortion tends to be cited as a prime example of the judicialization of politics in Latin America (Bergallo and Ramón Michelle 2016) and elsewhere (Hirschl 2008), there are no comparative studies on the judicial politics of abortion. This book fills that gap.

Starting with the landmark ruling by Colombia's Constitutional Court in 2006 (C355–2006), some Latin American apex courts began to hand down historic landmark rulings that liberalized access to abortion. Yet, in other cases, such as Costa Rica's Constitutional Chamber (*A.N. v. Costa Rica*) and the Dominican Republic's Constitutional Tribunal (TC/0599/15), some courts decided to maintain the status quo. In this book, I have explored these developments in an attempt to explain cross-national variance in the decriminalization of abortion in four countries by high courts. The central research question guiding this investigation was: *What explains variance in the liberalization of abortion by Latin American high courts during the First Wave of Abortion Decriminalization?* To answer this question, I selected four historic landmark decisions by Latin American constitutional tribunals that vary in the extent to which they liberalized access to abortion: the 2012 FAL case by Argentina's Supreme Court; the 2008 ruling by Mexico's Supreme Court (146/2007 and 147/2007); the 2007 (non)decision by Costa Rica's Constitutional Chamber (*A.N. v. Costa Rica*); and the 2006 C-355 ruling by the Colombian Constitutional Court.[1] These are tribunals that have been key players in Latin

America's process of judicialization and that share important similarities, such as strong constitutional review powers and judicial independence. In this conclusion, I review the main research findings and explore their practical and theoretical implications.

Restating the Argument

Based on extensive research that spanned over three years and included forty-seven interviews with sitting and retired justices and law clerks, the data suggest that variance in the type of decisions is primarily due to the presence of *strategic justices and law clerks who are able to assemble voting majorities on the bench in favor of reducing restrictions on abortion through the strategic deployment of arguments*. As I have shown, in the three cases in which high courts ruled in favor of decriminalizing abortion (Argentina, Colombia, and Mexico), a group of justices *and* law clerks took the initiative to convince the largest possible number of justices in each bench to vote in favor of decriminalizing access to abortion by presenting arguments they thought would produce a majority of votes. In the top constitutional tribunals of Argentina, Colombia, and Mexico, a small group of entrepreneurial justices and law clerks committed to the expansion of rights and democratic equality led well-coordinated efforts to build majorities by focusing on moderate justices. The similarities among the three cases are striking. In all three cases, we saw a justice, in close collaboration with their law clerks, take the lead in developing strategies to convince their peers to liberalize access to abortion: Raúl Zaffaroni in Argentina's Supreme Court, Justice Manuel José Cepeda Espinosa in Colombia's Constitutional Court, and José Ramón Cossío Díaz in Mexico's Supreme Court. The three justices, as we saw, led efforts to calibrate arguments strategically to convince wavering colleagues to strike down statutory provisions that criminalized access to abortion as historic constitutional challenges reached their courts. In the three cases, these groups carefully crafted lines of argumentation that they knew had the potential to bring uncommitted justices to their side. Even more striking is the profile of the three lead justices: they were highly respected (both inside and outside their courts) *garantista* jurists with strong academic backgrounds. The same was not true in Costa Rica. As we saw, while the 2007 bench was composed of justices with strong profiles, it was characterized by a notable level of homogeneity and a lack of strategic leadership from any one justice. Agency is therefore a key part of the story.

However, the types of decisions—what I refer to as their amplitude—are shaped by *the perception of a favorable political environment*. Likely unsurprising to most social scientists, this story involves the decades-old debate of agency versus structure. In this book, both are important. While the role played by individual justices and law clerks is crucial, the phenomenon under investigation is also the result of perceived specific structural conditions. The groups that led the efforts to declare the unconstitutionality of provisions criminalizing abortion acted within the perceived level of resistance and backlash from state and nonstate actors that a final ruling would provoke. This factor, I have argued, is key to explaining the variance in the *amplitude* of decriminalization in the rulings. As the reader may recall, in the three positive cases, the political context influenced both the types of strategic arguments deployed and the final content of each ruling. An analysis of the discussions and negotiations that took place after the cases reached the dockets reveals that, as the main actors carefully calibrated the drafting and deployment of arguments, they considered the political context—understood as both the position of other state actors outside the court (such as presidents and members of Congress) and debates in society at large—in deciding the reach of each decision.

In the case of Argentina, the FAL case reached the court during a favorable political environment shaped by *Kirchnerismo*. Those administrations were characterized by an emphasis on the expansion of human rights. The two areas in which they ensured the court did not vote against the executive's policy preferences were political economic matters and past human rights violations. The strategic group at the court that led the move to declare access to abortion constitutional was attuned to the social and political context and knew that it would be possible to aim for an expansive ruling. As a result, they assembled a majority that ruled not only on a moot file but also on aspects that went beyond the case at hand, decriminalizing abortion more broadly than the constitutional challenge demanded. The ruling declared that the practice of abortion in Argentina is constitutional.

In the cases of Colombia and Mexico, the political environments were more constrained, which explains the more limited scope of the rulings under study. In the case of Colombia, the strategic group of the lead justice and law clerks knew that, partly because of the credibility the Constitutional Court had earned with a prior ruling on the presidential reelection opposition to a ruling decriminalizing abortion from the conservative president would not be forthcoming. Indeed, the president himself said as much publicly. Nevertheless, they believed that a complete decriminalization of abortion would not be acceptable to either the other two branches of government or society at large. They therefore opted for a middle ground and worked on a ruling that would liberalize abortion only under certain circumstances. Similarly, in the case of Mexico, the group of strategic players behind the 2008 ruling knew that opposition to the liberalization of abortion would be strong, especially from the conservative administration at the federal level at that time. However, they knew that a narrower ruling—one based on jurisdictional aspects—would be better received. They did not seek to liberalize access to abortion with a larger reach that included a broader expansion of sexual and reproductive rights; rather, they focused the discussion on whether Mexico City had the jurisdiction to legislate in that area. Our non-case, Costa Rica, was markedly different; favorable political conditions were simply not present. As I detailed in chapter 6, the majority of justices even rejected the idea of discussing the abortion case for fear that they would be labeled an "abortionist" court by state and nonstate actors. As I tried to demonstrate, this was partly because of the country's "judicial tradition," which is characterized by deference to parliament.

Implications

The Politics of Abortion

These findings contribute to the debate on abortion politics in Latin America. As reviewed in the introduction, political science scholarship on abortion politics in the region has identified a variety of factors that explain changes in abortion policy. These explanations, as you might expect, are not monocausal and identify several factors that need to be aligned for policy change to occur. Additionally, as mentioned, existing scholarship has largely focused on policy change through legislatures. While this book is the first to examine the judiciary as the medium for policy change/stasis, it nonetheless contributes to these debates.

The first contribution concerns, of course, the role played by institutions. During the early stages of Latin America's process of democratization, scant attention was paid to the role institutions play in politics in general and policymaking in particular. Scholars have since increasingly shown that institutions matter, from the type of presidentialism to constitutions to decentralization (Franceschet and Díez 2012, 17–20). To state the obvious to the patient reader, in some Latin American countries, the judiciary matters, and it matters a lot. Courts can be a medium through which state and nonstate actors seek policy change in abortion regulatory regimes by challenging the constitutionality of criminal codes that restrict access to abortion. As we have seen, in the three positive cases I have covered, both state and nonstate actors relied on courts to liberalize abortion, and they did so successfully. The role courts play appears to be especially important when other venues, such as the executive and the legislature, are closed to change given the presence of conservative veto players (Marcus-Delgado 2020). The opportunity that the judicial route offers for policy change appears to take on special relevance given the conservative push against the expansion of sexual and reproductive rights that the region, as well as other democracies, has experienced over the last decade (Vaggione 2022; Payne et al. 2023). As conservative forces increase their representation in parliaments and presidencies, courts offer an alternative venue through which to bring about policy change (González Vélez and Jaramillo Sierra 2021; Machado 2023; Machado and Cook 2018).

For courts to matter, however, there must obviously be judicial independence (introduction), given the contentiousness of abortion as a policy area and the fierce opposition to reform in Latin America (chapter 2). The importance of judicial independence is directly connected to scholarly debates on the politics of abortion, especially regarding both the dispersion of power in political regimes and the presence of liberal actors in the executive office. Regarding the first point, scholars of Latin American politics have long emphasized the important role that strong executives play in the policymaking process due to the significant concentration of power (both formal and informal) in the president's hands, known as *presidencialismo* (Díez 2012). In terms of abortion politics, research has found that variation in abortion policy regimes is related to the "degree to which different government actors wield power independently of the presidency" (Marcus-Delgado 2020, 6). Because of the contentiousness of the issue, to my knowledge, not a single Latin American presidential candidate ran on such platform during the First Wave of Abortion Decriminalization. As you may recall from chapter 1, in some countries in the region, it was even taboo to speak publicly about abortion. Empowered and independent courts can thus serve as conduits for abortion liberalization, even in cases where the executive has taken a strong anti-choice position, such as in Mexico (chapter 5).

Institutional power decentralization is intrinsically related to the ideological positioning of governments. Research has underlined the important role "institutional leftist" governments have played in the liberalization of abortion over the last two decades: "We find that abortion liberalization proposals are more likely to get on the political agenda and passed in contexts of institutionalized partisan left governance" (Blofield and Ewig 2017, 482).[2] The role played by leftist governments in abortion liberalization during the First Wave appears to have been particularly important, given its coincidence with the emergence of the "Pink Tide." Nevertheless, the association between the Pink Tide and the expansion of sexual and reproductive rights has not been direct (Díez 2020). In the case of abortion, this book's findings show that change has occurred without the presence of leftist governance, institutional or otherwise. Because the level of the judicial independence that some Latin

American high courts have assumed, the liberalization of abortion through the judiciary can occur *despite* the presence of conservative governments in the executive, as we have seen in Colombia and Mexico. Independent courts can therefore be important institutions through which change can occur, even in the presence of conservative national governments. Based on the four cases I have analyzed, however, judicial independence appears to be a necessary but insufficient condition for policy change, as demonstrated by the case of Costa Rica.

The second area to which this book contributes is the importance of sociopolitical structures in the making of policy—what public policy and social movement scholarship often refers to as *political opportunity structures* (Díez 2013) and what, in this book, I have termed the political "environment or climate." Context matters. The findings in this book build on previous scholarship on abortion politics in Latin America, which has shown that context shapes the ability of pro-choice forces to advance their demands successfully. As Jane Marcus-Delgado has argued: "Political context is critical to the abortion debate" (2020, 6). From elections to tragic events that attract media attention to scandals that rock anti-choice forces, such as those in the Catholic Church (Díez 2013), social junctures open up opportunities for state and nonstate actors to push for reform. The preceding chapters demonstrate this clearly. Indeed, a crucial aspect of the strategic calibration of arguments, as I have detailed, is symbiotically related to the perceived openness of the political environment.

Among the structural and contextual factors, scholarship has identified a cultural variable as an explanation for changes in abortion policy. For example, to my knowledge, the most comprehensive comparative study on abortion policy reform in Latin America shows a relationship between public opinion and levels of social secularization as predictors of policy change (Blofield and Ewig 2017). The cultural explanation is surely familiar to the reader. The use of cultural approaches, primarily captured by public opinion data, is not surprising; despite the intense criticism it has received over the past few decades, there has been a revival of interest in these approaches. Some scholars argue that the cultural values, beliefs, and attitudes shared by societies are mostly responsible for driving political behavior and processes (Inglehart et al. 1998). For example, in some moral policy areas, such as queer rights, research has found a clear association between social development (measured by income and education, for instance), both at the individual and national levels, and support for same-sex marriage (Dion and Díez 2018).

At first glance, there appears to be an association between some key indicators of cultural values and the amplitude of the decisions I have analyzed in this book. In a 2007 poll (around the time of the rulings under study), participants were asked to respond to the statement, "Abortion is never justified." The findings indicate that 70.9 percent of respondents in Costa Rica agreed, compared with 72.6 percent in Colombia, 58.4 percent in Mexico, and 50.9 percent in Argentina.[3] While support for abortion could explain the difference in the amplitude of the ruling in Argentina compared to the rest, it does not account for the difference among the rest. Similarly, in a poll carried out in 2008, those who reported going to a religious service once a week made up 31.5 percent of respondents in Costa Rica, compared with 30.4 percent in Colombia, 38.5 percent in Mexico, and 17 percent in Argentina.[4] Again, religiosity can explain variance in amplitude of rulings between Argentina and the rest, but not among the rest. Nevertheless, the perception of where public opinion stood at the time did in fact play a role in the crafting and deployment of arguments by strategic actors within the four courts I have analyzed, as we have seen. Indeed, one of the main findings of this research is the extent to which justices and law clerks pay attention to the public mood and the positioning of other branches of government when developing arguments, deciding cases, and finally, signing onto a ruling. It is, as should be clear, a story about strategy.

Another area to which this book contributes is the role played by civil society. If we have learned one thing from decades of research on sexual and reproductive rights is that these rights are not extended but rather conquered. Work on abortion politics in Latin America has consistently emphasized the importance of women's mobilization in wresting abortion rights from the state (Marcus-Delgado 2020; Kane 2008; Blofield and Ewig 2017; Ruibal and Fernández Anderson 2020). The role that women's movements have played in the judicialization of abortion in Latin America has been detailed (Ruibal 2014b; González Vélez and Jaramillo Sierra 2021; Machado 2023; Machado and Cook 2018). This book builds on that important work and analyzes the processes of judicial decision-making *after* the files arrived at the courts. As such, it did not attempt to assess the role of social movements.

Nevertheless, my analysis provides important lessons. The first concerns the important role that feminist activists and organizations played in presenting data and arguments to the courts, primarily through the submission of *amicus curiae*. As strategic justices and law clerks weighed which arguments could help them win over votes, the availability of various lines of argumentation facilitated this task. The second lesson concerns the remarkable variance in the timing of when nonstate actors joined the processes. As we saw, in the cases of Argentina and Mexico, women's groups became active and applied pressure on the courts *once* the cases reached the court, mostly in the form of amicus curiae submissions. In Colombia, the entire case, from beginning to end, was mounted and pursued by civil society organizations led by activist Mónica Roa. Likely because of the speed with which the case was discarded (two days from submission to decision) and the desire of some justices not to attract any publicity to the case, there was essentially no discernible women's mobilization in our non-case.

The third lesson concerns resources. Surely familiar to the reader, there is a long tradition of scholarship on how resources (financial and otherwise) affect social movement success. Known as "resource mobilization," an approach to social movement research suggests that social mobilization is more likely to occur when groups and individuals can rely on strong leadership, organizational strength, and financial resources (Díez 2013, 215). In the area of judicial politics, resources are in fact a key explanatory variable behind the emergence of a "rights revolution" in Charles Epp's classic work (1998). According to his analysis, rights are more likely to be expanded when nonstate actors have the resources to litigate cases before the courts. The role that resources played in the cases under study is rather ambiguous. As you may recall, in the case of Argentina, the original amparo challenging the legal barriers to accessing abortion was submitted by the plaintiff's mother with the support of a local and relatively unknown lawyer. Once submitted, the case worked its way up to the Supreme Court. The result was the most expansive liberalization of abortion in the four countries studied. In the cases in which both state and nonstate actors appear to have relied on more resources, Colombia and Mexico, the amplitude of decisions was more moderate. A final and very important lesson is the significant role that certain state actors played in these processes. In effect, it appears that the presence of individuals with a *garantista* approach to rights in the judiciary is crucial. Interestingly, women justices, as we have seen, are not guaranteed to become allies in the cases.

The last main area to which this book's findings contribute is framing. Work on abortion politics in Latin America has underlined the importance that specific policy frames play in the liberalization of abortion (Marcus-Delgado 2020). The main finding of this book concerns the importance of the strategic development and deployment of lines of argumentation, or frames, by strategic actors within the courts. Framing is key. Upon the availability of a host of frames, often provided by nonstate actors, leading justices and their law clerks strategically chose augmentative frames that they knew would help them build majorities. A point worth highlighting is that, as other research has shown (Marcus-Delgado 2020), the deployment of frames that move away from moral arguments tends to be more effective—in this case, in convincing other justices to liberalize abortion. Whether a case is argued based on public health (Colombia and Argentina) or procedural issues (Mexico), wavering justices seem more likely to agree to liberalize abortion when the discussion moves away from moral arguments. Unsurprisingly, in the non-case of the book, justices were unable to move beyond arguments on when life begins.

Comparative Judicial Politics

The judicialization of politics in Latin America has resulted in important literature attempting to explain the origins, patterns, and consequences of this phenomenon. A line of inquiry within this subfield has focused on judicial behavior. Likely because of the similarities between Latin American presidential systems and that of the United States, this scholarship has attempted to explain the behavior of courts by applying various models, such as the attitudinal and strategic, as well as relying on broader political science approaches, such as institutionalism (Kapiszewski and Tiede 2021). Yet, to my knowledge, no work has opened the black box to uncover the decision-making processes that take place *within* collegiate high courts. This book has attempted to fill that gap. As mentioned in chapter 1, explanations of judicial behavior tend to rely on the individual coding of justices, derive conclusions from ecological inferences, or view courts as unitary actors. The internal dynamics of Latin American constitutional tribunals have not been studied in detail. My analysis does precisely that and can provide some potential lessons.

The first one is that internal bargaining matters, and it matters a great deal. Attempts at predicting judicial behavior in landmark and controversial cases that rely on justices' voting patterns or their known legal and policy preferences can be limiting in anticipating and explaining outcomes. As I have demonstrated, majority rulings are not simply the accumulation of signatures based on justices' positions on an issue. They are, rather, the result of carefully planned and executed strategies by a handful of justices and law clerks intended to secure the necessary number of votes to push policy in a certain direction. In the three positive cases that I cover in this book, the majorities needed to liberalize abortion were not there when the cases arrived at the dockets. Instead, they were assembled by strategic actors through effective argumentative persuasion. The positions of Justices Maqueda and Highton de Nolasco in Argentina, Justices Beltrán and Vargas in Colombia, and Justices Franco, Luna, and Valls in Mexico were unclear when the cases were admitted by their courts. Leading actors within these collegiate bodies persuaded colleagues by crafting and deploying arguments they thought had the potential to convince their peers. The strategic framing of arguments is therefore a central part of the explanation, and such framing depends on which justice the arguments are directed toward. Strategic actors seem to calibrate their arguments based on the policy and legal preferences of undecided justices, as well as their personal traits and established relationships. These can include practical, technical, and substantive arguments. The main lesson, then, is that internal bargaining matters, since not all justices have a clear position.

The importance of internal bargaining in collective decision-making, within the apex courts and in the cases I have analyzed, complicates the neat models that have been developed to study SCOTUS and their relevance to the study of Latin American high courts. As detailed in chapter 1, there are major issues with the transferability of these models outside the US context given the particularities of its high court. And while the strategic model may appear to be more suitable for explaining the processes I have studied, the manner in which it has been used to explain judicial behavior in Latin America has been exclusively based on actors' outward-looking strategic considerations. While these are important, they are only part of the story; they shape the framing of arguments deployed by strategic actors in collective decision-making. This does not mean that attitudinal and legal models should be discarded. Model busting does not seem to be in order. Rather, one can safely say that they have limited explanatory power, at least in some landmark cases, as policy and legal preferences are merely the foundations on which strategic planning partially begins.

The second main contribution this book makes to debates about judicial politics concerns the limitations of explanations for the judicialization of politics in Latin America based on the spread of neoconstitutionalism. As indicated in the introduction, some scholars view the phenomenon as a result of a structural progressive reorientation of justices' legal preferences. That is, the liberal turn and expanded role that some high courts have taken over the last quarter of a century have partly been caused by a move away from legal formalism and toward interpretivism. My analysis complicates that account. The variance I have sought to explain in this book is not directly associated with a neoconstitutional turn. Two of the courts that are widely seen as having become more active and liberal in the expansion of rights are Colombia's Constitutional Court and Costa Rica's Constitutional Chamber. Yet, as I have shown, in the area of sexual and reproductive rights, Costa Rica has been a laggard. The same applies to Mexico's Supreme Court, which is widely seen as not being a harbor of neoconstitutional thinking. Even after the 2011 human rights reform in Mexico (chapter 1), legal formalism has continued to guide the behavior of some justices at the court. Indeed, such has been the entrenchment of legal formalism in that court that some observers have begun speaking about "neo-formalism" (Díez and Ruíz Ramírez 2024). Yet, Mexico's constitutional tribunal, along with Colombia's, has expanded sexual and reproductive rights the most in the entire hemisphere in recent years. The expansion of rights can therefore occur through legal formalism. This does not mean that the spread of legal ideas and techniques does not play a role. It can. But only partially, as my analysis suggests.

A third contribution pertains to the debate about the appropriate role of courts in relation to counter-majoritarian concerns. Specifically, among socially conservative actors, there are concerns about "judicial activism" in the expansion of sexual and reproductive rights. As I have detailed, the idea of constitutional review—of having impartial arbiters to ensure that enshrined constitutional rights are respected—is as old as the Latin American republics themselves. This is not a new institutional feature. What we have witnessed is the use of that feature *along with* a gradual expansion of rights in a part of the world that has historically and notoriously been known for rather progressive constitutional texts. Some of these constitutional tribunals, like Colombia's, were specifically designed to prevent the violation of the numerous rights enumerated in the country's constitution. Its appropriate role seems to be confirmed by the high levels of confidence in the court that Colombians systematically express.

Nevertheless, just as with all scholarly work, this study has limitations. My analysis is based on highly controversial cases that resulted in landmark rulings. The extent to which the lessons drawn can be extrapolated to explore other judicial behaviors in other policy areas is limited, given the particularities of the policy area under study. Indeed, some cases, even the procedures followed during the deliberation of cases were rather irregular (e.g., setting up a working group in Argentina's Supreme Court and holding public forums by Mexico's Supreme Court). However, these are the very cases that most people are most interested in learning about: the most controversial and consequential ones.

The Americas in Comparative Perspective

Beyond the four cases analyzed in this book, more recent changes in abortion policy in Latin America are noteworthy. In terms of liberalization through the judiciary, four high courts have played a role, albeit an ancillary and limited one: Brazil's Federal Supreme Court (*Supremo Tribunal Federal*); Bolivia's Plurinational Constitutional Tribunal (*Tribunal Plurinacional Constitucional*); Ecuador's Constitutional Court (*Corte Constitucional*); and Chile's Constitutional Tribunal (*Tribunal Constitucional*).

In 2012, Brazil's Supreme Court ruled (ADPF 54/DF) that abortion should be authorized in cases of anencephalic fetuses. Then, in 2016, in light of a bill introduced in Congress to restrict access, the court ruled in a nonbinding decision (No. 84.025–6/RJ) that abortion "should not" be considered a crime during the first trimester because it violates women's rights, including equality rights. At the time of writing, conservative members of Congress had tabled a bill that would equate abortions after twenty-two weeks of pregnancy with homicide and establish sentences of up to twenty years in prison (*Reuters*, June 26, 2024). In Bolivia, after members of Congress submitted a constitutional challenge to various articles of the criminal code, the court ruled in 2014 (0206/2014) that the right to life is legally protected by Bolivia's constitution in all its facets, from the moment of conception, but that it is not protected with the same intensity. The court therefore ruled that the conditions of access to abortion established by the criminal code (rape and when the individual's life is at risk) are constitutional, and it declared the application of any penalties in these cases unconstitutional.

In the case of Ecuador, in 2021, its high court ruled (No. 34–19-IN/21) that the criminalization of abortion in cases of rape violates one's rights to personal integrity, free development of personality, equality, and nondiscrimination, as well as rights related (*conexos*) to women. It thus argued that, even when the right to life is a constitutional one, it "cannot be interpreted in an isolated or absolute manner, but, rather, it has to be understood systematically along with other rights and principles also established by the Constitution." Whereas the criminal code previously allowed access to abortion for women with a mental disability, it has now established that this provision must be extended to all pregnancies resulting from rape.[5]

Perhaps the most interesting case within this group is Chile's high court. Traditionally regarded as a rather timid tribunal since the country's return to democracy in 1990, despite having strong constitutional review powers, Chile's Constitutional Tribunal appears to have begun waking up from its own slumber. On two separate occasions in the 2000s, the high court ruled against the expansion of reproductive rights. In 2001, the tribunal handed down a ruling (Rol 2.186–2001) declaring that access to contraception was unconstitutional because the right to life was protected by Chile's constitution and that right extended to the unborn. It equated it to an abortion, which was criminalized in the country. With the same logic, the tribunal ruled in 2008 (Rol 740–07-CDS) that a program unveiled by Michelle Bachelet's first government (2006–10), through a decree, to promote the free distribution of the morning-after pill to individuals aged 14 and older was unconstitutional. The challenge was submitted to the tribunal by the government's conservative opposition. Citing the precedent set by the tribunal in 2001, they argued that the pill was essentially tantamount to abortion, a practice that is prohibited and criminalized in Chile. The tribunal agreed. Its position on reproductive rights appears to have begun to change, however. In 2017, with an important 6–4 ruling (STC Rol 3729–17), the tribunal upheld changes to Chile's criminal code that included exceptions for abortion (e.g., imminent risk to the mother's life, fetal disease, and pregnancy resulting from rape).[6] The challenges were submitted by conservative members of Congress from both chambers. The tribunal's main line of argument was primarily procedural and the majority opinion clearly refrained from engaging in debates about women's rights and the right to dignity.[7] In effect, the ruling stands out—especially in a comparative perspective—for its clear omission of women's rights. Furthermore, it allowed for conscientious objection, allowing one to refuse to perform an abortion.[8] However, the ruling likely suggests a possible shift in the position of a historically notorious conservative and passive high court. Just like Ecuador's case, it is a phenomenon that warrants detailed further investigation.[9] This book may provide some suggestions on how to do so.

The other Latin American high court that has played a role changing a country's abortion policy is the Dominican Republic's Constitutional Tribunal, as mentioned in the introduction. However, in this case, it upheld one of the most restrictive regimes in the world, banning the practice under any circumstance.[10] Under the administrations of President Danilo Medina (2012–20) of the leftist Liberation Party, a reform to the criminal code decriminalizing abortion under three conditions was enacted: when it poses a threat to a woman's life, in cases of incest and rape, and when fetal malformations exist that make pregnancies unviable. Approved by Congress on December 16, 2014 (Ley 550–14), this reform was subsequently challenged by conservative groups before the tribunal—which struck down those changes in 2016, declaring them unconstitutional (TC/0599/15). The tribunal therefore reestablished the total ban on abortion as specified in the 1884 criminal code.[11] The Dominican Republic remains among the four Latin American countries that have complete bans (along with Honduras, Nicaragua, and El Salvador).

This admittedly cursory overview of the state of abortion policy regimes would, of course, be incomplete without a reference to United States. Adhering to an informal tradition of handing down historic rulings in June of every year, on June 24, 2022, the US Supreme Court issued its historic decision in *Dobbs v. Jackson Women's Health Organization* (597 US 215). The case involved assessing the constitutionality of a law passed by the state of Mississippi in 2018 that banned most abortions after fifteen weeks of pregnancy. Jackson Women's Health Organization, the state's only abortion provider, had sued the state's health officer, Thomas D. Dobbs, for enforcing the law, arguing that it violated the constitutional right to abortion established in 1992 by the *Planned Parenthood v. Casey* ruling (505 US 833). That ruling disallowed states from banning abortions before fetal viability (twenty-four weeks). The majority ruling in *Planned Parenthood* argued that a woman's right to choose an abortion during this period of pregnancy was protected by the due process clause and the Fourteenth Amendment of the US Constitution. It built on the historic 1973 *Roe v. Wade* decision (410 US 113), which ruled that the right to an abortion was protected by the right to privacy embedded in the constitutional guarantees of liberty. In its 6–3 majority decision, drafted by Justice Samuel Alito, SCOTUS overturned both *Roe v. Wade* and *Planned Parenthood* with the main guiding argument that the constitution does not extend the right to an abortion: "The Constitution makes no reference to abortion, and no such right is implicitly protected by any constitutional provision." Alito further argued that rights not mentioned in the US Constitution can only be extended when they are "deeply rooted" in the country's history. Wading into the political and moving away from the argumentative, Justice Alito summed up his position rather clearly by stating, "Roe was egregiously wrong from the start. Its reasoning was exceptionally weak, and the decision has had damaging consequences. And far from bringing about a national settlement of the abortion issue, *Roe* and *Casey* have enflamed debate and deepened division."

The Dobbs decision, of course, did not put out the alleged fire, nor has it healed divisions: it has instead reignited the debate, placing the issue of abortion atop US politics. In practical terms, by rescinding the constitutional right to abortion that the previous cases had extended, the ruling unloaded the regulation of access to abortion to the states and unleashed the fragmentation of abortion politics at the subnational level. Almost overnight, a series of abortion bans was instituted in many states, recriminalizing the practice and stripping women and girls of full citizenship rights. Two years after the ruling, twenty-two states had implemented partial or full ban on abortions. In tandem with this phenomenon, the tragic stories of the obstacles US women and girls have encountered have become regular news stories. They strikingly reassemble many of the stories from Latin America I have covered in this book.

The Dobbs decision presents scholars of judicial politics with an opportunity to explore the factors that led to its drafting and, most importantly, to the construction of a majority of votes on the bench willing to sign onto a ruling that challenges the legal doctrine of *stare decisis*. Just as I have done in this book, research on the case can assess which of the models, or combination thereof, is best suited to explaining the outcome. Preliminary information on the process points to strategic planning by Justice Alito in securing a majority of votes (Kantor and Liptak 2023). It includes, for example, Alito's decision to delay hearing the case as much as possible in an attempt to convey the image that the conservative majority was not taking advantage of Justice Ruth Bader Ginsburg's death (on September 18, 2020) and her replacement with a social conservative justice (Amy Coney Barrett). More importantly, however, was the highly unusual decision to leak a draft of the opinion on May 2, 2022, in order to secure support from Chief Justice John G. Roberts (who was seeking a ruling with less amplitude) and Justice Barrett (who originally opposed hearing the case) (Kantor and Liptak 2023). By leaking a draft of the opinion (which did not undergo any significant changes), the two justices' positions would be solidified as they could not be challenged for changing their positions and sacrificing their conservative stance.

Courts and the Politics of Abortion

Some Latin American apex courts have been central to the ecosystems of abortion politics in the region. To state the obvious, this book shows that formal institutions matter. Scholarship on Latin America has traditionally held an ambivalent position on the role that institutions play in sociopolitical processes, given their perceived weakness—a weakness partly derived from the particular processes of state formation in the region. Scholars have therefore tended to look for broader structural independent variables, such as class structures, to explain political processes and policy outcomes. As the politics of post-transition Latin America stabilized in the 1990s, however, an increasing number of Latin American scholars devoted their attention to the study of institutions. There is now a widespread consensus that institutions matter in the politics of the region. My analysis may potentially broaden that consensus and include Latin American high courts more systematically.

For courts to matter, however, they need to enjoy a certain degree of judicial independence, which has historically been a rarity in Latin America. Indeed, one can possibly count on two hands the number of high courts in the region that can act independently vis-à-vis the preferences of other branches of government and state and nonstate actors. Judicial independence appears to be particularly crucial in the politics of abortion, given the contentiousness of the issue. Support for and opposition to final decisions from the courts can be strong, and their rulings can displease powerful actors. However, judicial independence can be an institutional characteristic in flux. In a part of the world that has historically seen a strong concentration of power in the executive branch and produced many populist leaders, it seems that the judicial independence of high courts is not a guaranteed feature of Latin American politics. Constitutional tribunals can become easy targets of *caudillismo*, as the administrations of Nayib Bukele of El Salvador (1999–present) and Andrés Manuel López Obrador of Mexico (2018–2024) have clearly shown. As the world experiences the spread and entrenchment of populism, it will be interesting to see which apex courts can resist attacks on their independence; its permanence is not guaranteed (Haggard and Tiede 2024). The case of Mexico does not augur well as the recent capturing of the high court by a populist regime shows. The June 1, 2025, election results for Supreme Court justices, following the 2024 constitutional reform that overhauled the judiciary by purging all federal justices and judges and forcing the election of new ones by popular vote, point to the practical end of judicial independence of the county's high court: amid widespread allegations of fraud, and with barely 13 percent of eligible votes cast, all newly elected justices for the high court are openly partisan political actors directly aligned with the governing populist regime.

Yet, while judicial independence is crucial for high courts to matter in contentious politics, the analysis I have presented in this book shows that high courts are deeply political institutions. The benches of these institutions are populated by keen political actors who have policy preferences, act strategically to pursue them, and are embedded in the social and political contexts that shape their behavior. If anything, this book's analysis calls for greater attention to the internal politics of high courts. These truly political institutions make consequential decisions. More attention is therefore needed to understand their inner workings, in the same manner that political scientists have looked at the inner workings of, for example, executive cabinets.

The increased importance of high courts in the politics of Latin America inevitably raises the question of the similarities and differences in policy changes made through legislatures and judiciaries. As mentioned, in some cases, courts are the only venue through which nonstate (and state) actors can pursue the expansion of sexual and reproductive rights, given that socially conservative players in parliaments systematically use their veto to block their attempts. Courts with sufficient political independence and *garantista* justices are a clear venue. They can also serve as a venue when executives are of the socially conservative variety, as we have seen. It appears that, based on the evidence we have so far, legislatures can be conduits for abortion policy change only when socially progressive and non-populist leftist governments are in power, as demonstrated by the cases of Argentina (2020), Chile (2016) and Uruguay (2012). However, given the processes through which justices are nominated and confirmed to high courts, the issue of the democratic legitimacy of these decisions, undergirded by the counter-majoritarian debate, arises. Those opposing the expansion of fuller citizenship can be heard calling these rulings antidemocratic. As I have pointed out, though, these historic decisions rely on the panoply of rights that have already been collectively debated and formally enshrined in Latin American constitutions. Indeed, a clear consequence of some of these expansive rulings is that they can further cement the enshrinement and potential exercise of these rights. That is a key difference with abortion policy changes enacted through legislatures: while social and parliamentary debates can be rather fierce during reform processes, the end result usually is minor changes to criminal codes.

The idea of the potential exercise of rights automatically brings one's thinking to practical considerations in a part of the world that has historically been characterized by wide gaps between legal formalism and compliance with the law. Indeed, a contradiction in contemporary Latin America is the expansion of all levels of formal rights within a context of extreme violence, where rights are routinely violated. The gap between legal formalism and compliance with the law in Latin America is tied to cultural traits, best captured by the adage "*obedezco pero no cumplo*" (I obey but I do not comply with), as well as weak state capacity in policy implementation (Díez 2015). A question therefore arises: Do these landmark rulings matter in practical terms? There is no doubt that in some cases, the implementation of the rulings has been an issue, as demonstrated by the case of Argentina (with some provinces failing to elaborate the mandated access protocols) and Colombia (with constant attempts at sabotage by the attorney general). It remains to be seen how the implementation of the most recent rulings will play out. However, as overviewed, evidence suggests that in those cases where policy changes brought about ample access to abortion procedures with guaranteed public health care support—what the 2008 ruling on Mexico City's reforms upheld—rulings matter a great deal: quite simply, countless lives are saved.

The fragility of formal rights in Latin America raises an additional issue: Just as judicial independence can at times be fleeting, can formal rights be retracted once expanded? To the surprise of many political scientists, myself included, who were trained with a teleological view of political development, it has become clear that rights can indeed be taken away once they are won. The current democratic backsliding that many Latin American countries have experienced (El Salvador, Mexico, Nicaragua, and Venezuela) demonstrates as much. In terms of sexual and reproductive rights, the possibility of the retraction of abortion rights within the context of a neoconservative backlash increases, as the election of Javier Milei in Argentina in 2023 shows. (His political party submitted a bill to Congress in early 2024 to repeal the 2020 law and criminalize abortion again.) Rights can clearly be fluid. This is especially important in a part of the world where the Catholic Church has its largest presence and its leadership's position on abortion is implacable. However, and perhaps differing from policy changes enacted through legislatures, it appears that the expansion of formal rights through the judiciary can *potentially* be more effective at securing the maintenance of established formal rights, at least in some cases. As we have seen most clearly in the cases of Colombia and Mexico, high courts can play an important role in shielding against attacks on expanded rights by restating their jurisprudence. In some cases, such as in Mexico, some of these rights are further shielded by unique constitutional features, such as the progressivity principle (*principio de pro-*

gresividad) adopted in 2011: legislators must interpret rights in the amplest possible way, and once a right is expanded, it cannot be retracted. But for courts to be guarantors of established rights, judicial independence must exist—a feature that, as mentioned, is also fluid. Courts, then, can be central in advancing and securing the full democratic citizenship of gestating individuals if judicial independence is not attacked or eroded. And that, alas, remains to be seen in our current age of populism.

Notes

Introduction

1. The data were obtained through forty-seven in-depth personal interviews with sitting and retired justices and law clerks in the four high courts carried out over a period of twenty-one nonconsecutive months between May 2016 and August 2019. It also comprised archival research. Funding for this research was provided by Canada's Social Sciences and Humanities Research Council (Grant 435–2016–1106). With the objective of facilitating candid discussions, none of the interviewees is identified.

Chapter 1

1. While scholars began to study judicial behavior earlier (Maveety 2003), its systematic analysis seems to have been sparked by Pritchett's (1968) publication as seen by subsequent works (Schubert 1965, 1974; Rohde and Spaeth 1976).

2. A major criticism of the model is that the index used to measure policy preferences is derived from newspaper editorializing, which tends to focus on civil rights cases that usually are more ideologically driven (Epstein and Mershon 1996).

3. Sunstein et al. (2004, 306), for example, finds a certain degree of ideological fluidity (ideological "dampening" and "amplification," depending on a panel's composition) in all areas except in abortion and capital punishment cases: "in each of these areas, judges apparently vote their convictions and are not affected by panel composition."

4. *Garantista*, which literally translates into "guarantor," refers to individuals committed to upholding and expending human rights.

5. During the heyday of legal formalism, in the latter part of the nineteenth century, law was considered a "science," consisting of certain principles and doctrines. Based on the case method, which is still in use today, students were asked to employ inductive reasoning to determine case outcomes by discovering legal principles.

6. Ronald Dworkin (1978, 1986) famously argued that the law includes principles and is therefore inextricably linked to questions of morality.

7. The authors identify five factors: job satisfaction, external satisfactions, leisure, salary/income, and promotion.

8. Three previous attempts at adopting a constitution in Argentina after independence failed mainly because of disagreement over the desired balance of power between the national and provincial governments. There have been only seven constitutional reforms since then. See Miller 1997 for a detailed discussion on how the US Constitution formed the basis for the drafting of Argentina's constitution.

9. It is a variant of the legal institution native to Latin American par excellence: the *recurso de amparo* (writ of amparo), also known as *tutela* in Colombia. First (formally)

established in 1841 by the State Constitution of Yucatán State, Mexico, it was later adopted by Mexico's 1857 Constitution. This mechanism is intended to protect individual rights with constitutional character. As the main legal mechanism to redress individual-rights violations, it is typically the most common way in which cases reach high courts through appeal. In Argentina, in addition to the extraordinary appeal and complaint proceeding, a 1994 constitutional reform (explored below) formally incorporated the writs of *amparo* (designed to protect constitutional rights), *habeas corpus* (when physical liberty is involved), and *habeas data* (when private information is involved). These provisions are specifically designed to enforce constitutional and international rights, as we shall see.

10. In the *Sojo* case, the CSJN (Argentine Supreme Court) declared unconstitutional Article 20 of Law 48 used by the Chamber of Deputies to issue a directive (*resolución*) to imprison a journalist, Eduardo Sojo, thereby establishing constitutional review *derecho difuso* (see Miller 1997, 1553–60, for a detailed discussion). The court reaffirmed its judicial-review powers the following year, in the *Municipalidad de la Capital c/Elortondo* case, when it struck down an expropriation law passed by Congress on constitutional grounds.

11. The clearest expression was articulated in the *Caporale, Susana* ruling in October 1995.

12. It literally means "addicted court."

13. Menem, in fact, took office before the official inauguration day because Alfonsín resigned, given his inability to deal with the crisis.

14. The Chamber of Deputies did not have the necessary quorum.

15. Justices Fayt and Petracchi publicly decried the move in a written document (*Acuerdo 44*), claiming an attack on judicial independence.

16. Bacqué has previously replaced Justice Carrió in 1985, when the latter retired for health reasons.

17. Constitutional reform in Argentina can only occur through the establishment of a constitutional convention, which in turn requires the passage of a declaratory law that needs a two-thirds majority in both congressional chambers.

18. These include the American Convention on Human Rights; the International Covenant on Economic, Social and Cultural Rights; the Convention on the Elimination of All Forms of Discrimination against Women; and the Convention against Torture and Other Cruel, Inhuman or Degrading Treatment of Punishment.

19. This was according to its ruling in the Horacio David Giroldi case (April 7, 1995).

20. The writ of amparo was recognized by the Supreme Court through two rulings in 1957 (*Siri* case) and 1958 (Kos case).

21. The reform also expanded the scope of these writs by conferring legal status to collective actors.

22. As in Mexico's case, 1810 has more symbolic weight. It is the year when independence was "declared" by leaders, even if the war was not won until 1819. It is the year when Colombians (like Mexicans) in fact celebrate their independence from Spain.

23. The territory was informally known as Gran Colombia when Nueva Granada, Venezuela, and Ecuador joined. The country officially gained its independence with the proclamation of a constitution (*Ley Fundamental de Colombia*) in 1821. It subsequently became Republic of New Granada in 1830 and the Grenadine Confederation in 1858.

24. In 2014, the Inter-American Court of Human Rights in fact condemned the armed forces for the manner in which it responded and accused the Colombian state of human-

rights violations (10.738) (*El País*, December 10, 2014). It made the Colombian state responsible for the killing of one justice and for the arrest, torture, and cruel treatment of others and the "disappearance" of ten individuals.

25. For a detailed account of the establishment and functioning of the National Constituent Assembly, see Silva 1998.

26. It is commonly translated into English by scholars of Colombia as a "social rule of law" or a "social state under the rule of law."

27. As we shall see below, in 2005, the CCC allowed for one immediate reelection.

28. Interview with a legal adviser to President César Gaviria (1990–94), Bogotá, June 18, 2018.

29. Members of the Supreme Court are selected by the court itself from lists prepared by the Council of Judicial Affairs (*Consejo Superior de la Judicatura*). Members of the Council of State are selected by the Supreme Court from a list of candidates proposed by the president.

30. To my knowledge, the first Latin American jurisdiction to have adopted judicial review was Colombia's Cundinamarca Province. While still officially under Spanish rule, its constitution of 1811 gave the Senate the ability to "censure and protection to sustain the Constitution and the rights of the people" (Eder 1960). The 1853 Constitution, amended in 1863, gave the Senate the power to declare acts of subnational states void when in violation of the national constitution. The 1886 Colombian Constitution only awarded the newly created Supreme Court these powers. Article 90 granted the president the power to veto a bill passed on unconstitutional grounds. If Congress overrode the presidential decision, the Supreme Court was given the power to decide on the constitutionality of the case (Ley 153,1887). A 1910 amendment to the 1886 Constitution confirmed judicial review by making the Supreme Court the "guardian of the integrity of the Constitution." It introduced a term that is commonly used in judicial circles in Colombia to this day—*exequibilidad* (constitutionality) of bills and laws.

31. Concrete review refers to an analysis of whether a law that has been applied, and for which there has been litigation, is constitutional. Abstract review refers to an analysis of the constitutionality of a law in general terms, without a specific set of facts or litigation.

32. For an excellent overview of the senatorial confirmation process, see Montoya 2013.

33. The 1811 Cundinamarca constitution, referred to above, allowed for judicial review prompted by an "individual complaint" (Grant 1948). The mechanism was reestablished in 1910 by a constitutional reform and turned over to the Supreme Court. The court's decision had *erga omnes* effects. It also introduced the "unconstitutionality exception" by which any judge or public official could decide not to apply laws they found unconstitutional (Cepeda-Espinosa 2004, 538). After the 1968 constitutional reform, the Supreme Court was granted *ex officio* review powers over presidential decrees during state siege and economic emergencies. However, the court systematically declared most decrees constitutional since then.

34. *Erga omnes* means that decisions have universal applicability.

35. It can also modify laws partially through what is called conditional constitutionality (*exequibilidad condicionada*). It establishes a new interpretation of the legislation.

36. The constitution also introduced two additional mechanisms: *acción de cumplimiento*, which forces administrative institutions to fulfill their mandates, and the *acción de grupo*, which is similar to the class-action procedure in the United States. The granting of tutelas went from less than 24 percent in 1993 to 63 percent in 2003 (Nunes 2010a, 82).

37. There are other important mechanisms such as the "insistencies" and "solicitudes ciudadanía de selección," both of which allow citizens to ask the CCC to hear certain tutela cases (see Jaramillo Sierra and Barreto Rozo 2010), and the popular action (*acción popular*), which is used for the protection of collective rights (Ley 472, 1988).

38. It also protected the right of a four-year-old girl to keep her preferred appearance (SU-642–098), and it allowed for the intersex operation of an older child (SU-337–099).

39. The court argued that such operations are considered a mutilation, which violates children's rights.

40. This bench sat from February 17, 1992, to February 28, 1993. It increased to its current size of nine justices in March 3, 1993. Three justices were appointed by the Supreme Court, the Council of State, and the attorney general (one each); the president appointed two additional justices; and the last two were selected by the CCC itself from two three-member lists submitted by the president.

41. This group refers to three justices: the president's two appointments to the bench, Ciro Angarita Barón and Alejandro Martínez Caballero, and a justice appointed by the attorney general, Eduardo Cifuentes Muñoz. All three, and some of their law clerks, had ties to the Faculty of Law at the elite, private Universidad de los Andes in Bogotá. The three justices had close ties with two individuals close to the president: Manuel José Cepeda, the president's legal adviser, and Minister of Government Humberto de la Calle. All five had ties to the prestigious Faculty of Law.

42. Author's calculations based on information accessed on June 10, 2018.

43. It replaced the *Supremo Tribunal de Justicia* (established during the brief imperial period of Agustín de Iturbide, 1821–23), which in turn had replaced the *Real Audiencia de México*, the highest tribunal during colonial Mexico, founded in 1527, when twelve judges were appointed by the king (Mendieta y Núñez 1992, 44–46).

44. It is important to note, as Jaime E. Rodríguez O. (2012) has so aptly reminded us, that contrary to the stylized view of colonial Latin America as superstitious, Catholic peoples having been completely dominated by autocratic rule from Spain, ideas of representative government were present in the region, and seeking access to justice through the courts was one of them. In effect, natives defended their interests and relied extensively on the judicial system to seek protection from other groups. And high courts were part of that system. See, for example, Woodrow 1983 and Owensby 2008. It may also be of interest to some readers to note that the Aztecs had a fairly developed judicial system that was administered by a "supreme magistrate" who operated under the authority of the king (*Tlatoani*).

45. This institution is mostly likely inspired by the idea (well elaborated by Benjamin Constant) of the need to establish a fourth institution capable of maintaining a balance between the three branches of government. Also known as a Moderating Power, Simón Bolivar was one of the main proponents of such an institution in Latin America during the early independent years (Barrón 2002). This differed from the Rousseauian idea of having the legislature or a permanent legislative committee as guardians of the constitution.

46. Different names were used for intermediate subnational jurisdictions during the nineteenth century in Mexico: departments, provinces, and states.

47. However, the "father of the *amparo*" was Manuel Cresencio Rejón y Alcalá. Inspired after having read the first translation into Spanish (1837) of Alexis de Tocqueville's *Democracy in America*, he proposed that it be incorporated into the constitution of Yucatan Province in 1841 as the main mechanism to defend its principles (Fernández Segado 2020,

chap. 3, 301–95). The first amparo was submitted on July 7, 1842, to a judge of first instance in the province. It should be noted that the amparo had a predecessor in Spanish law, a mechanism called *amparo indirecto*. Used during colonial Latin America, especially by Indigenous peoples, it was meant to protect people from abuses of power (Lira González 2017).

48. According to Article 192 of the Amparo Law (*Ley de Amparo*), when a qualified majority of justices (today, eight out of eleven) decide on an issue five consecutive times (*ejecutorias*) while sitting en banc, the interpretation becomes *jurisprudencia* (binding precedent) on all state and federal courts. It can only be overturned by a unanimous vote.

49. This was the second attempt. The first law to regulate the use of amparo was enacted in 1861, but it was mostly unimplemented because of instability caused by foreign intervention.

50. For example, a reform introduced in 1934 replaced life tenure for the justices with six-year terms coinciding with presidential terms and an unwritten rule established that all justices be PRI members.

51. Work by Rodrigo Meneses (2014, for example, shows that, by the mid-1960s, 66 percent of amparo cases submitted by informal vendors in Mexico City were won.

52. It should also be noted that the court also resolved fifty-five constitutional controversies from 1917 until 1994, although when the court was involved, it mostly favored the executive (Cossío 1998c).

53. For a detailed historical account see Díez 2006, 13–26.

54. The label was applied by the court's oldest weekly, the *Seminario Judicial de la Federación*. First published in 1871, it has divided the court's history along "eras" roughly coinciding with constitutional reforms that have affected its makeup; it publishes the court's rulings to provide direction to lower-level judges on set jurisprudence.

55. Its size was changed five times in the interim.

56. If the Senate does not select one candidate, the president can submit a second list. If the Senate does not select a candidate from the second list, the president can unilaterally confirm any candidate from that list.

57. A simple majority refers to a majority of legislators present at a given session.

58. It manages the appointment of lower-level federal judges, administers the judicial budget, and regulates merit and performance and mechanisms to deal with corruption.

59. The channel first aired on May 29, 2006 (*El Universal*, May 29, 2006). Ministers can meet in private when the issue at hand warrants it for "moral" or "public interest" reasons (Article 94 of the constitution).

60. The only way the court could previously ensure enforcement was by laying off the party refusing to abide by the ruling, a rather drastic measure. The new legal framework provides several alternatives, based on whether or not the action is excusable.

61. If it involves an intrusion of the federal government against a state or municipality, decisions supporting the federation's side have general effects if a majority of eight justices support it. If the decision supports a state's claim against the federal government, the invalidation of the law is only applicable in that state.

62. After a 1996 reform, the court was also given the power to decide on the constitutionality of federal and state electoral laws. All other electoral disputes are reviewed by the National Electoral Tribunal (*Tribunal Electoral del Poder Judicial de la Federación*), also established in that reform.

63. Various explanations of the Mexican case align well with the major theories in the judicialization literature, which address that most interesting of puzzles: Why do dominant elites empower courts and give up policymaking power? For Mexico, there may be various reasons. Some have argued that it is because of the "insurance policy," a delegation of power to hedge against possible losses (Finkel 2004a). Others cite the formation of a new government coalition (Ríos-Figueroa and Pozas-Loya 2010); the need to seek democratic legitimacy (Inclán 2009); a needed mechanism to manage further political crises (Magaloni 2003); and strategic thinking with the objective to earn international recognition and to increase the possibility to anchor policy legacies (Cortez Salinas and Salazar Rebolledo 2019).

64. Colloquially known in legal circles as the "human rights reform," in 2011 several articles of the Mexican Constitution were reformed to make the Mexican State the main guarantor of human rights by including international standards on human rights (making them similar in the constitution) and adopting the *pro homine* principle. The reform produced an increase in human rights cases on which the court has ruled. For a detailed description, see García Castillo 2015. For analyses of this reform, see Castilla Juárez 2011 and Carmona Tinoco 2011. For some authors, this reform completed Mexico's transition into a constitutional democracy (Salazar Ugarte 2012).

65. It is colloquially known as *Sala IV*, or Fourth Chamber, by Costa Ricans.

66. This early document would become the basis for two features of Costa Rica's Supreme Court that have remained to the present day: the establishment of substitute justices (*magistrados suplentes*), who are called in to vote on cases when a justice is absent (Article 134), and unlimited terms through automatic reelection (Article 132).

67. The text also introduced a variety of elements to reinforce judicial independence, such as limiting the political activity of justices.

68. For an excellent and concise review of the various constitutional and legal changes that affected the court in the first half of the twentieth century in Costa Rica, see Cascante Segura 2014.

69. Scholars have identified other factors as well, such as continuity of the political elite, ethnic and cultural homogeneity, a political culture that values legality, guaranteed and obligatory education and social security, and a weak colonial tradition, among others (see, for example, Alcántara Sáez, 2008).

70. The 1949 Constitution prohibited immediate reelection but allowed any president to run again after sitting out for two terms (eight years). A 1969 constitutional reform eliminated reelection entirely. A 2002 ruling by Costa Rica's Constitutional Chamber allowed for reelection.

71. This is an important prerogative because in many other Latin American countries, a "constitutional convention" is necessary to bring about constitutional reforms.

72. Decisions on amparo cases began after 1950, when the Amparo Law regulating the process was enacted.

73. Continuing with a previous provision, justices are automatically renewed unless the Legislative Assembly votes to deny another term.

74. The proposal suggested adding the Fourth Chamber to the other three in charge of administrative, commercial, and financial law (First Chamber); family, labor, private, and notarial law (Second Chamber); and criminal law (Third Chamber).

75. Out of the fifty-seven deputies, forty-three voted in favor and six against. Eight were absent.

76. The threshold changed to a two-thirds majority in 2003.

77. For an excellent, detailed overview, see Sagüés 1991.

78. The actions can also be brought before the Constitutional Chamber by parties in judicial cases when a constitutional question is raised or through ex officio referrals from lower courts when they have doubts regarding the constitutionality of statutes. The process is halted until the chamber decides on the question and has obligatory and res judicata effects (Articles 104 and 117).

79. Amparos can also be brought against individual actions or omissions, but in a restricted way to persons or corporations exercising public powers.

80. The reform changed Article 132 of the constitution (through Law No. 4349) allowing immediate reelection. The original text allowed reelection only after presidents sat out two four-year terms.

81. The ruling marked a reversal from a position the chamber held in 2000, when it had declared the 1969 reform constitutional. It followed the submission of a case by President Arias who had sought to run for office again in 2002. The case was resubmitted by a private citizen in 2002. For an excellent, detailed account of the process, see Treminio Sánchez 2013.

82. The overall numbers are simply astonishing: from September 1989 to September 2023, Costa Rica's Constitutional Chamber had heard over half a million (502,198) cases (author's calculations). According to Zamora Zamora 2007, approximately 30 percent of amparos relate to medications.

83. The percentage of amparo cases out of all of the cases submitted up until September 2023 was 87.1.

84. Tellingly, the (now) classic edited book on changing legal culture in Latin America (see Couso 2010) does not include Costa Rica as a case study.

85. In the first case, the chamber declared that checkpoints could only be used with preauthorization or in cases with an open investigation underway. In the second, the chamber canceled the TSE investigation of Deputy Maureen Ballestero for having used a government plane in an election campaign. The debate was whether her parliamentary immunity should be waived in the investigation.

86. Criticism of the high levels of rulings in favor of amparos requiring medications has mostly come from the national social security system (CCSS), which has expressed dissatisfaction with the financial costs these decisions have (Solano 2009).

87. Interview, justice, San José, March 20, 2018.

88. Interview, justice, San José, March 19, 2018.

89. Interview, justice, San José, March 22, 2018.

90. Interview, substitute justice, San José, January 30, 2018.

Chapter 3

1. The measures essentially converted all US deposits into Argentine pesos.

2. In this case, it was the congressional opposition that demanded the summary impeachment of all the justices.

3. Kirchner received 22.2 percent of the vote against 25.4 and 14.1 percent, respectively, for the Peronists Menem and Adolfo Rodríguez Sáa, and 16.4 and 14 percent, respectively, for the Radicals Ricardo López Murphy and Elisa Carrió. Both Menem and Kirchner qualified for the second round of voting in May 2002, but Menem decided not to run. Kirchner was consequently declared the winner.

4. The team included prominent figures such as Horacio Verbtisky, investigative reporter and director of the prestigious *Centro de Estudios Legales y Sociales* (Centre for Legal and Social Studies), and legal experts from the following organization and institutions: *Poder Ciudadano* (Citizen Power), *Fundación Ambiente y Recursos Ciudadanos* (Environmental and Natural Resource Foundation), *Institutto de Estudios Comparados en Ciencias Penales y Sociales* (Institute for Comparative Studies in Criminal and Social Sciences) and the *Unión de Usuarios y Consumidores* (Consumer and Users Union).

5. This position was created during the 1994 reforms. It is a ministry in charge of acting as the main liaison with Congress.

6. Commentary from individuals and organizations is collected by the justice minister within fifteen days of the nomination. Once vetted, the nominee moves onto the Senate for confirmation.

7. According to Hauser, officials held meetings with Justices Highton, Zaffaroni, and Lorenzetti prior to their nominations. Justice Argibay did not have a meeting because her term at the International Criminal Court for the former Yugoslavia had not ended.

8. Zaffaroni's independent thinking is well captured by his public criticism of a provincial constitutional reform that had allowed Kirchner to get reelected in Santa Cruz (Hauser 2016, 31).

9. In October 2006 the Supreme Court, in the *Bustos* case, ruled that the "pesification" (the pegging of the peso to the US dollar) was constitutional, declaring that a 2001 decree and emergency law was sound. Further, the court ruled in 2005 that the repeal of the two most important amnesty laws and pardons (passed in 2003 by Congress during the Alfonsín years) were constitutional.

10. The study looks at justices' votes in the most salient 500 rulings from 1984 to 2013. The first figure refers to the 2004–8 period and the second to the 2009–13 period.

11. Argentina was one of the first countries in the world to establish rape as an exception to punishable abortions, an idea that was subsequently incorporated into several Latin American criminal codes.

12. The country's first criminal code, enacted in 1886, made abortion punishable under all circumstances. A reform in 1903 allowed one exception: failed attempts at reform followed, until the reform undertaken in 1921.

13. It found that court hearings caused LMR's abortion to be delayed to the point that she required an illegal abortion. Such decision violated Article 2 in relation to Articles 3 (right to equality and nondiscrimination), Article 7 (right to be free from torture or cruel inhuman or degrading treatment), and Article 17 (right to privacy). LMR's right to privacy was violated by the court's unlawful interference into a decision that should have included only LMR, her guardian, VDA, and her doctor. Failing to protect LMR's right to an abortion under Argentinean law, and the resulting suffering, violated her rights under Article 7, which protects individuals from mental as well as physical suffering. The violation was particularly serious given her status as a person with a disability.

14. In fact, the stepfather had raped her repeatedly between the ages of eleven and fifteen (UN Doc. CCPR/C101/D/1608/2007).

15. These are urgent and autonomous ex parte measures used for cases in which there is a high probability that the request is meritorious. They are self-executing because, once granted, no other proceeding is necessary to satisfy the applicant's claim.

16. The number of secretariats has increased over the years. There were seven of them in 2010. There have been other secretariats in the court that are not judicial, such as the *Secretaría general de administración*, which is the main administrative unit.

17. Interview, Buenos Aires, November 12, 2018.

18. This view was shared by several law clerks in interviews.

19. Interview, Buenos Aires, December 13, 2018. The reference to "equal marriage" refers to the court's engagement of a constitutional challenge against the traditional definition of marriage in 2010, just before same-sex marriage was legalized by Argentina's Congress in 2010. As per leaked information (Díez 2015), a majority of justices were to rule in favor of same-sex marriage, and the reference here suggests that included Justice Fayt.

20. Interview, Buenos Aires, December 13, 2018. The rift between Gialdino and some justices appears to have grown over time, to the point that he was asked to tender his resignation two years later (*Cronista*, March 10, 2013).

21. The Tejerina case refers to a ruling in which Justices Zaffaroni and Maqueda voted (in the minority) in favor of reducing the sentence of Romina Tejerina, who allegedly killed a newborn who had been the product of a rape.

22. Interview, Buenos Aires, November 12, 2018.

23. Interview, Buenos Aires, December 5, 2018.

24. Interview, Buenos Aires, December 13, 2018.

25. Interview, Buenos Aires, December 4, 2018.

26. Interview, Buenos Aires, November 14, 2018.

27. Interviews with five law clerks and one justice involved in these discussions.

28. Interview, Buenos Aires, December 5, 2018.

29. Interview, Buenos Aires, November 14, 2018.

30. Interview, Buenos Aires, December 4, 2018.

31. Traditionally, justices convene every Tuesday morning at nine o'clock in the (beautiful) building's (*Tribunales*) conference room, where they hold a meeting (*plenario*) to come to decisions (*acuerdos*). These are called the *acordadas de los martes* (Tuesday agreements).

32. Interview, Buenos Aires, December 6, 2022.

33. Interview, Buenos Aires, Supreme Court Justice, November 14, 2018.

34. Interview, Buenos Aires, December 5, 2022.

35. It is difficult to establish the exact date. However, a review of the blog shows that it entered Justice Maqueda's chamber on March 14 and exited on March 16.

36. Law clerks stated that one of the other rare cases in which a working group was established was during discussion around the 2006 ALITT case in which the court ruled in favor of granting a transgender organization legal status (*personería jurídica*). For an excellent summary of the case, see *Página 12*, November 22, 2006.

37. Underlining that close professional relationship is the fact that Justice Zaffaroni had three law clerks with expertise in criminal law, yet he decided to designate as point person a clerk from Lorenzetti's chamber.

38. Ezequiel González-Ocantos refers to him as one of Argentina's most "influential legal minds" (2016, 94).

39. Interview, Buenos Aires, December 11, 2018.

40. Interview, Buenos Aires, November 14, 2018.

41. And this right is truly universal in the country since nonnationals have the right to access health care.

42. Interview, lead law clerk, Buenos Aires, November 28, 2018.

43. Interview, Buenos Aires, November 28, 2018.

44. Interview, Buenos Aires, November 28, 2018.

45. Interview, Buenos Aires, November 28, 2018.

46. Interview, Buenos Aires, November 28, 2018.

47. Maqueda served in many city and provincial positions in Cordoba before being elected to the Senate in 2002.

48. This case involved a ruling in which the court ordered that all prisons in the country should adhere to the minimal rules established by the United Nations in the treatment of prisoners. According to a law clerk, the justice's *virage* toward clear progressive positions occurred with the Tejerina case (referred to previously). His progressive stance was reiterated by his voting subsequent positions in controversial cases, such as the 2009 Arriola ruling, in which he sided with the majority in declaring unconstitutional the criminalization of the possession of cannabis for personal consumption.

49. Interview, law clerk, Maqueda's chamber, Buenos Aires, December 6, 2018.

50. Interview, lead law clerk, Buenos Aires, November 28, 2018.

51. Interview, Buenos Aires, December 6, 2018. See note 36 for a description of the ALITT case.

52. Interview, Buenos Aires, December 13, 2018.

53. Interview, lead law clerk, Buenos Aires, November 28, 2018.

54. Interview, lead law clerk, Buenos Aires, November 28, 2018.

55. Lorenzetti took several concrete steps to restore the court's legitimacy guided by the idea that it had to become closer to the people, such as allowing for public hearings, making it easier for nonstate actors to submit amicus curiae, establishing sustained interactions with nongovernmental organizations, holding public forums and regular news conferences, and allowing for online public access to rulings.

56. *Pansada* is the colloquial Argentine term to refer to a big meal, a feast.

57. Interview, lead law clerk, Buenos Aires, November 28, 2018.

58. Her feminist position is perhaps best captured by the intense questioning during her confirmation hearing by conservative senators (see *Página 12*, June 24, 2004) and the strong reaction from socially conservative nonstate actors, including the Catholic Church hierarchy, who labeled her an "atheist and abortionist" (Hauser 2016, 39).

59. This article of the code is the legal provision (referred to above) that allows Supreme Court justices not to hear cases when they are deemed as not having a federal character or when the issues at hand are either not "transcendental" or "substantial."

60. Interview, Buenos Aires, December 5, 2018. The arbitrariness principle essentially refers to the requirement to use the least level of discretion possible when interpreting the law. In Justice Argibay's case, she was greatly influenced by Alfredo Adrián Urteaga (interview, law clerk, Argibay's chamber, December 3, 2018), with whom she had worked previously in another federal court (*Cámara Federal de Casación Penal*) and who had made his

critical position of judicial discretion rather clear. For a detailed justification of Justice Argibay's position, based on Urteaga's reasoning, see Argibay 2008. For an overview of the arbitrary principle, see Urteaga 2006.

61. Interview, Buenos Aires, December 3, 2018.

62. Interview, Buenos Aires, December 5, 2018.

63. The two associations were *Profamilia*, the pro-family association, and the Corporation of Catholic Lawyers (*Corporación de Abogados Católicos*). They argued that Highton had made her pro-abortion position clear in a publication of the early 1990s (Highton 1993), to which she responded during her confirmation hearing that she had never said "that any legislation related to abortion was unconstitutional" (*Página 12*, June 1, 2004).

64. Interview, Buenos Aires, December 7, 2018.

65. Interview, Buenos Aires, November 28, 2018. The case involved Pablo Albarracini, whose wife, on religious grounds, refused that he be given a blood transfusion while in critical condition in a Buenos Aires hospital. The court sided with her, essentially arguing that a declaration the patient has previously signed, in which he had clearly and expressly stated his opposition to any blood transfusion, should be respected.

66. Interviews suggest that Fayt tended to self-identify with Alfredo Palacios, the first socialist elected to Congress in 1904. A lawyer and academic, Palacios was vocal in expressing an interest in helping the poor and in fact introduced trail-blazing labor legislation that included, among other things, limiting the working day to eight hours and prohibiting child labor.

67. Interview, Buenos Aires, November 28, 2018.

68. Interview, law clerk, Fayt chamber, Buenos Aires, December 13, 2018.

69. Examples are the 1984 Arezón case (in which he ruled against an ableist case), the 1986 Bazterrica case (in which he ruled against the criminalization of drug possession), and the 1986 Sejeán case (right to privacy in support of divorce).

70. Landmark cases included, for example, the 1991 Molinas case, the 1998 Fernández Prietto case, and the 2000 Manna case, the last one pitting him directly against the executive, where Petracchi voted against a presidential decree.

71. Interview, Buenos Aires, November 14, 2018.

72. Interview, Buenos Aires, November 14, 2018.

73. Interview, Buenos Aires, November 28, 2018.

74. This office is the public defender before the Supreme Court in civil and criminal trials.

75. Let us recall that the lead law clerk represented the chambers of Justices Lorenzetti and Zaffaroni. The following paragraphs, until note 77, are based on interviews with sixteen individuals at the rank of justice and law clerk, including the law clerks in charge of drafting the ruling.

76. However, interviews suggest that the law clerks who did the bulk of the work were the ones representing the Lorenzetti, Zaffaroni, and Maqueda chambers. Justice Highton's chamber was deferential, and Fayt's designated law clerk did not attend the meetings frequently.

77. Interview, Buenos Aires, December 5, 2018.

78. Interview, Buenos Aires, December 6, 2018.

79. Article 19 reads: "Private actions by men that in any way do not offend public moral or order, nor affect a third party, are reserved to God, and exempt from the authority of

judges. Not one citizen of the nation will be obliged to do what the law does not order, nor deprived from what it does not prohibit."

80. This refers to a 2008 case in which the court responded to a challenge by a group of residents living in "villa inflammable," an area in the Matanza-Riachuelo river basin in the province of Buenos Aires, claiming compensation from the Argentine government, the city government of Buenos Aires, and forty-four businesses for damages they had suffered because of the river's pollution. In that ruling, the court not only agreed to compensation but established a detailed environmental policy implementation plan and tasked an intergovernmental institution, the Authority of the Matanza-Riachuelo Basin (*Autoridad de Cuenca Matanza Riachuelo*), with carrying out specific improvements and works to clean up the river. For a great review, see Botero 2018.

81. Interview, Buenos Aires, November 28, 2018.

82. Interview, Buenos Aires, December 12, 2018.

83. Interview, Buenos Aires, November 13, 2018.

84. Interview, Buenos Aires, December 13, 2018.

Chapter 4

1. Research on appointments by the Council of State and Supreme Court suggest that some clear criteria appear to drive list selection decisions. The most important selection criterion by the Council of State appears to be a desire to strike a balance between Liberal and Conservative candidates, not in a partisan manner but rather on a freethinking/institutional status quo axis (Lamprea 2010). For the Supreme Court, on the other hand, the main selection criterion appears to be loyalty to the Supreme Court itself and its jurisprudence (Lamprea 2010).

2. This period refers to the administrations of presidents Virgilio Barco Vargas (1986–90), César Gaviria Trujillo (1990–94), and Ernesto Samper Pizano (1994–88).

3. The senatorial confirmation requirement within a fragmented political party system appears to foster a great deal of compromise in the selection process. For example, evidence points to only small differences in voting behavior on the constitutionality of legislation between justices appointed by Liberal or Conservative presidents (Tiede 2022, 146–47, 160–61).

4. He earned a master's degree in procedural law and subsequently a PhD in constitutional law.

5. Interview, Bogotá, June 12, 2018. In Latin American judicial circles, "legislator" is generally used in lieu of legislature.

6. He also supported the candidacy of Clara López to the mayoralty of Bogotá upon leaving the court in 2006. López belonged to the leftist *Polo Democrático* (Democratic Pole).

7. These cases include a hugely important decision on a program that indexed housing interest rates to interest rates in the broader economy to facilitate financing for the urban middle class. Economic crises pushed interest rates higher, punishing homebuyers. In a couple of majority opinions drafted by Beltrán (C-747–1999, C-383–1999), the court banned repayment penalties, disallowed the capitalization of interests, and prohibited the downward adjustment of interest-rate calculations. It also includes decisions to constrain constitutional amendments pushed by conservative president Álvaro Uribe Vélez (2002–10) to fight terrorism that would have restricted civil liberties, such as the home searches and the interception of communications without warrants. In a majority opinion penned by

Beltrán's chamber, several of these provisions were struck down (C-1024–2002). On a salient decision on divorce (C-074–04), which declared constitutional a legal provision that allowed judges to dissolve marriages (even those performed by the Catholic Church), he sided with the majority.

8. *La Silla Vacía* is a respected and independent online publication that, among other things, monitors voting patterns in the CCC and assigns scores to the justices based on their voting behavior (see https://www.lasillavacia.com/). *La Silla Vacía* was founded by Juanita León, a well-known lawyer and journalist (law degree from Los Andes University and a MA in journalism by Columbia University) who has worked as a reporter for *The Wall Street Journal* and Colombia's prestigious *El Tiempo* newspaper and as editor-in-chief of *Semana* magazine.

9. Rodríguez-Raga developed these scores based on responses obtained in a survey completed by forty-three public law professors across Colombia's law faculties (2011). The scores are like LSV's, with a score of 1 for the most liberal and 10 for the most conservative.

10. In a 1998 ruling (C-481–1998), Beltrán joined two other justices (Hernando Herrera Vergara and José Gregorio Hernández) in a dissenting opinion to a ruling that declared unconstitutional a law that discriminated against teachers because of their "homosexuality." Beltrán justified his position by arguing that the majority opinion would violate the rights of children and adolescents given that the law considered it to be a personal matter. Importantly for our purposes, Beltrán's argument was framed around the decision made by the legislator to protect children and adolescents from visible "homosexualism" and clearly argued that "a constitutional judge cannot substitute the legislator." He also voted against the expansion of LGBTQ+ rights in the 2001 decision (SU-623–01) on the expansion of social security benefits to same-sex couples and the 2001 decision (C-814–01) on LGBTQ+ adoption rights.

11. The three voted consistently against the expansion of LGBTQ+ rights before the 2007 decision (C-075) that expanded social security benefits to same-sex couples, including the three above-cited decisions, as well as the 2004 divorce decision.

12. Interview, law clerk, Tafur's chamber, Bogotá, May 9, 2018.

13. *Conjueces* are called in to vote on cases when justices must recuse themselves. They are selected from a list. However, there is no record that Cepeda was ever called in. He spent most of the 1990s in academia.

14. Pardo Schlesinger would eventually become justice.

15. Such as the planned (but unmaterialized) referendum of late 2000 that sought to allow the president to dissolve Congress due to some corruption scandals and legislative deadlock.

16. Interview, Bogotá, June 8, 2018.

17. *Acta del Congreso, Plenaria 27*, December 13, 2000.

18. Interview law clerk, May 12, 1998.

19. Monroy dissented from the 2004 ruling that relaxed divorced restrictions and, like Escobar, prior to 2007, he dissented in three rulings that expanded LGBTQ+ rights.

20. Monroy seems to have belonged to a conservative network of jurists, judges, and academics. He replaced the most conservative justice in the previous bench (Vladimiro Naranjo Mesa, with whom he had a close relationship) as the preferred choice of justice by conservative forces in Colombia. Once confirmed, Monroy recruited three conservative law clerks, two of whom (Cristina Pardo and Julio Ossa) had worked in Naranjo's chamber in

the previous bench. Pardo, as we shall later see, would be influential in the development of Monroy's arguments against the decriminalization of abortion. According to Pardo, in both Naranjo's and Monroy's chambers, conservative ideas dominated discussions, both politically and ideologically, and the justices and law clerks had respect for Catholic ideas and were influenced by natural law ideas (*iusnatiralistas*) (as cited by Azuero Quijano 2006). Pardo was inspired by her former husband's doctoral thesis "El derecho a la vida y al aborto," Universidad de Navarra 1984, under the supervision of the conservative legal theorist Javier Hervada Xiberta (studio canónico).

21. *Acta del Congreso, Plenaria 27*, December 13, 2000.

22. While the university as a whole can be considered leftist, its Faculty of Law is more mixed. As Jaramillo and Alfonso suggest (2008, 141), some areas, such as civil and commercial law (Vargas's areas of specialization), tend to be more conservative, while others are more liberal, such as criminal, administrative, and labor law.

23. He was also a candidate to become a member of the 1991 Constituent Assembly, backed by the Liberal Party.

24. In the 2001 ruling on adoption, he went beyond equality arguments and emphatically defended the rights of same-sex couple to adopt arguing that society need to move away from religious morality and into a laic one. He further argued that the court had interpreted incorrectly the constitution around the idea of the family, since it can have different configurations.

25. Interview, law clerk, Araújo's chamber, Bogotá, April 28, 2018.

26. Acting as vice-National Public Prosecutor in 1999, he cosponsored the reforms to the Criminal Code of 1999–2000 and had taken a position on the statue.

27. Except for other three occasions in which he recused himself, Córdoba voted in favor of LGBTQ+ rights and the liberalization of abortion and divorce every single time while at the court (LSV, April 7, 2015).

28. He received 51 votes compared to the 40 votes received by Caldas; the third candidate (Libardo Rodríguez) received no votes.

29. As discussed in the previous chapter, *garantista* in Latin America refers to individuals who believe in the expansion of rights.

30. The reference to the "institutional block" in Colombia is similar to the "constitutional plexus" in Argentina: it refers to the entirety of the legal structure derived from the national constitution, statues, *and* international treaties and agreements.

31. In this case, the plaintiff argued that legal provisions that allowed for mitigating factors in the sentencing of abortion cases (when resulting from rape or unconsented insemination) was unconstitutional as a result of flaws in the legislative process.

32. The court argued that the 1980 statue (which was enacted before 2000 criminal code) was constitutional because of protecting life from conception is a state responsibility, even if the fetus does not have "legal personality." It also argued that Congress has the authority to criminalize conduct that may cause harm to the unborn. However, three justices (Eduardo Cifuentes Muñoz, Carlos Gaviria Díaz, and Alejandro Martínez Caballero) signed a dissenting opinion in which they criticized the absolute nature of the criminal provisions being questioned during the first trimester of pregnancy. They also criticized the attribution of legal personhood to the fetus. The justices largely based their argument defending the notion of "procreative autonomy" taking a strong position on women's rights: "A pregnant woman enjoys the constitutional right to procreative autonomy. The State must

protect that right and take necessary measures so that it be effective or providing those who do not the scientific mechanisms to avoid the risk that clandestine abortions represent." In a ruling the following year (C-591–95), a majority argued that legal existence begins at birth, but they confirmed that life starts at the moment of contraception.

33. A 1997 decision (C-213–97) confirmed the previous decision as a constitutional *res judicata*, or reaffirming jurisprudence. For a detailed account of these 1990s decisions, see Bohórquez Monsalve et al. 2019.

34. The three justices who dissented from the C-133–094 majority also dissented here, especially on the majority's reliance on papal encyclicals to build its lines of argumentation.

35. A 2002 decision (C-198–02) was also a res judicata decision of the 2001 ruling.

36. The court had previously engaged the idea of the weighing of rights (C-133–94, C-475–97, and C-093–01). However, C-647–01 was, to my knowledge, the first time it was introduced in discussions around reproductive rights.

37. At its most basic level, proportionality analysis involves the application of three logical steps when two rights collide to arrive at a decision. Typically, the end pursued has to be sufficiently important; the means involving the restriction on the right has to be rationally related to the achievement of the end and not restrict its enjoyment more than necessary; and the social benefit in terms of the achievement of the end must outweigh the harm done by the restriction of the right (Landau 2005).

38. Recent work has challenged the idea that proportionality analysis spread from Germany almost mechanically to other parts of the world after World War II and shows how some Latin American judiciaries engaged in proportionality analysis in the first half of the twentieth century (Pou-Giménez et al. 2022).

39. In interviews, justices and law clerks often refer to Robert Alexy's work on proportionality theory (2010) when engaging the proportionality test. His work, which has been translated from German and is published by Colombian university presses, appears to be well read by many at the court. Jurists, some of whom have worked at the court, have built on Alexy's work to theorize on constitutional matters further (Arango 2005; Bernal 2009).

40. Decisions will eventually refer explicitly to the proportionality test. See, for example, C-1064–01, C-773–03, and C-144–15.

41. Interview, Bogotá, June 18, 2018.

42. For a detailed review of all the arguments and challenged statue provisions, see Jaramillo and Alfonso (2008, 64–71).

43. Information is based on a response dated August 27, 2008, from General Secretary Martha Victoria Sáchica Méndez to an access-to-information request (DSG-190/18); author's copy.

44. Interview, Bogotá, June 12, 2018. Nilson Pinilla was nominated by President Uribe and confirmed to the court by the Senate in June 2006, shortly after the May general elections, when Uribe was reelected. He filled the vacancy left by Justice Beltrán. While the candidate list was likely not known in January and February 2006, Pinilla had been mentioned as a likely contender because of his close ties to conservative groups. However, this justice's mention of Pinilla was certainly meant to capture the fact that the imminent vacancy was going to be filled with a conservative justice, given that it was President Uribe's turn to submit a list to the Senate.

45. Requests were submitted on January 23 by Brenda Rocha, on February 24 by Cristina Amparo Cárdenas de Bohórquez, and on March 7 by Sigifredo Corredor Rodríguez.

These were rejected on March 8 (communiqué 26, 2006), February 1 (communiqué 90, 2006), and February 24 (communiqué 91, 2006).

46. It urged the Court to declare unconstitutional Article 122 of the Criminal Code under the condition that "it not include the decriminalization" of abortion under three conditions: unconsented pregnancy, when the pregnancy poses a threat to the physical or mental health of the woman; when malformations or other conditions make the pregnancy inviable. As a result, his office recommended to declare unconstitutional Articles 122, 123 and 124 (Author's copy).

47. Interviews with law clerks, Bogotá, April 26 and June 27, 2018.

48. Interview, Bogotá, April 26, 2018.

49. Interview, Bogotá, June 27, 2018.

50. Interview, Bogotá, April 26, 2018.

51. Interview, Bogotá, June 27, 2018.

52. Interviews.

53. Interview, Bogotá, June 27, 2018.

54. Interview, Bogotá, June 27, 2018.

55. Interview with law clerk, Bogotá, April 26, 2018.

56. Interview with law clerk, Bogotá, April 26, 2018.

57. In interviews, team members referred to the intervention made by the Colombian Episcopal Conference (*Conferencia Episcopal Colombiana*) a few weeks later, which argued for rejecting the public action's demand because the criminal code protected the life, health, and integrity of the unborn. They also suggest that they predicted the same argument being deployed by conservative justices once the draft opinion was discussed.

58. Interview, Bogotá, June 27, 2018.

59. Interviews.

60. Interviews.

61. Interview, Bogotá, June 27, 2018.

62. Interview, Bogotá, June 18, 2018.

63. Interview, Bogotá, May 3, 2018.

64. Interview, Bogotá, April 26, 2018.

65. Interview, Bogotá, June 27, 2018.

66. Interview, Bogotá, May 3, 2018.

67. Interview, Bogotá, June 18, 2018.

68. Interview, Bogotá, June 27, 2018. Valledupar is in the Caribbean part of Colombia, and people from the Caribbean region are widely considered to be more plainspoken.

69. Interview, Bogotá, May 23, 2018.

70. Interview, Bogotá, May 24, 2018.

71. Interview, Bogotá, May 23, 2018.

72. Interview, Bogotá, May 23, 2018.

73. Interview, Bogotá, June 8, 2018.

74. Interview, Bogotá, May 3, 2018.

75. Interview, Bogotá, June 8, 2018. The reference is to Murphy's classic *Elements of Judicial Strategy* (1964), which is one of the first works on strategic judicial behavior.

76. Interview Bogotá, June 12, 2018.

77. Interview, Bogotá, May 31, 2018.

78. Interview, Bogotá, June 12, 2018.

79. Interview. Bogotá, June 8, 2018.

80. Interviews.

81. Interview, Bogotá, June 8, 2018.

82. Interview, Bogotá, June 12, 2018.

83. Interview, Bogotá, June 12, 2018.

84. Interview with Justice, Bogotá, June 8, 2018.

85. Interview, law clerk, Cepeda's chamber, May 3, 2018.

86. Interview, Bogotá, May 8, 2018. The interviewee mentioned that he was the "logical" justice to lead the discussion, in part because Justice Cepeda "was not a good communicator."

87. As per document DSG-190/18 provided by the court's General Secretariat.

88. Court records refer to two documents—*Acta 17, Sesión Plena de la Corte Constitucional, Mayo 9, 2006*, and *Acta 18, Sesión Plena de la Corte Constitucional, Mayo 10, 2006* that were provided by the General Secretariat on August 27, 2018, through an access-to-information request. Author's copies. According to General Secretary Martha Victoria Sáchica Méndez (who worked at the court from its establishment until June 2023), only she and the justices were present at these plenary sessions (personal interview, Bogotá, June 18, 2018). The secretary takes notes, and reports on the deliberations are filed for each session.

89. Such disagreements included not affording sufficient attention to the weight that life carries and the direct link between personal dignity and autonomy.

90. Justice Vargas was not present during the morning part of the session for personal reasons. The plenary was thus made by seven justices.

91. The draft paragraph reads: "To declare Article 122 of the Criminal Code constitutional with the understanding that an abortion crime is not committed, when, with the woman's willingness, the termination of pregnancy is undertaken in these cases: a) when the continuation of pregnancy represents a danger to a woman's life or health, certified by a doctor; b) when there exist malformations of the fetus which make its life unviable, certified by a doctor; c) when pregnancy is the result of a conduct, duly reported, that constitutes carnal access or a sexual act without consent, abusive or artificial or unconsented compensation [an apparent mistake most clearly meant to read "insemination"], or from incest" (*Acta 18*, 13).

92. Interview, Bogotá, April 26, 2018.

93. Information on interviews is withheld on the following quotations to protect possible personal identification.

94. Interview, Bogotá, June 27, 2018.

95. It states that there can be no "clinics, hospitals, health centers or whatever name they are given, that can declare conscientious objections to carry out the procedure when the stated conditions in this ruling are met."

Chapter 5

1. The PT's numbers were 10, 7, 1, and 1 over the same time frame; the PVEM had won 8 seats in 1997, and 5 and 5 in 2000 and 2003. The remaining seat in 2000 and 2003 went to a smaller new Convergence Party (*Convergencia*).

2. These reforms included the enshrinement of the protection for minorities in the constitution, the enactment of the first nondiscrimination legislation, the establishment of a national institute to combat discrimination, and national campaigns to fight homophobia.

3. Tellingly, the school was originally founded in 1955 as the National Jurisprudential School (*Escuela Nacional de Jurisprudencia*). Pilar Domingo calculates that, during PRI rule, some 70 percent of judges in Mexico came from that school (2000).

4. The authors code on the interpretivist-legalist continuum in three ways: overturning judicial precedent that limits judicial power; expanding the court's jurisdiction in a non-literal interpretation of the constitution; and ruling against a limited interpretation of standing (Sánchez et al. 2011, 33).

5. According to the measurement developed by Sánchez, Magaloni, and Magar (2009), Cossío would be the second most "legalist" justice on the 2008 bench.

6. The other was Juan Díaz Romero. He was one of the two justices who was forced to retire in 2006.

7. As in previous chapters, I refer to the justice's last name(s) depending on how they are usually referred to in the country by legal experts and journalists: sometimes they use one last name and sometimes more.

8. The most salient cases were 2146–2005 and 307–2007. The first one refers to a soldier who was forced to retire after his status was revealed during unconsented blood work. The second one was a broader question on the constitutionality of such dismissals. While the majority voted in favor against such actions based on discrimination, Azuela voted to support forced dismissals. See Pou Giménez 2012 for a detailed analysis of the cases. Azuela's social conservativism was perhaps best captured by a declaration he made at his retirement speech at the court at the end of his term, when he compared "good" law clerks to "good" wives: "When the wife is good, one lives in tranquility."

9. As explained in the previous chapters, the term "conventional control" refers to the requirement to adhere to international treaties in the adjudication of cases by high courts.

10. Interview, Mexico City, October 2, 2018.

11. Interview, Mexico City, October 2, 2018.

12. Interview, Mexico City, October 5, 2018.

13. Interview, Mexico City, October 2, 2018.

14. Controversia Constitucional 31/97, "Voto Particular," *Semanario Judicial de la Federación y Gaceta*, Tomo XI, January 2000, 738.

15. The case involved a challenge to poem written by Sergio Witz titled "(Invitation) The Motherland amid Shit"—*(Invitación) La Patria entre la mierda*—in which he expressed his desire to use the national flag as toilet paper. After a complaint filed by a nongovernmental organization, the Federal Public Prosecutor (*Ministerio Público Federal*) arraigned Witz before a district court for violating provisions in the Coat of Arms, Flag and National Anthem Law (*Ley sobre el Escudo, Bandera y el Himno Nacionales*). Charged by the judge, he submitted a writ of *amparo* arguing that his freedom of speech had been violated. It was denied. He subsequently appealed the decision. The appellate court forwarded the case to the Supreme Court to determine whether the provisions used in the federal criminal code to convict Witz were constitutional. The case (2676–2003) was heard by the First Chamber of the Court, which ruled, in a 3–2 majority, that the constitutional right to freedom of expression does not "include the right to dissent from a given national morality ridiculing national symbols." Justice Gudiño sided with the majority.

16. Interview, Mexico City, October 10, 2018.

17. The office, known as Constitutional Actions and Controversies (*Unidad de Controversias y Acciones Constitucionales*), was created in 2000, but Góngora significantly increased its resources during his term as chief justice. For detailed accounts of these changes, see Castillejos Aragón (2013, 147–48) and Cortez Salinas (2020, 123–28).

18. Interview, Mexico City, October 8, 2018.

19. The other vote went to Justice Sergio Valls.

20. Such closeness is captured by the fact that she was one of the three justices nominated to serve the longest terms with the newly established staggered system.

21. Acción in Inconstitucionalidad 2/2010, Plenary Session, August 5, 2010, 20.

22. AI 2/2010, Plenary Session, August 5, 2010, 63.

23. Tellingly, Justice Sánchez Cordero elaborates extensively in the preface to the Spanish translation of this author's work on gay marriage (Díez 2018) on the importance of supporting changes to the traditional definition of marriage based on ideas of liberty and social justice. (Disclosure: the publishing house, of its own volition, asked the then-retired justice to write the preface.) Referring to the court's first ruling (2–2010) on the subject, in which she joined the 8–2 majority in declaring Mexico City's enactment of gay marriage constitutional, she, for example, speaks about the "great satisfaction" she had in writing the preface because the book's content "involves me, and many other colleagues who, from different ambits, have worked in Mexico and other Latin American countries to overcome legislative paradigms that can break down arbitrary and unequal 'classifications' and to build policies that allow societies to live in freedom" (2018, 15).

24. Interview, Mexico City, September 12, 2018. Carbonell is one of the most famous jurists in Mexico and a clear neoconstitutionalist.

25. He was a collaborator in the campaign of President Miguel López Portillo (1976–82).

26. Acción de Inconstitucionalidad 8/2014, en sesión del 10 de agosto de 2015).

27. Acción de Inconstitucionalidad 8/2014, en sesión del 10 de agosto de 2015.

28. These justices were José Vicente Aguinaco Alemán and Juventino Castro y Castro.

29. The other two candidates on the list were María Teresa Martínez (who received six votes) and Teresita Rendón (who received two).

30. The center's primary mission is to foster research and education on political and constitutional questions to support democracy in Spain and Ibero American countries.

31. See Cortez Salinas's magnificent study (2020) for a detailed description.

32. The program included three facets: increasing judicial transparency, fostering interaction with the legal profession, and increasing the use of remedies to augment rights decisions (Castillejos-Aragón 2013, 150).

33. Please see chapter 1 for detailed description of this institutional feature.

34. The scandal, colloquially known as *PEMEXgate*, involved taking funds from the national oil company's workers union to fund the PRI presidential candidacy. The tribunal fined the PRI with the equivalent, at the time, of US$90 million.

35. Out of the 82 senators present, PRI cast 37 votes in favor of Luna. Twelve PAN senators voted for Díaz de León, and the remaining PRD and PAN votes went to De la Peza.

36. Fifteen PAN senators did not vote for her.

37. One example is the Castañeda case (743/2005).

38. Interview, Mexico City, May 31, 2019.

39. The other two were Felipe Borrego (former PRI senator and party leader) and Bernardo Sepúlveda (a former cabinet minister in the 1980s).

40. That refers to Sepúlveda, who with experience at the International Criminal Court, was considered a strong candidate. Twenty PAN and five other opposition senators did not vote for him.

41. Amparo Directo 6/2008, en sesión del 24 de noviembre de 2008, 16.

42. She had been cabinet minister in the first half of his administration and his legal counsel.

43. Franco had been legal counsel to President Salinas and deputy-minister to Zedillo as well as Fox.

44. Those negotiations became evident when Herrera Tello withdrew her candidacy before the confirmation vote before reinstating it later. She earned three votes and Sámano two.

45. He also served as a judge for a year with its predecessor, the Federal Electoral Institute.

46. Interview, Mexico City, May 31, 2019.

47. Interview, Mexico City, October 2, 2018. The reasonableness standard refers to a test whereby the judge asks whether decisions around lawmaking were made with legitimacy and designed to remedy a given situation.

48. Interview, Mexico City, October 12, 2018.

49. The states of Hidalgo and Tabasco were the first to begin this trend.

50. Before the reforms, Mexico City's leader, the regent, was appointed by the president following a constitutional reform passed in 1928 that abolished local governance.

51. Mexico City's first, full-fledged criminal code was enacted in 2002.

52. Robles, a cabinet minister in the city government, was elected by the assembly to replace PRD mayor Cuauhtémoc Cárdenas, who stepped down to seek the presidency in the 2000 federal elections.

53. For a great account, see MacDonald and Mills 2010.

54. Justices vote on parts or the entirety of a draft opinion. A justice may well vote on the constitutionality of one article but not on another one. Votes can include numerous decisions on various components of challenged legal provisions. Four types of decisions on various provisions are possible. Justices can vote to strike down, to uphold, to dismiss, or to reject (*desestimar*), which occurs when a majority votes to strike down legislation but does not reach the supermajority of eight justices.

55. At the Mexican Supreme Court, the Justice Rapporteur alone decides whether a case is admissible through a feature called "initial agreement" (*acuerdo inicial*). The case is dropped if found non-admissible. The plaintiff can present an appeal that is then decided by one of the two chambers or the full bench (depending on the case). In this instance, there were questions about the case's admissibility given the timing of the submission to the court (whether or not a business day could be counted in the set thirty-day window) and whether legislators-elect who had not been sworn in could file a constitutional action. Justice Sánchez Cordero decided that the case was admissible.

56. In favor of the draft opinion were Justices Azuela, Silva, Castro y Castro, Gudiño, Roman, Sánchez Cordero, and Góngora. Voting against it were Justices Aguirre, Díaz Romero, Aguinaco, and Ortiz Mayagoitia. In a second component of the opinion, justices

voted on the criminal proceedings code and whether public prosecutors could be permitted to authorize genetic abortions. In a 6–5 vote, the justices decided that they were not.

57. It must be noted that the original reform bill came from PRI legislator Armando Tonatiuh González, who presented it on November 23, 2007. A similar bill was submitted five days later by two legislators belonging to a "progressive alliance" called the Social-Democratic Parliamentary Coalition, which included the PRD. Both bills were subsequently submitted to the appropriate legislative committees for formal discussion and debate.

58. For analyses of the reform, see Sánchez Fuentes et al. 2008; MacDonald and Mills 2010; Becker and Díaz Olavarrieta 2013; and Lamas 2017, 44–48.

59. For a review of Ebrard's push for what he called the expansion of "full citizenship rights," see Díez 2015, 162–64.

60. As you may recall from the introduction, Uruguay decriminalized abortion in 2012, but in that case and unlike Mexico City, women must explain their decision to seek an abortion before a committee made up of three medical professionals (*La Nación*, October 22, 2012). Uruguayan women therefore need the state's approval to become full citizens.

61. For an excellent discussion on decision-making in Mexico's high court see Elizondo Mayer-Serra and Magaloni, 2011.

62. Public plenary meetings are usually held on Mondays, Tuesdays, and Thursdays at 11:00 a.m.

63. Interview, Mexico City, October 12, 2018. A "clear shaving blade" means shaving with no shaving cream—the expression is an allusion to making arguments with no filters. For the unfamiliar reader, breakfast meetings are a revered tradition by businesspeople and politicians in Mexico to discuss important matters.

64. Interview, Mexico City, October 5, 2018. Importantly, there appears to be little communication even between the chambers of justices who have close personal connections. For example, and according to one law clerk, a daughter of Justice Sánchez Cordero was married to a son of Justice Aguirre's, but the justices did not discuss the case (Interview, Mexico City, September, 2018).

65. Interview, Mexico City, October 8, 2018.

66. Interview, Mexico City, September 17, 2018.

67. Interview, Mexico City, September 12, 2018.

68. For the most comprehensive study of law clerks at Mexico's Supreme Court, see Cortez Salinas 2019.

69. Interview, Mexico City, October 8, 2018.

70. Interview, Mexico City, October 5, 2018.

71. Justice Raúl Carrancá y Rivas argued that Aguirre was incompetent to oversee the file given his religiosity (*Cimacnoticias*, June 26, 2007). Among the legislators objecting was Leticia Quezada Contreras, chair of the assembly's Equity and Gender Committee.

72. For a detailed account on many of these activities, see GIRE 2009, 27–29.

73. The decision to seek out input from these experts was to afford the report the most legitimacy possible and to move the arguments away from moral positions. Interview, Mexico City, August 31, 2018.

74. Author's copy. These individuals included Carla Huerta, Margarita Valdés, Marisa Belausteguigoitia, Ana Laura Magaloni, Martha Villareal, and Juan Luis Alvarez Gayud.

75. Such as Jorge Carpizo, Raúl Carrancá y Rivas, Lorenzo Córdova, and Alejandro Madrazo.

76. Author's copy. For a succinct summary, see *Proceso*, June 21, 2007.

77. Aguirre leveled a scathing criticism of the practice in the minority opinion he co-signed with Azuela and Góngora, stating that they opposed the majority opinion in part because it had taken into consideration information that had not been part of the case and that it was "not possible that this High Tribunal take into consideration medical evidence or opinions that were not part of the Amparo [that was] submitted to the district judge."

78. Titled "Questionnaire for expert opinion relation to conception and human life inside the womb," it was sent to four experts—María Cristina Castro Márquez Orozco, Alejandro Reyes Fuentes, Guillermo Soberón Andrade, and Ricardo Tapia Ibargüengoytia. Two of them declined to answer the questionnaire, apparently because of its biased nature (*La Jornada*, September 4, 2007). One of the questions, for example, asked what the difference is between an embryo at 11, 12, and 13 weeks. The experts were asked to answer the questionnaire during a closed-door meeting at the court on August 16 (*El Universal*, August 23, 2007).

79. Interview. "To place a *sambenito* on someone" is an old Spanish expression referring to the unjust accusation of a person.

80. Interview with justice, Mexico City, May 31, 2019.

81. Interview with justice, Mexico City, October 8, 2018.

82. Interview with law clerk, Justice Silva's chamber, Mexico City, September 13, 2018.

83. Interview, Mexico City, October 18, 2018.

84. Interview, law clerk, Justice Gudiño's chamber, Mexico City, October 10, 2018.

85. Interview, law clerk, Justice Valls's chamber, Mexico City, September 18, 2018.

86. Interview, Mexico City, October 5, 2018. Serrano Limón was the head of the organization *Provida* (mentioned above) and one of the most visible pro-life figures in Mexico. His image had been severely tarnished at this point because of press reports about the misuse of funds directed to set up care centers for women. He would later be charged and arrested when reports were confirmed by Mexican authorities (*El País*, February 18, 2016).

87. Interview, Mexico City, September 12, 2018.

88. Interview, Mexico City, September 11, 2018.

89. Interview, Mexico City, October 2, 2018.

90. Interview, Mexico City, October 4, 2-18. Beltrán was part of GIRE's legal team.

91. Interview, Mexico City, September 12, 2018.

92. Author's copy.

93. Interview, Mexico City, October 5, 2018.

94. Interview, Mexico City, September 12, 2018.

95. Interviews, Mexico City, September 17, 2018, and May 31, 2019.

96. Interview, Mexico City, September 12, 2018.

97. Interview, Mexico City, September 17, 2018.

98. Interview, Mexico City, October 5, 2018.

99. Interview, Mexico City, May 31, 2018.

100. It declared constitutional the reforms to Article 145 of the criminal code, which lessened the penalties for abortions committed beyond the twelve weeks.

101. Interview, Mexico City, August 8, 2018.

102. Interview, Mexico City, October 10, 2018.

103. Discarding the proportionality test is quite remarkable, given that it had just begun to be used by neoconstitutional law clerks and justices at the court at around that time (Pou 2012), and some work credits Cossío's innovative approach to the law with the introduction of the test to the court (Cortez Salinas 2020).

104. This refers to the vagueness doctrine (*Principio de Taxatividad*). The analysis meant to establish whether changes to the penalties were constitutional: the reforms lessened the penalties applied to women who have an abortion after the twelve-week period from one to three years in prison to three to six months or 300 days of labor (Article 145).

105. Interview, justice, Mexico City, May 31, 2019.

106. Interview, law clerk, Gudiño's chamber, Mexico City, October 10, 2018.

107. Interview, justice, Mexico City, October 3, 2018.

108. Interview, law clerk, Silva's chamber, Mexico City, September 13, 2018.

109. Interview, Mexico City, September 17, 2018.

110. Interview, Mexico City, September 13, 2018.

111. Interview, Mexico City, September 11, 2018.

112. Interview, Mexico City, September 12, 2018.

113. Interview, Mexico City, September 12, 2018.

114. Interview, Mexico City, October 2, 2018.

115. For two of the best analyses of the final decision that include the various arguments advanced in the concurrent opinions, see Adame 2009 and Pou 2009.

116. They also referred to a little know regulations (*norma*) enacted by the Health Ministry in 2005 (NOM-046-SSA2–2005) that requires federal hospitals to provide abortions to women and girls when allowed by state legislation.

117. This refers to the highly controversial "mandatory pretrial detention" (*prisión preventiva oficiosa*), a provision established by Article 19 of the constitution. It allows federal prosecutors to jail individuals suspected of having committed a crime while awaiting trial. After a long process, the Inter-American Court of Human Rights deemed the practice to be in violation of basic human rights and ordered the Mexican state to eliminate it from the legal system (IDH_CP-25/2023).

118. Ten votes were cast in favor. One justice was absent.

Chapter 6

1. From 2001 until 2013, the lists were supplied with a score based on candidates' experiences and credentials.

2. It increased from approximately 30 percent in 1998 to just under 35 percent in 2018 (Cascante Matamoros and Lara Escalante 2021).

3. Interview, San José, March 18, 1998.

4. The analysis looks at 2,733 AI cases for the decade including cases that were heard and voted on and rejected.

5. Interview, San José, March 14, 2018. A *chichicaste* is a Central American thorny weed.

6. Interview, Justice, March 22, 2018.

7. Interview, San José, March 21, 2018.

8. Interview, retired substitute justice, San José, February 2, 2018.

9. Interview, substitute justice, San José, January 30, 2018.

10. Interview, San José, February 3, 2018.

11. The decision culminated a very divisive yet significant process that must be mentioned. Arias supported signing the trade agreement but did not have enough support in the assembly for its ratification (recall that the authority to sign international treaties and agreements rests with the country's parliament). He thus decided to put the question to Costa Ricans through a referendum through an executive order. After the Electoral Tribunal endorsed the decision, a significant mobilization against the referendum ensued, which included constitutional challenges by civil society groups and parliamentarians before the CC. The ruling was a complex one, with the justices deciding on a variety of procedural and substantive questions, from whether triggering a referendum was constitutional to whether challenging its constitutionality should be admissible and whether the actual agreement, once adopted, would violate the constitution. On admissibility, Justice Calzada is the only one who cast a minority opinion arguing the challenge from the assembly should not be admissible. On proper legislative procedure, Justices Armijo and Cruz Castro voted in the minority, noting that there were unconstitutional aspects.

12. The case ultimately ended up at the Inter-American Court of Human Rights. Skirting the question of when life begins, in a historic ruling (C No. 257)—colloquially known as the *Artavia Murillo* case—it declared in 2012 that the prohibition of IVF violated the right to privacy and family life, personal liberty, and the integrity of the petitioners. While it ducked the question of when life starts, the court very importantly stated that governments could not give embryos and fetuses absolute protection under the American Convention on Human Rights.

13. This case was an AI brought to the chamber by an evangelical minister who challenged the constitutionality of provisions (Articles 23 and 24) of the family code, which restricts marriages not performed by Catholic priests from having automatic "civil effects" (Costa Rica is one of a handful of confessional states in Latin America, and Catholicism is its official religion). Marriages performed by priests, pastors, and leaders of other denominations do not have civil effects, and the parties must register their marriages at a civil registry. The plaintiff argued that the code violated equality principles enshrined in the constitution and international agreements. The majority ruling, penned by Mora Mora himself, argued, among other things, that the Article 23 of the constitution expressly gave the Catholic Church special status and that it is up to the legislator to decide on changes to it.

14. Calzada was elected chief justice in the 2008–13 period. In 2007, when the abortion case was discussed, she was acting justice. The chief justice at the time was Luis Fernando Soto Carrera, who held the position from 2005 until 2008.

15. Such as the Alberto Brenes Córdoba Award granted by Costa Rica's Law Society (*Colegio de Abogados y Abogadas de Costa Rica*) to the best publication in law and the Ulises Odio Santos Award granted by the Supreme Court for distinguished work in legal writing.

16. He also received the Ulises Odio Santos Award.

17. Chinchilla was a very influential figure within the PLN at the time. After her deputyship at the assembly in 2006, she served as cabinet minister (Public Security and Justice) and vice president in the second Arias administration (2006–10), and she was ultimately elected president of Costa Rica in 2010.

18. Later on, he would be promoted by the party to fill in a permanent vacancy at the chamber in 2009.

19. Interview, San José, March 12, 2018.

20. Interview, San José, March 14, 2018.

21. Interview, substitute justice, San José, June 19, 2019.

22. Interview, San José, March 21, 2018.

23. Interview, San José, March 22, 2018.

24. Interview, San José, March 20, 2018.

25. Interview, San José, March 14, 2018.

26. Interview, San José, March 14, 2018.

27. Interview, San José, March 19, 2018.

28. Interview, San José, June 24, 2019.

29. Interview, San José, March 16, 2018.

30. When asked "How much do you agree or disagree with the idea that the Constitutional Chamber has the power (*potestad* in Spanish) to decide on sexual and reproductive issues in our society?" most Costa Ricans (74 percent) disapproved in 2018. They selected 1, 2, and 3 on a scale of 5, where 0 indicated strong disapproval and 5 strong approval. In 2019, the disapproval rate was 66 percent. The question was inserted by Michelle Dion and the author into surveys carried out by the University of Costa Rica's Center for Political Studies (CIEP) on March 19–21, 2018 (CIEP 2018).

31. Interview, San José, February 2, 2018.

32. Interview, San José, February 6, 2018.

33. Interview, San José, June 9, 2019.

34. Interview, San José, March 16, 2018.

35. Interview, San José, March 21, 2018.

36. Named *Protocolo de Atención Clínica para el procedimiento médico vinculado con el Artículo 121 del Código Penal: Interrupción Terapéutica del Embarazo*.

37. For an excellent analysis, see Serrano Guzmán 2024.

Conclusion

1. Abortion policy reforms are mentioned in order of ruling amplitude, as presented in table I.1 in the introduction.

2. The authors rely on political-party typology in which "institutional" leftist parties are identified by a notable internal dispersion of power, compared to populist movements and machine leftists parties developed by Steven Levitsky and Kenneth Roberts (2011).

3. The 2007 poll was conducted by Latinobarómetro (https://www.latinobarometro.org).

4. The AmericasBarometer 2008 poll was conducted by the LAPOP Lab at Vanderbilt University (https://www.vanderbilt.edu/lapop/).

5. This decision is very interesting in light of a 2016 ruling by the same tribunal (No. 0014–2005-RA) that upheld a ban on emergency contraceptives, arguing that rights of women do not take precedence over the rights of the unborn after fertilization occurs. While the 2021 ruling is rather limited in scope, especially compared with the three positive cases analyzed in this book, it is nonetheless a change in the court's position over time, one that warrants further investigation.

6. This refers to legislation (Ley 21.030) enacted in September 2017.

7. For a great analysis of the ruling, see Undurraga Valdés (2019).

8. The tribunal reaffirmed its position on this issue in 2019, when its rulings were challenged (STC Rol No. 5572–18-CDS / 5650118-CDS, *acumuladas*) The ruling was a response to a constitutional challenge submitted by senators against regulations (Decree 67) drafted by the health ministry that would govern the practice.

9. A new constitution was put to Chileans in late 2022 through a plebiscite that included an article that would have enshrined in the right to have access to abortion. It was defeated.

10. The country changed Article 37 of its constitution in 2010 establishing a complete ban on abortion.

11. By mid-2024, a new bill that reaffirms the ban passed in the Senate and was being debated in the lower house.

Bibliography

Abraham, Margaret, Esther Ngan-ling Chow, Laura Maratou-Altipranti, and Evangelina Tastsoglou. 2011. "Rethinking Citizenship with Women in Focus." In *Contours of Citizenship: Women, Diversity and Practices of Citizenship*, edited by Margaret Abraham, Esther Ngan-ling Chow, Laura Maratou-Altipranti, and Evangelina Tastsoglou, 1–21. New York: Routledge.

Acemoglu, Daron, and James A. Robinson. 2020. *The Narrow Corridor: States, Societies, and The Fate of Liberty*. New York: Penguin Press.

Acevedo, Zoila. 1979. "Abortion in Early Latin America." *Women & Health* 4 (2): 159–67.

Adame Goddard, Jorge. 2009. "Análisis de la sentencia que declara constitucional a la Ley del Distrito Federal, que permite a la madre dar muerte al concebido menor de doce semanas." *Boletín Mexicano de Derecho Comparado*, no. 125: 1103–27.

Agudelo, Carlos Alberto. 2010. "Dialogos internos en la Corte Constitucional Colombiana sobre el modus operandi en la seleccion de Tutelas entre la informalidad, la politica y la academia." *Jurídicas* 7 (2): 53–78.

Albarracín, Juan, Alura Gamboa, and Scott Mainwaring. 2018. "Deinstitutionalization without Collapse: Colombia's Party System." In *Party Systems in Latin America*, edited by Scott Mainwaring, 227–54. New York: Cambridge University Press.

Alcántara Sáez, Manuel. 2008. *Sistemas politicos de América Latina*. 2nd ed. Madrid: Editorial Tecnos.

Alexy, Robert. 2010. *A Theory of Constitutional Rights*. New York: Oxford University Press.

Alvarez, Sonia. 1990. *Engendering Democracy in Brazil: Women's Movements in Transitional Politics*. Princeton, NJ: Princeton University Press.

Ansolabehere, Karina. 2008. "Legalistas, legalistas noderados y garantistas moderados." *Revista Mexicana de Sociología* 70 (2): 331–59.

Arango Rivadeneira, Rodolfo. 2005. *El concepto de derechos sociales fundamentales*. Bogotá: Legis Editores.

Arballo, Gustavo. 2015. "La Corte Suprema frente al Gobierno: Cuantificando datos sobre datos políticamente perfilados en el período 1984–2014." Paper presented at the XII Congreso Nacional de Ciencia Política, Universidad Nacional de Cuyo, Mendoza, August 12–15, 2015.

Argibay, Carmen. 2008. "La Balanza de la justicia: o cómo aprendí a desconfiar de la Doctrina de la Arbitrariedad." *Jurisprudencia Argentina* 2: 1322–23.

Arias Ramírez, Bernal. 2009. "Apreciaciones jurídicas sobre el referendo del 7 de Octubre de 2007 (Costa Rica)." *Revista de Ciencias Jurídicas* 118 (January–April): 13–44.

———. 2013. "Costa Rica. La consulta legislativa de constitucionalidad: Apuntes para la toma de decisión." *Revista Judicial* 109: 43–77.

Arroyo Navarrete, Larissa. 2018. "El aborto en Costa Rica: Siguiendo las reglas jurídicas de un tabú social." In *Taburía: El tabú en el derecho*, edited by Norberto E. Garay Boza and Melissa Benavides Víquez, 27–50. San José: Centro de Investigaciones Jurídicas.

Azuero Quijano, Alejandra. 2006. *Trasjudicialismo: redes de diálogo judicial transnacional al interior de la Corte Constitucional*. Tesis, Facultad de Derecho, Universidad de los Andes.

———. 2009. "Redes de diálogo judicial transnacional: Una aproximación empírica al caso de la Corte Constitucional." *Revista de Derecho Público* 22: 3-19.

Bailey, Michael A., and Forrest Maltzman. 2011. *The Constrained Court: Law, Politics, and the Decisions Justices Make*. Princeton, NJ: Princeton University Press.

Bárcena Arévalo, Erika. 2018. "El oficio de juzgar, la corte y su cortesanos: Estudio etnográfico de la Suprema Corte de Justicia de la Nación y su incorporación del derecho internacional de los derechos humanos." Tesis doctoral, México DF, Centro de Investigaciones y Estudios Superiores en Antropología Social.

Barrera, Leticia. 2014. *Una etnografía del mundo de la justicia: La Corte Suprema en escena*. Buenos Aires: Siglo XXI.

Barreto Rozo, Antonio, and Jorge González-Jácome. 2022. "Between Exception and Transition: Proportionality and Necessity in the Colombian Quest for Peace." In *Proportionality and Transformation: Theory and Practice from Latin America*, edited by F. Pou-Giménez, L. Clérico, and E. Restrepo-Saldarriaga, 223–42. Cambridge, UK: Cambridge University Press. https://doi.org/10.1017/9781009201797.014.

Barrón, Luis. 2002. "La tradición republicana y el nacimiento del Liberalismo en Hispanoamérica después de la independencia: Bolívar, Lucas Alamán y el 'Poder Conservador.'" In *El Republicanismo en Hispanoamérica: Ensayos de historia intelectual y política*, coordinated by J. Aguilar and R. Rojas, 244–88. México DF: Fondo de Cultura Económica, Centro de Investigación y Docencia Económica.

Basabe-Serrano, Santiago. 2012. "Judges without Robes and Judicial Voting in Contexts of Institutional Instability: The Case of Ecuador's Constitutional Court, 1999–2007." *Journal of Latin American Studies* 44 (1): 127–61.

Bashin, Kamla, and Nighat Said Khan. 1986. *Some Questions on Feminism and Its Relevance in South Asia*. Charlottesville: University of Virginia Press.

Beatty, David M. 1990. *Talking Heads and the Supremes: The Canadian Production of Constitutional Review*. Toronto: Carswell.

Becker, David, and Claudia Díaz Olivarrieta. 2013. "Decriminalization of Abortion in Mexico City: The Effects of Women's Reproductive Rights." *American Journal of Public Health* 103 (4): 585–89.

Bejarano, Ana María. 2011. *Precarious Democracies: Understanding Stability and Change in Colombia and Venezuela*. Notre Dame, IN: University of Notre Dame Press.

Bergallo, Paola. 2014. "The Struggle against Informal Rules on Abortion in Argentina." In *Abortion Law in Transnational Perspective: Cases and Controversies*, edited by Rebecca J. Cook, Joanna N. Erdman, and Bernard M. Dickens, 143–65. Philadelphia: University of Pennsylvania Press.

Bergallo, Paola, and Agustina Ramón Michel. 2016. "Abortion." In *The Latin American Casebook: Courts, Constitutions and Rights*, edited by Juan F. González-Bartomeu and Roberto Gargarella. New York: Routledge.

Bergara, Mario, Barak Richman, and Pablo T. Spiller. 2003. "Modeling Supreme Court Strategic Decision Making: The Congressional Constraint." *Legislative Studies Quarterly* 28 (2): 247–80.

Bernal Pulido, Carlos. 2009. *El Neoconstitucionalismo y la normatividad del derecho.* Bogotá: Universidad Externado de Colombia.

Bickel, Alexander M. 1962. *The Least Dangerous Branch: The Supreme Court at the Bar of Politics.* Indianapolis, IN: Bobbs-Merrill Company.

Blofield, Merike. 2001. *Legislating Moral Sin: The Politics of Abortion and Divorce in Catholic Chile.* Santiago: Flacso Nueva Serie.

———. 2006. *The Politics of Moral Sin: Abortion and Divorce in Spain, Chile and Argentina.* New York: Routledge.

Blofield, Merike, and Christina Ewig. 2017. "The Left Turn and Abortion Politics in Latin America." *Social Politics: International Studies in Gender, State and Society* 24 (4): 481–510.

Bohórquez Monsalve, Viviana, Jordi Díez, and Nora Picasso Uvalle. 2019. "La Judiciarisation de L'avortement en Amérique Latine et les limites de la citoyenneté." *Problèmes d'Amérique latine* 114 (3): 53–79.

Bonneau, Chris W., Thomas H. Hammond, Forest Maltzman, and Paul J. Wahlbeck. 2007. "Agenda Control, the Median Justice, and the Majority Opinion on the US Supreme Court." *American Journal of Political Science* 51 (4): 890–905.

Booth, John. 1998. *Costa Rica: Quest for Democracy.* Boulder, CO: Westview Press.

———. 2020. *Understanding Central America.* New York: Routledge.

Botero, Sandra. 2018. "Judges, Litigants, and the Politics of Rights Enforcement in Argentina." *Comparative Politics* 50 (2): 169–87.

———. 2020. "Confianza, apoyo a la democracia y corrupción: Una mirada a la Corte Constitucional en la opinion pública Colombiana." *Latin American Law Review* 4: 25–47.

Brenner, Saul. 1980. "Fluidity on the United States Supreme Court: A Reexamination." *American Journal of Political Science* 24 (3): 526–35.

Brenner, Saul, and Joseph M. Whitmeyer. 2009. *Strategy on the United States Supreme Court.* New York: Cambridge University Press.

Bressman, Jeremy. 2007. "A New Standard of Review: *Craig v. Boren* and Brennan's 'Heightened Scrutiny' Test in Historical Perspective." *Journal of Supreme Court History* 32 (1): 85–95.

Brinks, Daniel M. 2005. "Judicial Reform and Independence in Brazil and Argentina: The Beginning of a New Millennium?" *Texas International Law Journal* 40 (3): 595–622.

———. 2011. "'Faithful Servants of the Regime': The Brazilian Constitutional Court's Role under the 1988 Constitution." In *Courts in Latin America*, edited by Gretchen Helmke and Julio Ríos-Figueroa, 128–53. New York: Cambridge University Press.

Brinks, Daniel M., and Abby Blass. 2018. *The DNA of Constitutional Justice in Latin America: Politics, Governance, and Judicial Design.* New York: Cambridge University Press.

Bushnell, David. 1993. *The Making of Modern Colombia: A Nation Despite of Itself.* Stanford: University of California Press.

Bustillos, Jaime. 2009. *La justicia constitutcional en México: Análisis cuantitativo de las resoluciones judiciales en materia constitucional.* Mexico City: UNAM.

Caballero, José Antonio. 2009. "De la marginalidad a los reflectores. El renacimiento de la administración de justicia en México, 1967–2006." In *Una Historia Contemporánea de México*, edited by Ilán Bizberg and Lorenzo Meyer, 163–93. México DF: Océano-El Colegio de México.

Cairns, Alan C. 1993. "A Defence of the Citizens' Constitution Theory: A Response to Ian Brodie and Neil Nevitte." *Canadian Journal of Political Science* 26: 261–67.

Cano, Gabriela. 1990. "Una perspectiva del aborto en los años treinta: La propuesta Marxista = la propuesta del aborto de la CTM en 1936." *Debate Feminista* 2 (September).

Carmona Tinoco, Jorge Ulises. 2011. "La reforma y las normas de derechos humanos previstas en los tratados internacionales." In *La Reforma Constitucional de Derechos Humanos: Un Nuevo Paradigma*, edited by M. Carbonell and P. Salazar, 39–63. México DF: UNAM-IIJ.

Carreras, Miguel. 2012. "Party Systems in Latin America after the Third Wave: A Critical Re-assessment." *Journal of Politics in Latin America* 4 (1): 135–53.

Carroll, Lea Anne. 2011. *Violent Democratization: Social Movements, Elites, and Politics in Colombia's Rural War Zones, 1984–2008.* Notre Dame, IN: University of Notre Dame Press.

Carubba, Cliff, Barry Friedman, Andrew D. Martin, and Georg Vanberg. 2012. "Who Controls the Content of the Supreme Court Opinions?" *American Journal of Political Science* 56 (2): 400–412.

Casar, María Amparo. 1999. "Las relaciones entre el poder ejecutivo y el legisltaivo: El caso de México." *Política y Gobierno* 6 (1): 83–128.

Cascante Matamoros, María José, and Camacho Sánchez. 2019. "El sistema de patidos en los cantones: análisis de la distribución territorial de los apoyos (1953–2016)." *Revista de Derecho Electoral* 28 (11): 195–216.

Cascante Matamoros, Marías José, and Mónica Lara Escalante. 2021. "Intolerancia y desafección: transformaciones en el sistema de partidos de Costa Rica." In *Los partidos politicos en América Latina: ideología y estructura de la competencia*, edited by Sebastián Mantilla Bacca, 227–53. Quito: Centro Latinoamericano de Estudios Políticos.

Cascante Segura, Carlos Humberto. 2014. *Estudio histórico del Poder Judicial en el proceso de democratizacion de Costa Rica (1900–1990).* San José: Estudios de la Nación.

———. 2017. "Política y justicia constitucional: temas y líneas de votación de la sala constitucional de Costa Rica en las acciones de inconstitucionalidad." In *Informe Estado de la Justicia*, edited by Programa Estado de la Nación, 1–48. San José: Estado de la Nación.

Casper, Jonathan D. 1976. "The Supreme Court and National Policy Making." *American Political Science Review* 70 (1): 50–63.

Castagnola, Andrea. 2018. *Manipulating Courts in New Democracies: Forcing Judges off the Bench in Argentina.* New York: Routledge.

Castagnola, Andrea, and Saúl López Noriega. 2017. "Are Mexican Justices True Arbiters among Political Elites? An Empricial Analysis of the Court's Rulings from 2000–2011." In *Judicial Politics in Mexico: The Supreme Court and the Transition to Democracy*, edited by Andrea Castagnola and Saúl Lópex Noriega, 68–94. New York: Routledge.

Castilla Juárez, K. 2011. "Un nuevo panorama constitucional para el derecho international de los derechos humanos." *Estudios Constitucionales* 9 (2): 123–64.

Castillejos-Aragón, Mónica. 2013. "The Transformation of the Mexican Supreme Court into an Arena for Political Contestation." In *Consequential Courts—Judicial Roles in Global Perspective*, edited by Gordon Silverstein, Diane Kapiszewski, and Robert A. Kagan, 138–60. New York: Cambridge University Press.

CEDES. 2001. *El aborto en el Congreso: Argentina 2018-2020*. Buenos Aires: Centro de Estudios de Estado y Sociedad.

Cepeda-Espinosa, José Manuel. 1993. *La Asamblea Constituyente: Mitos y Realidades*. Bogotá: Imprenta Nacional.

———. 2004. "Judicial Activism in a Violent Context: The Origin, Role, and Impact of the Colombian Constitutional Court." *Washington University Global Studies Law Review* 3: 529–699.

———. 2007. *Polémicas Constitucionales*. Bogotá: Legis.

———. 2019. "Responsive Constitutionalism." *Annual Review of Law and Social Science* 15: 21–40.

Cerar, Dr. Miro. 2009. "The Relationship between Law and Politics." *Annual Survey of International and Comparative Law* 15 (1): article 3.

Chávez, Rebecca. 2004. *The Rule of Law in Nascent Democracies: Judicial Politics in Argentina*. Stanford, CA: Stanford University Press.

CIEP. 2018. *Cuestionario aleatorio, proyecto Estudios de Opinión, marzo 2018*. San José: Centro de Investigación de Estudios Políticos, Universidad de Costa Rica.

Clark, Tom S., and Benjamin Lauderdale. 2010. "Locating Supreme Court Opinions in Doctrine Space." *American Journal of Political Science* 54 (4): 871–90.

Cooter, Robert, and Tom Ginsburg. 1996. "Comparative Judicial Discretion: An Empirical Test of Economic Models." *International Review of Law and Economics* 16 (3): 295–313.

Corley, Pamela C., Amy Steigerwalt, and Artemus Ward. 2013. *The Puzzle of Unanimity: Consensus in the US Supreme Court*. Stanford, CA: Stanford Law Books.

Corrêa, Sonia, and Rosalind Petchesky. 2006. "Reproductive and Sexual Rights: A Feminist Perspective." In *Culture, Society and Sexuality: A Reader*, edited by Richard Parker and Peter Aggleton, 299–315. New York: Routledge.

Cortez Salinas, Josafat. 2019. "Secretarios de estudio y cuenta en la Suprema Corte de México: Un actor esencial pero olvidado." *Política y Gobierno* 26 (2): 219–36.

———. 2020. *Ideas, inovación y cambio organizacional en la Suprema Corte de Justicia de la Nación*. Mexico City: Universidad Nacional Autónoma de México.

Cortez Salinas, Josafat, and Grisel Salazar Rebolledo. 2019. "La construcción de la independencia y del poder de la Suprema Corte de Justicia en México. Explicando la reforma judicial de 1994." *Estudios Políticos (México)*, no. 46 (April): 213–33. https://www.scielo.org.mx/scielo.php?script=sci_arttext&pid=S0185-16162019000100213#B17.

Cossío Díaz, José Ramón. 1996. *Jurisdicción federal y carrera judicial en México*. Cuadernos para la Reforma de la Justicia 4. Ciudad Universitaria, DF: Instituto de Investigaciones Jurídicas, Universidad Nacional Autónoma de México.

———. 1998a. *Artículo 105. La Constitución Política de los Estados Unidos Mexicanos comentada*. México Distrito Federal: Porrúa.

———. 1998b. *Constitución, tribunales y emocracia*. México DF: Themis.

———. 1998c. *Dogmática constituicional y régimen autoritario.* México DF: Distribuciones Fontamara.

———. 2001. "La Suprema Corte y la teoría constitucional." *Política y Gobierno* 8 (1): 61–115.

———. 2002. *La teoría constitucional de la Suprema Corte de Justicia.* México DF: Fontamara.

Couso, Javier. 2010. "The Transformation of Constitutional Discourse and the Judicialization of Politics in Latin America." In *Cultures of Legality: Judicialization and Political Activism in Latin America*, edited by Javier Couso, Alexandra Huneeus, and Rachel Sieder, 141–60. New York: Cambridge University Press.

Crowley, Ethel. 2014. "Third World Women and the Inadequacies of Western Feminism." *Global Research*, March 8, 2014. https://www.globalresearch.ca/third-world-women -and-the-inadequacies-of-western-feminism/5372515.

Cruz Castro, Fernando. 2007. "Costa Rica's Constitutional Jurisprudence, Its Political Importance and International Human Rights Law: Examination of Some Decisions." *Duquesne Law Review* 45 (3): 557–76.

Daby, Mariela, and Mason Moseley. 2021. "Feminist Mobilization and the Abortion Debate in Latin America: Lessons from Argentina." *Politics & Gender* 18 (2): 1–35.

———. 2024. *Mobilizing for Abortion Rights in Latin America.* New York: Cambridge University Press.

Dagnino, Evelina. 2003. "Citizenship in Latin America: An Introduction." *Latin American Perspectives* 30 (2): 211–25.

Dahl, Ronald A. 1957. "Decision Making in a Democracy: The Supreme Court as a National Policy Maker." *Journal of Public Law* 6: 279–95.

Desposato, Scott W., Matthew C. Ingram, and Osmar P. Lannes, Jr. 2015. "Power, Composition, and Decision Making: The Behavioral Consequences of Institutional Reform on Brazil's Supremo Tribunal Federal." *Journal of Law, Economics, and Organization* 31 (3): 534–67.

Devins, Neal. 2004. "Is Judicial Policymaking Counter-Majoritarian?" In *Making Policy, Making Law: An Interbranch Perspective*, edited by Mark C. Miller and Jeb Barnes, 189–201. Washington, DC: Georgetown University Press.

Díaz, David. 2003. *Construcción de un estado moderno: Política, estado e identidad nacional en Costa Rica, 1821–1914.* Cuadernos de Historia de las Instituciones de Costa Rica 18. San José: Editorial de la Universidad de Costa Rica.

Díez, Jordi. 2006. *Political Change and Environmental Policymaking in Mexico.* New York: Routledge.

———. 2010. "The Importance of Policy Frames in Contentious Politics: Mexico's 2005 Anti-Homophobia Campaign." *Latin American Research Review* 45 (1): 33–54.

———. 2012. "Presidentialism and Policymaking in Latin America: The Case of Mexico." In *Comparative Public Policy in Latin America*, edited by Jordi Díez and Susan Franceschet, 34–53. Toronto: University of Toronto Press.

———. 2013. "Explaining Policy Outcomes: The Adoption of Same-Sex Unions in Buenos Aires and Mexico City." *Comparative Political Studies* 46 (2): 212–35.

———. 2015. *The Politics of Gay Marriage in Latin America: Argentina, Chile and Mexico.* New York: Cambridge University Press.

———. 2018. *La política del matrimonio gay en América Latina: Argentina, Chile y México.* México DF: Fondo de Cultura Económica.

———. 2020. "The Record of Latin America's Left on Sexual Citizenship." In *Legacies of the Left Turn Latin America: The Promise of Inclusive Citizenship*, edited by Manuel Balán and Françsoise Montambeault, 252–79. South Bend, IN: University of Notre Dame Press.

Díez, Jordi, and Alba Ruibal. 2025. "The Decriminalization of Abortion in Latin America: A Tale of Gradual Judicialization." *PS: Political Science & Politics* 58 (1): 1–4.

Díez, Jordi, and José Manuel Ruíz Ramírez. 2024. "Explaining the Liberal Turn of Mexico's Supreme Court." Latin American Studies Association, Annual Congress, Bogotá, June 12–15, 2024.

Dion, Michelle L., and Jordi Díez. 2018. "Democratic Values, Religiosity, and Support for Same-Sex Marriage in Latin America." *Latin American Politics and Society* 59 (4): 75–98.

Dobrowolsky, Alexandra, and Evangelia Tastsoglou, eds. 2006. "Crossing Boundaries and Making Connections." In *Women, Migration and Citizenship*. New York: Routledge.

Domingo, Pilar. 1999. "Judicial Independence and Judicial Reform in Latin America." In *The Self-Restraining State: Power and Accountability in New Democracies*, edited by Andreas Schedler, Larry Jay Diamond, and Marc F. Plattner, 151–75. Boulder, CO: Lynne Rienner.

———. 2000. "Judicial Independence: The Politics of the Supreme Court in Mexico." *Journal of Latin American Studies* 32 (3): 705–35.

Drinot, Paulo. 2020. *The Sexual Question: A History of Prostitution in Peru, 1850s–1950s.* New York: Cambridge University Press.

Duque Daza, Javier. 2019. "El Frente Nacional revisitado: El cambio institucional en Colombia y sus efectos no previstos." *Reflexión Política* 21 (42): 109–28.

Dworkin, Richard. 1978. *Taking Rights Seriously.* Cambridge, MA: Harvard University Press.

———. 1986. *Law's Empire.* Cambridge, MA: Harvard University Press.

Eder, Phanor J. 1960. "Judicial Review in Latin America Comparative Constitutional Law." *Ohio State Law Journal* 21 (4): 570–615.

Elizondo Mayer-Serra, Carlos, and Ana Laura Magaloni. 2010. "La fiorma es fondo: Cómo se nombran y deciden los ministros de la Suprema Corte de Justicia." *Cuestiones Constitucionales* 23 (July–December): 27–60.

Enns, Peter K., and Patrick C. Wohlfarth. 2013. "The Swing Justice." *Journal of Politics* 75 (4): 1089–107.

Epp, Charles R. 1998. *The Rights Revolution: Lawyers, Activists and Supreme Courts in Comparative Perspective.* Chicago: University of Chicago Press.

Epstein, Lee, and Jack Knight. 1998. *The Choices Justices Make.* Washington, DC: CQ Press.

———. 2013. "Reconsidering Judicial Preferences." *Annual Review of Political Science* 16 (1): 11–31.

Epstein, Lee, Jack Knight, and Andrew D. Martin. 2001. "The Supreme Court as a Strategic National Policy Maker." *Emory Law Journal* 50: 583–611.

Epstein, Lee, and Joseph F. Kobylka. 1992. *The Supreme Court and Legal Change.* Chapel Hill: University of North Carolina Press.

Epstein, Lee, and Carol Mershon. 1996. "Measuring Political Preferences." *American Journal of Political Science* (40) 1: 261–94.

Epstein, Lee, and Olga Shvestova. 2002. "Heresthetical Maneuvering on the US Supreme Court." *Journal of Theoretical Politics* 14: 93–122.

Eskridge, William N., Jr. 1991. "Overriding Supreme Court Statutory Interpretation Decisions." *Yale Law Journal* 101 (2): 331–455.

Eskridge, William N., Jr., and John Ferejohn. 1992. "The Article I, Section 7 Game." *Georgetown Law Journal* 80: 523–64.

Estado de la Nación. 2015. *Informe Justicia 2015.* San José: Programa Estado de la Nación.

Evans, Peter. 1995. *Embedded Autonomy: States and Industrial Transformation.* Princeton, NJ: Princeton University Press.

Farhang, Sean, Jonathan P. Kastellec, and Gregory J. Wawro. 2015. "The Politics of Opinion Assignment and Authorship on the US Courts of Appeals: Evidence from Sexual Harassment Cases." *Journal of Legal Studies* 44 (S1): 59–85.

Felitti, Karina, and María Rosario Encartes Ramírez Morales. 2020. "Pañuelos verdes por el aborto legal: Historia, significados y circulaciones en Argentina y México." *ENCARTES* 111 (2020).

Feoli Villalobos, Marco. 2012. "Activismo judicial y justicia constitucional: Los casos de Colombia y Costa Rica." Tesis, Facultad de Derecho, Universidad de Salamanca.

Ferejohn, John. 2002. "Judicializing Politics, Politicizing Law." *Law and Contemporary Problems* 65 (3): 41–68.

Fernández Anderson, Cora. 2016. "Decriminalizing Abortion in Uruguay: Women's Movements, Secularism, and Political Allies." *Journal of Women, Politics & Policy* 38.

Fernández Sanabría, Alejandro. 2010. "Así piensa la Sala IV." *El Financiero,* June 14–20, 4–5.

Fernández Segado, Francisco. 2020. *El juicio de amparo, la Constitución de Querétaro de 1917, y su influjo sobre la constitución de la Segunda República Española.* Mexico City: Instituto de Investigaciones Jurídicas, Universidad Nacional Autónoma de México. https://archivos.juridicas.unam.mx/www/bjv/libros/13/6320/1.pdf.

Finkel, Jodi S. 2003. "Supreme Court Decisions on Electoral Rules after Mexico's 1994 Reform An Empowered Court." *Journal of Latin American Studies* 35 (1): 1–23.

———. 2004a. "Judicial Reform as Insurance Policy: Mexico in the 1990s." *Latin American Politics and Society* 47 (1): 87–113.

———. 2004b. "Judicial Reform in Argentina in the 1990s: How Electoral Incentives Shape Institutional Change." *Latin American Research Review* 39 (3): 56–80.

Fix-Fierro, Héctor. 2003. "Judicial Reform in Mexico: What Next?" In *Beyond Common Knowledge: Empirical Approaches to the Rule of Law,* edited by Erik Jensen and Thomas Heller, 240–89. Stanford, CA: Stanford University Press.

Fix-Zamudio, Héctor. 1990. "La independencia judicial en el ordenamiento mexicano." In *Derecho constitucional comparado México-Estados Unidos,* edited by James Frank Smith, 1: 379–98. Mexico City: Universidad Nacional Autónoma de México.

Fox, Jonathan. 1994. "The Difficult Transition from Clientelism to Citizenship: Lessons from Mexico." *World Politics* 46 (2): 151–84.

Franceschet, Susan, and Jordi Díez. 2012. "Thinking about Politics and Policy-Making in Contemporary Latin America." In *Comparative Public Policy in Latin America*, edited by Jordi Díez and Susan Franceschet, 1–31. Toronto: University of Toronto Press.

Friedman, Marilyn. 2005. *Women and Citizenship*. Oxford, UK: Oxford University Press.

Galdámez Zelada, Liliana, Pedro Salazar Ugarte, Humberto Sierra Porto, and Farit Rojas Tudela. 2014. "Reforma constitucional y derechos humanos." *Anuario de Derechos Humanos*, no. 10 (June): 59–77.

García Castillo, Tonatiuh. 2015. "La reforma constitucional Mexicana del 2011 en materia de derechos humanos. Una lectura desde el derecho internacional." *Boletín Mexicano de Derecho Comparado*, no. 143 (August): 645–96.

García Villegas, Mauricio, and Rodrigo Uprimny, 2004. *Corte Constitucional y emancipación social en Colombia*. Bogotá: Editorial Norma.

Gargarella, Roberto. 2019. "Latin America's Contribution to Constitutionalism." In *Routledge Handbook of Law and Society in Latin America*, edited by Rachel Sieder, Karina Ansolabehere, and Tatiana Alfonso, 25–36. New York: Routledge.

Gargarella, Roberto, Pilar Domingo, and Theunis Roux, eds. 2006. *Courts and Social Transformation in New Democracies: An Institutional Voice for the Poor?* Burlington, VT: Ashgate.

Garrett, Geoffrey, R. Daniel Kelemen, and Heiner Schulz. 1998. "The European Court of Justice, National Governments, and Legal Integration in the European Union." *International Organization* 52 (1): 149–76.

Gely, Rafael, and Pablo T. Spiller. 1990. "A Rational Choice Theory of Supreme Court Statutory Decisions with Applications to the State Farm and Grove City Cases." *Journal of Law, Economics, and Organization* 6 (2): 263–300.

Getgen, Jocelyn E. 2007. "Reproductive Injustice: An Analysis of Nicaragua's Complete Abortion Ban." *Cornell International Law Journal* 41 (1): 143–76.

Gillman, Howard. 2001. "What's Law Got to Do with It? Judicial Behavioralists Test the 'Legal Model' of Judicial Decision Making." *Law and Social Inquiry* 26 (2): 465–504.

Gillman, Howard, and Cornell W. Clayton. 1999. "Beyond Judicial Attitudes: Institutional Approaches to Supreme Court Decision-Making." In *Supreme Court Decision-Making: New Institutional Approaches*, edited by Cornell W. Clayton and Howard Gillman, 1–12. Chicago: University of Chicago Press.

Ginsburg, Tom. 2003. *Judicial Review in New Democracies: Constitutional Courts in Asian Cases*. Cambridge, UK: Cambridge University Press.

GIRE. 2009. *Constitutcionalidad de la ley de aborto en la Ciudad de México*. México DF: Grupo de Información en Reproducción Asistida.

González-Bertomeu, Juan F. 2019. "Judicial Politics in Latin America." In *Routledge Handbook of Law and Society in Latin America*, edited by Rachel Sieder, Karina Ansolabehere, and Tatiana Alfonso, 169–86. New York: Routledge.

González-Ocantos, Ezequiel A. 2016. *Shifting Legal Visions: Judicial Change and Human Rights Trials in Latin America*. Cambridge, UK: Cambridge University Press.

———. 2019. "Courts in Latin American Politics." *Oxford Research Encyclopedia of Politics*. Oxford, UK: Oxford University Press.

González Ruiz, Edgar, and Gabriela Infante. 2004. "Perfiles del conservadurismo sexual." In *Encuentros y desencuentros en la salud Reproductiva: Políticas públicas, marcos normativos y actors sociales*, edited by Juan Guillermo Figueroa and Claudio Stern, 195–221. México DF: El Colegio de México.

González Vélez, Ana Cristina. 2005. "La situación del aborto en Colombia: Entre la legalidad y la realidad." *Cadernos de Saúde Pública* 21 (2): 624–28.

González Vélez, Ana Cristina, and Isabel Cristina Jaramillo Sierra. 2021. *La batalla por el aborto: El caso de la Mesa por la Vida y la Salud de las Mujeres*. Bogotá: Siglo del Hombre Editores.

Graber, Mark A. 1993. "The Nonmajoritarian Difficulty: Legislative Deference to the Judiciary." *Studies in American Political Development* 7 (1): 35–73.

Graff, David. 2012. "¿Se Volverá la Corte Conservadora?" Bogotá: La Silla Vacía.

Grant, J. A. C. 1948. "Judicial Review by Executive Reference prior to Promulgation: The Colombia Experience." *Southern California Law Review* 154 (1947–48): 154–71.

Gutiérrez de Colmenares, Carmen María. 2006. "Sistemas de elección y remoción de los magistrados de las salas y tribunales constitucionales en Centroamérica, evaluación crítica." *Estudios Constitucionales* 4 (2): 631–59. https://www.redalyc.org/articulo.oa?id=82040126.

Gutiérrez Gutiérrez, Carlos José. 1999. "La constitución 50 años después." In *Temas Claves de la Constitución Política*. San José: Investigaciones Jurídcas, S.A.

Gutiérrez Sanín, Francisco, ed. 2002. *Degradación o cambio: evolución del sistema político Colombiano*. Bogotá: Norma.

Guttmacher Institute. 2018. "Facts on Abortion in Latin America and the Caribbean." Fact Sheet. Guttmacher Institute.

Haas, Liesl. 2010. *Feminist Policymaking in Chile*. University Park: Pennsylvania State University Press.

Haggard, Stephen, and Lydia B. Tiede. 2024. "Judicial Backsliding: A Guide to Collapsing the Separation of Powers." *Democratization* 32 (2): 513–37.

Hagopian, Frances. 2007. "Latin American Citizenship and Democratic Theory." In *Citizenship in Latin America*, edited by Joseph S. Tulchin and Meg Ruthenburg, 11–56. Boulder, CO: Lynne Rienner.

Hall, Melinda Gann. 1990. "Opinion Assignment Procedures and Conference Practices in State Supreme Courts." *Judicature* 73: 209–14.

Hall, Pater A., and Rosemary C. R. Taylor. 1996. "Political Science and the Three Institutionalisms." *Political Studies* 44 (5): 936–57.

Hammond, Thomas H., Chris W. Bonneau, and Reginald S. Sheehan. 2005. *Strategic Behavior and Policy Choice on the US Supreme Court*. Palo Alto, CA: Stanford University Press.

Hart, H. L. A. 1961. *The Concept of the Law*. New York: Oxford University Press.

Hartlyn, Jonathan, and John Dugas. 1999. "Colombia: The Politics of Violence and Democratic Transformation." In *Democracy in Developing Countries: Latin America*, 2nd ed., edited by Larry Diamond, Jonathan Hartlyn, Juan J. Linz, and Seymour Martin Lipset, 249–307. Boulder, CO: Lynne Rienner.

Hauser, Irina. 2016. *Los supremos: historia secreta de la corte*. Buenos Aires: Planeta.

Helmke, Gretchen. 2004. *Courts under Constraints: Judges, Generals and Presidents in Argentina*. Cambridge, UK: Cambridge University Press.

Hernández Valle, Rubén. 1978. *El control de la constitucionalidad de las leyes*. San José: Editorial Juricentro.

———. 2009. "Costa Rica: La eclosión de amparo en Costa Rica. Problemas y posibles soluciones." In *La reforma del proceso de amparo: La experiencia comparada*, edited by Pablo Pérez Tremps and Samuel B Abad Yupanqui, 195–210. Lima: Palestra Editores. https://vlex.com.pe/vid/costa-rica-posibles-soluciones-371397906.

Hessini, Leila. 2005. "Global Progress in Abortion Advocacy and Policy: An Assessment of the Decade since ICPD." *Reproductive Health Matters* 13 (25): 88–100.

Hettinger, Virginia A., Stefanie A. Lindquist, and Wendy L. Martinek. 2004. "Comparing Attitudinal and Strategic Accounts of Dissenting Behavior on the US Courts of Appeals." *American Journal of Political Science* 48 (1): 123–37.

Highton, Elena I. 1993. "La salud, la vida, y la muerte. Un problema ético-jurídico: El difuso límite entre el daño y el beneficio de la persona." In *Revista de Derecho Privado y Comunitario*, edited by Hector Alegria, 165–214. Santa Fe: Rubinzal Culzoni.

Hilbink, Lisa. 2007. *Judges beyond Politics in Democracy and Dictatorship: Lessons from Chile*. New York: Cambridge University Press.

Hirschl, Ran. 2008. "The Judicialization of Mega-Politics and the Rise of Political Courts." *Annual Review of Political Science* 11 (1): 93–118.

Horowitz, Donald L. 1977. *The Courts and Social Policy*. Washington, DC: Brookings Institution Press.

Howard, Robert M., and Jeffrey A. Segal. 2002. "An Original Look at Originalism." *Law & Society Review* 36 (1): 113–38.

Htun, Mala. 2003. *Sex and the State: Abortion, Divorce, and the Family under Latin American Dictatorships and Democracies*. Cambridge, UK: Cambridge University Press.

Huneeus, Alexandra, Javier Couso, and Rachel Sieder. 2010. "Cultures of Legality: Judicialization and Political Activism in Contemporary Latin America." In *Cultures of Legality: Judicialization and Political Activism in Latin America*, edited by Javier Couso, Alexandra Huneeus, and Rachel Sieder, 3–21. New York: Cambridge University Press.

Iaryczower, Matias, Pablo Spiller, and Mariano Tommasi. 2002. "Judicial Independence in Unstable Environments, Argentina 1935–1998." *American Journal of Political Science* 46 (4): 699.

Inclán Oseguera, Silvia. 2009. "Judicial Reform in Mexico: Political Insurance or the Search for Political Legitimacy?" *Political Research Quarterly* 62 (4): 753–66.

Inglehart, Ronald F., Miguel Basáñez, and Alejandro Moreno. 1998. *Human Values and Beliefs: A Cross-Cultural Sourcebook*. Ann Arbor: University of Michigan Press.

Ingram, Matthew C. 2015. "Judicial Power in Latin America." *Latin American Research Review* 50 (1): 250–60.

Jaramillo Sierra, Isabel. 2023. "The New Colombian Law on Abortion." *International Journal of Gynecology & Obstetrics* 160: 345–50.

Jaramillo Sierra, Isabel, and Anotion Barreto Rozo. 2010. "El problema del procesamiento de información en la selección de tutelas por la Corte Constitucional, con especial atención al papel de las insistencies." *Colombia Internacional* 72 (July–December): 83–86.

Jaramillo Sierra, Isabel, and Tatiana Alfonso Sierra. 2008. *Mujeres, cortes y medios: La reforma judicial del aborto*. Bogotá: Siglo del Hombre Editores, Universidad de Los Andes.

Jelin, Elizabeth, and Eric Hershberg, eds. 1996. *Constructing Democracy: Human Rights, Citizenship, and Society in Latin America*. New York: Routledge.

Jesudason, Sujatha, and Tracy Weitz. 2015. "Eggs and Abortion: 'Women-Protective' Language Used by Opponents in Legislative Debates over Reproductive Health." *Journal of Law, Medicine & Ethics* 43 (2): 259–69.

Johnstone, Rachael. 2017. *After Morgentaler: The Politics of Abortion in Canada*. Vancouver: University of British Columbia Press.

Kane, Gillian. 2008. "Abortion Law Reform in Latin America: Lessons for Advocacy." *Gender and Development* 16 (2): 361–75.

Kantor, Jodi, and Adam Liptak. 2023. "Behind the Scenes at the Dismantling of *Roe v. Wade*." *New York Times*, December 15, 2023.

Kapiszewski, Diana. 2011. "Tactical Balancing: High Court Decision Making on Politically Crucial Cases." *Law & Society Review* 45 (2): 471–506.

Kapiszewski, Diana, and Matthew M. Taylor. 2008. "Doing Courts Justice? Studying Judicial Politics in Latin America." *Perspectives on Politics* 6 (4): 741–67.

Kapiszewski, Diana, and Lydia B. Tiede. 2021. "Empirical Studies of the Behavior of Justices and High Courts in Latin America: An Overview." In *High Courts in Global Perspective: Evidence, Methodologies, and Findings*, edited by Nuno Garoupa, Rebecca D. Gill, and Lydia B. Tiede, 199–231. Charlottesville: University of Virginia Press.

Kerber, Linda L. 1980. *Women of the Republic: Intellect and Ideology in Revolutionary America*. Chapel Hill: University of North Carolina Press.

Koblitz, Ann Hibner. 2014. *Sex and Herbs and Birth Control: Women and Fertility Regulation through the Ages*. Seattle, WA: Kovalevskaia Fund.

Kritzer, Herbert M., and Mark J. Richards. 2003. "Jurisprudential Regimes and Supreme Court Decisionmaking: The Lemon Regime and the Establishment Clause Cases." *Law & Society Review* 37 (4): 827–40.

Kulczycki, A. 2007. "The Abortion Debate in Mexico" Realities and Stalled Policy Reform." *Bulletin of Latin American Research* 26 (1): 50–68.

Lamas, Marta. 2017. *La interrupción legal del embarazo: El caso de la Ciudad de México*. México DF: Fondo de Cultura Económica.

Lamprea, Everaldo. 2010. "When Accountability Meets Judicial Independence: A Case Study of the Colombian Constitutional Court's Nominations." *Global Jurist* 10 (1). https://doi.org/10.2202/1934-2640.1347.

Landau, David. 2005. "The Two Discourses in Colombian Constitutional Jurisprudence: A New Approach to Modeling Judicial Behavior in Latin America." *George Washington International Law Review* 37 (3): 687–744.

———. 2012. "The Reality of Socio-Economic Rights Enforcement." *Harvard International Law Journal* 53 (1): 319–78.

———. 2015. *Beyond Judicial Independence: The Construction of Judicial Power in Colombia*. Doctoral thesis, Harvard University, Cambridge, MA.

Lauderdale, Benjamin E., and Tom S. Clark. 2013. "The Supreme Court's Many Median Justices." *American Political Science Review* 106 (4): 847–66.

Lax, Jeffrey R. 2011. "The New Judicial Politics of Legal Doctrine." *Annual Review of Political Science* 14 (1): 131–57.

Lehoucq, Fabrice Edouard. 1998. *Instituciones democráticas y conflictos políticos en Costa Rica*. Heredia, Costa Rica: Editorial Universidad Nacional.

Lemaitre, Julieta. 2005. "Los derechos de los homosexuales y la Corte Constitucional: (Casi) una narrativa de progreso." In *Hacia un nuevo derecho constitucional*, edited by Daniel Bonilla and Manuel Iturralde, 181–217. Bogotá: Universidad de los Andes.

———. 2009. *El Derecho como conjuro: Fetichismo legal, violencia y movimientos sociales*. Bogotá: Grupo IDEAS, Facultad de Derecho Universidad de los Andes.

———. 2014a. "Constitution or Barbarism? How to Rethink Law in 'Lawless' Spaces." In *Law and Society in Latin America: A New Map*, edited by César Rodríguez Garavito, 43–62. London: Routledge.

———. 2014b. "El sexo, las mujeres y el inicio de la vida humana en el constitutcionalismo católico." In *El aborto en el derecho internacional*, edited by Rebecca J. Cook, Joanna N. Edman, and Bernard M. Dickens, 306–31. México DF: Fondo de Cultura Económica.

Lemaitre, Julieta, and Rache Sieder. 2017. "The Moderating Influence of International Courts on Social Movements: Evidence from the IVF Case against Costa Rica." *Health Human Rights* 19 (1): 149–60.

Levitsky, Steven, and Kenneth M. Roberts, eds., 2011. *The Resurgence of the Latin American Left*. Baltimore: Johns Hopkins University Press.

Lind, Amy. 2012. "'Revolution with a Woman's Face'? Family Norms, Constitutional Reform, and the Politics of Redistribution in Post-Neoliberal Ecuador." *Rethinking Marxism* 24 (4): 536–55.

Lira González, Andrés. 1972. *El amparo colonial y el juicio de amparo Mexicano: antecedentes novohispanos del juicio de amparo*. México DF: Fondo de Cultural Económica.

Llewellyn, Karl N. 1931. "Some Realism about Realism." *Harvard Law Review* 44 (8): 1222–64.

Lombo, Juan Sebastián. 2021. "Dios, Religión y la Constitución de 1991." *El Espectador*, April 2, 2021.

López-Ayllón, Sergio, and Héctor F. Fix-Fierro. 2003. "Faraway, So Close!' The Rule of Law and Legal Change in Mexico 1970–2000." In *Legal Culture in the Age of Globalization: Latin America and Latin Europe*, edited by Lawrence M. Friedman and Rogelio Pérez Perdomo, 285–351. Palo Alto, CA: Stanford University Press.

López Aylón, Sergio, and Florencia Valladares. 2009. "Las acciones de insconstitucionalidad en la constitución Mexicana: Análisis empírico de 12 años de ejercicio." *Cuestiones Constitucionales* 21 (2): 175–212.

López Bajo, Lizett Paola. 2017. "Límites constitucionales, activismo judicial e incidencia de las organizaciones civiles: las controvertidas decisiones de la Corte Constitucional Colombiana sobre derechos humanos." Tesis de maestría, Facultad Latinoamericana de Ciencias Sociales.

López Medina, Diego. 2004. *La teoría impura del derecho*. Bogotá: Legis.

Lopreite, Debora. 2014. "Explaining Policy Outcomes in Federal Contexts: The Politics of Reproductive Rights in Argentina and Mexico." *Bulletin of Latin American Research* 33 (4): 389–404.

Lösing, Norbert. 2002. *Die Verfassungsgerichtsbarkeit in Lateinamerika*. Berlin: Konrad Adenauer Stiftung.

MacDonald, Laura, and Lisa Mills. 2010. "Gender, Democracy and Federalism in Mexico: Implications for Reproductive Rights and Social Policy." In *Federalism, Feminism and Multilevel Governance*, edited by Melissa Haussman, Marian Sawer, and Jill Vickers, 187–98. London: Ashgate.

Machado, Marta. 2023. "Antiabortion Legal Mobilization in Brazil: Human Rights as a Field of Contention." *International Journal of Constitutional Law* 21 (1): 308–38.

Machado, Marta, and Rebecca Cook. 2018. "Constitucionalização de Aborto no Brasil." *Revista de Investigações Constitutcionais* 5 (3): 185–231.

Madrazo, Alejandro, and Estefanía Vela. 2011. "The Mexican Supreme Court's (Sexual) Rights Revolution?" *Texas Law Review* 89 (7): 1863–94.

Magaloni, Beatriz. 2003. "Authoritarianism, Democracy and the Supreme Court: Horizontal Exchange and the Rule of Law in Mexico." In *Democratic Accountability and in Latin America*, edited by Scott Mainwaring and Christopher Welna. New York: Oxford University Press.

———. 2008. "Enforcing the Autocratic Political Order and the Role of Courts: The Case of Mexico." In *Rule by Law: The Politics of Courts in Authoritarian Regimes*, edited by Tom Ginsburg and Tamir Moustafa, 180–206. Cambridge, UK: Cambridge University Press.

Mainwaring, Scott, Guillermo O'Donnell, and Samuel Valenzuela, eds. 1992. *Issues in Democratic Consolidation: The New South American Democracies*. Notre Dame, IN: University of Notre Dame Press.

Mainwaring, Scott, and Sober Shugart, eds. 1997. *Presidentialism and Democracy in Latin America*. New York: Cambridge University Press.

Mainwaring, Scott, and Christopher Welna, eds. 2003. *Democratic Accountability in Latin America*. Oxford, UK: Oxford University Press.

Maldonado Castañeda, Oscar. 2014. "Cortes, expertos y grupos de interés: Movilización y localización del conocimiento del experto en la Sentencia C 355 de 2006." *Universitas Humanística* 77 (January–June): 327–53.

Maltzman, Forrest, James F. Spriggs II, and Paul J. Wahlbeck. 2000. *Crafting Law on the Supreme Court: The Collegial Game*. New York: Cambridge University Press.

Maltzman, Forrest, and Paul J. Wahlbeck. 1996. "May It Please the Chief? Opinion Assignment in the Rehnquist Court." *American Journal of Political Science* 40: 421–23.

Marcus-Delgado, Jane. 2020. *The Politics of Abortion in Latin America: Public Debates, Private Lives*. Boulder, CO: Lynne Rienner.

Marino, Katherine M. 2019. *Feminism in the Americas: The Making of an International Human Rights Movement*. Chapel Hill: University of North Carolina Press.

Marks, Brian A. 2012. "A Model of Judicial Influence on Congressional Policy Making: Grove City College v. Bell." *Journal of Law, Economics, and Organization* 31 (4): 843–75.

Marshall, T. H. 1950. *Citizenship and Social Class, and Other Essays*. Cambridge, UK: Cambridge University Press.

Martin, Andrew D., and Kevin M. Quinn. 2002. "Dynamic Ideal Point Estimation via Markov Chain Monte Carlo for the US Supreme Court, 1953–1999." *Political Analysis* 10 (2): 134–53.

Martin, Andrew D., Kevin Quinn, and Lee Epstein. 2005. "The Median Justice on the US Supreme Court." *North Carolina Law Review* 83 (5): 1275–322.

Maveety, Nancy, ed. 2003. *The Pioneers of Judicial Behavior*. Ann Arbor: University of Michigan Press.

McAtee, Andrea, and Kevin T. McGuire. 2007. "Lawyers, Justices, and Issue Salience: When and How Do Legal Arguments Affect the US Supreme Court?" *Law & Society Review* 41 (2): 259–78.

McGuire, Kevin T., and James A. Stimson. 2004. "The Least Dangerous Branch Revisited: New Evidence on Supreme Court Responsiveness to Public Opinion." *Journal of Politics* 66 (4): 1018–35.

Mendieta González, David. 2010."La Acción Pública de Inconstitucionalidad: a Propósito de los 100 Años de su vigencia en Colombia." *Vniversitas* 120 (January–June): 61–84.

Mendieta y Núñez, Lucio. 1992. *El derecho precolonial*. México DF: Porrúa.

Meneses, Rodrigo. 2014. "Los litigios por la calle: el ambulantaje en la Ciudad de México y la justicia federal." *Estudios Sociológicos* 32 (94): 73–102.

Mijangos y González, Pablo. 2022. *Historia minima de la Suprema Corte de Justicia de México*. Mexico City: El Colegio de México.

Miller, Dorothy. 1990. *Women and Social Welfare: A Feminist Analysis*. New York: Praeger.

Miller, Jonathan M. 1997. "The Authority of a Foreign Talisman." *American University Law Review* 46, no. 5 (June): 1483–572.

Minow, Martha. 1987. "Interpreting Rights: An Essay for Robert Cover." *Yale Law Review* 96: 1860–915.

Mohanty, Chandra Talpade. 1995. "Feminist Encounters: Locating the Politics of Experience." In *Social Postmodernism: Beyond Identity Politics*, edited by Linda Nicholson and Steven Seidman, 68–86. New York: Cambridge University Press.

Mollmann, Marianne. 2005. "Decisions Denied: Women's Access to Contraceptives and Abortion in Argentina." *Human Rights Watch* 17 (1B): 1–87.

Montoya, Ana María. 2013. "'Si no vas al Senado, no te eligen magistrado.' Instituciones informales y criterios de selección de los magistrados de la Corte Constitucional Colombiana en el Senado (1992–2009)." *Colombia Internacional* 1 (79): 155–90. https://doi.org/10.7440/colombiaint79.2013.06.

Mora Mora, Luis Paulino. 2001. *Historia del poder judicial en la segunda mitad del Siglo XX y sus retos futuros*. San José: EUNED.

Morgan, Lynn M. 2018. "'Human Life Is Inviolable': Costa Rica's Human Rights Crucible." *Medical Anthropology* 38 (6): 493–507. https://doi.org/10.1080/01459740.2018.1510394.

Morgan, Lynn M., and Elizabeth F. S. Roberts. 2012. "Reproductive Governance in Latin America." *Anthropology & Medicine* 19 (2): 241–54.

Müller, Wolfgang P. 2012. *The Criminalization of Abortion in the West: Its Origins in Medieval Law*. Ithaca, NY: Cornell University Press.

Muñoz Portillo, Juan Manuel. 2014. *Política e independencia judicial: Los mecanismos de elección de magistradas y magistrados en Costa Rica, 1990–2013*. Informe Final. San José: Programa Estado de la Nación.

Murphy, Walter F. 1964. *Elements of Judicial Strategy*. Chicago: University of Chicago Press.

Navia, Patricio, and Julio Rios-Figueroa. 2005. "The Constitutional Adjudication Mosaic of Latin America." *Comparative Political Studies* 38 (2): 189–217.

Noonan, John. 1967. "Abortion and the Catholic Church: A Summary History." *Natural Law Forum* 126: 85–131.

Nossiff, Rosemary. 2007. "Gendered Citizenship: Women, Equality and Abortion." *New Political Science* 29 (1): 61–76.

Nunes, Rodrigo M. 2010a. "Ideational Origins of Progressive Judicial Activism: The Colombian Constitutional Court and the Right to Health." *Latin American Politics and Society* 52 (3): 67–97.

———. 2010b. "Politics without Insurance: Democratic Competition and Judicial Reform in Brazil." *Comparative Politics* 42 (3): 313–31.

Offe, Claus. 1998. "'Homogeneity' and Constitutional Democracy: Coping with Identity Conflicts through Group Rights." *Journal of Political Philosophy* 6 (2): 113–41.

Okin, Susan Moller. 1979. *Women in Western Political Thought*. Princeton, NJ: Princeton University Press.

———. 1989. *Gender, Justice, and the Family*. New York: Basic Books.

Ovalle Favela, José. 2011. "Las controversias constitucionales y los órganos autónomos." *Cuestiones Constitucionales*, no. 25 (December): 101–27. https://www.scielo.org.mx/scielo.php?script=sci_arttext&pid=S1405-91932011000200004.

Owensby, Brian P. 2008. *Empire of Law and Indian Justice in Colonial Mexico*. Stanford: Standford University Press.

Palacios, Marco. 2006. *Between Legitimacy and Violence: A History of Colombia, 1875–2002*. Durham, NC: Duke University Press.

Pateman, Carole. 1988. *The Sexual Contract*. Cambridge, UK: Polity Press.

Payne, Leigh A., Julia Zuliver, and Simón Escoffier, eds. 2023. *The Right against Rights in Latin America*. New York: Oxford University Press.

Pérez-Liñán, Aníbal, and Andrea Castagnola. 2009. "Presidential Control of High Courts in Latin America: A Long-Term View (1904–2006)." *Journal of Politics in Latin America* 1 (2): 87–114.

———. 2016. "Judicial Instability and Endogenous Constitutional Change: Lessons from Latin America." *British Journal of Political Science* 46 (2): 395–416.

Pianesi, Maria Emilia. 2024. "Argentina's Abortion Law Three Years Later." Think Global Health, Council on Foreign Relations.

Pizarro Leongomez, Eduardo. 2002. "La atomización partidista en Colombia: El fenómeno de las microempresas electorales." In *Degradación o cambio: Evolución del sistema político colombiano*, edited by Francisco Gutiérrez Sanín, 351–401. Santo Domingo: Grupo Editorial Norma. https://www.academia.edu/35855813/La_atomizaci%C3%B3n_partidista_en_Colombia_el_fen%C3%B3meno_de_las_microempresas_electorales.

Pou Giménez, Francisca. 2009. "El aborto en México: El debate en la Corte Suprema sobre la normativa del Distrito Federal." *Anuario de Derechos Humanos* 5: 137–52.

———. 2012. "Las casos de los militares con VIH: El impacto del conocimiento médico en el análisis constitucional sobre discriminación." *Gaceta Medica de México* 148: 194–200.

Pou-Giménez, Francisca, Laura Clérico, and Esteban Restrepo-Saldarriaga, eds. 2022. *Proportionality and Transformation: Theory and Practice from Latin America*. ASCL

Studies in Comparative Law. Cambridge, UK: Cambridge University Press. https://doi .org/10.1017/9781009201797.

Pritchett, Herman C. 1968. "Public Law and Judicial Behavior." *Journal of Politics* 30 (2): 480–509.

Ragin, Chales C. 1987. *The Comparative Method: Moving beyond Qualitative and Quantitative Strategies.* Palo Alto: University of California Press.

Rahman, Anika, Laura Katzive, and Stanley K. Henshaw. 1998. "A Global Review of Laws on Induced Abortion, 1985–1997." *International Family Planning Perspectives and Digest* 24 (2): 56–64.

Raventós Vorst, Ciska, and Olman Ramírez Moreira. 2006. "Transición política y electoral en Costa Rica (1998–2006)." Encuentro de Latinoamericanistas Españoles, Santander.

Reuterswärd, Camilla. 2019. "¡Malas Madres, Malas Mujeres, Malas Todas! The Incarceration of Women for Abortion-Related Crimes in Mexico." In *Gender, Global Health and Violence: Feminist Perspectives on Peace and Disease,* edited by Catia Confortini and Tiina Vaittinen, 139–58. Lanham, MD: Rowman & Littlefield.

Reuterswärd, Camilla, Pär Zetterberg, Suruchi Thapar-Bjorkert, and Maxine Molyneux. 2011. "Abortion Law Reforms in Colombia and Nicaragua: Issue Networks and Opportunity Contexts." *Development and Change* 42 (3): 805–31.

Ríos-Figueroa, Julio. 2007. "Fragmentation of Power and the Emergence of an Effective Judiciary in Mexico, 1994–2002." *Latin American Politics and Society* 49 (1): 31–57.

Ríos-Figueroa, Julio, and Andrea Pozas-Loyo. 2010. "Enacting Constitutionalism. The Origins of Independent Judicial Institutions in Latin America." *Comparative Politics* 42 (3): 293–311.

Rodríguez O., Jaime E. 2012. "Democracy from Independence to Revolution." In *The Oxford Handbook of Mexican Politics,* 31–52. Oxford, UK: Oxford University Press.

Rodríguez-Raga, Juan Carlos. 2011. "Strategic Deference in the Colombian Constitutional Court, 1992–2006." In *Courts in Latin America,* edited by Gretchen Helmke and Julio Ríos-Figueroa, 81–98. New York: Cambridge University Press.

Rohde, David W., and Harold J. Spaeth. 1976. *Supreme Court Decision Making.* San Francisco: W. H. Freeman.

Ross, Loretta, and Rickie Solinger. 2017. *Reproductive Justice: An Introduction.* Stanford: University of California Press.

Roth, Cassia. 2020. *A Miscarriage of Justice: Women's Reproductive Lives and the Law in Early-Twentieth Century Brazil.* Stanford, CA: Stanford University Press.

Rozo Barragán, Luz Zoraida. 1997. "Origen y Evolución del Regimen de Control Constitucional en Colombia." *Revista Derecho del Estado* 3 (December): 45–61.

Rubiano Galvis, Sebastián. 2009. "La Corte Constitucional: Entre la independencia judicial y la captura política." In *Mayorías sin democracia: Desequilibrio de poderes y estado de derecho en Colombia, 2002–2009,* edited by Mauricio García Villegas and Javier Eduardo Revelo Rebolledo, 84–145. Bogotá: Dejusticia.

Rueda, Pablo. 2010. "Legal Language and Social Change during Colombia's Economic Crisis." In *Cultures of Legality: Judicialization and Political Activism in Latin America,* edited by Javier Couso, Alexandra Huneeus, and Rachel Sieder, 25–50. New York: Cambridge University Press.

Ruibal, Alba María. 2009. "Self-Restraint in Search of Legitimacy: The Reform of the Argentine Supreme Court." *Latin American Politics and Society* 51 (3): 59–86.

———. 2014a. "Movement and Countermovement: A History of Abortion Law Reform and the Backlash in Colombia 2006–2014." *Reproductive Health Matters* 22 (44): 42–51.

———. 2014b. "Social Mobilization and Legal Change: Legal Mobilization and Counter-Mobilization in the Field of Abortion Law in Latin America." Doctoral thesis, European University Institute, Florence.

———. 2018a. "Federalism, Two-Level Games and the Politics of Abortion Rights Implementation in Subnational Argentina." *Reproductive Health Matters* 26 (54): 137–44.

———. 2018b. "Federalisms and Subnational Legal Mobilization: Feminist Legal Mobilization: Feminist Litigation Strategies in Salta, Argentina." *Law & Society Review* 52 (4): 928–59.

Ruibal, Alba María, and Cora Fernández Anderson. 2020. "Legal Obstacles and Social Change: Strategies of the Abortion Rights Movement in Argentina." *Politics, Groups and Identities* 8 (4): 698–713.

Sagües, Néstor Pedro. 1991. "La Jurisdicción Constitucional en Costa Rica." *Revista de Estudios Políticos* 74 (October–December): 471–95.

———. 1998. "La Corte Suprema y el Control Jurisdiccional de Constitucionalidad en Argentina." *Ius et Praxis* 4 (1): 85–101.

Sáenz Carbonell, Jorge Francisco, and Mauricio Masís Pinto. 2006. *Historia de la Corte Suprema de Costa Rica: 180 Aniversario.* San José: Editorama.

Salazar Ugarte, P. 2012. "Camino a la Democracia Constitucional en México." *Isonomía* 36: 189–206.

Saldivia Menajovsky, Laura. 2021. "Argentina, Trans Persons and the Development of a Human Rights Discourse." In *Trans Rights and Wrongs: A Comparative Study of Legal Reform Concerning Trans Persons*, edited by Isabel C. Jaramillo and Laura Carlson, 335–63. New York: Springer.

Sánchez, Arianna, Beatriz Magaloni, and Eric Magar. 2011. "Legalist vs. Interpretivist: The Supreme Court and the Democratic Transition in Mexico." Stanford Public Law Working Paper No. 1499490.

Sánchez Fuentes, María Luisa, Jennifer Paine, and Brook Elliott-Buettner. 2008. "The Decriminalisation of Abortion in Mexico City: How Did Abortion Rights Become a Political Priority?" *Gender and Development* 16 (2): 345–60.

Schiebinger, Londa. 2004. *Plants and Empire: Colonial Bioprospecting in the Atlantic World.* Cambridge, MA: Harvard University Press.

Schor, Miguel. 2008. "Mapping Comparative Judicial Review." *Washington University Global Studies Law Review* 7 (2): 257–87.

Schubert, Glendon. 1965. *The Judicial Mind: The Attitudes and Ideologies of Supreme Court Justices, 1946–1963.* Evanston, IL: Northwestern University Press.

———. 1974. *The Judicial Mind Revisited: Psychometric Analysis of Supreme Court Ideology.* New York: Oxford University Press.

SCJN. 2008a. "Contenido de la versión taquigráfica de la sesión pública extraordinaria del Pleno de la Suprema Corte de Justicia de la Nación, celebrada el lunes veinticinco de agosto de dos mil ocho. *Versiones taquigráficas.* https://www.scjn.gob.mx/multimedia/versiones-taquigraficas.

———. 2008b. "Contenido de la versión taquigráfica de la sesión pública extraordinaria del Pleno de la Suprema Corte de Justicia de la Nación, celebrada el martes veintiseis

de agosto de dos mil ocho." *Versiones taquigráficas*. https://www.scjn.gob.mx
/multimedia/versiones-taquigraficas.

———. 2008c. "Contenido de la versión taquigráfica de la sesión pública extraordinaria
del Pleno de la Suprema Corte de Justicia de la Nación, celebrada el veintisiete de
agosto de dos mil ocho." *Versiones taquigráficas*. https://www.scjn.gob.mx/multimedia
/versiones-taquigraficas.

———. 2008d. "Contenido de la versión taquigráfica de la sesión pública extraordinaria
del Pleno de la Suprema Corte de Justicia de la Nación, celebrada el lunes veintiocho de
agosto de dos mil ocho." *Versiones taquigráficas*. https://www.scjn.gob.mx/multimedia
/versiones-taquigraficas.

———. 2021. "Contenido de la versión taquigráfica de la sesión pública extraordinaria
del Pleno de la Suprema Corte de Justicia de la Nación, celebrada el martes siete de
septiembre de dos mil veintiuno." *Versiones taquigráficas*. https://www.scjn.gob.mx
/multimedia/versiones-taquigraficas.

Scribner, Druscilla. 2011. "Courts, Power, and Rights in Argentina and Chile." In *Courts
in Latin America*, edited by Gretchen Helmke and Julio Ríos-Figueroa, 248–77. New
York: Cambridge University Press.

Segal, Jeffrey A., and Harold J. Spaeth. 2002. *The Supreme Court and the Attitudinal
Model Revisited*. Cambridge, UK: Cambridge University Press.

Serrano Guzmá, Silvia. 2024. "The Transformative Case of the Artavia Murillo Case on
In Vitro Fertilization." In *The Impact of the Inter-American Human Rights System:
Transformations on the Ground*, edited by Armin von Bogdandy, Flávia Piovesan,
Eduardo Ferrer Mac-Gregor, and Mariela Morales Antoniazzi, 285–302. New York:
Oxford University Press.

Sheldon, Sally. 1997. *Beyond Control: Medical Power and Abortion Law*. London: Pluto
Press.

Siegel, Reva B. 2012. "Abortion and the 'Woman Question.'" *Indiana Law Journal* 89 (4).

Sierra Porto, Humberto Antonio, Paula Robledo Silva, and Diego Andrés González
Medida. 2022. *Justicia constitucional a debate. Vol 1: Crónicas jurisprudenciales del
2021*. Bogotá: Universidad Externado de Colombia. https://bdigital.uexternado.edu.co
/server/api/core/bitstreams/88e16ab7-ef87-48a2-a876-8e71c0b08112/content.

Silva, Miguel. 1998. "La Asamblea Constituyente de 1991." In *Nueva historia de Colombia:
Historia política desde 1986*, edited by Álvaro Tirado Mejía, 107–21. Bogotá: Planeta
Colombiana Editorial.

Smith, Rogers M. 1988. "Political Jurisprudence, the 'New Institutionalism,' and the
Future of Public Law." *American Political Science Review* 82 (1): 89–108.

Smulovitz, Catalina. 2012. "Public Policy by Other Means: Playing the Judicial Arena."
In *Comparative Public Policy in Latin America*, edited by Jordi Díez and Susan
Franceschet, 105–25. Toronto: University of Toronto Press.

Smulovitz, Catalina, and Enrique Peruzzotti. 2003. "Societal and Horizontal Controls:
Two Cases of a Fruitful Relationship." In *Democratic Accountability in Latin America*,
edited by Scott Mainwaring and Christopher Welna, 309–31. Oxford, UK: Oxford
University Press.

Solano, Luis Fernando. 2009. "A veinte años de la Sala Constitucional: Relfexiones sobre
impactos, riesgos y desafíos." In *Estado de la Nación en Desarrollo Humano Sostenible*,
343–63. San José: Programa Estado de la Nación.

Songer, Donald R., Susan W. Johnson, Cynthia L. Ostberg, and Matthew E. Wetstein. 2012. *Law, Ideology, and Collegiality: Judicial Behaviour in the Supreme Court of Canada*. Montreal: McGill-Queen's University Press.

Spaeth, Harold J., and Jeffrey A. Segal. 1999. *Majority Rule or Minority Will: Adherence to Precedent on the US Supreme Court*. New York: Cambridge University Press.

Spiller, Pablo T., and Matthew L. Spitzer. 1992. "Judicial Choice of Legal Doctrines." *Journal of Law, Economics, and Organization* 8 (1): 8–46.

Staton, Jeffrey K. 2010. *Judicial Power and Strategic Communication in Mexico*. New York: Cambridge University Press.

Suárez Avila, Alberto Abda. 2014. *Protección de los derechos fundamentales en la Novena Epoca de la Suprema Corte*. México DF: Porrúa.

Sunstein, Cass R., David Schkade, and Lisa Michelle Ellman. 2004. "Ideological Voting on Federal Courts of Appeals: A Preliminary Investigation." *Virginia Law Review* 90 (1): 301–54.

Sutton, Barbara, and Elizabeth Borland. 2013. "Framing Abortion Rights in Argentina's Encuentros Nacionales de Mujeres." *Feminist Studies* 39 (1): 194–234.

Tabbush, Constanza, María Constanza Díaz, Catalina Trebisacce, and Victoria Keller. 2016. "Matrimonio Igualitario, identidad de género y disputas por el derecho al aborto en Argentina. La política sexual durante el Kirchnerismo (2003–2015)." *Sexualidad, Salud y Sociedad (Rio de Janeiro)*, no. 22: 22–55.

Tate, C. Neal, and Torbjorn Vallinder. 1995. *The Global Expansion of Judicial Power*. New York: New York University Press.

Teichman, Judith. 2001. *The Politics of Freeing Markets in Latin America: Argentina, Chile and Mexico*. Chapel Hill: University of North Carolina Press.

Thelen, Kathleen, and Sven Steinmo. 1992. "Historical Institutionalism in Comparative Politics." In *Structuring Politics: Historical Institutionalism in Comparative Analysis*, edited by Sven Steinmo, Kathleen Thelen, and Frank Longstreth, 1–32. New York: Cambridge University Press.

Tiede, Lydia Brashear. 2022. *Judicial Vetoes: Decision-Making on Mixed Selection Constitutional Courts*. Cambridge, UK: Cambridge University Press.

Torres-Ruiz, Antonio. 2011. "HIV/AIDS and Sexual Minorities in Mexico: A Globalized Struggle for the Protection of Human Rights" *Latin American Research Review* 46 (1): 30–53.

Treminio Sánchez, Ika. 2013. "Llegaron para quedarse . . . Los procesos de reforma de la reelección presidencial en América Latina 1999–2001." Tesis doctoral, Facultad de Derecho, Universidad de Salamanca.

UBA Derecho. 1998. "Entrevista al Dr. Petracchi." *Revista Lecciones y Ensayos* 49. Buenos Aires: Facultad de Derecho, Universidad de Buenos Aires. http://www.derecho.uba.ar/publicaciones/lye/pub_lye_entrevista_petracchi.php.

Unah, Isaac, and Ange-Marie Hancock. 2006. "U.S. Supreme Court Decision Making, Case Salience, and the Attitudinal Model." *Law & Policy* 28 (3): 295–320.

Undurraga Valdés, Verónica. 2019. "La sentencia de aborto del Tribunal Constitucional de Chile: Evitando la excepcionalidad en el trato de la mujer embarazada como sujeto de derecho." In *Aborto en tres causales en Chile: Lecturas del proceso de penalización*, edited by Lidia Casas Becerra and Gloria María Vargas, 121–50. Santiago: Centro de Derechos Humanos, Facultad de Derecho, Universidad Diego Portales.

United Nations. 1995. *Beijing Declaration and Platform for Action: The Fourth World Conference on Women.* Beijing: UN.

United Nations Population Fund (UNFPA). 2017. *Worlds Apart: Reproductive Health and Rights in an Age of Inequality.* New York: UNFPA.

Uprimny, Rodrigo. 2014. "The Recent Transformation of Constitutional Law in Latin America: Trends and Challenges." In *Law and Society in Latin America: A New Map*, edited by César Rodríguez Garavito, 63–82. New York: Routledge.

Uprimny, Rodrigo, and Mauricio García Villegas. 2004. "Corte Constitucional y emancipación social en Colombia." In *Democratizar la Democracia: Los Caminos de la Democracia Participativa*, edited by Bonaventura De Sousa Santos and Mauricio García Villegas, 255–88. Bogotá: Grupo Editorial Norma.

Urcuyo Fournier, Constantino. 1995. *Presidencialismo versus parlamentarismo: Una falsa confrontación.* San José: Asamblea Legislativa.

Urteaga, Alfredo Adriá. 2006. "La doctrina de la arbitrariedad de sentencias: Una crítica." *Jurisprudencia Argentina* 2:1394.

Vaggione, Juan Marco. 2022. "El entramado neoconservador en América Latina. La instrumentalización de la ideologia de género en las democracias contemporaneas." *Revista Internacional de Filosofía Política* 11 (1).

Valverde Díaz, María Fernanda. 2018. "Seguimiento a la recomendación No. 33 del año 2011 del Comité CEDAW en Costa Rica: Análisis jurídico-filosófico del estado actual del aborto en Costa Rica y una propuesta de cumplimiento desde un planteamiento feminista." Tesis para la optar por el grado de Licenciatura en Derecho, San José, Universidad de Costa Rica.

Vela, Estefanía. 2011. *La Suprema Corte y el matrimonio: Una relación de amor.* Tesispara Obtener el Título de Licenciada en Derecho. Mexico City: CIDE.

Verbitsky, Horacio. 1993. *Hacer la corte. La construcción de un poder absoluto sin justicia ni control.* Buenos Aires: Edición Planeta.

Viterna, Jocelyn. 2012. "The Left and 'Life' in El Salvador." *Politics & Gender* 8 (2): 248–54.

Volcansek, Mary L. 2001. "Constitutional Courts as Veto Players: Divorce and Decrees in Italy." *European Journal of Political Research* 39 (3): 347–72.

Wahlbeck, Paul J. 2006. "Strategy and Constraints on Supreme Court Opinion Assignment." *University of Pennsylvania Law Review* 154 (6): 1729–56.

Waldron, Jeremy. 2002. "Citizenship and Dignity." In *Understanding Human Dignity*, edited by Christopher McCrudden, 327–44. New York: Oxford University Press.

Walzer, Michael. 1989. "Citizenship." In *Political Innovation and Conceptual Change*, edited by Terrence Ball, James Farr, and Russell L. Hanson, 211–20. New York: Cambridge University Press.

Wasby, Stephen L. 1988. *The Supreme Court in the Federal Justice System.* Chicago: Nelson-Hall.

Whittington, Keith E. 2000. "Once More unto the Breach: Post-Behavioralist Approaches to Judicial Politics." *Law & Social Inquiry* 25 (2): 601–34.

WHO. 2012. Information Sheet. *Unsafe Abortion Incidence and Mortality.* World Health Organization.

Wilson, Bruce. 2005. "Changing Dynamics: The Political Impact of Costa Rica's Constitutional Court." In *The Judicialization of Politics in Latin America*, edited by Rachel Sieder, Lime Schjolden and Alan Angell, 47–65. London: Palgrave Macmillan.

———. 2007. "Claiming Individual Rights through a Constitutional Court: The Example of Gays in Costa Rica." *International Journal of Constitutional Law* 5 (2): 346–61.

———. 2009. "Rights Revolutions in Unlikely Places: Costa Rica and Colombia." *Journal of Politics in Latin America* 1 (2): 59–85.

———. 2011. "Enforcing Rights and Exercising an Accountability Function: Costa Rica's Constitutional Chamber of the Supreme Court." In *Courts in Latin America*, edited by Gretchen Helmke and Julio Rios-Figueroa, 55–80. New York: Cambridge University Press.

Wilson, Bruce, and Juan Carlos Rodríguez Cordero. 2006. "Legal Opportunity Structures and Social Movements: The Effects of Institutional Change on Costa Rican Politics." *Comparative Political Studies* 39 (3): 325–51.

Wilson, Bruce, Juan Carlos Rodríguez Cordero, and Roger Handberg. 2004. "Judicial Reform in Latin America: Evidence from Costa Rica." *Journal of Latin American Studies* 36 (3): 507–31.

Wood, Susan, Lilián Abracinskas, Sonia Corrêa, and Mario Pecheny. 2016. "Reform of Abortion Law in Uruguay: Context, Process and Lessons Learned." *Reproductive Health Matters* 24 (48): 102–10.

Woodrow, Borah. 1983. *Justice by Insurance: The General Indian Court of Colonial Mexico and the Legal Aides of the Half-Real.* Stanford: University of California Press.

Yamin, Alicia, and Agustina Ramón Michel. 2023. "Using Rights to Deepen Democracy: Making Sense of the Road to Legal Abortion in Argentina." *Fordham International Law Journal* 46 (3): 377–424.

Yashar, Deborah. 2005. *Contesting Citizenship in Latin America: The Rise of Indigenous Movements and the Postliberal Challenge.* Cambridge, UK: Cambridge University Press.

Young, Iris Marion. 1990. "The Politics of Difference: A Critique of the Ideal of Universal Citizenship." *Ethics* 99: 250–74.

Zaller, John. 1992. *The Nature and Origins of Mass Opinion.* New York: Cambridge University Press.

Zamora Zamora, Carlos. 2007. "Los recursos de amparo y recursos de inconstitucionalidad contra la Caja Costarricense de Seguro Social de 1989 a 2005." In *Gaceta Médica de Costa Rica* 9 (2): 130–34.

Index

abortion: health consequences of, 72, 99; and jurisdictional authority, 194, 198–201; and religion, 64, 143, 189–90, 233; therapeutic, 4, 216, 227–28, 230, 237–40; unsafe, 1, 72, 75, 106, 182; voluntary, 66, 96, 134, 158. *See also* abortion, access to; criminal code, abortion; policy, abortion; regulation, abortion

abortion, access to, 64, 143, 189–90, 233; in Argentina, 10–14, 85, 92, 100–103, 111–12; in Colombia, 128, 130, 156–60; in Costa Rica, 216, 233, 235; in Mexico, 182, 210–12, 238

abortion decriminalization, first wave of, 81, 128, 158, 240–42

abortionists, 189, 233–34, 247

advisory opinions, 45, 58

Aguirre Anguiano, Sergio Salvador, 164, 167–71, 179, 187–91, 198–202, 208. *See also* conservative justice

amicus curiae, 41, 105–6, 134, 186–87, 192, 219

amnesty laws, 55, 88–89

amparo, 42, 58, 94, 170, 195, 210–11, 223, 230–36, 267n48; case, 49, 60–62, 167, 212–15, 225, 229, 251; and constitution, 45–46, 238; decision, 220; establishment of, 43–44; and judicial review, 48

antiabortionists, 92, 106, 192, 194, 198

antiabortion movements, 74, 92

A.N. v. Costa Rica, 4, 12, 50, 216, 220, 229–30, 238. *See also* constitutional court

appointment process, 37, 48, 63, 164, 178, 216–20

Araújo Rentería, Jaime, 138, 141–48

Argentina Golden Court, 86, 91

Argentina Impeachment Jury (Jurado de Enjuiciamiento), 17

Argentina National Judicial Council, 31

Argentina Supreme Court, 5, 26–27, 37–39, 88, 94, 160; and 2006 LMR Case, 91–92, 270n13; and 2012 FAL Case, 3, 85, 91–94, 113–16, 246. *See also* Lorenzetti, Ricardo

Argentine Feminist Union, 70

attitudinal model, 18–19, 253

Attorney General of Argentina, 4, 106

Attorney General of Colombia, 40, 134, 136, 159

Attorney General of Costa Rica, 52, 58, 226

Attorney General of Mexico, 48, 181–83, 212–13

Aurora case, Costa Rica, 238–39

Azuela, Mariano, 167–68, 171, 177–79, 184, 202–4. *See also* conservative justice; Mexico Supreme Court

bodily autonomy, 65, 70, 73, 182, 213–15

Bonifaz, Leticia, 187, 193

Calzada, Ana Virginia, 216, 222–24, 231–34, 237

centralization, 33, 36, 45, 247

centrist justice, 51, 124, 138, 142, 149, 153, 161, 176–77

Cepeda, Manuel José, 138–41, 148, 151

Colombia Supreme Court, 119–20, 124

concurring opinions, 41, 109–11, 117, 152, 186

conservative justice, 10, 18, 20, 120, 124–25, 145, 152, 167, 190

constitutions, 2, 6, 21, 67–68, 259; in Argentina, 27, 31–37, 41, 99, 107, 263n8; in Colombia, 118, 122, 138, 141, 146, 155–60; in Costa Rica, 51–58, 216, 228, 230; interpretation of, 22, 122, 141; in Mexico, 41–47, 174, 181, 183, 201–4, 211, 268n64. *See also* constitutional reform constitutional court, 17, 21, 32, 37–38, 40, 134; in Argentina, 5, 12, 128–30, 138, 160; in Colombia, 5, 12, 128, 137, 150, 159–60; in Costa Rica, 269n82, 286n11. *See also A.N. v. Costa Rica*; C-355 2006 case

constitutional reform, 6, 26, 30–35, 49, 55–59, 94, 144, 166, 188, 259

conventional control, 31, 61, 97, 168, 179, 198

corte adicta (co-opted court), 28, 88

Cossío Díaz, José Ramón, 162, 173–74, 194. *See also* Mexico Supreme Court

Costa Rica Supreme Court, 55, 58, 61

criminal code, abortion in, 70; in Argentina, 91, 93–94, 99, 112; in Colombia, 128, 230, 149, 155, 159–60; in Costa Rica, 227–28, 240; in Mexico, 179–81, 201, 210, 212–15. *See also* reproductive rights

Cruz Castro, Fernando, 62, 216, 224–25, 231–32, 237. See also *A.N. v. Costa Rica*

C-355 case, Colombia Constitutional Court 2006, 4, 118, 130, 158–61. *See also* Roa, Mónica

C-647 case, Colombia Constitutional Court 2001, 154. *See also* decriminalization of abortion

decentralization, 27–33, 180, 248

decriminalization of abortion, 8–13, 71–75, 246, 278n46; in Argentina, 91, 95, 118; in Colombia, 128–30, 134, 139, 142–44, 151–54, 159; in Mexico, 4, 70, 182, 192, 201, 204, 208, 215. *See also* abortion decriminalization, first wave of; therapeutic abortion

De la Rúa, Fernando, 86–87

democratic backsliding, 260

democratic citizenship, 5, 14, 65–67, 71, 75, 80–81

democratic debt, 14, 65, 75, 79, 81

democratic legitimacy, 18, 47, 57, 195, 197, 259

Democratic Revolutionary Party, 162

democratization, 1, 14, 65, 75–76, 165, 247; and reproductive justice, 72–73; third wave of, 1, 65, 80, 242

deregulation, 2, 6, 9, 20

Dobbs decision, 256-57. See also *Roe v. Wade*

draft opinions: in Argentina, 10, 103, 105, 109; in Colombia, 134–37, 145–52; in Mexico, 180–81, 186, 189, 198–204, 206; revised, 146–52

erga omnes, 27, 38, 43, 48–49, 55–58, 213

feminism, 67–72, 80, 102, 158, 239; waves of, 70

golden court, 85–86, 90–91

green wave, 114–16

guerrilla groups, 34–35, 123, 144; mobilization of, 71; movement of, 47

habeas corpus, 32, 53, 55, 58, 62, 264n10

health consequences of abortion, 72, 99. *See also* abortion decriminalization, first wave of

Highton de Nolasco, Elena, 90, 103, 107, 113

hospital protocols, 4, 111

human rights commission, 4, 49, 183, 188, 209

human rights court, 32, 39

Institutional Revolutionary Party (Partido Revolucionario Institucional, PRI), 162–67, 175, 177

internal bargaining, 10, 23, 26, 252–53

international treaties, 3–4, 36, 45, 58, 60, 99, 110, 146, 176–79, 188

interpretivist justice, 22–23, 59–61, 120, 126, 138, 165–67, 173–77, 203

judicial independence, 6, 44, 248; in Argentina, 91, 248, 258–59; in Colombia, 125; in Costa Rica, 52, 56–59; in Mexico, 42–45, 48, 55, 186, 194

judicial interpretation, 22, 30, 44, 138, 179

judicial philosophy, 22, 99, 165, 168, 219

jurisdictional argument, 195–97, 200, 205–7, 210

jurisdictional authority and abortion, 194, 198–201

www.ingramcontent.com/pod-product-compliance
Lightning Source LLC
Chambersburg PA
CBHW021214270326
41929CB00010B/1132